THE NEW NATURAL

CW00765626

A SURVEY OF BRITISH NA

HEDGEHOG

THE NEW NATURALIST LIBRARY

HEDGEHOG

PAT MORRIS

WILLIAM
COLLINS

This edition published in 2018 by William Collins,
An imprint of HarperCollins Publishers

HarperCollins Publishers
1 London Bridge Street
London SE1 9GF
WilliamCollinsBooks.com

First published 2018

© Pat Morris, 2018

A CIP catalogue record for this book is available
from the British Library.

Set in FF Nexus, designed and produced by
Tom Cabot/ketchup

All photos by the author unless otherwise credited.

Printed in China by RR Donnelley APS

Hardback
ISBN 978-0-00-823570-3

Paperback
ISBN 978-0-00-823573-4

Contents

Editors' Preface

SINCE THE NEW NATURALIST MONOGRAPHS ceased publication, the policy of the New Naturalist Library has been to base those volumes concerned with animals and plants, on groups of related species, rather than individuals, other than in exceptional circumstances. The first of these exceptions was NN 114 *Badger* by Timothy Roper. The badger is a well-known animal, popular with many, as an attractive component of our countryside – feared, and even hated, by some because of its associations with bovine TB in cattle.

This volume, *Hedgehog* (NN 137) by Pat Morris, is the second exception – and, ironically, badgers are the hedgehog's main predator. Hedgehogs are popular, even iconic creatures, as familiar as the badger to us all from childhood (Beatrix Potter's *Mrs Tiggy-Winkle*, for example) with accounts of their natural history of varying accuracy – or, better, inaccuracy – dating back over two millennia to Aristotle and Pliny. As Pat Morris puts it, 'the stories so often told are more picturesque than trustworthy'.

Over 13 chapters the author explores in detail the current state of knowledge on every aspect of hedgehog natural history, 'one of the least studied of our common mammals' – including distribution, feeding, breeding and mortality, with a particularly fascinating (and widely useful) account of hibernation in Chapter Six.

Pat Morris could not be better placed to write this comprehensive account of hedgehog natural history, with almost a lifetime's research involvement in all aspects of it. He draws on a comprehensive international network of colleagues and hedgehog enthusiasts, and is well versed in communication skills – his typical audiences range from Womens' Institutes, through students, to learned academic societies. Readers of this volume will enjoy these skills as well as his knowledge, and cannot fail to be fascinated (or, become even more fascinated) by hedgehogs and thus become far better informed about them at the end of an excellent read.

Author's Foreword and Acknowledgements

ANY PEOPLE HAVE ASSISTED ME in pursuit of a better understanding of mammals, my friend the late Derek Vaiden foremost among them. I am grateful for contributions made by my research students who studied hedgehogs, particularly Nigel Reeve and Andrew Wroot, also many undergraduates who helped with fieldwork (including George Bemment, Simone Bullion, Steve Carter, Samantha Craig-Wood, Warren Cresswell, Penny Goodridge, Richard Leishman, Kim Matthews, Kathy Meakin, Samantha Munn, Susan Sharafi, Ruth Temple. Guy Troughton also created artwork for this book and Chloe Metcalfe the graphs. Nigel Reeve read a draft and made many suggestions for improvement. I also acknowledge the friendly assistance of Hugh Warwick and support from Pat Campbell and Bob Brockie in New Zealand. I thank Dru Burdon for her assistance with fieldwork in Jersey and for access to her records. The Late Major Adrian Coles (founder of the British Hedgehog Preservation Society) provided research funds at a critical time, as did the RSPCA. A gift from Mrs Coulthard-Bayley in memory of her husband enabled an early computer programme to be written for calculating home range sizes. I am also grateful to many landowners who allowed access to study sites and various gamekeepers who collected dead hedgehogs for me. Pat Holtham provided help and access to data on my visit to the Uists. In retrospect I also now realise how important were particular encounters with Maurice Burton, Percy Butler and Ian Linn half a century ago. My late parents were always strongly supportive, despite having no background in wildlife matters, and my wife Mary has provided unswerving dedication, even to the extent of attending my hedgehog lectures more times than we could possibly count.

CHAPTER 1

Introducing Our Knowledge of Hedgehogs

W RITTEN ACCOUNTS OF THE HEDGEHOG (*Erinaceus* sp.) date back at least 2,300 years to the Greek philosopher Aristotle. The Roman naturalist Pliny the Elder also wrote about it in the first century CE. Several of the mediaeval animal bestiaries, or 'books of beasts', mention hedgehogs too, but all of these early accounts, even the encyclopaedic *Historia Animalium* published by Conrad Gesner in the mid-1600s, were heavily focused on the usefulness of animals and their supposed medicinal value rather than their life and general natural history. The early accounts also include elements of folklore, but it is often difficult to assess the reliability of what was said and some hedgehog stories may originally have referred to the porcupine (*Hystrix* sp.), causing confusion when translations were made into English. It is also hard to know how much of what was said is just imaginary or inappropriately crediting the hedgehog with anthropomorphic behaviour.

For centuries, the animal remained a very familiar creature, but with real details of its biology poorly known. The result was that authors tended just to copy out what had been said previously. From Aristotle onwards, many of the stories so often told are more picturesque than trustworthy. For example, William Barlow in 1658 enlarged on Pliny's earlier account of hedgehogs carrying fruit on their spines to state that 'having been abroad to provide their store and returning home laden with nuts and fruit, if the least filbert fall but off, they will in a pettish humour bring down all the rest and beat the ground for very anger with their bristles.' When 'facts' were supplied in such detail, why should later authors not believe them and incorporate them into their own writings if they didn't know any better? This seems to have happened a lot with hedgehogs, despite the obvious untruth of the story above and many others. A frustrated hedgehog is unlikely to lose its temper as described and filberts are nuts and unlikely to adhere to a hedgehog's spines. Nor are they especially appealing as hedgehog food, and nobody in recent times has encountered food stored by hedgehogs. Occasional fruits found in hedgehog nests are likely to have been imported by rats (*Rattus* spp.) or wood mice (*Apodemus* spp.). So the whole account is misconceived and yet published with an air of authority along with similar tales, many of which have been repeated over and over, well into modern times. The seemingly improbable story that hedgehogs carry fruit about on their spines has an ancient origin and is widely reported in the literature (see Chapter 4) and Pliny's story that a captured hedgehog will defend itself by urinating copiously was another of his assertions that appeared repeatedly in print down the ages with no substantiation whatever. Captured hedgehogs are no more likely to wet themselves than any other frightened mammal, including humans.

The first significant account of hedgehogs, written in English, appeared in *The History of Four-footed Beasts and Serpents* by Edward Topsel published in 1658. It was largely copied from Gesner and the ancient Greek and Roman authors, and the text remained focused on the animal's utility, especially for medicinal purposes (see Chapter 13). Various later authors included the hedgehog in their general accounts of British wildlife, often adding observations and commentary that gradually helped to create a more rounded description of the species, but much was still based on speculation and anecdote. Over the years, respected authors such as Gilbert White (1789), Thomas Bewick (1807), Thomas

FIG 1. Topsel (1658) was the first natural history book published in English and included several pages about the hedgehog. The woodcut illustration has the spines disarranged in a way that is not seen in the living animal.

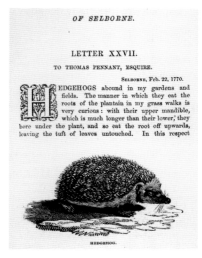

FIGS 2 & 3. (left) Gilbert White's *The Natural History and Antiquities of Selborne* is one of the most famous natural history books ever published. This illustration is from J. E. Harting's edition of 1875. (right) The woodcuts in Thomas Bell's *A History of British Quadrupeds* (1874 edition) depict the hedgehog's spines as short bristles, often seen in illustrations by many subsequent artists. It makes the animal seem more appealing and less defensive/unapproachable.

Pennant (1776), Thomas Bell (1837) and Sir Harry Johnston (1903) all wrote authoritative books about British wildlife, especially mammals, but their accounts of the hedgehog were brief and often featured the same old tales about carrying fruit, suckling cows and fighting adders (*Vipera berus*), but little else. Curiously, Gilbert White's *The Natural History and Antiquities of Selborne* provided one of the most accurate and detailed of these early accounts in the form of a letter to Thomas Pennant written in 1770. In the third edition of his own book *British Zoology* published six years later, Pennant used some of this

FIG 4. Illustrations of the hedgehog in J. G. Millais' *The Mammals of Great Britain and Ireland* (1904) included three accurate sketches by himself and also the first coloured plate of a hedgehog in a serious natural history book. It was based on a painting by Archibald Thorburn (1860–1935).

FIG 5. Major Gerald Edwin Hamilton Barrett-Hamilton died in 1914 and never completed his massive compilation on British mammals. The artist for many of the plates, including the hedgehog, was the naturalist Edward A. Wilson, who died alongside Captain Scott in the Antarctic in 1912.

material, but in a 'new edition' in 1812 he seems to have ignored practically all of it.

A longer description of the hedgehog's life and activities appeared in Millais' massive three-volume work *The Mammals of Great Britain and Ireland* in 1904, but the first really thorough and reliable treatment of this species in Britain filled 30 pages in *British Mammals* (Barrett-Hamilton & Hinton, 1910), a comprehensive account that was issued in sections over several years and became the basic reference on British mammals for over half a century. The hedgehog's anatomy and general behaviour were better known by then and there were plenty of anecdotes about its depredations on bird eggs and its resistance to snake bites to evaluate. Otherwise, relatively little new information was added to the hedgehog's story, especially about its ecology and life in the wild. In parallel with this rather slow development of the hedgehog's scientific literature, it became an increasingly favourite topic for popular nature writers in newspapers and magazines during the nineteenth and twentieth centuries. Beatrix Potter's *The Tale of Mrs Tiggy-Winkle* (Potter, 1905) did much to propel this species to the forefront of public popularity, which continues unabated to this day (see Chapter 13).

During the first half of the twentieth century there were occasional research publications in scientific journals that focussed on particular issues to do with hedgehog biology. Notably, these include the work of Ruth Deanesly and Marjorie Allanson that formed part of a systematic survey of reproductive organs in various mammals carried out in the 1930s (see Chapter 7). They used histological methods to study seasonal changes, offering limited insights into associated patterns of reproductive behaviour. Thirty years later Bryn Morris (no relation of mine), at the University of Nottingham, used the hedgehog as a 'primitive mammal' to investigate transmission of immunity from mother to young for comparison with the process in evolutionarily more advanced species. Although this was experimental laboratory-based work, it did involve quite large samples of animals. Many of these were bred in captivity and provided some important insights into hedgehog reproductive physiology and behaviour.

Despite these advances, the hedgehog remained for years as one of the least-studied of our common mammals. It was Konrad Herter who published the first book wholly about hedgehogs. His monograph, *Die Biologie der Europäischen Igel* (Herter, 1938) was in German and appeared just before the Second World War, so it was another 27 years before his work became more widely known when an abbreviated version, *Hedgehogs*, was published in English (Herter, 1965). Despite its subtitle – *a comprehensive study* – that book still ran to only 69 small pages.

It was 1969 before we had the first genuinely comprehensive hedgehog book in English, based on observations in Britain and extending to more than 100 pages. This was *The Hedgehog* by Maurice Burton (Burton, 1969), who had been a world authority on sponges for 30 years, based at what was then the British Museum (Natural History). In parallel with his professional life, Maurice Burton had developed a strong personal interest in hedgehogs and published some detailed information about their behaviour (Burton, 1957) and many short popular accounts of the species. He also produced several popular natural history books and had a regular nature

FIG 6. The first book in English devoted to the hedgehog, a translation of Herter's original monograph published in 1938.

FIG 7. Burton's book, published in 1969, was the first really thorough treatment of the species. It included many original observations from members of the public.

HEDGEHOGS

Nigel Reeve

POYSER NATURAL HISTORY

FIG 8. Nigel Reeve was one of my PhD students and compiled this major review of the literature, published in 1994. It is a book that I should have written myself, but somehow never found the time. Anyway, Nigel did the job more thoroughly than I would have done, not least because of his mother's facility with other European languages!

column in the *Daily Telegraph* that continued well into his retirement. His consequent fame as a naturalist attracted a substantial correspondence from his many readers. This provided him with a large file of letters describing observations by ordinary people over many years and much of the information he gained by this route found its way into his writings. As a result, *The Hedgehog* formed a very personal and informative account, written in a very readable, conversational style. But the lack of academic studies in those days meant that there remained little new information, especially about the animal's ecology and survival, until I began to publish my own research in the 1970s. The hedgehog was simply not amenable to detailed investigation using the customary methods available at that time, so it had been by passed by zoologists concentrating on other species that were easier to study.

A similar low-key approach to hedgehog research was also apparent in other countries. The lack of knowledge was not just in Britain, but evident across Europe too, a point that was explicitly highlighted by James Fairley in his review of Irish mammals (Fairley, 2001). But from the 1970s onwards, people began to take more interest, both in Britain and abroad. Several authors tackled aspects of hedgehog ecology in France, Germany and Scandinavia, with a sustained focus in Finland on laboratory studies of hibernation physiology (see Chapter 6). Meanwhile in New Zealand, where hedgehogs had flourished since their introduction in the nineteenth century, Bob Brockie had begun a lifetime's engagement with this species and a number of key studies were made there of wild populations, slowly building up a broader picture of the animal's life and summarised in the two editions of the *Handbook of New Zealand Mammals* (King, 1990, 2005). By the 1990s, a substantial body of information had become available regarding hedgehog biology throughout much of its geographical range, comprehensively reviewed by Nigel Reeve. His monograph, *Hedgehogs*, extended to 313 pages (Reeve, 1994) and became the basic reference for all those who followed.

The problem with studying hedgehogs in the wild has always been one of practicality. For example, its secretive nocturnal habits and keen sense of hearing hamper close observation, ruling out simple direct visual studies like those that had been carried out successfully on rabbits and deer. Grid trapping, the standard method for studying small mammals like mice and voles since the 1930s, is also impractical as too many traps would be needed to obtain even quite small samples of hedgehogs. Nesting sites are hard to detect, unlike badger (*Meles meles*) setts or rabbit (*Oryctolagus cuniculus*) warrens, and searching for active individuals at night is very laborious and often unproductive. The hedgehog's spines and habit of rolling up make handling them difficult and compromises the collection of physical data in the field. In captivity, the animals are often frustratingly obtuse and their behaviour is also very variable, with the prospect of getting results that are statistically non-significant. Many of these problems remain. It is hard to work at night and not just because it is dark. In urban areas, local residents and the police may not be sympathetic to furtive investigations late at night. Nocturnal fieldworkers need somewhere quiet to sleep during the day and are faced with expectations among friends and work colleagues that do not allow for the 'working day' having ended at breakfast time. In our safety-conscious age, difficulties also arise with using student helpers working alone, yet working in pairs costs twice as much. It is also often surprisingly difficult to find enough animals to make a representative study.

The other major impediment to hedgehog research was that there seemed to be no real need for it. Hedgehogs do not carry serious diseases, unlike foxes with rabies or badgers with bovine tuberculosis. Nor do they devastate farmers' crops as rabbits do, or damage forestry plantations like deer. Unlike rats and mice, they do not cause serious economic losses in houses or food stores. Nobody had a pressing reason to learn more about hedgehogs in order to help get rid of them. Conversely, hedgehogs are not a significant economic resource. They do not provide valuable furs or useful supplies of meat, so there is nothing to be gained by investing in studying them. They were routinely considered to be a familiar, common and widespread species so there was no obvious need for research aimed at their protection and conservation. They were welcome as consumers of garden pests, but these could be easily destroyed by using cheap chemicals. Anyway, for decades, there was little money available to support field studies and no apparent need to do more than just tolerate the hedgehog and enjoy its bumbling presence.

FIGS 9 & 10. (left) Royal Holloway College (part of the University of London) where the Zoology Department in the 1960s specialised in research and teaching that centred on mammals and ecology. This tradition continued during my time there, attracting many excellent students with interests in these areas and providing me with a regular supply of new and highly motivated fieldwork assistants. (right) My first 'Big Cheque' from the BHPS, which paid for fieldwork on hedgehogs and also astonished the college accountant who was unable to decide what to do with it.

This is where I began a three-year PhD project in 1965 based in the Zoology Department of Royal Holloway College (University of London), in those days one of Britain's few centres specialising in the study of mammals. My supervisor, the late John Clevedon-Brown, sent me off with a cheerful assurance that he would not trouble me if I did not bother him. I was on my own. Rather desperately, I sought to identify lines of enquiry that might prove fruitful, given all the practical obstacles in the way and an absence of money to pay for any equipment required. Like all new researchers, I read the available literature, although that didn't take very long. I also visited the people who had recently published on the hedgehog in Britain, all three of them! One of these was Maurice Burton, of course. Having retired from the Natural History Museum as Deputy Keeper in Zoology, he was a very senior zoologist, a tall, patrician figure living in a large house in Surrey, where his study was lined with bookshelves, floor to ceiling (Fig. 11). He might easily have been intimidating towards a young and eager PhD student, but instead proved both agreeable and very encouraging, sharing his enthusiasm and interest in a broad range of wildlife interests, and willingly offered me access to his invaluable files of correspondence on hedgehogs.

A second established expert was my namesake, Bryn Morris, who had been breeding hedgehogs for use in his studies of immunity transmission at the University of Nottingham. He seemed wary of my intrusion and declined my request for help in establishing age criteria for the species. The third contemporary hedgehog author was Maxwell Knight, who had been a senior spymaster at MI5, the model for 'M' in the original James Bond stories. In his retirement, he had published various magazine articles and a small booklet about hedgehogs (Knight, 1962). So I visited him one afternoon and he gave me a cup of tea.

Fortunately I had inadvertently stumbled upon a site in a west London park where hedgehogs congregated to hibernate and I had already begun to monitor the construction and use of hibernacula there (see Chapter 6). I was strongly encouraged to continue this by Ian Linn, a prominent figure in the mammal world, and patiently assisted by my old school friend Derek Yalden, a key

FIG 11. Dr. Maurice Burton in 1988. He was a senior zoologist and widely known popular natural history author. He was also very helpful and encouraging to me as a fresh PhD student in 1965. (Courtesy of his son Robert Burton)

FIGS 12 & 13. (left) My friend and fellow zoologist Derek Yalden helping to check winter nests of hedgehogs in Bushy Park in 1964; (right) Derek, as President of the Mammal Society. He and I were at school together and for more than 40 years provided mutual support and encouragement in the study of British mammals.

mentor throughout my career. I monitored the nests for six successive winters. This would become a completely new area of investigation, filling a crucial gap in knowledge of the hedgehog's ecology, but it would not be enough to fill a PhD thesis.

I toyed with the idea of studying hedgehog spines, but this had been done in the nineteenth century and failed to address any new questions so I gave that up. I was then lucky in meeting Mary English, a pathologist at Bristol Royal Infirmary. She was interested in fungal infections of the skin and knew the hedgehog to be a potential source of a condition occasionally seen in humans. She readily agreed to 'see what we could find out' and was delighted with the unexpectedly extensive results of our partnership (see Chapter 11). I was relieved to create another section for my thesis.

People often asked me how long would a hedgehog live and I had read about age determination methods based on counting growth rings in the teeth of fur seals, but I could find nothing in the microscopic structure of hedgehog teeth that seemed to offer a way forward. In desperation, I showed some tooth sections to my Head of Department, Professor Percy Butler. He was a world authority on fossil teeth, an arcane topic that I considered of little use to anyone, but I was lucky that day. He agreed that growth lines were not consistently visible in hedgehog tooth cement or dentine, but pointed out that my sections showed very prominent incremental lines in the bone of the lower jaw. This proved to be the key that would later open up a whole new field of hedgehog biology, leading to an understanding of population structure and survival rates. And it would make my thesis a bit thicker.

I had also been asked many times about hedgehog movements – where did they go at night and how far would they travel? Again, nobody knew. Somehow I came across an American paper describing for the first time (in 1959) how a radio transmitter could be attached to an animal allowing its movements to be tracked continuously from a distance. This looked promising and I visited R. M. Newson, a Government scientist who was studying coypu (*Myocastor coypus*) and had apparently tried this technique. He told me that the transmitters were unsuitable for his work and that the equipment had cost £250. That was five times more than my entire research allowance for a whole year and out of the question. But in another serendipitous development, I discovered that a member of the Royal Holloway College staff, John Pontin, was a keen flyer of radio-controlled model aircraft. He taught me how to build cheap transmitters myself. I then faced ridicule at the idea of attaching them to hedgehogs and an obstructive element of officialdom keen to point out that all radio transmitters had to be licensed under the Wireless and Telegraphy Act of 1949, which had somehow omitted to take account of hedgehog research. After a few months argument, some inventive

FIGS 14 & 15. (left) The first hedgehog radio-tracking experiments in 1966 involved using a home-made transmitter attached to the animal by a loop of bra elastic. Signals were transmitted on the model aircraft frequency but had a range of barely 100 m; (right) My crude 1966 radio-tracking equipment. The receiver weighed over 7 kg and the whole system failed to detect hedgehogs at more than 100 m away. Nevertheless, new information was obtained, pointing the way towards answering key questions about hedgehog life once better equipment became available.

FIG 16. Official approval to begin radio-tracking hedgehogs made a good story in the local newspaper.

discussion over the use of words enabled my animals to be licensed to operate on the model aircraft frequency as 'Testing and Development Stations', but I had to keep a log of everything said during transmissions! Nowadays, radio-tracking is an accepted mainstream activity and there is a blanket licence to use particular radio frequencies for the purpose. Whilst my radio-tracking efforts in 1966 were pioneering (in Britain at least), they were also ineffectual. Principally, this was because the hedgehogs quickly went out of range of the legally restricted signal strength of my transmitters. The technique had to await advances in technology before there would be any real progress on the hedgehog radio-tracking front (see Chapter 5), but another innovative chapter for my thesis was born. I thus had four lines of enquiry to pursue in the hope that at least one would actually generate some results. The university then rejected my PhD project title on the grounds that it was 'too broad'. Fortunately that problem was resolved by another manipulation of words. My PhD was delivered in 1969 less than three months late, in marked contrast to the norm. It was the first PhD thesis based solely on wild hedgehogs. I had finished almost on time despite spending several weeks away in Ethiopia as a key advisor on a big Army expedition. For that sin, I was ordered to repay my student grant on the grounds that I had not been studying hedgehogs, the task for which I was being paid. Fortunately this too was another dispute with officialdom that could be resolved with an alternative interpretation of words and a threat to pursue the argument at ministerial level.

I have described this autobiographical context here because it formed the background to breaking into the hedgehog's secrets and became the bedrock upon which many other things have been built. It is also in marked contrast to the way that PhD studies are initiated and supervised today. Indeed, looking back, it is important to appreciate just how great the changes have been in terms of research resources and scientific ethos. But change came slowly. After I became a member of staff at Royal Holloway, I could bid for money to buy equipment that would help my research and assist in speedy publication of its results. I persuaded my colleagues to buy the Department's first electronic calculator, a miraculous device the size of a house brick that could actually add up and multiply just by pressing buttons! It speeded data analysis, but when I tried for an upgrade to a machine that would do square roots (for statistical calculations), I had to fill in official Government forms to explain why foreign currency was being spent on buying equipment from Japan. In those days, foreign expenditure greater than £50 had to be specially authorised. In addition to building my own radio transmitters, I had to make my own microscope slides and take and develop X-rays myself; all good training perhaps, but a slow way to learn about hedgehogs.

After a few years, I was able to supervise a PhD student myself. Nigel Reeve had been one of my undergraduates and was keen to pursue the idea of studying hedgehog movements using radio-tracking. Major technological advances made that a more practical proposition than previously, but there was still no money for hedgehogs and he too had to build his own equipment and cobble together a system for receiving VHF signals based on a modified domestic transistor radio and some car radio aerials (Fig. 17). He also had to raise his own fees and everyday support money for three years (1977–79). But for the first time anywhere,

FIG 17. By the 1970s, improvements in transistor technology enabled Nigel Reeve to build far better equipment and begin gathering systematic data on hedgehog movements for the first time anywhere in Europe.

FIG 18. For many years I struggled to find funds for studying hedgehogs and turned to other species instead, notably the hazel dormouse (*Muscardinus avellanarius*). This proved more successful, but hedgehogs got neglected.

not just in Britain, his work gained detailed insights into aspects of hedgehog movements, nesting and population density (see Chapter 5).

I sought a grant from the Natural Environmental Research Council, to be told that they had a policy of only funding studies of systems, not individual species. During the 1980s and onwards, the philosophy behind ecological research increasingly moved towards testing principles and ideas, erecting hypotheses and exploring broad concepts that might apply widely across species and ecosystems. The hedgehog had little place in this kind of approach, although Andy Wroot, another of my PhD students, did try to study hedgehogs in relation to ideas about optimum foraging theory that were being developed by ornithologists, and Patrick Doncaster (at the University of Oxford) gained useful information about the species whilst exploring the issue of intraguild predation (Doncaster, 1992). Studies in which the hedgehog would be little more than a tool could yield interesting new information about its life, aided by modelling and powerful new statistical techniques, but this was an avenue that I felt poorly qualified to follow and I remained focused on answering simple questions about how hedgehogs live. Over the years, the study of animals has become more ideas-oriented and less focused on species. Massive advances in computing and data handling have also led to competence in statistical analysis overtaking the fieldwork skills needed to acquire data in the first place. Cutting-edge scientific enquiry slowly left me behind, but many of the same old questions remain.

One of the consequences of the evolving scientific paradigm has been that a lot of basic data was not published as front-line research moved on. Studying something simple like body weights is not regarded as important or is assumed to have been done already, even when it has not. Yet body weights are a vital factor in the hedgehog's life (see Chapter 6). Most of our understanding of hedgehog winter nesting, another key aspect of its life, is based on just one study now overlooked or ignored as it was carried out more than half a century ago. It has never been repeated. Much of what else we know about hedgehogs today comes from a very few investigations, many of them based on small numbers of animals and few alternative sites. We cannot be certain how valid are the data that we now use for twenty-first-century science such as elaborate population modelling, but it's all that we have. Basic studies have become unfashionable, unlikely to be funded and even less likely to be published in the journals from which modellers draw their basic input data. This is becoming not just a hedgehog problem, but an issue with many species where key

FIG 19. Hugh Warwick on one of our studies following up hedgehogs that were released in Devon after a period in veterinary care.

facts are needed upon which to base conservation management plans or model the potential spread of disease, for example. This problem is discussed further in later chapters (8, 9 and 10). One is left with the feeling that researchers need to spend less time on their computers and more time in the field gathering reliable and up-to-date data.

Whilst the hedgehog remained an unsuitable basis for major research grants, small amounts of money became available to investigate welfare issues such as the effect of supplementary feeding and also what happens to 'rehabilitated' hedgehogs after release from a period in veterinary care. I made a series of studies aided by seven of my students (see Chapter 11), funded by animal charities, including the Royal Society for the Prevention of Cruelty to Animals (RSPCA). One of those projects led me to employ Hugh Warwick (Fig. 19), who had completed an interesting investigation of hedgehogs that had been translocated to North Ronaldsay (see Chapters 4 and 12) and he has since managed to carve out a successful and effective career as the hedgehog's high-profile champion in print (Warwick, 2008) and on social media. But these are not the sort of issues that play a leading role in advanced university level research and I was running out of hedgehog questions that could be investigated with minimal funding. Longer-term studies were needed, requiring significant resources of time and money. Based on setting up PhD studentships, they would cost at least £90,000 over three years, a level of funding that was unlikely to become available very often.

Hedgehogs live at relatively low population densities in the wild, so it is difficult to obtain large enough samples to generate statistically reliable results, a disaster for anyone attempting a PhD or seeking to have their research published in a respectable scientific journal. As a result of all this, few researchers have attempted to investigate this species and most have swiftly discovered the hard way the many practical difficulties associated with small sample sizes, nocturnal fieldwork and uncooperative animals. With the exception of a mere handful of often underfunded three-year PhD studies (probably fewer than a dozen nationally), with students often working alone and without help in the field, there has been very little concentrated research on wild hedgehogs in Britain. It's not just me who found it difficult working on these animals. Although ultimately successful, two PhD studies on arable land (by Anouschka Hof and Carly Pettett) nearly foundered because it was so hard to find enough animals, and Amy Haigh's PhD study in Ireland resulted in a paper on methods of detecting hedgehogs that was published in the *Journal of Negative Results*! (Haigh *et al.*, 2012a)

An important exception to this story of inadequately resourced research concerns studies on the Hebridean islands of North and South Uist, and Benbecula that lies between them. In 1974, four hedgehogs had been taken from the mainland to South Uist, with a few more added the following year. Within a decade or so, there was alleged to be a population of 5,000 hedgehogs on the three islands causing significant damage to internationally important populations of ground-nesting birds, particularly waders such as redshank (*Tringa totanus*), dunlin (*Calidris alpina*) and lapwing (*Vanellus vanellus*). Digger Jackson, funded by the Royal Society for the Protection of Birds (RSPB), was engaged to carry out extensive fieldwork because it was suddenly important to know a lot more about hedgehog ecology. Significant effort was put into conducting detailed studies of hedgehog activities, based on large samples of animals and with the benefits of modern technical facilities. The Uist story crops up frequently in this book because it is one of the few times that major national resources have been invested in work on hedgehogs, in this case focused on their activities as a predator of bird colonies, but also leading to useful insights into other aspects of its biology (Jackson & Green, 2000;

Jackson, 2006, 2007). The arrival of hedgehogs and their subsequent activities resulted in important research efforts in the Uists, but also generated a major area of controversy and public engagement, described in Chapters 12 and 13.

There have been many smaller studies published, some of which have usefully extended our understanding of hedgehogs and some that have not. The paucity of formal research on hedgehogs contrasts with the huge volume of magazine articles and newspaper features that reflect ongoing popular interest in this species. I attempted to summarise the hedgehog's story in a popular book (Morris, 1983, 2014) enhanced with amusing cartoons by another of my students, Guy Troughton (Fig. 20). This concept was initially rejected by publishers, confused as to whether I was writing a serous account or a joke book. But for most people hedgehogs are interesting and

FIG 20. The first edition of my popular book published by Whittet Books in 1983. It included jokes and cartoons, a concept which mainstream publishers had rejected. It has remained in print, regularly updated and enlarged, for longer than any other book on the hedgehog ... or any other British mammal!

fun, not merely a subject for scientific enquiry. That book has remained in print, enlarged and updated, for longer than any other on a British mammal, testimony to the widespread public interest in hedgehogs. Today, use of the internet enables much information to be disseminated among enthusiasts. Some of it is very helpful, but 'buyer beware'! There is much out there that has little real foundation and some that is misleading or just plain wrong.

By the 1980s, my old-fashioned approach to mammal research was no longer academically appropriate to a leading university, whose institutional requirement for large research grants was unlikely to be satisfied by pursuing small spiny mammals of little consequence. I changed tack and returned to where I had started, trying to study a species in which practical problems had resulted in little or no ecological information being available. For 20 years, aided

FIG 21. Major Adrian Coles, founder of the British Hedgehog Preservation Society in 1982, seen here in a publicity photograph illustrating his campaign to get hedgehog escape ramps fitted to cattle grids. On the right is a circular car sticker issued by the BHPS.

by Paul Bright (another of my ex-students), I set about filling the huge gaps in knowledge about the hazel dormouse. This uncommon species did attract research grants and generated a respectable series of published papers. It also drew me into the challenge of studying the introduced edible dormouse (*Glis glis*) and I started a ball rolling for water voles (*Arvicola terrestris*) based on an analysis of works which had nationwide consequences for the conservation of this species (Jefferies, Morris & Mulleneux, 1989). Hedgehogs got left behind and my academic career ended in 2003 with timely voluntary early retirement. But my engagement with these animals has continued, working closely with two key charities whose activities feature frequently in this book, the People's Trust for Endangered Species (PTES), founded in 1977 (see Chapter 13) and the British Hedgehog Preservation Society (BHPS), another key player.

The BHPS was established in 1982 by Major Adrian Coles, one of its objectives being to raise funds for hedgehog research (Fig. 21). My slightly aggressive request for some of his money resulted in the first of several small studies being funded that way, bypassing the obstacles involved with getting funds from academic sources. With research funding no longer entirely at the whim of changing scientific fashion, alternative ways of supporting research have emerged, enabling bigger and better hedgehog studies. Some of these have been supported jointly by BHPS and the PTES, from whom I had sought funds for a study of red squirrels (*Sciurus vulgaris*) and subsequently fostered a partnership with the Mammal Society that drove forward initiatives that we would now describe as 'Citizen Science'. A legacy from Dilys Breese (the BBC producer of *The Great Hedgehog Mystery*) helped to forge a partnership between the PTES and BHPS (Fig. 22). This arrangement, under the project name 'Hedgehog Street', has been exceptionally successful in harnessing modern communication media to develop a huge popular base for hedgehog support and the application of Citizen Science to the study of hedgehog populations (see Chapters 11 and 13). Both charities supported hedgehog research by Paul Bright, Steve Carter and Anouschka Hof at Royal Holloway after my retirement, and studies at other universities too. The BHPS also began to employ 'Hedgehog Officers' to be based with county wildlife trusts with the aim of promoting the species locally in high-profile initiatives to raise awareness of hedgehogs and their needs in the increasingly challenging environment of our towns and cities.

Another significant development has been the huge increase in the number of wildlife rescue centres, where the hedgehog has become the most frequent mammal brought in for treatment. The rescue centres offer the prospect of gaining and collating a lot of basic information about hedgehogs, although that potential has not yet been fulfilled. There has also been a massive increase in public engagement

FIG 22. The BBC producer Dilys Breese in 1981 filming a story about hedgehogs carrying fruit on their spines as part of *The Great Hedgehog Mystery*, a programme for 'Wildlife on One', a popular wildlife TV series. This attracted a bigger audience than the BBC's *Match of the Day*, its principal sporting programe of that time.

in the form of many independent volunteer 'carers' who specialise in rescuing and rehabilitating sick and injured hedgehogs (see Chapter 11). The BHPS lists no fewer than 800 of them.

As the scientific hedgehog literature has expanded, so has the range of popular publications. Since the 1970s, public interest in hedgehogs has blossomed, supporting the sale of many small and inexpensive books about the species, benefitting from the greater availability of photographs and cheap colour printing. Some offered accounts of direct personal observations on hedgehog behaviour, such as *Secret Life of the Hedgehog* (Bomford, 1979). Mostly, they were unremarkable and soon vanished from the shops, but they still managed to leave buyers and

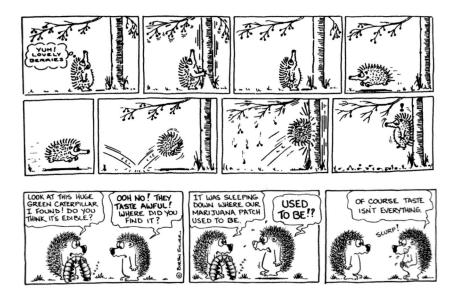

FIG 23. The Bogor cartoon strips by Burton Silver featured a whimsical woodman and his hedgehog companion. They were published weekly in New Zealand, with an annual compilation in book form. (Courtesy of Burton Silver)

readers better informed about hedgehogs. A few of these books show genuine originality, like the anthology of hedgehog poems (Anon, 1992) published in association with the BHPS, with its attractive watercolour illustrations. A similar spectrum of small publications can be found among the popular books published on the Continent, ranging from personal observation of pet hedgehogs (Poduschka & Poduschka, 1980) to publicly available PhD theses (Berthoud, 1982, for example) and various translations of my own Whittet Books monograph (Morris, 1983), often enhanced by contributions from a local author.

A very readable book by Hugh Warwick, *A Prickly Affair* (Warwick, 2008), tells of his involvement with these animals as a field researcher and his engagement with an extraordinary range of people dedicated to hedgehogs in captivity and in the wild. A second book, *Hedgehog*, is a thorough and entertaining review of hedgehog iconography and human engagement with these animals (Warwick, 2014). The popular literature also includes the wonderful cartoons by Burton Silver, published in New Zealand. They depict Bogor, a lonely lovesick woodsman and his hedgehog companion whose mind is strongly focused on cannabis plants

(Silver, 1994) (Fig. 23). These cartoons in *The Listener* continued for 21 years, the longest-running cartoon strip ever published in New Zealand. It is a shame that European readers have not had an opportunity to chuckle over the perceptive and endearing humour in these weekly stories, which were also published annually in book form. The vital importance of popularity and public support for the hedgehog is discussed more fully in Chapter 13.

CONCLUSION

For the first half of the twentieth century, existing literature consisted mainly of accounts and information copied from previous publications, some dating from centuries earlier with little new added. Although a few authors did substantiate their embellishments, much information was published without evidence of its reliability (sample sizes or who made the observations, for example). The hedgehog is one of our most widespread and easily recognised species, but the practical difficulty of studying them meant that few attempts were made and reliable information about the life of our only spiny mammal remained elusive. Hedgehog research stayed very much in the background in the second half of the twentieth century compared with major ongoing studies of foxes, badgers, deer and species of common small mammals. Even today, much that we think we know about this animal is based on only a small number of studies, most of them not repeated or corroborated by similar work in another place. Meanwhile, the hedgehog has gained hugely in public prominence. Support from key charities has enabled a significant enhancement in research activity and professionalism that continues to illuminate the life of this very special species. Charities increasingly facilitate a wider public engagement with these interesting and iconic animals.

CHAPTER 2

The Hedgehog's Origins and Distribution

T HE HEDGEHOG REALLY NEEDS NO introduction. We can all recognise Britain's only spiny mammal; we know what it is and what it looks like. However there are many details about this animal that are probably unfamiliar to most people and add up to it being a rather special creature.

The hedgehog's spines immediately suggest an affinity with porcupines (Fig. 24), spiny mice (*Acomys* spp.) and maybe the spiny anteaters (*Zaglossus* and

FIG 24. Despite their spiny coats, porcupines are no more related to hedgehogs than are monkeys or seals. They belong to a completely different order of mammals, the Rodentia.

FIGS 25–7. Hedgehogs belong to the mammalian order Insectivora, along with various species of moles (*Talpa europaea*, top left) and other creatures that mostly feed on large invertebrates. Shrews, both the red-toothed and white-toothed (*Crocidura suaveolens*, top right) varieties, are the most numerous of the hedgehog's relatives. The rare solenodons of the West Indies (*Solenodon paradoxus*, left) are among the most primitive mammals alive today and closely resemble the hedgehog's ancient ancestors and also today's spineless hairy hedgehogs of the Far East.

Tachyglossus) of Australia. Actually those animals all belong to very different groups of mammals (rodents and monotremes respectively), they simply share the same evolutionary development in which hairs have become stiffened and thickened into defensive structures. This is a process referred to as 'convergent evolution', where unrelated animals come to resemble each other through developing similar structures in response to similar ecological pressures. A more clear-cut example might be the webbed feet of otters, seals, ducks and frogs. They have all evolved to have webbing between their toes, benefitting from improved swimming capabilities, but obviously they are not closely related at all. Wings are found in bats, birds and butterflies, but they are not evidence of being close relatives. Camouflage colouration is another example, found in birds, frogs and many invertebrates. It's the same with spines; superficial similarity does not necessarily imply close evolutionary relationships.

Hedgehogs are mammals of course, hairy animals that characteristically give birth to active young and feed them on milk. Traditionally, since 1816, they have been assigned to an order of mammals called the Insectivora, lumping them together with various other odd groups of species that eat insects and small prey,

FIG 28. Among the tenrecs of Madagascar, some species, like this lesser hedgehog tenrec (*Echinops telfairi*), have evolved a spiny coat very similar to that of the hedgehog.

but these animals have little else in common. Other mammalian orders include distinctive groups like the whales (Cetacea), bats (Chiroptera) and elephants (Proboscidea). By contrast, the Insectivora are a rather disparate assortment of animals (including moles, shrews, the West Indian solenodons and Madagascan tenrecs (Fig. 28) that appear to share only the distinction of not belonging to any other group of mammals (although two genera of tenrecs, *Setifer* and *Echinops*, are spiny animals and look rather like hedgehogs). Attempts to refine the classification by seeking evidence of affinities using morphological methods or DNA analysis have yielded confusing and contradictory results. Modern classifications sometimes split off some groups, leaving the rest as the Lipotyphla (or Eulipotyphla), within which the hedgehog's nearest relatives are still moles (classified as a single family, Talpidae) and shrews (Soricidae). Anatomical similarities indicate that the lipotyphlan Insectivora evolved from a single ancestor, but molecular evidence suggests otherwise. Actually, the hedgehog's nearest relatives are other hedgehogs and they all belong to their own family of mammals, the Erinaceidae, largely defined by the nature of their dentition and lack of specialised skeletal features. This may seem a little perverse, but the study of evolutionary origins needs to be based on fossils and it is the teeth and bones that fossilise best and allow detailed examination. Classifying animals on superficial features (like spines, for example) limits what we can learn from the fossil record and also risks assembling artificial groups of unrelated animals like 'spiny mammals' (see above!).

Following the system devised by the Swedish botanist Carl von Linné (usually known as 'Linnaeus'), animals and plants are given a scientific (Latin) name that is recognised across the world to save the confusion that arises from the multifarious names used in many different languages. There are at least 30 different regional names for the hedgehog in Europe alone, but only one scientific name and this is recognised by everyone. Each scientific name is in two parts, the genus and species, just as each of us is identified by a family name ('surname', shared with close relatives) and a given name that is personal to each of us as individuals. Linnaeus formally named our familiar hedgehog *Erinaceus europaeus* in 1758. Subsequent authors tried to distinguish local geographical races as subspecies (designated by adding a third name in Latin). Often these diagnoses were based on small samples of animals, frequently with incomplete skulls, and were focussed on particular features that are anyway highly variable. In fact the detailed anatomy of *E. europaeus* is sufficiently inconsistent across its geographical range that none of these regional distinctions is regarded as valid these days and the descriptions of subspecies that have been published in the past are now normally ignored. That goes for the 'special' British sub-species, *Erinaceus europaeus occidentalis*, described by the eminent mammalogist G. E. H. Barrett-Hamilton in 1900 and dismissed as nonsense by a Swedish biologist within just a few weeks.

Some of the family Erinaceidae have no spines, just a coat of coarse hair. There are about six kinds of these 'hairy hedgehogs' or 'moonrats' (assigned to the genera *Hylomys*, *Podogymnura* and *Echinosorex*) which live on the ground in the evergreen forests of China, the Malay Peninsula, Indonesia and the Philippines. They closely resemble what the earliest hedgehogs would have looked like when they first evolved in the Miocene epoch about 20 million years ago, around the time when the first grasslands began to develop. Spines came later, but even so, our hedgehog is among the most ancient types of mammal still alive today. The ancestors of our hedgehogs were snuffling about much earlier than our own; indeed, the first 'ape men' would probably have found and eaten them from time to time. The Erinaceidae evolved well before the woolly mammoths and sabre-toothed cats that became extinct thousands of years ago, so hedgehogs are clearly ancient and successful animals, although they face many new challenges in the modern world.

The spiny members of the Erinaceidae all look rather similar and are separated into four distinct genera (Macdonald, 2001) which survive in rather different conditions to those found in western Europe, and most have not been studied in much detail. The long-eared hedgehogs (*Hemiechinus*) comprise six species that occur in desert regions of the Middle East and Central Asia (Fig. 29). Four species of *Atelerix* are mostly found in the sub-Saharan areas of Africa (Fig. 30), although one (*A. algirus*) occurs in North Africa and in a few places in Spain. Two species of steppe hedgehog (*Mesechinus*) live in Mongolia and parts of China. Nearer to home, the genus *Erinaceus* includes our own western European hedgehog (*E. europaeus*) (Fig. 31) and there is another species (*E. amurensis*)

FIG 29. The long-eared hedgehog (*Hemiechinus*) is a desert species found from the eastern Mediterranean eastwards to India.

FIG 30. African pygmy hedgehogs are widely distributed on that continent and captive-bred varieties are now often kept as pets.

FIG 31. The familiar western European hedgehog, *Erinaceus europaeus*.

that lives in China. This makes a total of about 15 spiny species in the family Erinaceidae, depending, for example, upon whether or not the white-throated hedgehogs of eastern Europe are considered sufficiently different from their western counterparts to be classified as separate species, *Erinaceus concolor* or *E. roumanicus*. Most authorities these days say they are and DNA analysis shows

FIG 32. European hedgehog *Erinaceus europaeus* – subadult.

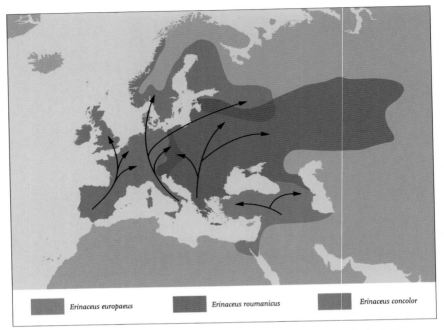

| Erinaceus europaeus | Erinaceus roumanicus | Erinaceus concolor |

FIG 33. During the last Ice Age, hedgehogs retreated south into separate refugia. As the climate improved they spread northwards: some recolonised western regions as *Erinaceus europaeus*, others migrated northwards and eastwards from the Balkans and Middle East to form the white-fronted species *Erinaceus concolor* and *Erinaceus roumanicus* (which are often regarded as a single species). Based on Bolfíková & Hulva, 2012.

separate genetic clades developing about 4 million years ago. Genetic studies also suggest that Spain, Italy and Sicily provided climatic refuges for populations of *E. europaeus* during the last Ice Age, from which they colonised western Europe as the climate ameliorated about 10,000 years ago. Similarly, the white-breasted forms spread from refugia in the Balkans and Middle East (Bolfíková & Hulva, 2012) to colonise eastern Europe. The eastern and western species of *Erinaceus* overlap in the Czech Republic, north to Poland and the Baltic countries, and also in southern Russia (Fig. 33). Both eastern and western species of *Erinaceus* have the same number of chromosomes (48) and can hybridise, both in captivity and in the wild, but any differences in their behaviour or their ecology remain obscure. British hedgehogs seem to belong to the same karyotypic race as *E. europaeus* of western Europe (Searle & Erskine, 1985).

PRIMITIVE?

Despite being long-term survivors and successfully widespread, hedgehogs are considered to be primitive animals. This is because their anatomy remains very basic without significant modifications for a specialised way of life. For example, they have five fingers and toes, each with a long but blunt claw, and they walk on flat (plantigrade) feet (Fig. 34). They have small collar bones (clavicles) and prominent cheek bones (zygomatic arches), which are often reduced or absent in more advanced mammals. In males, the testes do not descend into an external pouch (the scrotum) in the breeding season, as they do in many more highly evolved species. The brain is relatively small and also simple in form with a smooth surface that lacks the folded structure associated with complex behaviour, and with its principal development in the region associated with the sense of smell rather than vision or hearing (Clark, 1932). All of these features would have characterised the anatomy of the earliest mammals to evolve back in the Jurassic epoch when dinosaurs roamed the Earth. But alongside the primitive features of hedgehogs, we see their characteristic spiny coat. In this respect, they are very highly developed animals, as the spines and associated skin muscles are more complex in their structure than in any other mammals.

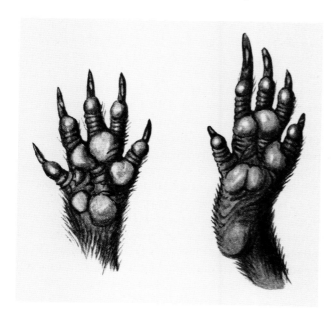

FIG 34. The hedgehog's feet have well-developed fleshy pads on the soles and there are five fingers and toes, each furnished with a long claw.

HEDGEHOGS IN BRITAIN – THEIR HISTORY AND DISTRIBUTION

Fossil remains of hedgehogs from the Pleistocene epoch are rare, even from the warm interglacial periods when hyaenas lived in southern Britain and hippos basked by the rivers. This could be because much of the land was forested at that time, a habitat that seems to be used relatively infrequently by hedgehogs even today. Our knowledge of the early history of the British fauna after the last Ice Age ended and humans began to settle here relies heavily on evidence obtained by archaeologists excavating cave shelters and ancient settlements (Yalden, 1999). Hedgehogs had arrived here by the Mesolithic era (the Middle Stone Age) and their remains have been found at Star Carr, the largest Mesolithic settlement so far excavated, in what is now the Vale of Pickering in East Yorkshire. That community lived beside a shallow lake about 10,000 years ago and used flint tools and antler picks. Most of the bones that have been excavated there were from large mammals, probably food remains from animals that had been hunted and killed. Perhaps Mesolithic people ate a few hedgehogs too? Another Middle Stone Age site in lightly wooded terrain at Thatcham in Berkshire had hedgehog remains among the excavated bones, along with those of its possible predators the lynx (*Lynx lynx*) and wolf (*Canis lupus*). Generally speaking, ancient hedgehog remains are few, partly because archaeologists in the past rarely bothered with sieving the soil they dug up to check for the bones and teeth of small mammals. The prehistoric record is thus fragmentary, especially so for hedgehogs, which were never as common as rodents and domestic animals.

During the Neolithic era (New Stone Age), forested areas were progressively cleared by the use of stone tools and the nibbling teeth of domestic animals like sheep and cattle. This process continued for centuries and would have created more open and patchy habitats, a change that is likely to have favoured hedgehogs. They were present in Roman Exeter about 300 CE and the continuing expansion of farming in Saxon times created an expanding mosaic of small-scale open-field systems with grasslands, crops, human habitation and a diversity of grazing activities that offered increasing opportunities for the species to prosper. From Norman times onwards, there was a steady reduction in reliance on the hunting and eating of wild animals and a localised focus on some sporting species like deer and commercially managed rabbits. Bears (*Ursus arctos*) and then wolves were vigorously exterminated, removing two of the hedgehog's few natural predators (by Saxon times and the 1700s respectively). From the reign of Queen Elizabeth I, for 300 years, the hedgehog was regarded officially as a pest and very large numbers were killed by people (see Chapter 12).

FIG 35. The distribution of *Erinaceus europaeus* in Britain and Ireland. Blank areas represent regions of poor or unsuitable habitat where few would be expected to live.

Figure 35 shows the present distribution of hedgehogs within the British Isles. Today, they are found in Ireland and on the Isle of Man, begging the question of how that came about when so many other common animals are absent from one or both. There are no moles in Ireland, nor field voles (*Microtus agrestis*) or snakes, for example. These absences are due to conditions at the end of the last Ice age. As the climate improved in the late Pleistocene epoch, our ice-bound landscape slowly became more richly vegetated, offering opportunities for animals to colonise the land by spreading north and west from the Continent, overland into southern England and beyond. But the melting ice and associated rising sea level opened up the English Channel about 9,500 years ago, preventing many species from reaching mainland Britain. Rising sea levels also compromised the colonisation of Ireland by land animals, leaving it with an impoverished fauna. Although hedgehogs had arrived in England by about 10,000 years ago, they are climate-sensitive (which is why they hibernate in winter) and are unlikely to have been among the leading pioneers of western colonisation and probably reached western Britain too late to colonise Ireland naturally.

Giraldus Cambrensis wrote a lengthy and famous account of his visits to Ireland in the twelfth-century, *Topographica Hibernica*, and explicitly stated that hedgehogs were absent there. However, he said the same about stoats (*Mustela erminea*), which are undoubtedly present. Much else in his book is biological nonsense, despite the credence paid by historians to Giraldus. It is nevertheless likely that the present-day occurrence of hedgehogs in Ireland (and on many lesser islands around Britain) is a result of being taken there long ago in the course of coastal trade since the Middle Ages, perhaps by being carried accidentally in a shipment of fodder or thatching material. It may seem unlikely that hedgehogs would be transported unknowingly, but in 1974 one arrived in a Bournemouth ironmonger's shop having travelled from Poland in a shipment of kettles (Fairley, 1975) and there are plenty of documented accounts of deliberate transport of hedgehogs to islands.

Translocation by humans accounts for hedgehogs being present on at least 31 of the Scottish islands, where bleak and treeless landscapes may have meant that importing building materials and winter fodder for farm animals from the mainland was necessary for the continued existence of island communities. Hedgehogs could easily have been gathered up and carried along too, even perhaps deliberately as useful food items. Sometimes the actual date of introduction is known – 1860 in the case of Shetland for example, and 1870 in Orkney (with multiple twentieth-century releases). Many other deliberate translocations have occurred, establishing the hedgehog on islands that it could never have reached naturally. Most of the Scottish islands are surrounded by deep water and have probably been separated from the mainland since the end of the last Ice Age, so their hedgehogs could not have arrived unaided.

Some English offshore islands (such as the Isle of Wight) have only shallow water between them and the mainland, so the hedgehog population might have originated long ago through natural immigration, perhaps aided by swimming short distances when sea levels were lower. However, it is known that deliberate or accidental introduction is responsible for the present-day populations on Steepholm (fewer than six released in 1975–76, but scarce by the 1980s and extinct by 2017) and Caldey Island (nine animals brought from Wembley in London, some still present in 2017). In the Channel Islands, hedgehogs are present in Jersey where they were probably introduced in the 1880s (Le Sueur, 1976) and are now widespread there (Morris & Burdon, 2008). They are also on Guernsey, Alderney (present population established by the 1960s) (Fig. 36) and Sark (introduced in July 1984). They were released on St. Mary's (Isles of Scilly) in 1985 and were still

FIG 36. On Alderney, one of the Channel Islands, both the cow and the hedgehog are special local varieties characteristic of that island (see Chapter 3). Both were introduced to the island, although at different times.

present in 2013 (Groves, 2013). Hedgehogs were probably also taken to the Isle of Man in historical times as there are no ancient Manx names for this animal. Their arrival is thought to have occurred sometime in the nineteenth century, although that remains in doubt. One story has it that a schooner called *Hooton* was wrecked at Roo Point and a crate of hedgehogs belonging to a passenger was cast ashore and the locals took in the animals as pets. Why anyone would have been shipping a crate of hedgehogs to the Isle of Man remains a mystery.

In the nineteenth century, it was reported that hedgehogs were absent from all of northern Scotland, but the animals have spread there now, in many cases with human help. In 1888, for example, two pairs escaped from a garden at Kintradwell and in 1900 at Inverbroom in Wester Ross the sudden appearance of hedgehogs was attributed to accidental transport in baled hay. By 1988, they were well established as far north as Thurso, where one of my correspondents enjoyed their presence in her garden.

Since 1860, there have been multiple introductions to Shetland and to at least seven of its offshore islands. Clearly there has been much enthusiasm for the idea of assisting the expansion of the hedgehog's geographical distribution. Translocations to islands or within mainland Britain often involved just a few animals, taken in order to combat garden pests or simply because these familiar and lovable creatures were absent and it would be nice to have them around. Many of these released animals have given rise to island populations that have resulted in serious problems for the native wildlife, leading to major controversy and heavy costs when attempting to remove them (see Chapter 12). Today, we consider it unwise to release animals in places where they do not occur naturally because of the ecological damage that may result. But in the late nineteenth century, led by some very senior scientists and wealthy landowners, there was much enthusiasm for enhancing impoverished faunas to make up for natural absences or to introduce species that might play some beneficial economic role. This is why Britain gained muntjac deer (*Muntiacus reevesi*) and grey squirrels (*Sciurus carolinensis*), for example (Lever, 2009). Translocations were regarded in a positive light and we should not be surprised that hedgehogs can now be found on so many islands, where their presence would otherwise seem unlikely.

TABLE 1. Some islands and dates for hedgehogs being released there. Some of the dates originate in publications, others in letters whose accuracy cannot be easily verified.

Island	Date	Source of information
Jersey, Channel Islands	1880s	Le Sueur (1976)
Steepholm, Bristol Channel	1975/6	Kenneth Allsop Memorial Trust*
Arran	Present in 1994*	
Lewis	Present in 1994*	
Orkney	c. 1870 and many subsequent dates	Berry (1985)
Caldey, Dyfed	1984	From London*
North Ronaldsay	1972	Warwick (2008)

* denotes information from a correspondent; otherwise, the source reference is given.

Similar motives prompted the export of British hedgehogs to New Zealand, encouraged by acclimatisation societies dedicated to filling perceived vacancies in New Zealand's habitats and stocking up with familiar creatures reminiscent of life back home in Europe. The hedgehog was also seen as a potentially useful means of reducing the number of insect larvae that were damaging the grass

FIG 37. This is a New Zealand hedgehog. It looks just like one of ours because the present population there is based on animals imported from Britain in the nineteenth century.

that underpinned the country's increasingly important sheep industry. The first two arrived in 1870, followed by multiple batches over the next few years (Fig. 37). The climate, particularly of North Island, proved very favourable for hedgehogs, moist like England, but warm like Spain, and they prospered. They were welcomed as consumers of slugs and insects that otherwise damaged crops and they quickly spread, with plenty of officially sanctioned human assistance. Within a 100 years, hedgehogs had attained population densities that appear far higher than in their British homeland. However, official attitudes changed and in 1939 a bounty of three pence per snout (increased to sixpence in 1940) was paid to encourage their destruction. By 1948, over 58,000 bounties had been paid out, itself an indication of how abundant hedgehogs had become within 80 years of their arrival (Wodzicki, 1950). The success of British hedgehogs in New Zealand and their response to differing climatic conditions prompts some interesting comparisons with their relatives back home in Britain, showing this to be a very adaptable species.

Attempts have been made to export hedgehogs from New Zealand for the American pet market (although the African species are better suited for this way of life). In 1994, a shipment of 120 European hedgehogs to American zoos was denied entry to the USA and sent back on the grounds that the animals may have been carrying bovine tuberculosis. There appear to have been no major releases elsewhere in the world. Hedgehog distribution is therefore confined to the Old World, with none living wild in the Americas or in Australia, and there are no spiny hedgehogs in tropical Asia.

BOX 1. The Hedgehog in New Zealand

New Zealand is a long way away and seems remote from the focus of this book. However, the hedgehog population there is derived from British specimens and has been intensively studied over a long period of time. This provides comparative information of considerable interest and relevance to the situation in Britain (Moss & Sanders, 2001; King, 2005). Until the arrival of humans a thousand years ago, there were no terrestrial mammals in New Zealand. Rats and domestic animals came later and in the nineteenth century, acclimatisation societies deliberately imported mammals and birds to diversify the local fauna. The first recorded hedgehogs were delivered to Canterbury (South Island) on the *Hydaspes* in 1870, with more brought in to other areas over the subsequent 20 years. They are all thought to have come from Britain, with at least one shipment known to have been dispatched from Perth in Scotland. Importation was originally motivated by sentiment, but by the 1890s the hedgehog's role as a potential controller of pests was firmly established and further releases were made, including on North Island. Hedgehogs have spread widely since, but remain scarce in the uplands and where there are more than 250 frosty days per year or where annual rainfall exceeds 2,500 mm. They are particularly abundant in suburban areas and on dairy farmland where there is plenty of invertebrate food. Unlike in Britain, lizards sometimes feature strongly in the diet (up to 28 per cent of faeces contain their remains) and also the large native grasshoppers called 'wetas', a potential threat to populations of these unique creatures. As in Britain, hedgehogs have caused significant losses in colonies of ground-nesting birds such as the black-fronted tern (*Chlidonias albostriatus*) and banded dotterel (*Charadrius bicinctus*). Hedgehogs might also compete for food with the declining population of kiwis (*Apteryx* spp). The hedgehog is now accorded pest status in areas where the conservation of key native species is a priority and large numbers are removed by trapping.

Adult body weights normally average 620–700 g, with 10 per cent lost as fat reserves are consumed during (often brief) hibernation periods. Body colouration is similar to what we see in Britain, with occasional albinos (estimated to be about 1 in 10,000 animals). The milder climate, especially in North Island, affects the duration of hibernation and extends the breeding season, enabling two and sometimes even

---

Where it does occur, here and abroad, the hedgehog often lives in close association with people, inhabiting gardens, parks and farmland. Securely protected by its spines, the animal appears bold and confiding, perhaps accounting for its popularity with humans. People put out food to encourage hedgehogs to visit their gardens, probably increasing local abundance. Indeed, hedgehogs may be more numerous in some urban areas than in many parts

FIG 38. The hedgehog has become one of the common road casualties in New Zealand, like this one in the suburbs of Auckland.

three litters per year. New Zealand hedgehogs lack fleas, which were somehow shed (or were removed) during the long sea voyage south, but they appear to suffer more heavily from mite infestations than elsewhere. Despite lower traffic flows, road kills are much more frequent than in Britain. In 1987, my wife and I counted an average of 5.3 per 100 km in South Island and 11.1 per 100 km in North Island (and in some areas three times as many!). That compared with 4.1 per 100 km in our similar surveys in Britain during the same year (Morris & Morris, 1988). This suggests a much higher population density in New Zealand, confirmed in some areas by high levels of trapping success in control operations. New Zealand has a low human population density, plenty of foraging areas, no serious hedgehog predators (although cats and polecats occasionally eat them or scavenge their remains). There is a favourable climate and very little arable farming, creating ideal circumstances for hedgehogs to prosper, yet their population appears to have begun an inexplicable decline in recent years. There was an 82 per cent reduction in the number killed on the same stretch of road across North Island between 1994 and 2005 (Brockie et al., 2009), although numbers apparently remain high in South Island.

of the countryside, especially where arable farming predominates (Pettett et al., 2017b). People also find sick and injured hedgehogs more often than other species and can easily pick them up and take them to a care centre without getting bitten (as they would for almost any other wild mammal). There is therefore a close and mostly positive relationship between hedgehogs and humans, which is explored more fully in Chapter 13.

PRESENT-DAY DISTRIBUTION

Erinaceus europaeus extends across the Continent from Ireland in the west to central Europe. Its geographical limits are probably determined by a lack of suitable food and also an absence of the necessary materials with which to construct a secure winter nest. Similar factors limit the hedgehog's distribution within Britain, where they are seldom encountered on open moorland, heathland or in dense conifer forests. They are rarely found on mountains, although there are occasional reports of hedgehogs being seen above 500 m, including one at 1,067 m (3,435 ft) near the summit of Ben Lawers (Arnold, 1993). In New Zealand, it is said that hedgehogs are absent where there are more than 250 frosty days in the year, but few places in Britain are that cold and parts of the hedgehog's range in Scandinavia have a more severe climate than here. Temperatures are probably not the main controller of hedgehog distribution in Britain.

Here, within the British mainland, hedgehogs are very widely distributed, although there appear to be distinct differences in local abundance. There are also large and consistent regional differences in the numbers killed on the roads (see Chapter 9). Local variations in abundance are suggested by a fourfold difference in the number of dead hedgehogs seen per 100 km of road between northeast England and the southeast, with fewest in the southwest.

Hedgehogs are commonly encountered in mixed farmland, grasslands, some forested sites and even in heavily urbanised areas. Surveys in towns and cities often reveal hedgehogs to be plentiful there, like urban foxes, the latter being formerly often attributed to escaped pets (Fitter, 1949). But few city dwellers keep pet hedgehogs or foxes, so their presence in parks and gardens is a result of natural colonisation or the persistence of existing populations that were engulfed by spreading urban development. Towns offer a refuge from predators such as the badger, abundant food near bird tables and at pet feeding bowls, plus the food that is often put out specially for hedgehogs. There are also many potential nesting sites, especially in the suburbs where there are extensive gardens, often with areas that are left largely undisturbed. In the 1960s, hedgehogs were widespread even in central London, particularly around parks and public gardens (Morris, 1966), but their occurrence is steadily diminishing. They still hang on in the inner suburbs of Hampstead, Rotherhithe, Hackney (Victoria Park) and Barnes (Fig. 39). They are still present in Regent's Park too, but that appears now to be the last remaining population in central London ('Zone 1' in local public transport terms). Although formerly present, hedgehogs have become extinct in Hyde Park and St. James' Park. The latter was the probable source

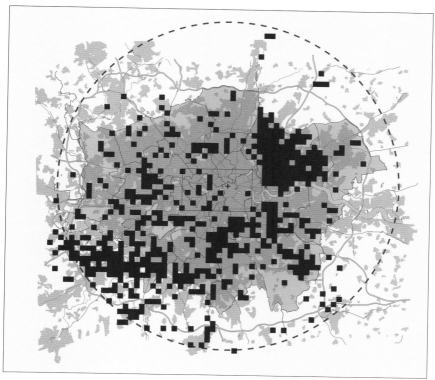

FIG 39. Hedgehog distribution in London over 50 years ago, based on Morris (1966), with the addition of data from Essex a few years later. It is unlikely that hedgehogs are so widespread in the inner suburbs nowadays and they are now absent from the inner London sites apart from Regent's Park. The dashed circle represent a 20-mile radius based on St Paul's cathedral.

of one reported in *The Times* in 1961 as having been found wandering about in the Foreign Mail section of the Admiralty building in Whitehall. In those days, hedgehogs were also common and widely distributed in the boroughs of east London (Barking, Newham, Redbridge and Waltham Forest; Plant, 1979) and across the suburbs of south London (Wimbledon, Streatham, Dulwich, Camberwell), but the replacement of large houses and their extensive grounds with new buildings will have severely reduced hedgehog numbers and they are now mainly associated with the remaining parks and open spaces. There was still at least one hedgehog living in Chelsea in 1983, but potential foraging and nesting areas are slowly being lost. Surveys reveal the importance of green spaces as vital reservoirs for remnant populations in many urban areas, but barriers to free movement between them make these isolated groups vulnerable to local extinction. Piecemeal removal of potential foraging sites also constrains urban hedgehog populations. Already, large numbers of front gardens in London have been taken over for off-street car parking, and in Solihull nearly a third of all front gardens have been lost in this way. Many other urban areas are probably also following a similar pattern, with a progressive decrease in hedgehog numbers and distribution, both nationally and at local level (see Chapter 10). Across Europe, a similar pattern is emerging. Urban hedgehogs suffer from reductions in the availability of supportive habitat, smaller localised populations and increasing isolation of those that remain.

Hedgehogs were never common on heathland, moorland or in dense forest (especially conifer plantations), but they used to be relatively abundant on farmland. However, progressive intensification of farming, especially in arable areas, appears to have reduced their numbers over large parts of the countryside. In arable landscapes, they appear to be largely confined to field margins and fail to use the landscape as a whole. This impacts on their overall distribution and numbers because arable farming is now the principal form of land use for more than a quarter of the countryside. Several recent surveys have indicated that rural hedgehogs tend to be clustered around villages and farms. In open landscapes, hedgehog road casualties will often be concentrated where a road passes through villages (something also noted on the Continent; Göransson et al., 1976). This is some indication that hedgehogs are not evenly distributed across the landscape and certain regions and habitats appear to have more hedgehogs than others. Agri-environment schemes that offer farmers subsidies to encourage biodiversity

FIG 40. Large-scale removal of hedges, ploughing, pesticide application and seasonal harvesting on arable farmland, create a habitat that offers little scope for hedgehogs across much of Britain's countryside today, even where the crop is simply grass as in this case.

FIG 41. Locally, hedgehog populations in Britain are becoming increasingly focused on gardens and the vicinity of buildings; critically, they now depend very much on what we do to support them or at least avoid making their continued survival more difficult.

do seem to benefit hedgehogs, but this may be offset somewhat by the increasing numbers of badgers (see Chapter 9). There is evidence that badgers now play a significant role in affecting our traditional impression of hedgehog distribution and abundance. Preliminary results from a national survey using tracking tunnels suggest that the probability of hedgehogs being present is sharply reduced where badgers occur, but they may also be absent from a third of suitable sites, even where there are no badgers (Williams & Yarnell, pers. comm.). This suggests that other factors are also affecting hedgehogs and they have become barely detectable across large areas of arable farmland, for example, whereas this was once a relatively favourable habitat for them. Grazing land remained a favourite hedgehog habitat for a long time, but in 2006 a survey by the Central Science Laboratory found hedgehogs on only 3 per cent of 125 pasture fields, compared with 26 per cent of a similar number of amenity grassland areas (mostly suburban parks). However, changes in the way that recreational grasslands were managed a decade later (see Chapter 9) may now have severely reduced the numbers there too. A simulation exercise (Moorhouse *et al.*, 2014) creating a virtual countryside, in which the availability of various habitat features could be varied, showed that virtual hedgehogs were particularly favoured by a mosaic of abundant hedgerows associated with small areas of pasture, the kind of farmland that has largely disappeared since the 1950s. Hedgehog populations seem to be increasingly fragmented and focused around buildings, gardens and suburban open spaces. They appear to be dwindling across large areas of the countryside.

CONCLUSION

The hedgehog is a primitive but specialised creature, familiar to all. It is a native species that reached Britain of its own accord over 10,000 years ago and has now been helped by humans to reach many remote places. It has had a chequered career, having gone from being a tentative new arrival as the last Ice Age ebbed, to being vilified and persecuted in the Middle Ages, and becoming now a legally protected species. For centuries, it was regarded as a noxious creature of the night, given to stealing eggs and sucking milk from cows, but it was voted the most popular British animal in the early twenty-first century, despite its negative impact on a few important bird colonies. Nationally, the hedgehog remains fairly widespread, albeit rather patchily distributed compared with the past, and with its abundance nationally significantly reduced. Populations have tended to become fragmented and centred on favourable sites such as gardens, allotments, parks and large cemeteries. There is increasing evidence that what was once a rural species is becoming less abundant in the countryside, relying more on survival in the urban fringe and around human habitation in rural areas, particularly where predation risk is lower. It is no longer entirely appropriate to dismiss the species as 'common and widespread', a frequent assessment in most of the previous literature on British mammals. These issues are explored more fully in the later chapters of this book and also the hedgehog's special relationship special relationship with ourselves in modern times.

CHAPTER 3

The Hedgehog Up Close

THE HEDGEHOG IS A COMPACT-LOOKING animal with a wide body and shorter neck than any other British mammal. Its spiny coat is very distinctive of course, with no fur among the spines that cover the dorsal surface (Fig. 42). The belly and legs have no spines, just a covering of long, coarse and rather sparse hair. This combination offers poor insulation, but coarse hair is probably easier than fluffy fur to keep clean and not become matted, vital properties given the hedgehog's habit of walking with its belly brushing along in wet grass or soil. In view of that habit perhaps, it is also helpful not to have a male's testes scraping along the ground in a dangling scrotum. The spines offer little comfort in cold weather, but the hedgehog's dorsal skin is thick and has few blood vessels near the surface via which to lose warmth to the air. There are

FIG 42. Bristling hedgehog spines. There is no underfur or hair between the spines, just bare skin, so the hedgehog has virtually no external insulation.

 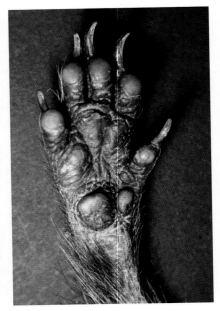

FIG 43. The hedgehog's feet each have five blunt claws that cannot be retracted like those of a cat.

FIG 44. The feet have large soft pads that must make it uncomfortable to walk on rough surfaces, like roads and gravel paths.

also no sweat or sebaceous glands in the skin of the animal's back and few on the belly, so heat loss by evaporation is minimal. There are glands on the soles of the feet and around the anus that probably release scent. The hands and feet each have five toes, all with prominent pads and claws (Figs. 43 & 44). The latter are especially long on the hind feet, but none of the claws are sharp, nor are they retractable as they are in cats.

The hedgehog has quite long legs, yet we are rarely aware of this because they are hidden behind the fringe of long hairs that grow along the lower edge of the spiny skin (Fig. 45). The baggy skin also hangs down along the animal's flanks, hiding the legs. The hedgehog tends to 'walk low' on its limbs, keeping its belly close to the ground, adding to the impression of being short-legged. Actually it can extend its legs and run quite fast when necessary. That is when the tail (about 2 cm long) may become visible from behind, although even then it will be hard to see as this is a nocturnal species, conducting its business under cover of darkness (Fig. 46). Most people are unaware that this familiar creature has a tail at all.

FIG 45. A fringe of long, coarse hairs along the hedgehog's flanks acts like a skirt, hiding its feet and legs except when it is moving.

FIG 46. When walking fast or running, the hind legs may project and become vulnerable to attack by a predator. Skin wounds on the hind legs are quite common, resulting from an aggressive rival hedgehog biting a fleeing adversary at the end of a fight.

Close inspection is also impeded by the hedgehog's characteristic caution which results in its curling up at the least sign of danger or interference with its activities. So, although we are very familiar with this iconic animal, closer inspection of its distinctive features reveals much of interest that is not so familiar after all.

ANATOMY: SKULL AND TEETH

The hedgehog's skull has prominent cheek bones and, unusually for mammals in general, two quite large apertures towards the rear of the palate (Fig. 47). The snout is prominent, accommodating the sensitive areas of tissue associated with the animal's well-developed olfactory capabilities. A particular feature of hedgehog

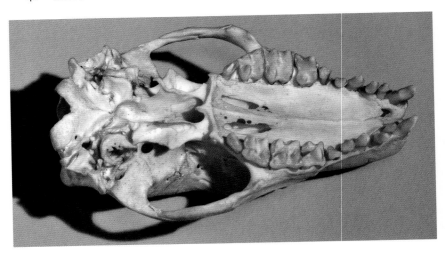

FIG 47. The molars have sharp cusps but these soon become rounded as the teeth become worn in older animals. The large palatal vacuities are unusual among placental mammals, although common in marsupials.

dentition is the peculiar way that the front lower incisors lie almost horizontal ('procumbent'). Instead of biting upwards against the sharp edges of the upper incisors, as seen in humans, they bite in between the two long stabbing incisors at the front of the upper jaw (Fig. 48). What appears to be a long canine tooth in the upper jaw is actually the first incisor; the true canine (defined as the first tooth on the maxillary bone) is small and looks like the premolars that lie posterior to it. This arrangement probably makes it easier to nip and pick up small prey, using the tips of the lower incisors like tweezers, but it also means that hedgehogs cannot deliver a very powerful bite. They rarely bite humans and are unlikely to draw blood if they do. They also cannot easily tackle snails with tough shells (see Chapter 4). The molars are square in outline with several sharp-pointed cusps well suited to chomping up prey into small pieces ready for digestion. However, the cusps get worn down fairly soon because the typical ground-living prey often includes a lot of gritty worms and many beetles with a tough exoskeleton. The teeth can be quite variable in their shape, and especially in the number of roots they have, sometimes even a twin root for the canine (not a feature of many other mammals). Otherwise, the dentition is very basic: typically, the full set of teeth has a dental formula of: 3–1–3–3/2–1–2–3 = 36 altogether, but it is very variable and there may be as many as 38 teeth in total. More advanced mammals tend to have a reduced number (humans have only 32 teeth, for example).

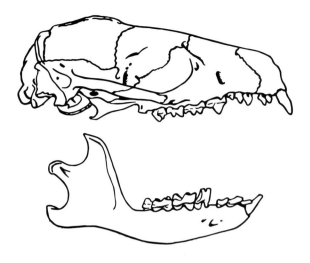

FIG 48. The prominent teeth at the front of a hedgehog's skull are incisors, not canines, and the procumbent lower incisors bite upwards between them.

Hedgehogs seem not to actually need them all anyway as many individuals have missing teeth. It is common for a few to be absent, either as a result of accident or never growing in the first place. Abnormalities were found in 13 per cent of 202 specimens collected from across Europe (Ruprecht, 1965). Nearly half the hedgehogs in New Zealand also have dental anomalies like this and many British ones have teeth missing too (Brockie, 1964). Despite this variability, the apparent absence of the odd tooth or two sometimes causes well-meaning hedgehog carers to become concerned about an individual's ability to feed properly.

SPINES

The hedgehog's most distinctive feature is its coat of about 5,000 spines. Regarded as a form of hair by Aristotle, there has long been a debate as to whether spines are single hairs or formed from several of them fused together. Either way, instead of being straight, stiffened hairs like those of spiny rodents (including porcupines), hedgehog spines are tapering with a distinctive bend (the 'neck') where the spine emerges from the skin. The spine itself is made of keratin, a stiff but flexible material that also forms claws and hair. Each one is about 2 cm long with a very sharp tip. The other end terminates in a bulbous shape embedded in the muscles of the skin (Fig. 50). Seen in cross section, the spines are not solid, but have a hollow core surrounded by longitudinal ridges that strengthen the inner walls of the spine, like columns of boxes. This

FIG 49. The proximal ('body end') of each spine ends in a bulbous structure to which tiny muscles attach that allow the spine to be erected when necessary. The narrow 'neck' of the spine can flex to absorb the harmful forces caused by a fall or predator's jaws.

FIG 50. The bulbous end to a hedgehog's spine where it embeds into the skin, and the massive thickness of the *panniculus carnosus* muscle, prevents it being driven back into the body when the animal is attacked or suffers a fall. (Guy Troughton)

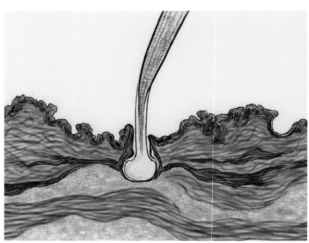

creates a light but extremely strong and rigid structure which nevertheless remains slightly flexible. The core of the spine has crosslinks in places, so that it sometimes appears to be filled with low-density foam (Fig. 51). This internal structure allows the spine to resist buckling despite being hollow, thus enabling the spines to absorb large amounts of mechanical energy by deforming elastically. The spines can also bend (at the 'neck') rather than break, enabling a hedgehog to resist quite severe impacts (up to 4 kg on a single spine) without damage to the animal's softer parts or driving the spine back into the skin. The mushroom-shaped end of the hedgehog's spines buried in the skin also spreads the force of impact. No other spiny mammals have spines like this. The length of the spine is greater in adult animals, but also directly proportional to its diameter. In other words longer spines are thicker and not weaker.

These properties probably explain why hedgehogs appear not to fear heights and will often climb surprisingly far off the ground. If that sounds unlikely, here is an eyewitness account sent to the BBC by Mrs Brenda Keeley of Chipstead in Surrey: 'Today, about mid-morning, I was astonished to see *and hear* a hedgehog clambering over the top and down my 5 ft wattle hurdle fence. It made such a noise I thought it was a squirrel and then saw its body

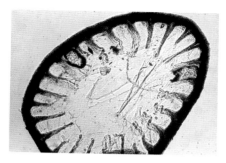

FIG 51. In cross section the spines are seen to be hollow with a series of longitudinal ridges that strengthen the walls.

flattened out on the wattle and its four legs gripping like mad. It was all over in a flash and it disappeared into the ground cover below.' There are plenty of other stories about hedgehogs falling off tables or walls, dropping 3 m or more, and I have been told several times about hedgehogs climbing flights of stairs inside houses. It is unclear why they should do this, or climb anything else much, but if they fall, their bristling spines cushion the effect of landing and the animal walks off as though nothing had happened. The spines of porcupines are much longer and thinner and less able to deliver this kind of protection.

Rolling up into a spiny ball has long been recognised as the hedgehog's most distinctive behaviour, graphically described in *The Schoole of Beastes* (1585): 'when the foxe pursueth him, the hedg-hogge rowleth him selfe (as men say) within his prickles as the chestnut is enclosed within his hull. And by that means he keepeth him there enclosed, so that he cannot be any whit hurted' (White, 1954). Despite its reputation for prickliness, during its normal activities an unworried hedgehog has its spines lying flat, but each one has tiny muscles attached to its bulbous base which allow it to be erected at will. Making the spines stand collectively upright generates a bristling protective mass which the animal can direct this way or that by variably contracting the different muscles attached to each one (Figs. 52 & 53). By doing this, and, to some extent, moving the skin from one area to another (the way we can frown or move our scalp skin about), the hedgehog can bunch up its spines at the point of attack, increasing their defensive value. Other skin muscles allow the hedgehog to roll up more effectively and more completely than any other spiny mammal. Paired muscles draw the bristling spiny skin forwards over the animal's face. Another pair of muscles pull in the hind quarters, then a circular muscle (the *orbicularis*), running around the junction between the spiny

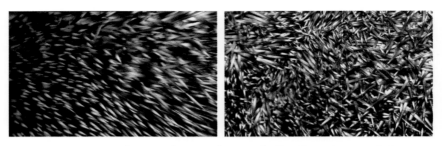

FIGS 52 & 53. At rest and in normal activity, the spines lie flat, all pointing towards the rear of the animal; when alarmed, the hedgehog adopts a defensive position in which the muscles to each spine are contracted, causing the spines to bristle in every direction. Other spiny mammals lack the musculature that enables this.

skin and hairy underside, contracts like the drawstring of a bag to close up the animal (Fig. 54). A fully rolled up hedgehog is thereby completely enclosed in its spiny skin, with its head, legs and soft underbelly tucked away safely inside its prickly protection. The *orbicularis* muscle appears to have special structural and physiological properties that enable it to remain contracted for long periods without getting tired. So a rolled-up hedgehog can stay that way for long enough to wait for danger to depart (Fig. 55).

In order for the hedgehog to roll up completely, the vertebral column has to bend in a steep arc (Fig. 56) and the skin has to be quite loose-fitting in order to accommodate the legs and head. The skin of a fully grown hedgehog needs to

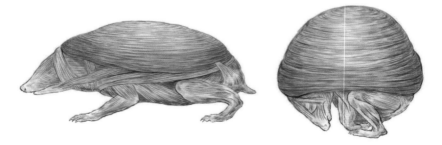

FIG 54. Underlying the dorsal skin is the *panniculus carnosus* muscle that enables the spiny part of the skin to be moved about relative to the body. Around its periphery (corresponding to the fringe of long hairs on the flanks), lies the *orbicularis* muscle, which plays a vital role in the rolling-up process. (Guy Troughton)

FIG 55. A rolled-up hedgehog is protected on all sides. This one is lying on its back, which would normally expose its legs and soft underbelly. No other spiny mammal can roll up so completely.

be more voluminous than we might expect for an animal that big, almost like a human wearing a woolly jumper that is two sizes too large. This is why stuffed hedgehogs often appear to have a large hump because too much stuffing has been inserted in order to fully stretch the skin. Stuffed hedgehogs are also often depicted as though walking about with their spines bristling. This is not natural and the skin and spines normally lie flat on the animal's back. In juveniles, the skin is less baggy and the muscles weaker, so they are unable to roll up tightly and this renders them more vulnerable to predators. So, the hedgehog's most obvious feature, its principal survival mechanism for millions of years, is not just its spines, but their integration within a highly developed system of skin muscles unmatched by any other species.

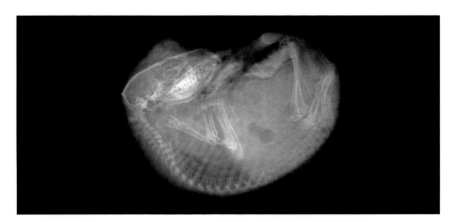

FIG 56. This x-ray shows how the hedgehog's nose is brought close to its feet and when fully rolled up there will be no gap between them and the outside.

FIG 57. Spines are moulted irregularly and at long intervals. This batch shows how variable they can be. They are from a juvenile animal; adult spines are thicker and more robust.

The spines are not moulted seasonally like the coat of most mammals. Instead, they grow and fall out more or less all the time, although not during hibernation. The stump of a clipped spine can remain visible, still embedded in the skin, for over a year. This suggests that the replacement process is a slow one and also ensures that hedgehogs do not suddenly find themselves defenceless while a new prickly coat is grown (not like geese that moult all their primary wing

FIG 58. When a hedgehog is challenged, it can move its skin towards the threat, effectively increasing the density of protective spines where they are needed most.

feathers at once and cannot fly for a week or so while new ones grow into place). The spines are moulted intact, complete with their bulbous inner end. Finding a few of these in a hedgehog's cage may have given rise to the idea that they can 'shoot their spines out' like arrows as a form of defence. This is a common piece of folklore often associated with porcupines, but is completely false. A functional hedgehog spine is very firmly embedded in the skin and cannot even be pulled out deliberately without causing severe distress, greater even than that associated with pulling out a bunch of human hairs (Fig. 57).

As the hedgehog grows, it adds more spines to its dorsal surface to maintain an effective density. Various attempts to count how many spines there are on a hedgehog have resulted in different estimates in the literature. This is partly because a living hedgehog can use its skin muscles to bunch up spines at any point where it is being touched (Fig. 58). Counting the number per square inch on a living animal and scaling up for the body size will then result in an inflated figure (allegedly as many as 16,000!). To resolve the matter, I removed all the spines from a few dead hedgehogs of different ages and counted them. When it first becomes independent, the juvenile hedgehog has about 3,000 spines, increasing to about 5,000 as it reaches adulthood, and a really large adult has about 7,000 of them. These figures have been confirmed by similar counts in *Erinaceus concolor* (Kratochvil, 1974). The spines of juvenile hedgehogs tend to be thinner than those of adults.

Each spine is creamy-coloured, with a broad dark brown band towards its sharp end which normally has a white tip (Fig. 59). This banded pattern imparts a grizzled appearance to the animal overall, with a more contrasting dark zone in juveniles. Some adults have quite pale spines, almost fawn in colour and some have single white spines or patches of them among the normally coloured ones

FIG 59. Each spine has a detailed structure more complex than in other spiny mammals. It is generally a cream colour with a brown zone towards the tip, giving the whole animal a more distinctive appearance than if the spines were all the same colour throughout their length.

FIG 60. Some adult hedgehogs may have white spines in patches, or scattered throughout the normal ones.

(Fig. 60). Albino hedgehogs occur surprisingly often, perhaps because the spines are such good protection that the added conspicuousness of a white coat that would swiftly attract the attention of a predator is less of a disadvantage than it would be in a white vole or shrew, for example. Press reports of albinos are frequent, often accompanied by amusing captions about their ghostly appearance (Fig. 61). It is interesting that such reports usually show only single animals, an odd albino in the family; two seen together is unusual. A true albino has completely white spines and fur. It also has pink eyes because dark pigments have failed to form anywhere in the body. Whilst pale brown or white hedgehogs can be seen from time to time, fully black ones appear to be extremely rare or even perhaps non-existent. I have never seen one reported. This is a little surprising as black colour variants are found in many other mammals, including water voles, rabbits, squirrels and even the dormouse.

FIG 61. Albinos, with white spines and pink eyes, occur fairly frequently.

FIG 62. Very occasionally, a hedgehog turns up with no spines at all, perhaps as a result of infection or a genetic failure to produce keratin like this one, which has no claws or whiskers either.

Very occasionally, a hedgehog turns up with no spines at all. I have only ever seen two of them alive among the thousands of hedgehogs that I have come across (although another one was illustrated in *The Times* in October 2017, irreverently referred to as 'Baldy'). Close inspection reveals that these weird-looking creatures have a healthy skin and a few (maybe a dozen or so) wispy or stunted spines. One that I saw, christened 'The Blob', had no fur, whiskers or claws (Fig. 62). It is fairly clear that there had been a failure to produce the keratin needed to form those structures. Thanks to Mr and Mrs Tony Thomas of Luton, I saw another case. Their animal had been named 'Alice'. She was a juvenile, apparently normal in early life, but by November her spines had fallen out, leaving an otherwise healthy skin with normal hair on the belly and flanks and about ten tiny malformed spines remaining. The claws were normal, so this

FIG 63. A spineless hedgehog is an extremely vulnerable creature. This one, 'Alice', had spines when it was young, but they all fell out at an age of about six weeks.

FIG 64. This allegedly spineless hedgehog was exhibited at a scientific meeting, but it was probably a taxidermist's fraud.

A HEDGEHOG (*Erinaceus europaeus*) WITH HAIRS INSTEAD OF SPINES

(*This block is kindly lent by Prof. A. Fritsch*)

was not the same syndrome as seen in The Blob and it is hard to see why spines should have been absent, but with hair and claws remaining normal (Fig. 63). In 1898, a picture was published that showed what purported to be a spineless stuffed hedgehog with fully furred body, but no spiny dorsal surface (Anon, 1898). Although this specimen was exhibited by a Professor Fritsch at a scientific meeting, it was probably a taxidermist's fraud. It is comparatively easy to cut away the spiny part of the skin in a dead hedgehog, stitch the animal up along its back and produce a hairy aberration like this (Fig. 64).

Fakes or not, one thing is clear, a spineless hedgehog is a very vulnerable creature, and would easily fall prey to any passing predator, including cats, dogs and even magpies. It is therefore unlikely that this spineless trait would persist in the population and is only manifest as an infrequent genetic or biochemical anomaly. Nevertheless, pictures sometimes appear in newspapers and magazines showing hedgehogs with varying degrees of spine loss and looking very sorry for themselves. However, it is quite common for hedgehogs to have extensive bare patches of skin, with few spines or none at all across several square centimetres of the body, yet still possess normal hair around the face and flanks. This form of spinelessness is almost certainly due to a skin infection, probably by ringworm or mites (or both), which leaves the bare skin rather flaky (see Chapter 11). The condition is curable and accounts for a few stories in the press suggesting that spineless animals may sometimes recover (in one case with the help of a hedgehog hypnotist!). The Royal College of Surgeons' collection of preserved animals has a bald hedgehog dating from 1908. It has only about 50 full-sized healthy spines and its whiskers appear normal. This too was probably a pathological condition.

Sometimes a hedgehog will be found that is pale creamy colour, not white, and it has normal dark eyes so it is not an albino. These so-called 'blonde' animals are technically known as 'leucistic' and they constitute another genetically arising colour variant, just like true albinos. They are very scarce on the mainland, but residents on the island of Alderney in the Channel Islands reported a high proportion of leucistic individuals in the 1990s and sometimes as many as half the hedgehogs seen visiting their gardens were pale ones (Fig. 65). That could be due to the same few blonde animals repeatedly coming back to the same place, creating a false impression of abundance. However, in 1993 my student Alison Tutt and her husband attempted to determine the true proportion of leucistic hedgehogs by walking over 81 km of sampling transects at night. They encountered 67 hedgehogs, of which 17 (25 per cent) were blonde ones. There was no statistically significant difference between the distance at which pale and normal hedgehogs were sighted, so the abundance of leucistic animals was not simply due to their being more conspicuous in the dark. The colour difference was not related to sex or age: proportions of males and females, young and old did not differ significantly between normal and variant hedgehogs (Morris &

FIG 65. A quarter of the population of hedgehogs on the island of Alderney are 'blonde' like this one. They have normal dark eyes, so are not albinos. These leucistic varieties are very rare on the British mainland.

ALDERNEY
Bailiwick of Guernsey

Erinaceus europaeus

FIG 66. The blonde hedgehogs of Alderney are so special that they were featured on local postage stamps.

Tutt, 1996). These blonde hedgehogs were deemed so noteworthy that they featured on a special issue of the island's postage stamps (Fig. 66). Alderney is only about 15 km off the coast of France, but it is unlikely that the hedgehog population is native to the island. They were explicitly stated to be absent there in 1810, and must have been introduced to the island sometime after that. Elderly residents reported that the local hedgehogs were normal brown animals at the time of the First World War. Due to the privations of the Second World War, that population is likely to have become extinct by the 1950s or earlier and the present one derives from a postwar introduction. According to a survey among local residents, at least three people had imported hedgehogs in the 1960s, one pair having been purchased from Harrod's pet shop in London. Others may have come from the nearby island of Guernsey.

The genetic basis for coat colouration in hedgehogs is unknown, but the scarcity of leucistic animals on the mainland suggests that this colour variant may be the result of a rare recessive gene, normally having no visible effect because brown is dominant. However, whatever their source, translocations to islands will almost inevitably involve small numbers of animals and inbreeding (mating between close relatives) would be inevitable for the first few generations. It is possible that one of the original founder members of the present-day Alderney population was the normal colour, but carrying a recessive 'blonde gene'. That could then be passed to at least one of its young and if the adult then mated with one of its own family carrying the recessive blonde gene, perhaps the following year after maturity had been reached, then the offspring of that mating would have two blonde genes. That would cause it to become a leucistic individual. The Mendelian principles of inheritance patterns would predict that, in such circumstances, a quarter of the offspring from such matings would carry two of the pale genes and grow up as blondes. This is exactly the proportion that was observed on Alderney in the 1990s. There are no ground predators on the island,

FIG 67. Occasional individual hedgehogs may develop a distinctive patch of white fur somewhere on their body, possibly as a result of injury. This one also has a pale pink nose.

so being conspicuously pale would not necessarily be a much of a disadvantage and we might therefore expect this trait to persist. On the other hand, if the blonde character really is simply due to a recessive gene, perhaps pale colouration will slowly disappear. Brown animals were more abundant anyway and over time the population may revert to normal colouration as dominant genes begin to suppress the occurrence of pale-coloured animals. It is possible that the genetics are more complex and also possible that more animals will be transported to Alderney. Either would affect the rate of change, but future surveys would be of special interest as this situation seems not to have occurred with other hedgehog translocations, although up to a third of hedgehogs found by Hugh Warwick on North Ronaldsay were also pale in colour. Meanwhile, the Alderney hedgehogs, like those taken to New Zealand, appear to have had their fleas removed at some stage on the journey to their new home.

BODY SIZE

Although hedgehogs generally all look fairly similar, they do vary in detail. Some have a more pointed face, others may have darker fur. These differences are not necessarily a distinction between male and female, despite many assertions to the contrary. They also vary a lot in size. Juveniles leaving the nest are about 150 mm long, adults are 200–250 mm, but hedgehogs also show enormous seasonal changes in weight associated with hibernation, another of their distinctive features. During their first season, juveniles grow from about 120 g to around

500 g as they fatten up ready for the winter, but adults (especially older males) can sometimes exceed 1,500 g in the autumn (see Chapter 6). Overfed in captivity, some individuals will top 2 kg, but this is exceptional in the wild and obese captives released into natural conditions usually lose weight rapidly until they closely match a more normal weight for their age. Over winter, hibernating hedgehogs will shed 20–30 per cent of their mass as their fat reserves are consumed, again demonstrating how flexible and variable these animals can be. Continental hedgehogs seem to be somewhat larger than their British counterparts, but it is hard to generalise with such a variable animal.

TABLE 2. Descriptive statistics for the hedgehog based on 17 dead animals (From Barrett-Hamilton & Hinton, 1910). Larger samples are difficult to obtain and reliably measuring live ones is almost impossible.

	Males (n=7)		Females (n=10)	
	Mean	Range	Mean	Range
Head and body (mm)	230	188–263	217	179–257
Tail (mm)	26	17–35	23.5	17–31
Weight (g)	—	900–1,200	—	800–1,025

Table 2 gives measurements and weight ranges as published in 1911 and repeated in subsequent literature. These might seem out of date, but hedgehogs are extremely variable so that sample figures like this are almost meaningless anyway, especially as they are likely to be based on relatively small samples of animals. Average weights, for example, will depend entirely upon the proportion of young and old animals included and the time of year that the sample was weighed. Just prior to hibernation, a few of the older males may exceed 1,500 g and at the end of winter even adults may sometimes weigh less than a third of that. Unlike studying small mammals like mice and voles, it is not easy to obtain enough hedgehogs to gather a statistically robust sample. Plenty of them are brought into animal hospitals, but their weights would be biased by over-representation of sickly animals and towards young 'orphans', especially late in the season. However, the systematic capture of hedgehogs on the Uists (see Chapter 12) has resulted in the largest-ever sample of wild and healthy hedgehogs, captured more or less randomly, and Figure 68 can be regarded as a reliable snapshot of a population's weight profile at the end of winter. Most of those weighing more than about 600 g are likely to be entering their third summer season and those weighing less than that will mostly be young from

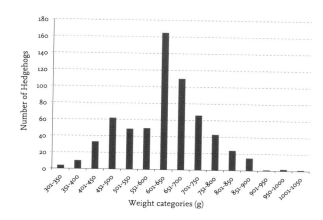

FIG **68.** Weight distribution of hedgehogs collected in April from the Hebrides, mostly South Uist, 2008–16 inclusive (n = 635 animals). (Courtesy of Pat Holtham and Scottish Natural Heritage)

the previous year approaching their first birthday. A few of the animals had overwintered and were still alive at less than 400 g, having lost a quarter of their mass in hibernation, an important fact given the discussions in Chapter 6. Some of the oldest animals weighed more than 850 g, even at the end of winter, and one weighed over 1 kg. It is possible that conditions in the Hebrides are particularly favourable, and also possible that the population is not representative because it is based upon a small number taken to the islands. However, a very similar overall pattern was evident among the dead hedgehogs I obtained from gamekeepers and as road casualties collected widely in the south and east of England. Figure 69 shows the typical pattern of weights in September.

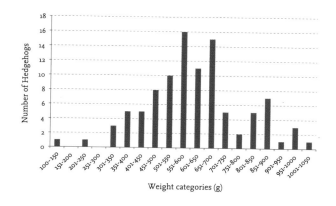

FIG **69.** Size distribution (a sample of 99 animals) among the Uist hedgehogs in the autumn. (Courtesy of Pat Holtham and Scottish Natural Heritage)

TABLE 3. Weights of adult urban hedgehogs from Regent's Park, London, confirming that it is wrong to suppose that males are normally larger than females. (courtesy of Nigel Reeve)

Males	Females
Range 700–1,220 g	700–1,450 g
Average in May 840 g (n=26)	Average in May 927 g (n=34)
Average in September 959 g (n=18)	Average in September 1,019 g (n=34)

BEHAVIOUR

Being a primitive animal means that the hedgehog has not evolved many of the complex features often associated with mammals. There is no real social behaviour (unlike monkeys or whales, for example), no play among the young (unlike badgers or dogs), no elaborate courtship rituals (unlike many ungulates) or specialised feeding adaptations (unlike anteaters), no using tools (unlike apes); indeed, hedgehogs seem to lack most of the behavioural features that generally make mammals interesting! However, they do what they do under cover of darkness and much of it may use scent and olfaction as the medium for communication, a system that we humans are poorly equipped to investigate or understand. A lot may be going on that we are unable to appreciate. It is clear from the way that hedgehogs behave in the normal course of foraging that they rely heavily on a well-developed sense of smell (Fig. 70).

FIG 70. Hedgehogs have an extremely keen sense of smell, their primary sense, and the associated olfactory region of the brain is very well developed.

Gentle experiments confirm that hedgehogs are extremely sensitive to sounds, particularly those with a high ultrasonic component. Sharp clicks or a metallic jangling noise will elicit an instant flinching response. This reaction can be used to test a hedgehog's sensitivity to high frequencies, suggesting that they can respond to sounds way above the upper limit of human hearing (20 kHz). They may even be able to hear sounds at 45 kHz, well into the spectrum of ultrasounds used by bats for echolocation. High-frequency sounds have a short wavelength and (if they can be heard at all) this helps to identify their source more accurately. This could assist a hedgehog seeking food, as a beetle may well make tiny ultrasonic creaking or scratching noises as it moves about. Perhaps more important, hedgehogs have extremely sensitive hearing and are able to detect very quiet noises whatever their frequency. According to Konrad Herter, his hedgehogs could hear a beetle from five metres away.

Vision is generally poor and hedgehogs are probably unable to distinguish colours to any great extent, although colour vision would anyway be of little use in the dark (Fig. 71). In some of Herter's experiments, carried out in daylight, certain hedgehogs appeared to be capable of discriminating between colours and also learning to tell shapes apart. There is plenty of scope here for more basic (and very simple) research. Other behavioural tests indicate abilities to see and discriminate, also to learn (for example, Schäfer, 1980). In one of my own studies, we frequently followed a blind wild hedgehog. He had one eye half closed and the other was badly shrivelled. He barely reacted to a flashgun or torch and frequently bumped into things, yet he was a very regular visitor to the

FIG 71. Eyes, so important to humans, are of limited use to hedgehogs. They are close to the ground and therefore unable to see distant views most of the time, especially in the dark.

FIG 72. 'No. 28' was a blind hedgehog that we radio-tracked for many nights, seen here running rapidly towards a distant food bowl. He coped well without the use of his eyes and still travelled as far as uninjured normal hedgehogs at the study site.

study garden, coming in from a nest 500 m away on the far side of a nearby golf course. It appeared not to matter to him that it was still daylight and the golfers had to wait while 'No. 28' pottered across the fairways. He also led a very active love life, briskly pursuing females (Fig. 72). All of which testifies to vision being a relatively unimportant sense for hedgehogs. Actually, eyes would be of limited use so close to the ground, and with the horizon obscured even by relatively short grass. Unlike humans that use vision as their primary sense, there is no doubt that hedgehogs rely much more on hearing, to detect the faint sounds of worms and other prey moving about, and they also have a very keen sense of smell. The oral mucosa is richly supplied with nerves and taste buds (Quilliam, 1972). From this we may assume that the hedgehog is capable of reacting to chemical stimuli and potentially able to select food based upon its taste, although hedgehogs seem not to be deterred by the nasty defensive secretions produced by some of its prey (see Chapter 4).

LEARNING CAPABILITY

Some simple experiments by Konrad Herter in the 1930s led him to claim that hedgehogs have much better sight than their behaviour in the wild would suggest and that they could also learn simple tasks and distinguish between a black symbol and one made up of four equal segments. A hedgehog would recognise its own reflection in a mirror as another of its own kind and set about fighting it. As in humans, the rates of learning and reaction varied between individual hedgehogs. He said that animals were capable of learning to pull rods about 30 cm long through the bars of the cage if they had a cockchafer beetle fastened to the outer end. One hedgehog learned to curl up and uncurl on the word of command and I too have met a pet hedgehog that would come when it was called. Herter kept four animals in the same cage, one of which (Female 3) became dominant and her aggressive nature prevailed whenever there was friction, leading to butting and biting. Female 2 was only dominated by 3 and was herself dominant over 4 and 11. It is hard to know the extent to which these accounts, and many other stories of individual hedgehog actions, translate into natural behaviour in the wild. It also has to be said that Herter's results are rather anecdotal and it would be good to see some better experimental designs applied to larger samples of animals to establish what does or does not reflect the hedgehog's normal behavioural capabilities. My own experience suggests that hedgehogs are very individualistic, so that generalisations are likely to be invalid unless they are based on quite large numbers of different animals.

THE INTERNAL ANATOMY

A hedgehog's internal anatomy is unremarkable. Its skeleton is very basic and shows no major developments associated with a specialised way of life, apart from minor modifications of the vertebrae allowing it to roll up tightly (Fig. 73). It has a simple stomach and its intestines are about a metre or so in length. Studies with captive animals suggest that food is not retained in the stomach for very long and passes quickly through the rest of the digestive tract within 12–16 hours, leaving little time for microbial digestion. There is no caecum, the blind-ending bag in which many herbivores digest the bulk of their food with the help of symbiotic microorganisms. This, and rapid passage through the gut, means that if a hedgehog eats plant material (see Chapter 4), little of it will be digested. Other mammals often slow the movement of ingested food in the caecum or gut and may also have a longer intestine, enabling more time for food

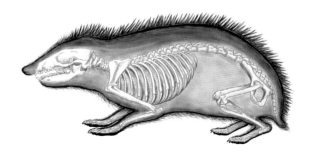

FIG 73. The simple, unspecialised skeleton of a hedgehog within its highly specialised skin. (Guy Troughton)

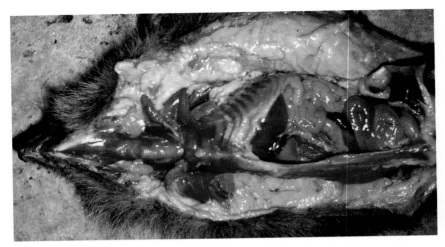

FIG 74. During the autumn, hedgehogs accumulate masses of white fat under the skin and also around the gut. It is this that sustains the animal through several months of hibernation, but also results in huge annual fluctuations in body mass.

to be exposed to digestive enzymes and consequently enabling a more complete breakdown of ingested materials, especially plants. But the hedgehog's diet is mostly easily digestible 'meat' in the form of insect and worm tissues, mixed with completely indigestible material such as soil or beetle exoskeletons where no amount of enzyme activity will increase the amount of food energy that can be extracted. It is these indigestible elements that make hedgehog droppings so easily recognisable, distinguished from those of cats and dogs because these are usually fed on pet food that contains no bones, fur or insects (see Chapter 4 and Appendix).

CONCLUSION

The hedgehog is a primitive but specialised creature, widespread and familiar to us all. Its spiny coat represents a highly integrated system of muscles, skin and modified hairs that make it one of Britain's most distinctive animals. The ability to roll up tightly surrounded by bristling spines makes this one of the few species that normally has little to fear from predators. The rest of the hedgehog's anatomy is relatively unspecialised, with its primary senses being those of hearing and smell rather than vision as in humans.

CHAPTER 4

Food and Feeding

LTHOUGH THE HEDGEHOG IS FORMALLY classified as a member of the mammalian order Insectivora (see Chapter 2) this does not mean that it eats only insects, far from it. In fact the hedgehog is almost omnivorous, eating virtually anything edible that it can find at ground level. That may even include some plant material, ripe fruits and bird-table debris. There have been many attempts to be more explicit, but few detailed studies have been carried out in Britain. Thorough investigations face the tiresome problem of identifying small bits of small prey chewed into tiny fragments, which is not a way that many people want to spend their time.

Moreover, making lists is all very well, but there are then several ways of interpreting what they might mean. The usual and least intrusive way of analysing an animal's diet is to collect samples of droppings and identify the fragments within. This is a painstaking task, not to everyone's liking and relatively few extensive investigations into hedgehog faeces have been made. My former student Andy Wroot used this method and said that it sometimes took him up to a week to identify and count all the things he found in a single faecal pellet. Dealing with large samples was therefore a very time-consuming job, but small samples were unlikely to provide a comprehensive view of the hedgehog's very varied diet.

However, even a superficial glance at a hedgehog's droppings will reveal many fragments of beetles, millipedes and other items, imparting a crinkly appearance to the faecal pellet (Fig. 75). This makes it easy to recognise hedgehog faeces and tell them apart from those of cats and dogs, both of which normally eat processed foods that contain few recognisable fragments of harder material. Such droppings then appear smooth and uniform in colour. Moreover, they are

FIG 75. Hedgehog droppings often contain easily recognisable fragments of beetles as these are the most frequent prey items.

quite large and fat, often thumb-sized, whereas those of hedgehogs are the size of one's little finger and usually deposited singly, not in heaps. This kind of superficial inspection is important as hedgehog droppings found on our lawns are conspicuous and often the first real evidence that they might be living nearby.

Most of the things that hedgehogs eat most often are arthropods such as beetles and other insects. These have a tough exoskeleton made of chitin, one of the most indestructible of natural products. Chitinous bits pass through the digestive system unchanged except for being broken into fragments by the teeth. So even a superficial examination of hedgehog droppings using a hand lens will often reveal the jointed legs from beetles and shiny bits of their elytra (wing cases) or tiny hoop-like rings from the exoskeletons of millipedes. For a more detailed analysis of the diet, the faecal pellet has to be soaked in water and gently teased apart under a binocular microscope. Then the broken fragments must be compared with pieces from known types of insects and other invertebrates in order to decide exactly what has been eaten. With a more powerful microscope,

FIG 76. Hedgehogs may consume large amounts of pet food or bread and milk which leave no visible traces in their droppings. This makes dietary analyses based on faeces incomplete.

some of the bristly hairs (called 'chaetae') embedded in the skin of earthworms may also be detected, but how many worms were eaten or how big they were remains obscure, an important issue, since worms often form a major part of a hedgehog's diet. That said, Andy Wroot devised a system that enabled chaetae to be measured, and from that a worm's size and probable weight could be deduced in order to quantify just how much worm 'meat' might have been eaten and thus indicate how important worms were in the diet relative to other food items (Wroot, 1985). Faecal analysis is not an activity for the impatient or faint-hearted.

Another problem with faecal analysis (with hedgehogs and everything else) is that, despite all the effort involved, it does not really show what has been eaten, only what has not been digested. For example, pet food, table scraps or bread and milk may be eaten in quantity, even becoming the major intake one night, but nothing recognisable will be left in the droppings (Fig. 76). In another faecal pellet,

TABLE 4. Various food items in order of frequency of occurrence among 137 hedgehog stomachs containing food (based on Yalden, 1976).

Food items	Percentage occurrence (137 stomachs)
Beetles (mostly carabids)	73.3
Earwigs	57.7
Caterpillars	48.9
Millipedes	40.1
Worms	34.3
Slugs	22.6
Bees etc.	17.5
Harvestmen	17.5
Spiders	17.5
Birds (feathers)	16.1
Diptera (adult flies)	11.7
Mammals	11.7
Birds (eggshell)	11.0
Mites	7.3
Diptera (Tipulid larvae)	4.4
Snails	3.6
Woodlice	2.2
Centipedes	1.5

there might be some vole or rabbit fur present, but no indication of how much of the animal was eaten. To find out what a hedgehog actually ate, rather than what it defaecated, it is better to examine stomach contents. A hedgehog's teeth will chomp up prey, but not shred it, so the pieces in the stomach will often be larger than if they had already been through the whole digestive process. Bigger bits, often still joined together, will also be easier to identify. Moreover, one might reasonably assume that a stomach full of food represents what was eaten during all or part of a single night just before the animal died, whereas it is not clear how much foraging is represented in a single faecal pellet. So the analysis of stomach contents is likely to be easier and generate more reliable results, although it is more difficult to obtain a large and representative sample of stomachs.

The most extensive study of hedgehog stomachs was carried out by Derek Yalden, using 177 of them, mostly from my sample of hedgehogs that had been killed in traps set by gamekeepers, but also including about 25 road casualties (Yalden, 1976). About a quarter of them were empty, but in the rest, food fragments as small as the antennae of a millipede were identified, so little is likely to have been overlooked. The simplest way of presenting the results (used in most studies of animal diets, including faecal pellets and stomach contents) is to show what percentage of samples included one or more fragments of each food category (Fig. 77). In effect, this describes the range of prey tackled and perhaps what hedgehogs eat most often, but it doesn't really reflect what is most important to them. A few animals might regularly gorge themselves on millipedes, but if the rest ignore these, or don't forage where they occur, then this category will appear to be a relatively minor component of the diet in a larger sample of hedgehogs.

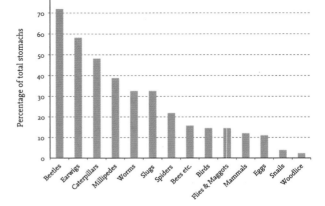

FIG 77. The proportion of 137 hedgehog stomachs that contained various types of prey, based on Yalden (1976).

FIG 78. Earthworms are nutritious, easy to catch and desirable food items, but difficult to find in dry weather when they retreat deeper into the soil.

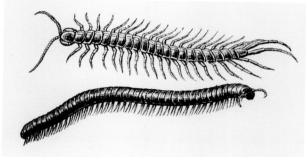

FIG 79. Centipedes and millipedes are common where hedgehogs forage, but the former are eaten far less often than the latter.

Another way of presenting the information is to record the percentage of the total number of fragments that came from this or that type of animal. But this is somewhat unrealistic too because a small insect may crop up in half the stomachs, but represent an insignificant contribution to the diet compared with a large type of beetle that is recorded in only a few. Earthworm chaetae might be found in many stomachs, but it is hard to know how many of those animals were consumed (Fig. 78). Bird eggs will only be recorded if bits of shell are present in the stomach. So, even Derek Yalden's massive study must be regarded as indicative rather than definitive. Bearing these caveats in mind, and disregarding the 40 stomachs that were empty, his study found beetles (Coleoptera) in nearly three quarters of all the stomachs. Clearly beetles were the most frequent items taken, with earwigs in over half of stomachs and caterpillars in 49 per cent of them. Worms, slugs and millipedes had also been eaten by many of the hedgehogs. An attempt was made to estimate how many actual animals had been eaten and this too showed the importance of beetles (34 per cent of the total number of prey taken), caterpillars (21 per cent) and earwigs (13 per cent).

FIG 80. Slugs such as *Limax maculatus*, are often eaten although the larger adults may be rejected as being too tough and slimy.

FIG 81. Snails are eaten far less often than slugs, probably due to their protective shell, which may grow to become impregnable in areas with calcareous soils.

Slugs were also important, appearing in about a quarter of the stomachs and comprising 8 per cent of the 1,726 whole animals eaten (Fig. 80). But this leaves out earthworms, despite their obvious importance, because the number of individuals could not be determined. Studies in other countries, including New Zealand, also show beetles as the most prominent category of hedgehog food, but their importance may be exaggerated because their fragmented remains are the most durable and most easily recognised food remnants. However, about one third of the calorific content of a beetle is locked up in its chitinous exoskeleton, which cannot be digested to liberate energy. So although carabid beetles are abundant and often predominate in hedgehog diets, they may contribute less than 15 per cent of the hedgehog's usable energy intake.

Slugs were about ten times more important than snails in the samples that Derek analysed, probably because their shell makes the latter more difficult to eat. Some snails live in areas with plenty of calcium in the soil that helps them to build an even stronger shell (Fig. 81). Millipedes were found in 40 per cent of stomachs, but centipedes in only 1.5 per cent. This too probably reflects practical issues as centipedes can run quite fast and they also bite. Hedgehogs will find them less easy to catch and also probably less agreeable to eat, regardless of their local abundance. Slugs and worms are easy to catch, but large slugs are very tough and slimy. The big black or orange slugs (*Arion* sp.) that we often see on the lawn on a moist summer night are probably rather difficult to tackle, and most of the slugs eaten will be smaller types (*Limax*, for example) or young individuals of the large species (and perhaps their eggs). Despite their abundance in the wild, woodlice were infrequently eaten. They may well be distasteful because of noxious secretions from their skin. However, millipedes are supposed to be similarly protected by chemical deterrents, but hedgehogs eat lots of them. Hedgehogs will also eat certain beetles that exude a nasty substance when attacked, a form of chemical defence for the hapless victim, but evidently not very effective in deterring a hungry hedgehog. Grasshoppers were infrequently eaten, despite their abundance in the field, probably because they are likely to leap away at the slightest disturbance (Fig. 82).

Earwigs (Dermaptera) are another common invertebrate in the sort of places that hedgehogs forage. Derek Yalden found them in over half of the stomachs he examined, with one animal having eaten 22 of them more or less in one go. But there is not much meat on an earwig, so they contributed less than 10 per

FIG 82. Grasshoppers are common enough but rarely eaten by hedgehogs as they will leap out of reach at the slightest disturbance.

FIG 83. Caterpillars are very frequent prey items. They are nutritious, easy to catch and often clustered in groups on their particular food plant.

FIG 84. Juicy beetle larvae and 'leatherjackets' (the larvae of crane flies) will be frequently encountered by a hedgehog nosing about under dead leaves and in the surface layers of the soil.

FIG 85. The pupae of butterflies and moths will make a welcome meal, but they will be infrequently found as they are widely scattered and buried in the soil.

cent of the energy intake. Similarly, although spiders and harvestmen were consumed quite frequently, they made only a small contribution to the diet. So another way of looking at the hedgehog's food intake is to consider the relative size of prey items, recognising that a big beetle will contribute more to its energy requirements than a small one or a tiny aphid. Size can be estimated by measuring prey fragments and comparing those measurements with similar pieces of animals of known body size. For example, by measuring the size of rat jaws in owl pellets, it is possible to estimate what those animals weighed when an owl swallowed them (Morris, 1985). Derek Yalden used the same principle to discover the size of caterpillars taken by urban kestrels, based on measuring the mandibles in regurgitated pellets and comparing them with caterpillars of known size and weight (Yalden, 1980). This approach applied to food remains in hedgehog stomachs suggests that caterpillars can be as important to hedgehogs as worms and beetles, even if they crop up less often in the stomachs, with other prey contributing very little (Fig. 83). It remains difficult to take account of the fur or feathers that reveal larger vertebrate prey being eaten, yet provide no indication of how much of the animal might have been consumed.

Derek found one stomach that contained 20 cranefly larvae (leatherjackets), showing that a hedgehog had been in the right place at the right time to get them easily, something it may never experience again. It is also true that a hedgehog might one night find a wasp or bumblebee nest and gorge on the larvae inside. It will expend little effort to get an excellent meal, but is unlikely to be that lucky very often. This kind of 'one-off' event, where a large pupa or beetle larva (Figs. 84 & 85) was encountered and provided a generous meal, could easily be missed in a sample of stomachs or droppings, or its occurrence in the sample could distort the overall picture provided by a diet analysis unless very large numbers of stomachs or faeces were available for study.

Another study of stomach contents, based on 87 dead animals collected from the suburbs of Oxford and nearby countryside, found a change in diet with increasing age, suggesting an element of choice in the hedgehog's feeding behaviour (Dickman, 1988). Older animals tended to prey on larger invertebrates such as slugs, caterpillars and beetles. They appeared not to bother much with smaller quarry like spiders (Fig. 86), which were treated as not being worth the effort, whereas younger animals ate a broader range of prey. As that study suggested, hedgehogs may indeed show a small shift in the spectrum of prey taken as they grow older, but perhaps this was because the youngsters were still learning what was best to eat. Anyway the differences are likely to be small and with a species that takes such a wide variety of food, foraging in a variety of different places, even a sample of 87 animals may not be enough to confirm that this is a regular and significant aspect of the hedgehog's life and behaviour. After all, each stomach represents only a snapshot of what that animal had eaten in the short time before it was killed on the road (the main source of animals for

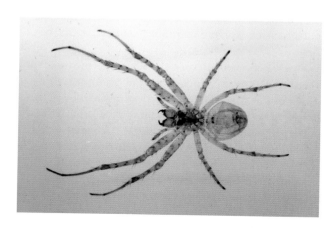

FIG 86. Spiders and harvestmen are mostly too small to make a worthwhile meal, although their remains were found in nearly one fifth of hedgehog stomachs.

Dickman's study). If it had been killed the day before, it might have been feeding somewhere quite different, with a different range of prey on offer. But this is just a general problem of sampling and also one of the difficulties with describing the life of the hedgehog when its feeding behaviour is so variable and so few detailed studies have been made.

Using captive animals, Elizabeth Dimelow set up experiments to investigate the extent to which hedgehogs prefer some foods to others (Dimelow, 1963). She found that her captives eagerly ate millipedes at every opportunity, but rejected woodlice. This surprising fact was also evident in the stomach analyses by Derek Yalden. Apart from those woodlice, they ate everything offered in 122 tests. However, her hedgehogs did also show a degree of preference for certain foods. Millipedes were a favourite, despite their distasteful secretions that are supposed to deter predators. In fact, the smell of those secretions may even help a hedgehog to locate the millipedes. Beetles were eaten, but some species can run fast enough to escape, reducing their likely frequency in the diet under more natural conditions. Nearly all the small slugs offered (especially *Limax* species) were eaten, despite their slimy secretions, although larger ones of the genus *Arion* could escape consumption because of their thicker skin. Earthworms were consumed, although they were often not first choice. Snails were rejected, especially those with a thick shell. Dimelow's results closely match what would be expected with wild hedgehogs based upon stomach and faecal analyses, but do not tally with some other studies which suggest millipedes are not taken very often in relation to their availability. One problem with using captive hedgehogs for behavioural studies like this is that, as many hedgehog keepers will know, the animals might learn what is going on. This could then affect their response when presented with unfamiliar foods. However, Dimelow's captives spent time turning over leaves and displacing small stones and pieces of wood, suggesting that in the wild they might be actively searching for things, not just relying on accidental contact with prey.

There will also be seasonal variations in diet and the results of any study will be biased according to when samples were collected. Andy Wroot found more earwigs and beetle larvae in warm weather and fewer earthworms in the dry periods, presumably because worms then retire deeper into the soil and are less likely to be found at the surface than after a shower of rain. He also demonstrated that hedgehogs did not feed opportunistically, but tried to select food that maximised their energy intake. All this complex detail shows just how difficult it is to describe the food of the hedgehog. It is clear from studies here and elsewhere that hedgehogs are very flexible in their diet and take a broad range of food items. Overall, the results of studies in Britain suggest that there are about

FIG 87. 'Mealworms' are beetle larvae, excellent hedgehog food and now available commercially to be offered in quantity to garden birds. They are likely to become more frequent in the diet of urban hedgehogs, but, like any foodstuff, should not be given in excess. (Rose Goodwin/BHPS)

ten categories of potential natural prey, but hedgehogs mainly rely on only about four or five of them – beetles, leatherjackets, caterpillars, slugs and earthworms – with other things being eaten only sporadically.

Maybe hedgehogs engage in 'optimal foraging'? This is a concept that has generated a lot of discussion among bird ecologists. The idea is that an animal will find a good place to feed and then keep looking for food there until most of it has been eaten. It will then move on to another good place once the law of diminishing returns begins to apply and the animal finds itself spending more time and effort searching for food with less and less reward to repay the effort involved. At some point, it will not be worth continuing the search in that place and it will be better to expend energy in going to try somewhere else. A humming bird, for example, might hover in front of a cluster of flowers, sucking nectar from each in turn until most of the flowers are empty. Before it risks spending more energy in hovering than it gets from the decreasing number of flowers still containing nectar, it buzzes away to feed at another group of plants. It may well come back later, by which time the nectar supply might have been replenished. Watching a hedgehog foraging at night often suggests that it may be behaving in a similar way. The animal will dither about, snuffling hither and thither until it finds something to eat (difficult to know what). Then it continues meticulously poking about, seeking more in the immediate vicinity. It may remain in the same feeding area for a while, then suddenly move on to somewhere else. These bursts of movement, in between zig zagging and gyrating in a small area, do certainly suggest that it is not feeding randomly by simply walking steadily along hoovering up whatever it comes across. However, it is hard to say for sure that hedgehogs are optimising their feeding or that they are pursuing any particular strategy, but clearly they do succeed in getting enough to eat.

Numbers eaten or frequency of occurrence may indicate actual choice (i.e. the animal going out of its way to deliberately find and eat worms, for example) or simply reflect the abundance of this or that in the environment (like finding a lot of beetles in one place around horse dung, or maggots in a rotting carcass). So, do hedgehogs exercise choice and seek out the things that appear to be most often present in their diet, or are they feeding opportunistically on whatever they come across in their nocturnal wanderings? Andy Wroot tried to establish from his analyses of faecal pellets whether hedgehogs are opportunists or if they did actively select certain types of prey. He compared what was in samples of faeces with what was available in mid-summer on his study site (a golf course), based upon what fell into pitfall traps and the worms that could be found in the soil (by watering a patch with a chemical irritant that makes them come to the surface). His observations did suggest that the hedgehogs were feeding selectively, not entirely opportunistically. They chose to eat more soft-bodied food items like worms, caterpillars and cranefly larvae than would be expected if they had simply eaten whatever they found in the same proportions as they encountered the prey. He also calculated the calorific values of prey items and showed that worms contained nine times as much energy as most other foods, which is a good reason for preferring to eat them. However, in a dry period, worms became scarce and many more beetles were taken instead.

In summary, Andy's study (and others too) suggest that most of a hedgehog's encounters with food are likely to be rather random and they will eat what they can get, but it also appears that they will exercise a degree of choice if they can. Some things will be rejected if they are highly distasteful or if there is an abundance of more attractive items available. It is also likely that individual hedgehogs will discover a good place and feed there extensively, picking up lots of the same prey and perhaps returning the following night. This would account for the large numbers sometimes found at once, such as 63 caterpillars in one stomach or 144 ground beetles in a single dropping.

Then there is the question of how much does a hedgehog need to eat in a night. Andy Wroot tried answering this too, by estimating the animal's energy requirements based on measuring the amount of carbon dioxide that was produced as a result of its metabolic activity. On this basis, an average-sized adult (weighing 500–700 g) uses about 90–140 kcal (377–586 kJ) per day to power its body (a similar figure to that suggested by Struck, 1995). It could get this amount by eating about 60–90 g (wet weight) of typical hedgehog food. This is quite close to the typical daily intake of 71 g suggested by Hans Kruuk, based on feeding experiments with captive hedgehogs (Kruuk, 1964). Hedgehogs studied in the laboratory by my namesake (Morris and Steel, 1967) ate somewhat less, about 57 g per day. However, his animals probably did not need as much food as wild ones because they were kept in cages where they were reasonably warm indoors and needed little energy to maintain their body temperature and none at all to sustain long foraging excursions.

A full hedgehog stomach contains about 30–35 g of food (Yalden, 1976), implying that it will need to be filled at least twice each night in order to process sufficient to fulfil its energy requirements. That would account for the bursts of feeding sometimes reported, where the animal forages quickly and effectively early in the night and then has a bit of a rest while it digests what it has eaten. As the food moves on from its stomach, the hedgehog will become more active again and begin a fresh bout of feeding activity. It will need to remain pretty busy all night because 60–90 g is equivalent to dozens of leatherjackets, beetles and caterpillars, rather a lot of individual prey items to find and consume. In practice, of course, there will be much variation in the amounts eaten. The adult males in early summer are preoccupied with finding females rather than food, so they probably spend less time looking for it and stay hungry for much of the time. Lactating females will need to eat about three times as much food as non-breeders in order to meet the energy costs of feeding their offspring. A cold night might well reduce the amounts available and a happy encounter with a nest of baby voles would be a real feast and require little further searching that night. Thus, there will always be much variation in the amounts eaten as well as in the actual food items consumed.

It is also likely that hedgehogs will eat as much as much as possible and that can add up to quite a lot. In normal foraging, they increase their body weight by about 1.3 per cent per hour or 15 per cent in a whole night (Jackson, 2006). But where generous people put out plates of food in their garden, large amounts may

FIG 88. Hedgehogs benefit enormously from the extra food available in town gardens, put out for pets and garden birds – and for the hedgehogs themselves. (Hedgehog Street)

be consumed gluttonously in a short time, averaging 7.1 g per minute in one of my studies (1.4 per cent of body weight every 60 seconds!). The maximum amount of bread and milk ingested in one continuous feed by a single hedgehog was 94 g, equivalent to more than 10 per cent of its body weight (Morris, 1985). In the same study, hedgehogs visiting a food bowl normally ate about 50 g at a time, but some returned for additional feeds later, so that up to 157 g could be consumed by a single individual in one night. This was in addition to the natural food items that were encountered, plus any extra consumption if those animals had also fed at food bowls in adjacent gardens. Clearly, food supplements offered by well-meaning householders can add substantially both to the amount available and the amount eaten, but still leave little trace in the stomach or faeces (Fig. 88).

Diet analyses, with their different approaches all suggest that the hedgehog's food intake is a reflection of availability, choice and food value. Just how choosy hedgehogs are is hard to say, but they certainly eat a very wide range of things, given the opportunity. Casual observations suggest that hedgehogs are fond of hard-boiled eggs, omelette, cooked chicken, liquorice allsorts and mealworms. They will also eat peanuts that spill from bird feeders (and may suffer when these get stuck in the animal's palate). One was observed eating a squashed Mars bar and another was seen in London licking a discarded car battery. In 2015, a Dutch hedgehog was reported to have found a broken bottle of advocaat (a liqueur made from brandy, sugar and eggs) and became happily inebriated. Basically hedgehogs eat what they can get, being selective where they can and rejecting very little. Broad generalisations are possible, but are not much improved by obtaining greater detail. What all the diet analyses do reveal is that the hedgehog is a beneficial creature to have around. The bulk of the food items that it eats most frequently are the very creatures that gardeners and farmers would most like to have removed from their land. The importance of slugs and caterpillars in the hedgehog's diet is a good example, as these are a real problem for gardeners and for those trying to grow their own their own vegetables. In New Zealand, it is thought that hedgehogs may consume up to 40 per cent of the beetle larvae that destroy grass roots in the pastures that are so vital to the sheep farming industry. This was one of the reasons why their introduction was regarded as an economic benefit to that country.

VERTEBRATE PREY

The presence of feathers in 16 per cent and mammal fur in 12 per cent of the stomachs studied by Derek Yalden begs the question of whether or not hedgehogs are active predators of vertebrates. In the case of that particular study, we must remember that the majority of the stomachs came from hedgehogs trapped by gamekeepers. It is likely that dead pigeons and rabbits were often used as bait, whose remains would later be found in the stomachs and create a misleading impression of how important rabbits and pigeons (or other birds and mammals) might be as hedgehog food. Hedgehogs will certainly take carrion where it becomes available, which is why they so easily fall victim to gamekeeper's traps baited with rabbit entrails or dead chicks. With vertebrate prey, it is hard to be sure whether the remains found in droppings or in a stomach represent active killing or simply scavenging on a dead body. Derek's study found hairs from mouse and shrew, perhaps caught and killed, but the mole fur he encountered was almost certainly from a dead one because moles are strong animals with sharp teeth and a live one would put up a vigorous fight if attacked by a hedgehog. Incidentally, both moles and shrews have skin glands that make these animals distasteful to normal mammalian predators such as cats and dogs.

As for hedgehogs being actively predacious, in November 1969 an article by J. K. Stanford in the *Shooting Times* described a hedgehog that ran after a baby rabbit and killed it. This prompted a spate of letters to the magazine reporting similar cases, including one eyewitness account of a hedgehog killing a starling and further notes from Stanford about a hedgehog attacking a broody hen and another seen eating a leveret. In some of the older literature describing hedgehog behaviour, there are stories from 'country folk' attesting to occasional

FIG **89.** Hen's eggs are too large and smooth to tackle easily, although they may get broken if the hedgehog crushes them together. (Elizabeth Bomford/Ardea)

bloodthirsty activity by hedgehogs, including catching and killing rats and attempting to kill chickens. Sometimes the stories are told as from an eyewitness, so they are hard to disbelieve, but many are also hard to accept purely on grounds of improbability. Here, for example, is the author of a popular little book published in 1912 and reissued in 1926 without changing a word of this particular story: 'I have known it [the hedgehog] to carry off a dozen pheasant eggs from under a brooding hen, and after purloining the whole clutch, endeavour to kill and eat the fowl itself' (Simpson, 1912). How does a hedgehog carry off such large eggs, where to and why so many? Would the bird not defend itself, being probably at least as large as its attacker? Was the story really true or did the author just make it up, and if so, why?

Despite hedgehogs' heavy predation on eggs, Digger Jackson suggested that they took relatively few chicks from the nests of shorebirds on the Uists, perhaps because plover and wader nestlings are precocial and capable of running away and dispersing almost immediately they hatch (Fig. 90). However, there is direct gruesome and reliable evidence that hedgehogs will occasionally find and consume the chicks of ground-nesting birds such as gulls, seizing them by

FIG 90. A black-headed gull egg and chick. Chicks of ground nesting birds are able to run away soon after hatching, so the main damage is through consumption of the eggs.

the back legs as they try to escape and gradually crunching their way forwards. Presumably they will also eat the nestlings of mice and voles if they come across them. According to Frank Buckland in his annotated edition of *The Natural History and Antiquities of Selborne* (White, 1883), one of his reliable informants insisted that hedgehogs would eat fresh-killed mice 'with avidity' and also young larks from their nest. Buckland also commented that they were 'very fond of bread and milk'.

Frogs and toads are eaten occasionally (Fig. 91) and small lizards feature on the hedgehog's menu in New Zealand. It may happen in Britain too. There are also plenty of picturesque stories in the older European literature (and some eyewitness accounts) to the effect that hedgehogs will certainly kill and eat reptiles. It is even asserted, rather frequently, that they will prey on adders, escaping fatal retaliation because of their dense coat of protective spines. According to the seventeenth-century naturalist Edward Topsel, there is 'mortal hatred between the Serpent and the hedgehog' and he went on to describe in dramatic detail how a snake may seek out and attack a hedgehog in its den, only to be impaled on its spines and finally devoured, having the flesh torn from its bones. Apparently the snake 'biteth in vain, for the more she laboureth ... the more she is wounded

FIG 91. A hedgehog eating a toad despite its distasteful skin secretions. (Barbara Witowska/Hedgehog Street)

and harmeth herself, yet notwithstanding the height of her minde and hate of her heart, does not ... let go her hold until one or both parties be destroyed' (Fig. 92). Knowing this ancient tale, the nineteenth-century naturalist Frank Buckland staged a gladiatorial contest between a hedgehog and an adder to test the story about antipathy between the two species. He reported that,

> *the viper struck the hedgehog two or three times in the face, where there were no bristles; the blows were well aimed, and meant to do business, as at the moment the hedgehog was munching the viper's tail. The hedgehog did not suffer in the least; on the contrary, he ate up the viper leaving not a trace behind.*

FIG 92. Stories of hedgehogs fighting adders and eating them date back hundreds of years.

Other fights staged between adders and hedgehogs are also reported in the old literature and end up with the snake being eaten, having exhausted its venom in fruitless attempts to bite the hedgehog's skin among its sharp spines (just as Topsel alleged). It is probably also true that hedgehogs can kill snakes by grasping the head end and then rolling up, using their powerful skin muscles to exert enough force on the snake to dislocate its vertebrae. It is also true that tests with hedgehog blood suggest a degree of immunity to adder venom, at least in some individuals, and hedgehog muscles contain a substance ('erinacin') that neutralises the effect of haemorrhagic toxins in the venom of several snake species (Omori-Satoh et al., 2016). However, it is hard to see how this might have evolved, as predation on snakes cannot be a common event, especially as they are active in the day and hedgehogs at night. But maybe hedgehogs sometimes come across reptiles after dark and can attack the sleepy creatures, whose movements will be slow due to the lower ambient night-time temperatures.

New methods of diet analysis include the possibility of using DNA in faeces to identify what an animal has eaten. One such study by Carly Pettett confirmed that all the usual things were being consumed by hedgehogs, but also cows and pigs! This presumably represents meat in the form of pet food put out for cats or dogs. We need to recognise the increasing importance of pet food in supporting urban hedgehogs and also remember that without the benefit of DNA analysis, there would be no trace of this important dietary component whose significance may consequently have been greatly underestimated in the past (Fig. 93).

Another unnatural form of nourishment (which also would not show up in a traditional diet analysis) is the bread and milk that well-wishers frequently offer to animals. For largely practical reasons, this seems to have become the default option for feeding sick and injured mammals brought into captivity. It is also put

FIG 93. Hedgehog eating dog food. They like it and in some urban areas the hedgehog population may benefit considerably from the provision of supplementary food like this.

FIG 94. Traditionally, people have put out bread and milk for their garden wildlife and hedgehogs will travel considerable distances to eat it, although the milk causes them to have diarrhoea.

out in large quantities as supplementary food for the benefit of wildlife, especially garden hedgehogs (Fig. 94). The relative abundance of hedgehogs in urban areas probably owes much to the provision of supplementary food and also the pet food and bird table offerings available in many suburban gardens. The problem is that the hedgehog appears to be poorly adapted to cope with cow's milk. This contains certain lactose sugars which irritate the hedgehog's intestine, causing diarrhoea. Lactose intolerance is also found in some humans, often developing with increasing age. With hedgehogs kept under captive conditions, this causes messy and highly undesirable results in the form of sloppy, green faecal material and excessive water loss, a serious issue especially for any young hoglets that are being raised to independence on a milky diet. This familiar and very visible problem with captive hedgehogs has led to highly publicised campaigns in the media, highlighting the dangers of cow's milk as though it was actually poisonous. The result has been widespread dismay among the many householders who put out food bowls in their gardens and now fear they may have caused suffering among their hedgehog visitors. On the one hand, there is diarrhoea and potential death among hedgehogs in captivity, but on the other hand, wild hedgehogs clearly like eating bread and milk and stories have been told for centuries about the efforts they make to suckle cows. Studies reveal that wild hedgehogs will travel considerable distances in order to visit a garden and consume a plate of bread and milk. Moreover, they will continue to come, night after night, and reappear the following year after hibernating, ready to resume a diet supplemented with bread and milk. Despite being unnatural food for hedgehogs, bread and milk is clearly not poisonous and does not disrupt normal behaviour patterns (see Chapter 5), nor do discernible harm. Indeed, bread and milk may be a valuable addition to natural food for wild hedgehogs, especially during periods of dry weather.

Nevertheless it remains true that feeding hedgehogs in captivity on bread and milk is very undesirable and potentially dangerous, especially for young hoglets. There are plenty of better, commercially available balanced diets for hedgehogs held temporarily in captivity ('Spike's Dinner' is an example). It would be better if wild hedgehogs could be given goat's milk instead of cow's milk, thereby avoiding harmful lactose sugars in the latter. But goat's milk is expensive and not readily available, so this advice is impractical although frequently given. A compromise, and better than nothing, might be to continue offering bread and milk to wild hedgehogs, especially in dry weather, but watered down to dilute its harmful components whilst retaining the benefits of its other constituents and continuing

FIG 95. Hedgehogs enjoy eating bread and milk and they will travel considerable distances to do so, despite its drawbacks. However, no trace will be found in a traditional analysis of hedgehog droppings and it is hard to know the extent to which this material acts as a dietary supplement locally or nationally.

to provide a valuable, moist supplement to the hedgehog's natural diet. This may be a crucial aid to survival, especially when mothers are attempting to raise young. But a better course of action would be to avoid offering milk altogether and put out a readily available brand of meaty dog food (such as 'Pedigree Chum'), supplemented with bread or broken dog biscuits and thoroughly diluted with water.

Hedgehogs probably do not need to make special journeys to drink, except perhaps in very dry weather. Normally their food will include the body fluids of their prey and they can always lick dew or rain drops from grass stems as they pass by. In captivity of course, they must be provided with water. At least one author has suggested that hedgehogs 'will drink beer to intoxication', but perhaps this should not be encouraged.

PLANT MATERIAL

Bits of grass can often be seen in hedgehog droppings, but they were probably stuck to one of the worms or slugs that had been eaten. This would be especially likely if the hedgehog had been foraging on a freshly mown lawn with plenty of loose grass cuttings. They cannot digest grass, any more than we can, so there would be little point in eating it deliberately. However, hedgehogs are capable of digesting processed starch products such as bread (Struck, 1995). Some of the green plant fragments found in stomachs may be from the guts of caterpillars. Similarly, quantities of grit will be from inside the earthworms that have been ingested. Although present, plants will be contributing little to the hedgehog's energy budget. Derek Yalden did not report finding fruit in any of the many stomachs he examined, although others have found fruit remains, including blackberry and plum (Dickman, 1988) and I have seen small peas in a hedgehog stomach. Sometimes it is assumed that plant material is an incidental occurrence, because hedgehogs are 'insectivores' and the hedgehog is presumed to have been mainly attracted by some maggots or worms feeding on rotting fruit and eaten them, along with some of the fruit as well. That way, the ingestion of fruit may be accidental, just like the occasional tiny mites found in hedgehog stomachs that were almost certainly swallowed whilst the animal was grooming its fur. On the other hand, it may be that the fruit itself is an acceptable or even attractive food item, being sweet, easy to chew and unlikely to run away. Any maggots that might be swallowed at the same time constitute a bonus. Obviously fruit-eating is more likely to happen in suburban gardens with fruit trees or where there are commercial orchards in the countryside. It is also obvious that it is more likely in the autumn when there is ripe fruit about and squashy apples often lie on the ground in an orchard. It is hard to say just how important fruit might be for hedgehogs in general. For some individuals, at some times and in some places fruit could form a significant part of the diet, but frugivory is probably not a frequent or universal activity, nor will there be much evidence of it in conventional studies of hedgehog faeces or stomachs

Despite this, there are persistent legends dating back a thousand years or more to the effect that hedgehogs will gather fruit and carry it away on their spines (a detailed review was published by Christy, 1919). One of the earliest depictions of the European hedgehog is a figurine found during excavations in Greece dating from the fourth century BCE which has fruit impaled on its spines. These stories are not just English or even European folklore, but form part of the verbal and written heritage of many different countries, even as far away as China. They usually refer to apples, but also mention strawberries, grapes, figs and other soft fruit. Pliny wrote about this behaviour in the first century CE and the story was elaborated by Claudius Aelianus, another Latin scribe, who said that the animals would climb trees in order to dislodge fruit (figs in that case) and then pick up on their spines. There are several mediaeval accounts too, some of them with very explicit illustrations of fruit-carrying activity (Fig. 96). The story was told yet again by Gesner in his *Historia Animalium* (1620), widely regarded at the time as a fundamental authority. A detailed version was later published by Topsel

FIG 96. The ancient tale of hedgehogs carrying food on their spines is depicted here in a mediaeval manuscript.

in his *The History of Four-footed Beasts and Serpents*, the first major natural history book published in English: 'In the summer time they keep near vineyards and bushy places and gather fruite, laying it up against the winter', a statement that had been repeated down the ages from Pliny's time. Topsel went on:

When he findeth apples or grapes on the earth he rowlleth himself upon them untill he have filled all his prickles and then carryeth them home to his den never bearing above one in his mouth. And if it fortune that one of them fall off by the way he likewise shaketh off all the residue and walloweth upon them afresh untill they be all setled upon his back again so forth he goeth making a noise like a cartwheele.

It looks as though, for centuries, authors have copied uncritically from a previous writer, sometimes adding further embellishments of their own. Such widespread and persistent tales surely cannot all be imaginary, and yet fruit rarely appears in studies of hedgehog diets. Although one can forcibly impale fruit on a hedgehog's spiny back, it is hard to see how that could be achieved by the animal

FIG 97. It is possible to press an apple on to a hedgehog's spines, but it soon falls off if the animal attempts to carry it away. Hedgehogs are unlikely to be able to pick up apples unaided, but perhaps the story originally referred to smaller and softer fruits.

itself without help as its spines lie flat during normal activity (Fig. 97). The fruit also easily falls off as soon as the hedgehog begins to walk away. Old illustrations of this behaviour depict multiple fruits in place, even though that would be still more difficult for the animal to accomplish on its own. But why should a hedgehog want to do that anyway? If fruit is not normally a significant part of their diet and hedgehogs do not store food in their nests the way some rodents do, why bother to collect it at all? In winter, when they are most in need of stored food, their hibernation nests never contain fruit; instead, hedgehogs draw upon fat stored under the skin in order to survive.

More food-related folklore, similarly widespread and persistent, has hedgehogs enhancing their calorific intake by sucking milk from cows. This claim was ridiculed by Robert Smith as long ago as the eighteenth century, pointing out that a hedgehog's mouth is too small and its teeth too sharp to avoid aggravating the cow, whose udder is anyway too far off the ground for the animal to reach. In spite of these objections, reviewed by many authors and no doubt discussed in many rural pubs, stealing milk remained one of the crimes for which the hedgehog was blamed and used to justify its continued persecution down the centuries. A vet even published a paper blaming the hedgehog for two cases in which some injuries had been found on a cow's teats (Corcoran, 1967), and farmworkers have often claimed to have seen it actually happening. One of the most graphic descriptions was given by a Welsh farmer's son who had seen a hedgehog gripping a cow's teat in its mouth when the cows were being brought in to the milking parlour about four in the afternoon. As the cow stood up, the hedgehog was seen clinging to the inside of the cow's leg, with its mouth firmly clamped on the teat. The cow ran away, making repeated attempts to dislodge its tormentor. Eventually, the hedgehog fell off and was killed; the cow showed no sign of injury. Another worker on the same farm had seen a hedgehog sucking at the teat of a cow as it lay among the grass (Bean, 1982).

Overall, the milk-stealing story is easier to accept than the one about carrying fruit. Not only are there reasonably reliable modern eyewitness accounts, but a cow with a full udder will ooze milk and if she is lying down, the teats would be within a hedgehog's reach or it could lap up exuded droplets from the grass. There is also no doubt that hedgehogs do like cow's milk regardless of the diarrhoea that it may cause. Milk is very nourishing too and perhaps better food value than many of the more normal items that hedgehogs might consume. But of course, milk will not be evident in analyses such as those described earlier because it will leave no recognisable traces in the stomach or droppings, so we have no way of knowing how prevalent milk theft is likely to be, assuming it does really happen.

EGGS

When assessing the hedgehog's diet in relation to human interests, we cannot ignore the occurrence of eggshell in the analyses described above. Derek Yalden found eggshell in more than one in ten of the stomachs he examined, although this may represent an exaggerated prevalence if gamekeepers had used eggs to bait the traps from which his specimens had come. On the other hand, some studies in New Zealand using video recording show hedgehogs licking out an egg's contents without swallowing bits of shell, implying that egg predation may be under-recorded rather than exaggerated. Nevertheless, gamekeepers have traditionally counted hedgehogs as vermin and sought to reduce their numbers by regular trapping in the firm belief that this will enable greater reproductive success among their pheasants (*Phasianus colchicus*) and partridges (*Perdix perdix*). But data gathered by the Game Conservancy Trust suggests that only about 10 per cent of pheasant nests destroyed by predators had been raided by hedgehogs (Fig. 98). Foxes and crows accounted for almost two-thirds of the losses. Studies of partridges on farmland showed that more nests were destroyed by dogs and carelessly operated mowing machines than by hedgehogs. In the case of game birds, one could argue that the amount of egg consumption by hedgehogs does not justify the cost and effort involved in trying to remove them

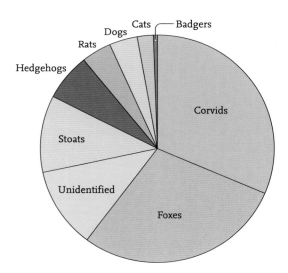

FIG 98. Data from the Game Conservancy Trust indicate that the hedgehog is not the main predator causing losses among pheasant nests.

in order to increase the availability of birds to be shot, although this kind of pressure on hedgehog populations has been intense in the past. For example, early in the twentieth century, some 20,000 hedgehogs were killed in 50 years on a single estate in East Anglia.

A study by Hugh Cott set out to establish whether the eggs of some species of birds were more appealing to hedgehogs than others (Cott, 1951). This was of interest because relative palatability had been part of the discussion among oologists and ornithologists as to why some eggs were more cryptically coloured than others. That was the principal purpose of Cott's study – hedgehogs were just a tool – but it also offered an opportunity to establish whether or not they are capable of detecting subtle differences in the taste of foods that they eat. Four hedgehogs were used in 332 tests. Samples of raw egg (without the shell) were offered in pairs, one bird species versus another, covering 25 different types of birds. Some of the species tested were unlikely to be taken by hedgehogs in the wild – gannets (*Sula bassana*) and kittiwakes (*Rissa tridactyla*), for example. However, the tests did show a preference for eggs of lapwings and common terns (*Sterna hirundo*), two ground-nesting species that hedgehogs can easily find and rob (Fig. 99). They liked chicken (*Gallus* sp.) eggs too. Conversely, those of blackbird (*Turdus merula*), linnet (*Acanthis cannabina*) and some of the warblers were treated as comparatively distasteful. So hedgehogs can tell the difference between foods that are as similar as the

FIG 99. Lapwings were among the birds that suffered from hedgehogs robbing their nests on the Uists, although their nests are usually dispersed, lessening the probability of being found.

egg whites from different species of birds. This adds nothing to the discussion about cryptic colouration in bird eggs, but does tell us a little more about a hedgehog's sensory capabilities.

Choosy or not, hedgehogs certainly do eat eggs, but it may well be behaviour that is learned by some individuals and not others. How does a hedgehog know what an egg is? An egg is a smooth hard object, quite unlike anything else on the hedgehog's menu. In captivity, hedgehogs will often ignore eggs completely, especially large ones that they cannot easily bite into, but having once tasted the forbidden fruit, so to speak, they will return to rob bird nests repeatedly and perhaps chicken coops too. This causes a problem where birds gather to nest on the ground in large colonies, and hedgehogs have been blamed for eating substantial numbers of the eggs of gulls and terns on nature reserves, even to the point of threatening local extinction of these ground-nesting birds. Careful study by Hans Kruuk at Ravenglass in Cumbria showed that, contrary to previous assertions, hedgehogs could break open and eat eggs as big as those of the black-headed gull (*Larus ridibundus*). He also suggested that some individuals in the nesting season might specialise in killing chicks or taking eggs (eating up to about six or seven per night), and could do so night after night (Kruuk, 1964).

Even so, the losses for which hedgehogs were responsible amounted to only about 2–3 per cent of the 8,000 broods on the Ravenglass peninsula. Foxes took far more, plus about 5 per cent of the adult birds in the colony.

Natural selection appears to have caused gulls and terns to synchronise their courtship behaviour, stimulated by the large numbers of birds in the colony and

TABLE 5. Analysis of 33 hedgehog faecal pellets collected near nesting colonies of black-headed gulls. (Based on Kruuk, 1964)

Prey type	Per cent occurrence among the 33 faecal samples
Insects	94
Snails (*Cepaea*)	21
Sandhoppers (*Talitrus & Talorchestia*)	18
Vegetable material (maybe eaten attached to animal food items)	58
Gull chicks' down	30
Adult gull feathers (carrion, maybe not from live birds?)	9
Eggshell	21

TABLE **6.** The number of nest failures attributed to hedgehogs and other causes on the Uists (including agricultural machines and flooding), based on Jackson & Green (2000). Losses among each of the first three species were greater in the 1990s, by which time hedgehog numbers had substantially increased.

	Period	Hedgehog	Other predator	Other causes
Dunlin (*Calidris alpina*)	1985–87	o	27	4
Dunlin	1996–97	44	30	1
Redshank (*Tringa totanus*)	1985–87	o	19	o
Redshank	1996–97	7	4	o
Ringed plover (*Charadrius hiaticula*)	1985–87	o	70	4
Ringed plover	1996–97	4	39	5
Snipe (*Gallinago gallinago*)	1996–97	2	1	o
Lapwing (*Vanellus vanellus*)	1996–97	25	35	10
Oystercatcher (*Haematopus ostralegus*)	1996–97	o	16	3

mating all at the same time. That results in almost all of them laying their eggs within a few days, creating so much food that the predators are overwhelmed and many clutches will escape being eaten. Any birds that breed later will be more exposed and have their nest robbed. This is an excellent example of natural selection, an evolutionary force driving colonial ground-nesting birds to breed all at once in order to reduce the impact of predation on the population as a whole. So long as the colony remains large enough, the impact of marauding hedgehogs will be relatively minor.

Smaller bird colonies are less likely to swamp the predators with food abundance and may suffer proportionately greater losses as a consequence. This appears to have been the case on Shetland, where nesting success was studied at a colony of about 500 pairs of Arctic terns (*Sterna paradisaea*). Evidence of nest predation attributed to introduced hedgehogs was plentiful (damage to the nest lining at night and large eggshell fragments left behind). As they moved through the colony, hedgehogs were also seen to cause considerable disturbance, which in turn upset other terns in the closely packed nesting area and resulted in nests being deserted by the parent birds. The hedgehogs remained untroubled by the noise of angry terns and their physical attacks, even though those birds can deliver a very sharp peck. At the end of summer, less than 10 per cent of the eggs that

FIG 100. A marauding hedgehog will be particularly damaging to colonial nesters like terns because it doesn't have far to walk before it finds another nest to rob and the eggs are laid in very exposed situations.

were laid that season had hatched successfully, compared to nearly 100 per cent at another colony from which hedgehogs were absent (Uttley *et al.*, 1981).

Damage has been attributed to hedgehogs where a nest has been plundered leaving large pieces of eggshell trampled into a disrupted nest lining, along with remains of egg white and yolk. The logic behind asserting that this was the work of a hedgehog is that larger predators like foxes and crows normally carry whole eggs away and do not leave behind slimy egg white or eggshell fragments. If the broken eggshell had been left by a hatching chick, all the yolk and white would have been consumed, leaving none in the nest. These diagnostic features have been verified using video cameras and led to several major studies that implicated the hedgehog as a significant predator in colonies of ground nesting birds. But predation by mink or polecats might also leave similar evidence that could be wrongly attributed to hedgehogs. In New Zealand, the reliability of this type of diagnosis has been questioned (again on the basis of video surveillance), so perhaps the degree of damage attributed to hedgehogs may have been overstated in some cases.

CONCLUSION

Dietary studies are fraught with difficulty, not least because of the many and confusingly different ways in which their results can be interpreted. Nevertheless, it is clear, from many studies and varied ways of considering their results that hedgehogs subsist on a wide variety of prey and other food items, but are not completely opportunistic feeders that just eat randomly whatever they come across. They do show a degree of selectivity and choice, although it is hard to imagine that they would pass up anything that was edible unless there was an abundance of food available. Mostly, they depend on common invertebrates, many of which are regarded as garden and agricultural pests. They also benefit from food put out for wildlife by supportive householders, although it is difficult to estimate just how significant this benefit is and little effort has been made to find out. Where hedgehogs gain access to the eggs of ground-nesting birds, their depredations make them highly unpopular and (locally at least) may even threaten the survival of certain vulnerable bird species. The consumption of eggs (and chicks) by hedgehogs raiding bird colonies cannot be denied and may also have an impact on non-colonial farmland birds such as skylarks and lapwings, whose numbers are already declining for other reasons. But in gardens, any damage is offset by the hedgehog's beneficial effects as a predator of horticultural pests and anyway there are few garden birds that nest on the ground where they might fall victim to hedgehogs.

CHAPTER 5

Activity: Movements, Home Range and Behaviour

A S A HIBERNATOR, ONE OF the few that we have in Britain apart from bats, the hedgehog shows a very strong seasonal pattern in its behaviour. Few are active before the end of March and most have gone into hibernation by late October (see Chapter 6). This pattern of activity is very clear from records of road casualties, and consistent from year to year when records are collected annually from the same area (Massey, 1972). Whenever regular surveys have been undertaken, road casualty counts also confirm that hedgehogs can be active even in January during temporary periods of arousal from hibernation, but their main period of activity is from April until September (Fig. 101). In many studies, including my own, samples of hedgehogs collected seasonally also often show a very skewed sex ratio, again reflecting changing activity patterns. Males predominate in spring and early summer, females later in the year just prior to hibernation. This corresponds to changes in behaviour, with the males being more active (and therefore more likely to be trapped, seen or run over) in early summer. By late summer, males will be preparing

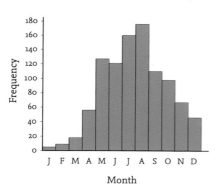

FIG 101. The number of hedgehogs reported for each month of the year in London reflects their annual pattern of activity. These 992 observations were made over half a century ago, long before climate change became a topic of discussion, yet they show winter activity is normal, although at a very reduced level.

for hibernation, or may have already become inactive, but females will still need to be fully out and about well into the autumn in order to replenish fat reserves lost during lactation. Some females may be still raising offspring in September, actually losing fat at a time when they need to be gaining it ready for the oncoming winter. Females will therefore typically be more active in the autumn than males, and for longer, so there is a preponderance of them in samples collected at this time. There is no evidence to suggest that an apparent skewed sex ratio is anything more than a reflection of this difference in behaviour.

The hedgehog is a nocturnal species whose detailed behaviour is difficult to observe in the dark. Any attempt to use a torch or approach closely typically results in a wary response. The animal will stop still and raise the spines on the crown of its head. If it becomes more suspicious, it will hunch its head down between the shoulders and raise more spines on its back. Loud sounds – the click of a camera shutter, for example – or close approach will also prompt this kind of reaction, exactly as Shakespeare described in *The Tempest*, Act 2, Scene 2, Line 10: 'Then like tumbling hedgehogs in my barefoot way and mount their pricks at my footfall.'

The hedgehog will remain motionless for long periods waiting for the perceived danger to go away and frustrating any attempt to study its behaviour. If it is touched or provoked, it may well roll up, completely encased in its spiny covering, and stay that way, obstinately waiting to be left alone. This highly characteristic action, so long identified with the hedgehog, is a form of passive defence that will deter most predators (see Chapter 9) but results in many being killed on the roads. Despite all the difficulties of direct observation, it is possible to follow hedgehogs and watch what they do. Some will behave in a very cautious manner, while others can be quite bold and even aggressively bad-tempered. On the other hand, some pet hedgehogs become very tame and will even come when they are called.

GENERAL BEHAVIOUR

Hedgehogs normally begin their activities about an hour after sunset, probably later in areas where there is a lot of disturbance. Its effective spiny defence might make us wonder why the hedgehog is nocturnal at all when it could manage just as well being active during the day. We regard that as a normal behaviour pattern because we humans are primates, most of which are diurnal: daytime activity is the norm for them and for ourselves. However, the hedgehog comes from an ancient line of mammals and the earliest species were nocturnal. Its lineage has

FIG. 102 Most of the hedgehog's normal prey are active at night, like this grey slug (*Limax* sp.), snails, worms and many species of beetle.

remained so, probably because most of the things upon which hedgehogs feed also emerge at night (Fig. 102). That is because creatures like worms and slugs are liable to lose water through their permeable skin when exposed to warm sunshine. They avoid this fate by coming out at night when cooler air results in moist surroundings and even dewfall. Many creatures that are potential hedgehog food are also nocturnal because in the dark they are more likely to escape predation by birds, most of which are active during the day. During dry spells, hedgehogs will usually not set out until after the dew has fallen, probably because there is little to eat on dry ground.

Activity often follows a bimodal pattern, with much moving about soon after emerging at dusk and during the early part of the night. Later, there will be another bout of activity once the animal's stomach has emptied and it is time to go foraging again. Lactating females will need more food than non-breeders and may have to be more continuously busy. Blood pressure rises as the animal gets going for the night and is highest just after the second period of general activity towards the end of the night. Hedgehogs sleep during the day and are said to dream a lot, more than sloths anyway, but it's hard to know what about (Grist, 1983).

During its nocturnal ramblings, a hedgehog will normally potter about taking a minute or two to cover little more than a metre, meticulously searching for food and frequently sniffing quite loudly as though using scent to locate edible items. Its progress is often surprisingly noisy, especially among dry leaves, almost as though its spiny coat gives the animal a feeling of confidence and invulnerability, reducing the need for caution and wariness that characterise the movements of most other mammals. A hedgehog's progression seemingly involves 'dithering about', often doubling back on its tracks as though a navigational error had just been realised. Then suddenly the animal may pick up a scent trail and scoot off in a different direction. In normal foraging the hedgehog will snuffle about, poking its nose into the ground, lifting dead leaves and occasionally pausing to sniff the air (Fig. 103). Shaking, yawning, stretching and arching the back are all common behaviours.

Watching a hedgehog moving around over open ground, it seems to have short legs. Actually they are quite long and enable the animal to run surprisingly fast. Averaged over half an hour or more, a foraging hedgehog travels at about 2–4 m per minute, but when it wants to it can scuttle along about as fast as a human can walk without breaking into a run. Nigel Reeve timed some of his male hedgehogs travelling at average speeds of 3.2–3.7 m per minute, females and youngsters around 2.2 m per minute. In short bursts, some hedgehogs managed speeds in excess of 30 m per minute for several minutes at a stretch, although these speedy individuals were all males. One was observed crossing the golf course fairway, covering at least 60 m in one minute, but this was the fastest that any hedgehog seemed to run.

FIG 103. When out foraging, a hedgehog will typically pause to sniff the air at frequent intervals. (Rose Goodwin/BHPS)

Evidence is sometimes offered to suggest that hedgehogs may use a regular route on their nocturnal forays. For example, the German biologist Walter Lindeman used to take two of his pet hedgehogs for a walk and reported that 'Eri' followed her favourite path on 47 per cent of her outings and 'Jossy' 52 per cent (Lindeman, 1951), but observations like this may be just a case of the animal following familiar linear features like a fence line or the edge of a lawn. Hedgehogs are also often found run over at the same point on a road, again suggesting a regular pathway or crossing point, but overall it seems that activity is not confined to particular routes, at least not for any significant distance. If it rains heavily, the animal will curtail its business and retire to cover, normally by the most direct route rather than follow a particular track back to its nest.

Even at mating time, hedgehogs seem to be mainly solitary. They do not call to each other or use sound for aggressive or social purposes, although young ones may occasionally emit a high-pitched chirping noise and very occasionally a distressed hedgehog can give vent to a loud squeal that sounds just like a pig. On the other hand, although non-vocal, hedgehogs are surprisingly noisy creatures in other ways, trampling and rustling leaves, pushing aside twigs and other obstacles. They wander hither and thither, their nose sniffing and poking at the

FIG 104. Some hedgehogs become adept at coaxing worms out of their burrow. Pulling too hard or too soon will cause the worm to break, reducing its value as food. (Brian Bevan/Ardea)

ground, forever searching and investigating until they retire to their nest about an hour before dawn. Sometimes a hedgehog will make a short dash to grab a fleeing beetle or maybe seize upon a worm. Some have learned not to pull too hard or the animal will snap and half of it will be lost. Instead, the worm will be gripped with the teeth and in a gentle rocking motion eased out of its burrow so the whole thing can be consumed (Fig. 104). One forefoot may be used to wipe off the gritty earth that will be sticking to it, but paws are otherwise not used to grasp food as a squirrel does when holding nuts. Occasionally the hedgehog will pause to groom itself, particularly soon after leaving its nest. It uses the long claw on one of its hind toes, lifting the foot and balancing on the other three. The animal can reach its flanks and also the back and middle of the body and behind its ears by twisting itself sideways to scratch between the spines. It can also lick the forelegs and the abdominal fur, aided by the extraordinary mobility of the skin, which can be pulled around backwards or sideways by the underlying muscles.

Scent-marking, to leave a social message or demarcate territory, is an important activity among many species of mammals, but not hedgehogs. While dogs mark lamp posts with their urine very frequently, the hedgehog appears to urinate at random. Otters (*Lutra lutra*) use their faeces to dispose of undigested food remains, but as these 'spraints' are carefully deposited by the otter they are augmented with secretions from scent glands to leave a signal to others of their species. Badgers stake out their clan territories with small dung pits around the territorial boundaries. The hedgehog does none of this and its droppings appear to be left at random, and not as part of an elaborate olfactory dimension to their social behaviour. It is rare to find more than a single faecal pellet in one place and other hedgehogs do not add further contributions as they pass by. This makes it all the more peculiar that accumulations of 50 or more hedgehog faecal pellets have been reported in New Zealand (Jones & Jackson, 2009). It is unclear whether more than one animal contributed, or why they should have been deposited in the particular locations recorded, and it seems not to have been observed elsewhere.

Hedgehogs can be quite aggressive and one will often attempt to bite another's legs where the skin is thin and unprotected by spines. The hind leg is particularly vulnerable as it is exposed from under the spiny umbrella when the animal tries to run away. Another form of belligerence is to use the spines as weapons in active attacks, the hedgehog attempting to butt rivals with its spine-covered forehead and trying to bowl over any animal whose presence is unwelcome. In response, the victim will move more of its skin and spines over towards the attacker, presenting an increasingly robust and challenging target. One animal may take the hint and swiftly depart or they might both give up and

FIG 105. Hedgehogs
can swim and will
readily take to the
water, but they easily
become exhausted and
drown, even in a small
garden pond, if they
cannot get back on to
dry land.

go their own way. Many people who put out food for hedgehogs in the garden
often describe something resembling a peck order, even suggesting that the
animals may form a sort of queue at the food bowl, headed by the most dominant
individuals. Sometimes a particularly large and aggressive hedgehog will briskly
dispatch others from the food. On other occasions, several hedgehogs may
feed together amicably. Overall there seems to be little evidence of a regular or
structured social system among wild hedgehogs, although a dominance hierarchy
has been described by several authors, based on observations of hedgehogs in
captivity where the physical constraints on space and access to food may distort
patterns of natural activity. Fighting and the appearance of dominant behaviour
have encouraged speculation that hedgehogs may be territorial, a matter
discussed later in this chapter.

FIG 106. Although they cannot grip with their paws the way monkeys or squirrels do, hedgehogs are capable of climbing walls and fences.

When necessary, a hedgehog can swim moderately well and there are reports of them crossing rivers in this way, even a wide one like the River Thames at Henley (Fig. 105). But if they cannot get ashore, or climb out of an artificial pond, they will become exhausted and drown just like any other animal. Hedgehogs can also dig and climb, easily scaling wire mesh fences and occasionally brick or stone walls. In this, and in tree climbing, they are aided if the obstacle lies at a slope rather than being fully vertical (Fig. 106). There are stories of hedgehogs climbing ivy-clad walls and even nesting in a thatched roof. I have been told several times about them climbing upstairs in houses, although it is hard to see what motive there would be for scaling an indoor staircase. A climbing hedgehog seems to have no fear of falling, probably because it can roll over and have a hard landing cushioned by its springy spines.

SELF-ANOINTING

Unlike many mammals, hedgehogs seem to spend no time in play, not even the young ones. They may interrupt normal activity for occasional stops to groom or indulge in sexual activity, but their active hours are normally devoted almost entirely to the serious business of seeking food. It is therefore all the more remarkable when an animal stops what it is doing and begins to indulge in what appears to be a very energetic, but completely pointless, activity that we now call 'self anointing'. This bizarre and somewhat alarming, almost manic, behaviour on the part of hedgehogs seems to have been first described in 1912 by Ludwig Heck, a German zoologist who named it *Selbstbespucken*, meaning 'self-spitting'. Konrad Herter later dealt with the subject only briefly and other German, French and Danish authors also subsequently described this behaviour without elaborating further. It was Maurice Burton who wrote the first detailed account (Burton, 1957), and coined the term 'self anointing' to describe it.

What happens is that a hedgehog will stop its normal activity and begin to salivate copiously, often stimulated by chewing at a variety of objects. When it has a frothy mass of saliva on its tongue, it twists the body and throws its head over its shoulder sufficiently far to flick the froth onto its spines. Sometimes this involves lifting one foot off the ground or leaning so far to one side that the animal may actually fall over. Undeterred, it continues with this extraordinary performance, spreading saliva on both its flanks and on its back. Its eyes are wide open and the creature appears deeply engrossed in what it is doing and totally

FIG 107. A hedgehog in the act of self-anointing seems almost manic in its efforts to spread saliva over its body, ignoring all else, including the flash of a camera.

FIG 108. The hedgehog spreads frothy saliva over its fur and spines, twisting the body to an extent that seems barely possible.

disengaged from its surroundings (Fig. 107). Burton expressed surprise that this startling and conspicuous behaviour had gone unreported anywhere until 1912, yet when he published his own observations in the 1950s there was an immediate flurry of response from many other people who had seen the same thing, usually with pet hedgehogs. The distracted behaviour and violent contortions caused some observers to fear that the animal was suffering from epilepsy or having a fit. Burton described a hedgehog called 'Rufus' who spent a lot of time self-anointing and seemed to be stimulated by contact with almost anything. The carpet, wool, rugs, glazed tiles, human sweat, the varnish on a wooden bookcase, garden plants, insulating tape, glue, the bristles of a brush, earthworms and dog excrement would all set him going. As Rufus continued self-anointing, he seemed to develop a frenzy and after a while would use his teeth, biting as well as licking. This frantic behaviour could go on for 20 minutes or more, although other hedgehogs self-anointed only briefly and most did not do it at all.

Maurice Burton's correspondence files revealed a wide variety of items that had set off a hedgehog's bout of self-anointing and the list continued to lengthen as still more observers contributed comments. The reported stimulants included the skin of a dead toad, a clean handkerchief, cigar butt and an empty cigarette

FIG 109. It's not only the adults that engage in self-anointing; this hand-reared baby is doing so with food mixed with its saliva. (Melissa Ilston/BHPS)

packet, as well as leather goods and at least 20 other different and completely unrelated things. The list includes various astringent or aromatic substances that might well stimulate salivary flow, but self-anointing has also been initiated by contact with nothing more exciting than distilled water. It was frequently reported that a hedgehog would sniff assiduously at the surface of an object before starting to lick it and at intervals would often return to exactly the same spot to lick it again. Among pet hedgehogs, there are some that would only self-anoint on the same few things, whereas for others there was an almost unlimited list of substances and objects that turned them on. A few hedgehogs were reported to perform only occasionally, but the majority seemed never to engage in self anointing at all. The action seems to occur in both sexes, possibly slightly more often by males. It has even been reported to occur among hand-reared nestlings and juveniles (Figs. 109).

This behaviour is so bizarre that it would be easy to assume that it was an artefact brought on by the unfamiliar and perhaps stressful conditions of captivity. But Burton observed that dried spittle also occurred on the spines of wild hedgehogs. Bob Brockie inspected 929 hedgehogs during his field studies in New Zealand and observed saliva on 19 of them (Brockie, 1976). He said they had (to him) a distinct smell and suggested that self-anointing might have some sort of sexual function, but offered no evidence in support of that idea. In three years, Nigel Reeve found only nine wild hedgehogs that showed clear evidence of recent self-anointing, confirming that it is a normal but infrequent behaviour. Three of his animals were sub-adults and two had covered themselves in dog faeces. Nigel also made the first direct observation of wild hedgehogs actually engaged in self-anointing. He found evidence of it outside the breeding season and not associated with courtship behaviour. 'Emily', his tame hedgehog, self-anointed at all times of the year, confounding Brockie's speculation. A study based on a larger sample of 194 wild hedgehogs in Belgium found a higher proportion of animals indulging (at least 11 per cent) and confirmed that self-anointing occurred among both young and old animals. Indeed the sub-adults seem to have been much more active in this behaviour than the older generations. Males engaged in the behaviour significantly more often than females and there was a peak of activity in July among the adults, but not in the younger animals (D'Have *et al.*, 2005).

The long list of potential stimulants is matched by the diversity of speculative explanations for this extraordinary activity. Almost every suggestion that matches one aspect of this behaviour is ruled out by another observation. For example, one idea was that it was some form of greeting, but hedgehogs normally self-

FIG 110. Self-anointing by a juvenile hedgehog, probably only about ten weeks old. (Graeme Thompson/BHPS)

anoint alone. Another suggestion was that it makes the hedgehog unpalatable to its predators, although these are few and observations show them more likely to be deterred by the sharp spines. One of Burton's correspondents mentioned a hedgehog that self-anointed only with boiled beetroot and went about coloured purple, but this cannot be a universal explanation, for the behaviour especially as colours are meaningless in the dark. Some people have suggested that it might be a means of getting rid of fleas and ticks, but if so it is remarkably ineffective. Anyway why concentrate on adding saliva to the spines when many of the skin parasites live on the legs and belly, which are easier for the tongue to reach? Another suggestion was that self-anointing was a means of keeping the spines supple, but why? Spines are better protection if they are stiff and firm. Yet another idea, prompted by the use of toad skin (Brodie, 1977), is that saliva contaminated with the toad's natural skin poison placed on the spines would make them more effective against enemies. But hedgehogs don't normally find or seek out a convenient toad and the spines are usually so sharp and numerous they form effective protection regardless of their taste or smell. It has even been suggested (with no supportive evidence) that self-anointing may be some form of residual behaviour aimed at keeping the hedgehog cool, dating from millions of years ago when hedgehogs first evolved in tropical climates.

None of these explanations seems very likely, given that only a minority of hedgehogs perform this behaviour and do so only on rare occasions. Moreover the behaviour has also been reported from at least three other species of hedgehog which live in such a variety of conditions and circumstances that it is difficult to imagine any of these explanations could apply to them all. In the absence of any scientific evidence or proof, the most likely function of self-anointing seems to be to provide an enhanced form of olfactory recognition. Perhaps, instead of scent-marking a lamp post or depositing scent-filled faeces as markers, the hedgehog is scent-marking itself. Maybe self-anointing serves to signal 'here I am' to other hedgehogs? The hedgehog's spines provide an enormous surface area from which scent from evaporating saliva could be wafted on the air. Perhaps the saliva is enhanced by the addition of pheromones from secretory glands under the tongue like we find in pigs. In that connection, it may be noted that several observers have pointed out that the hedgehog licks with the upper surface of the tongue to accumulate material, then uses the underside when actually anointing the spines and fur, but that could be due to anatomical limitations of not having a longer tongue and may also not always be what happens. It may be relevant that Madagascan tenrecs (similar to hedgehogs in many other ways) spread a mixture of urine and saliva on their spines and bush babies urinate on their hands then transfer that scent-laden substance to

FIG 111. A juvenile hedgehog, barely old enough to have left its mother's nest, self-anointing so vigorously that it is in danger of falling over. (Julien Crowther/BHPS)

their fur and to the surfaces where they walk. Perhaps these behaviours serve to enhance and diversify the olfactory regime within which many mammals operate, unrecognised by ourselves due to the relatively inferior sense of smell possessed by humans.

Hedgehogs have a very well-developed sense of smell and in addition there are suggestions that they may have a functional Jacobson's organ in the roof of the mouth. In snakes this structure plays an important part in detecting scent. Many male deer and antelope engage in a behaviour known as 'flehmen' in which the lips are raised and the air around potentially fertile females is sampled by sucking it into the mouth, there to be analysed in the Jacobson's organ. Maybe hedgehogs do something similar, depositing saliva, enhanced or not, on their spines to liberate an odour that can be detected by the Jacobson's organ of another individual. That might help them convey messages to each other about their identity and location. Hedgehogs appear not to be territorial, so they do not need to put down markers to defend where they live. Maybe instead of using a lamp post like a dog to announce its presence, the hedgehog uses its own body. Its spiny coat probably compensates for the additional risk of drawing attention to itself. But this remains just speculation, confounded by the observation that relatively few hedgehogs engage in self-anointing and those that do include both sexes as well as juveniles and adults. The behaviour is also not limited to the breeding season, when it might seem to be most useful for them to be sending out social signals.

Baffled by all the contrary observations he received, Maurice Burton toyed with the idea that self-anointing might actually have no purpose at all. He suggested that it could be comparable to the habit in some birds of frolicking among colonies of ants or in clouds of smoke. He also suggested that what cats do in the presence of catmint was also behaviour with no obvious functional benefit and wondered if self-anointing by hedgehogs could be similarly pointless (to humans at least) or just a form of play. The problem with the idea of it being 'non-adaptive' is that there would be no evolutionary pressure for it to develop if there was no benefit in doing so. On the other hand, we humans do an awful lot of things that appear to convey little or no biological benefit, ranging from abstract art to playing golf!

RUNNING IN CIRCLES

Another apparently pointless behaviour described by various people is where a hedgehog keeps running in circles. The most detailed account was published by the Reverend Boys Smith based on observing a hedgehog that regularly visited his garden at the Master's Lodge of St. John's College, Cambridge. Over a period of a month, almost every night when it was not raining, this hedgehog took to running in a large circle about 14 m in diameter. The activity went on for long periods in the same part of the garden, invariably running anticlockwise. The animal ran quite fast (he thought about 130 m per minute) across a grassy lawn and a gravel drive. The running began soon after dusk, but the hedgehog also performed its circulatory ritual at various times later in the night, apparently completely absorbed in what it was doing (Boys Smith, 1967). This story was widely publicised and discussed at the time. As a result, I received many letters on the subject and one of my correspondents, Cherry Johnstone, reported a hedgehog that regularly travelled in a circle in the same part of a garden in Canterbury. Apparently it did 31 circuits one night. Others wrote to me with similar stories, describing circuits extending to 20 m or more in diameter, and with the hedgehog running so vigorously and so frequently that a deep track would be beaten into the ground (Figs. 112 & 113). More incidents were reported in letters to newspapers (Burton, 1969). Similar behaviour was also observed in captive hedgehogs (Dimelow, 1963), with the same animal always running either clockwise or anticlockwise.

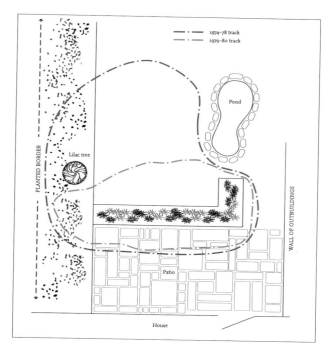

- - · - 1974–78 track
--- · - 1979–80 track

Pond

PLANTED BORDER

Lilac tree

WALL OF OUTBUILDINGS

Patio

House

FIG 112. One of my correspondents, Alan Brack, sent me this diagram of his circling hedgehog's activities. It would run clockwise non-stop for the 20-m circuits, sometimes 10 to 12 circuits without a pause.

FIG 113. He also sent a photograph showing how the hedgehog had beaten a trail into the grass during its rapid running. It would sometimes break off to feed elsewhere, then return to its regular track, night after night.

Manic running in circles is unlikely to be normal behaviour and is probably the result of some form of sickness in the animal. In the 1960s, it was quite common to find wild animals in a disoriented state, apparently unable to walk or fly properly. This was often the result of pesticide poisoning. In those days, various organochlorine compounds were widely used for timber preservation and for killing insect pests on agricultural land. These man-made chemicals do not readily decompose in natural systems and small amounts accumulated in animals that then became concentrated in the bodies of predators higher up the food chain. Instead of killing these larger animals outright, the toxic residues caused sickness and sterility, with impaired locomotory abilities and a lingering death. The reported cases of hedgehogs running in circles seem to have come mainly from the period when such chemicals were in widespread use. There appear to have been few, if any, reports from earlier than the 1960s, despite this being such a conspicuous form of behaviour that it would surely have been noticed and described in earlier books about mammals if it were commonplace. Also, few such stories are coming to light now that the most harmful cumulative poisons have been withdrawn from use. So it is possible that some hedgehogs accumulated residues of DDT, Dieldrin, Lindane or similar compounds through ingesting minute quantities in the individual prey items that they ate. Over time, the toxic residues could build up in the body and disrupt normal behaviour.

However, it is not clear why that kind of poisoning should be manifest in the form of circulatory ambulations. An association with agricultural chemicals was pure speculation, so when I was presented with a hedgehog that ran in circles, I decided to have it euthanased and autopsied in order to resolve the question. A bacterial infection in the middle ear was found. This offers a very plausible explanation for running in circles because the middle ear is the part of the sensory system that enables vertebrates to orientate themselves and maintain their balance when they move about. If one ear became infected and no longer operated in synchrony with the other, an animal would find it hard to travel in a straight line. Running in circles in an agitated manner would be a likely consequence. The pain associated with a severe infection might well result in a hedgehog adopting a distracted state, uncaring of what was going on in its surroundings and behaving exactly as described by many observers. One test of this hypothesis would be to treat a 'circle-running' hedgehog with antibiotics and see if it became cured of the affliction, but I have never been given another circling hedgehog upon which to experiment (perhaps because of what I had done with the first one).

SUMMER NESTING

At the end of a night's activity, the hedgehog withdraws to a sheltered place to rest for the ensuing day. Unlike the large hibernation nests which are relatively easy to see in the sparse vegetation of winter (see Chapter 6), summer nests are very hard to make out. We must rely on radio-tracking to discover where hedgehogs normally lie up each day and even then it may not be possible to find exactly where the animal is sleeping without excessive disturbance and destruction of the surrounding vegetation. Most of the early accounts of hedgehog ecology made casual references to lying up in shrubbery or thick vegetation during summer days, based upon occasionally and accidentally coming across them. The first systematic observations are from Nigel Reeve's study on Ashford Manor golf course in 1978 and 1979, with various subsequent studies elsewhere serving to confirm that his observations represent normal hedgehog behaviour (Reeve, 1982; Reeve & Morris, 1985). Nigel's radio-tracked animals usually spent the day in a specially constructed nest, although they sometimes merely used a sheltered place in thick vegetation (which he referred to as a 'lair'). Other authors, including myself, have also sometimes found hedgehogs merely sheltering in long grass or other dense vegetation, with no evidence of nesting material. This may be quite common in fine weather conditions, as Elizabeth Dimelow's captive hedgehogs often did not bother to make a nest when the temperature exceeded 16°C (Dimelow, 1963).

Nigel Reeve located 67 daytime resting places in one summer, but only 58 of them were sufficiently accessible to permit close inspection without undue disturbance. Two-thirds were well supported externally, such as those that were sited under bramble bushes or tucked up against solid objects. One nest was at the end of a passage into a tree stump and four were in burrows. These were tunnels a metre or so in length with a single entrance. They could have been dug by the hedgehogs themselves, but were more likely to have been excavated by rabbits. The use of rabbit burrows for nesting has been widely reported before and they are probably an important form of shelter in open and treeless landscapes.

Only 41 of Nigel's nests could be inspected closely enough to discover their precise composition. They were mostly (83 per cent) formed from naturally fallen leaves, creating a small mound, the rest being made of grass and leaves or grass alone. The nests were usually well constructed, implying that feeding time had been sacrificed in favour of nest construction. This suggests that nests are important to the animals in summer as well as in winter, and the availability

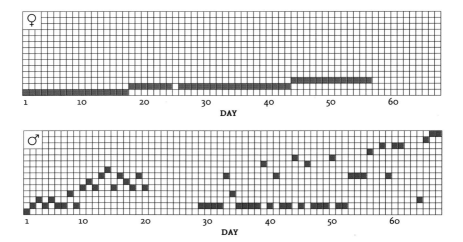

FIG 114. Comparative use of summer nests by male and female hedgehogs. Each horizontal row in these diagrams represents a different nest. Females tend to return to the same nest night after night for long periods (top, in green), whereas males (above, in red) use a variety of nests, enabling them to range over a wider area on consecutive nights.

of suitable sites and materials may be an ecologically limiting factor in some habitats (see Chapter 6). Summer nests tend to be smaller and less substantial than hibernation nests, although they are usually constructed using similar materials. They are used periodically throughout the active season, often abandoned and then reoccupied later or possibly used by a different hedgehog. Occasionally the same nest may serve as a hibernaculum during the ensuing winter and in a few cases Nigel found the same sites being used in consecutive summers, although probably not exactly the same nest.

During the active season, a hedgehog will use several different nests. One of Nigel's males occupied 10 different nests in 118 days, widely distributed within its summer home range of 39 ha. Another male used 14 nests in 68 days (with one day in a lair), within a home range of similar size (Fig. 114). A female used only 5 nests in 88 days, clustered more centrally in her smaller 14 ha of summer home range. There was a clear tendency for both sexes to use a nest only once before moving to another: of the 136 periods of occupancy recorded, two thirds were for one day only among the males and about half among females. There is much individual variation in the frequency with which a hedgehog changes its nest, but several studies have shown that males move from one nest to another significantly more often than females. In Nigel's study, males changed their nesting place about every three days. Three males used at least 10 nests each in the same summer, one of them making 42 changes among 11 nests in 4 months. By contrast, non-breeding females spent an average of 9.6 days in the same nest before moving on and several used the same nest every day for 2 weeks or more. In another study, hedgehogs were tracked in woodland and in 3 weeks 1 female used at least 3 different daytime resting places and changed her nest 4 times, while the male made 6 changes among 4 different nests in 19 days (Morris, 1986). Mothers will normally remain at the same nest throughout the time that they are rearing young, often more than a month, although they will sometimes move their family to another place. In a longer study (in Ireland), Amy Haigh found a total of 117

TABLE 7. Number of summer nests used and frequency of changes; data from two seasons combined. * indicates juvenile. (Based on Reeve & Morris, 1985).

	Animal no.	Tracking period (days)	Number of nests and 'lairs' used	Number of nest changes	Average number of days per nest
Males	106	39	10	26	3.9
	117	49	7	15	7.0
	105	72	4	15	18.0
	106	118	11	42	10.7
	108	32	4	25	8.0
	117	68	15	41	4.5
	136	7	2	1	3.5
	173	9	2	4	4.5
	176*	42	3	13	14.0
Females	107	29	2	4	14.5
	111	42	6	10	7.0
	139	14	9	8	1.5
	150*	33	6	7	5.5
	107	88	6	27	14.7
	111	29	3	11	9.7
	133	56	3	2	18.7
	139	40	4	3	10.0
	180*	73	3	6	24.3

different day nests, with individual hedgehogs using up to 11 nests during the summer and returning to a particular nest up to seven times. Her hedgehogs built both day nests and hibernacula in farmland hedgerows (Haigh *et al.*, 2012b).

In most studies, hedgehogs have built a nest, used it for a while and then gone away. Some would return to it again later, suggesting that they 'know their way around' and may perhaps have a selection of nests that could be used as needed. This would make sense, given that valuable time will have been spent in nest construction and it would be more efficient if an existing nest could be found and used again instead of making a new one. Exactly this behaviour was observed among rehabilitated hedgehogs released at unfamiliar sites after a period of veterinary care. They soon learned their way about in their new home and, having built nests, went directly back to them at the end of a night's foraging. Nest construction appears to be instinctive, as juveniles with no previous experience of life in the wild behave the same way as adults (Morris *et al.*, 1992; Morris & Warwick, 1994).

Hedgehogs will also use rabbit burrows, in summer and in winter. Even with radio-tracking they are hard to locate underground, so the importance of burrows may have been overlooked. At sites in New Zealand where rabbits were numerous, more than half of resting hedgehogs spent the day in a rabbit burrow.

Captive hedgehogs will often share the same nest during the summer, but there is no published information suggesting that this is a frequent occurrence among hedgehogs in the wild, a potentially vital activity in sustaining the life cycle of their parasites (see Chapter 11). Nigel found no instances of hedgehogs living together, but observed seven cases of non-simultaneous nest sharing where one hedgehog used a nest that had been previously occupied by another. In six of these, the 'visitor' was a male; all the nests being visited had been occupied by a female. No female ever occupied a nest known to have been used previously by a male. This type of 'home visiting' will have been under-recorded because it can only be evident among the few radio-tagged animals being studied at a particular time. Visits by non-radio-tagged animals would pass unnoticed. We also do not know whose nest it was initially unless a radio-tagged animal was actually observed to build it. There must be plenty of existing nests available to freely moving hedgehogs if only they can find them. However, there seems to be no organised pattern of use comparable with the satellite setts of a badger main sett, for example. Several nests are potentially available to a hedgehog at any one time and their use is spasmodic and unpredictable.

The tendency for males to change their nests more often than females may be connected with the larger home range of the former. It is expedient to have several widely dispersed nests instead of having to return repeatedly over long distances to the same one. This would allow a male hedgehog to range more widely in search of females and also enable him to exploit potential feeding areas that were a long way from the centre of his normal activities. Meanwhile female summer nests will include those that they use to raise their young. These must be bigger and more robust structures than the temporary nests that are only occupied for a day or two. Nursery nests are often large and resemble hibernation nests, frequently with the inclusion of paper and soft fabrics torn to pieces with the teeth while being held down by the front feet. Once the young are born, the nest will be used every day for about a month. Although a mother will sometimes move her young to another nest, she will cease her normal behaviour of frequent nest-changing until her offspring are weaned. In one of my studies, a female had a nest with five young, estimated to be five to seven days old as they were still blind and dependent upon their mother for milk. She had been out of the nest foraging every night for the preceding five nights, which almost certainly spanned the births, but she did not appear to have returned to feed her litter during the hours of darkness (Morris, 1986).

NOCTURNAL WANDERINGS

Hedgehogs can clearly learn the geography of their surroundings, finding their way back to a previously used nest for example. Experiments show that they will also learn good places to feed, perhaps using visual cues, and will return there repeatedly (Cassini & Krebs, 1994). They will go back to a regularly placed food bowl in the garden even after it has been removed. Displaced animals can also find their way back to a garden from a distance of more than 1 km, and a reader's letter in *Woman* magazine in 1956 reported a hedgehog that had returned from 3 km away. Several studies of marked hedgehogs suggest that some remain faithful to their normal home area year after year, while others may disperse over long distances, especially in unfavourable habitat. Patrick Doncaster found some of his animals travelled up to 3.8 km away (Doncaster *et al.*, 2001), even dispersing through an existing population instead of joining it. At least three animals 'homed' by returning to their release point. A hedgehog that I marked in Jersey travelled over 5 km from where it had been first found, apparently prevented from going further by its arrival at the coast. A marked hedgehog released in Devon was reported to me having apparently gone 15 km, crossing roads and other challenging obstacles on the way, and it probably never went back. It is possible that the disturbance associated with capture or marking (and sometimes translocation) of these animals caused them to disperse further than

TABLE 8. Evidence of dispersal movements. Returns from a small project carried out with the help of the BHPS where numbered tags were attached to 123 hedgehogs due for release by hedgehog carers. The tags bore a telephone number to report sightings and 11 were seen again after release (a 9 per cent rate of returns). The distances covered in relatively short periods suggest much more activity than is normally thought likely for hedgehogs, although the reported dispersal of 15 km is so remarkable as to invite speculation that the tag number was misread, especially as it was a female and these do not usually travel so far as males. No. 00784 crossed a major road and a river.

Tag No.	Sex	Released	Seen again	Minimum survival time	Distance travelled	County
00073	M	14 Mar	28 Mar	2 weeks	3 km	Shropshire
00321	F	26 Apr	8 May	12 days	350 m	Merseyside
00336	M	28 May	22 May	2 days	'Nearby'	Devon
00340	?	10 May	12 June	1 month	50 m	Devon
00346	M	22 Apr	21 May	1 month	c. 200 m	Devon
00349	M	7 May	19 May	12 days	6 km	Devon
00533	?	27 July	18 August	23 days	400 m	Lincolnshire
00677	M	23 June	11 August	7 weeks	500 m	Devon
00680	F	4 July	14 August	7 weeks	15 km	Devon
00780	M	13 Sept	15 Oct	1 month	4 km	Devon
00784	M	12 Sept	21 Sept	9 days	4.8 km	Devon

TABLE 9. Dispersal movements by hedgehogs released after a period of confinement in captivity. All were released into unfamiliar locations and might be expected to scatter widely as a result. Some remained close to the original release point, and others may have gone further than indicated after contact was lost or after two months when the study ended. Clearly, even hedgehogs with no previous experience of independent life in the wild can and do undertake surprisingly long-distance movements.

Author	Study date	Number released	Dispersals 0.5 km or more
Morris	1991, Suffolk	8	4,3 & 2 km
Morris	1993, Devon	12	2, 0.5 & 0.5 km; all juveniles with no previous experience in the wild.
Morris	1995, Jersey	13	5.2 km
Reeve	1996, Surrey	12	1, 2, 2.6, 2.7, 2.8 km; all dispersing away from the woodland in which they were released.

they might otherwise have done. In New Zealand, several dispersed more than 5 km, one managed 10 km in 6 months and another was found 12 km away after 26 months. Dispersal ensures that the hedgehog population is well spread out, reducing competition for food and ensuring genetic diversity is maintained. After hedgehogs were released on South Uist, the population spread at about 1 km per year on average for six years and 2 km per year thereafter. Dispersal and long-distance movements appear to be a natural part of hedgehog ecology, at least for some individuals, which is all the more reason to be concerned about the creation of artificial barriers to free movement as discussed later.

MOVEMENTS: HOME RANGE

Occasional dispersal movements or returning from far away are one thing, but what about normal activities? The hedgehog is a species of woodland margins, gardens, hedgerows and farmland, all habitats that are characterised by great physical and biological diversity. Prime hedgehog areas include mixtures of long grass, short pasture, bushes and trees offering a wide selection of potential food items and also suitable nesting sites. This much has been known for centuries, but exactly how a hedgehog behaves in these places, how far it travels and how much space it needs have all been key questions, frequently asked, but with the answers obscured by the cloak of darkness under which hedgehogs operate.

My own ineffective attempts at radio-tracking in 1966 were intended to throw light on the subject, but actually revealed little. Nevertheless, it became clear that hedgehogs (at least 24 of them in the space of a few weeks) would congregate in profitable feeding areas where the short-grazed turf made foraging more fruitful. Few remained in the hibernation areas that they had used the previous winter, as though a seasonal change in range area had occurred. One animal was followed for 300 m from its daytime nest to a favoured feeding area and it returned later in the night to the same nest, finding its way in the dark across ground traversed by the scent trails of countless people, dogs and deer (Fig. 115). I also found that some animals would use a different nest at the end of each night. All this was new information, with the promise of much more to be discovered once better equipment became available. But it would be another ten years before that happened, when new types of transmitters and receivers began to offer the prospect of studying movements and home range in the sort of detail needed.

The concept of 'home range' was devised by an American mammalogist keen to make sense of patterns of recaptures in studies of small mammals caught in a grid pattern of regularly spaced 'live catch' traps and then released and captured

FIG 115. A combination of radio-tracking and mark-recapture showed six hedgehogs that wintered in the plantations at the edge of Bushy Park in 1967 travelled to an open area of grassland to feed in the following summer. Female 113 had a nest with young in a patch of bracken in October of 1967, commuting between it and the feeding area during the night.

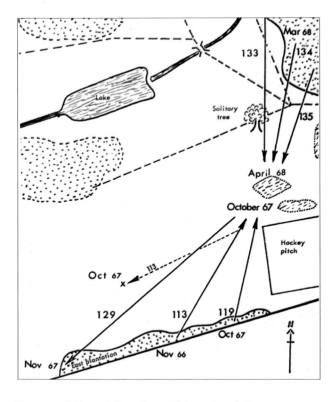

again somewhere else. Traps could be set for a few nights and each time an animal was caught this could be marked on a map of the trap grid. After a few nights, one could draw a line linking all the capture points for a particular animal and show where it had been, its 'home range', and compare this with other individuals or different species. But using traps like this means only one capture could normally be marked on the map for each trapping period. Even checking the traps every couple of hours (and disturbing the animals in the process) still gives only a snapshot of the general areas visited. With the development of radio-tracking in the 1960s, the movements of animals could be explored further and in more explicit detail. Home range became widely accepted as a description of an animal's 'normally used area'. As a radio-tagged animal walked about, its location could be determined very frequently, giving a much more realistic reflection of its spatial activity. With improvements in equipment and techniques of analysis, the home range concept was extended and elaborated upon to paint a very detailed picture of an animal's movements.

FIG 116. Nigel Reeve with his home-made radio-tracking equipment following hedgehogs at night on Ashford Manor golf course.

My own attempts at using radio-tracking involved crude home-made equipment which was not only heavy and impractical, but my hedgehogs quickly carried their transmitters out of range of the receiver. I was never going to learn much about how hedgehogs spent their time. Nigel Reeve took up the challenge ten years later, benefitting from a better system that could detect tagged hedgehogs more than 200 m away (Reeve, 1979). This made it possible to follow several animals at once and from far enough away as not to influence their behaviour (Fig. 116). Several position fixes could be obtained for each animal every night and plotted on a map. The usual way of describing the results of such studies was to join up all the outermost points visited, forming a convex polygon whose area could then be calculated to represent the animal's home range.

Nigel's study focused on the hedgehogs that inhabited Ashford Manor golf course, an area of approximately 40 ha, and its adjacent gardens. For the first time anywhere, not just in Britain, he was able to gather information about how much space hedgehogs used and how far they travelled in a night. The main

FIG. 117 Over time, radio-tracking equipment improved, with longer range, longer battery life and smaller transmitters. This one has a luminous tag attached to help locate the animal more precisely in the dark without approaching too closely and disturbing it.

study area comprised mown grass with small patches of woodland and shrubbery separating the fairways. The hedgehogs' calculated range areas were based on all the sightings and position fixes obtained during one active season – i.e. a yearly range. On average, it was about 32 ha in males and 10 ha for females. This can be visualised as males using the whole of the 18-hole golf course and females about half of it or less. Although there was considerable variation in range area between individuals, males generally appeared to use about two to three times as much space as females, a statistically significant difference. Similar results have been obtained in many subsequent studies.

The basic problem with any estimates of home range size is that the figure obtained is hugely dependent upon the number of observations used to calculate it. If an animal is located three times, its apparent home range is a triangle of a certain size. If it is seen a fourth time, the range area is increased, perhaps substantially so if it is found way off to one side, creating a rectangular range area. None of Nigel's home range estimates were based on fewer than 30 location fixes and most used more than that (up to 532), but they were spread over an entire season. It is tempting to list all the subsequent published estimates of home range size for comparison, but are they really comparable when they have all persisted for varying lengths of time and used different methods for analysing their results?

TABLE 10. A selection of 'average home ranges', based on observations carried out over a week or more. A much smaller area would be used on a single night.

	Average female range (Hectares)	Average male range (Hectares)
Morris (1988): pasture, Isle of Wight, about 30 location fixes each	10	37
Reeve (1992): golf course, west London, at least 30 location fixes each	10	32
Amy Haigh (pers comm.)	16.5	56
Kristiansson (1984): rural village, Sweden	19	46

But these are home ranges based upon studies that lasted weeks or even months. What do hedgehogs do in a normal single activity period? It seems unlikely that a hedgehog could patrol 30 ha in one night (almost the entire area of Nigel's 18-hole golf course). In a small study of hedgehogs in woodland, two females averaged 1–2 ha per night and a male 2.4 ha (Morris, 1986). This might suggest that hedgehogs in woodland could have smaller home ranges than those on the golf course, perhaps because the animals move about more easily in the

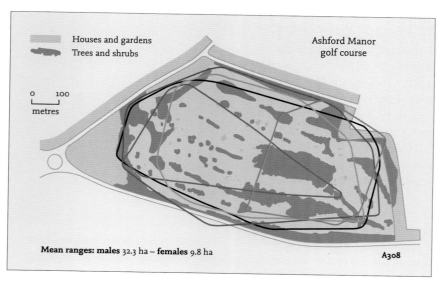

FIG 118. Areas used by five adult males in the course of one summer, showing they are not territorial. Males ranged over about three times more of the golf course than females.

FIG 119. The village of Newtown on the Isle of Wight, surrounded by farmland and isolated by tidal creeks. Here, we tracked hedgehogs that used a typical assortment of fields and gardens.

open habitat than in woodland. But activity on a single night should surely not be compared directly with a whole year's observations. And which of those figures best represents a hedgehog's home range – the 'normally used area'? On different nights the animals visited different places, not always the same localities. Adding position fixes from successive nights and measuring the progressively enlarging polygon enclosed by the outermost points provided an estimate of the minimum total area familiar to each animal in that woodland study. The largest 'cumulative home range' thus obtained in the woodland was 11 ha, the 'normally used area' beyond which the animal seemed not to go. Again it suggests smaller home ranges than on the golf course. But this was based on only a three-week study; the golf-course figure was for the whole summer season. Field studies tend

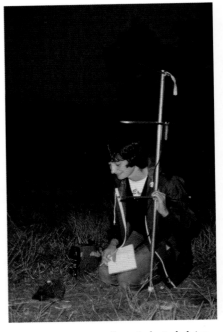

FIG 120. Penny, one of my students, helping to track hedgehogs at Newtown. By 1987, radio-tracking equipment had vastly improved and the receiver was small enough to be carried about quite comfortably.

to last for different lengths of time, driven by the needs and convenience of the investigator. When seeking comparative data in the literature, it also becomes evident that investigators may not have stayed up all night and their calculated home ranges will be incomplete. Clearly the time dimension needs to be considered and information given about hedgehog movements and home range needs to be taken with a pinch of salt.

In an attempt to obtain data in a structured manner, a group of my students radio-tracked five hedgehogs fairly continuously for three weeks on the Isle of Wight (Morris, 1988). The aim was to find each animal at least six times per night, spread across six hours. In practice, it sometimes proved difficult to achieve even this as the animals scattered widely. Nevertheless the study showed that there was considerable variation in range area used per night, twice as large on some nights as on others. It became clear the two females that were being closely monitored were generally using about 2–5 ha per night, but sometimes more than 20 ha for a very active male (Fig. 121). But the animals were not always visiting exactly the same places each night. So their cumulative home range was also estimated by adding new locations to those already obtained. After the sixth night, the animals rarely ventured far outside the area within which they had already been found. Plotted on a graph, the asymptote occurred at about

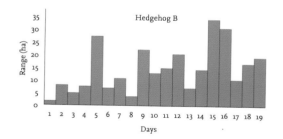

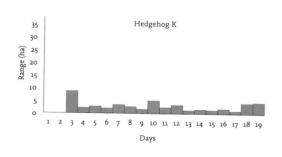

FIG 121. Range areas used each night by 'B', our most active male hedgehog. They varied considerably in both size and location. By contrast, the female hedgehog 'K' ranged more consistently each night over a smaller area and mostly in the same places each night. These differences between males and females are typical of all the studies undertaken so far.

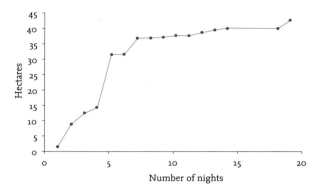

FIG 122. After six to seven nights, hedgehog 'B' seemed not to enlarge his area of activity by very much, so his 'cumulative home range' was about 40 ha.

Number of nights

10 ha for the females, and this could reasonably be regarded as the 'normally used area', i.e. home range in conventional terms. The very active adult male was also closely tracked and his cumulative asymptotic home range area was approximately 37 ha, reached after the seventh night (Fig. 122). (In another study by one of my students, asymptotes showing cumulative range sizes were also all established within ten days or less.) Since the protocol followed was the same as for the study in woodland, the results can be directly compared, although sample sizes were small. It appears that about 2 ha is a normal amount of space used in a night, for females at least. Males are likely to range over a much larger area and are far more variable in the extent of their activity. Winter nesting may occur elsewhere, owing to different habitat requirements, so the total area used in a year may be larger still.

Most of the published information about hedgehog movements is based on radio-tracking carried out in the middle of summer. Since activity varies seasonally (Rautio *et al.*, 2013a), figures for average home range size can be no more than a rough guide. When home range areas are determined by drawing polygons on a map, they will offer only a crude reflection of reality, not least because they often include areas that the hedgehog will never visit. They do, however, give a rough idea of how much space an animal needs and what is familiar to it, and these are factors that we need to know if we are to understand how to help hedgehogs survive in our increasingly human-dominated landscapes. All of the studies so far published, involving various habitats, indicate that hedgehogs travel more widely than previously realised and males travel further than females, although this differences persist only until the end of the breeding season.

TERRITORIALITY

Territory is defended space. Animals may defend it actively by interacting aggressively with intruders or passively by setting out scent markers to signal possession (with an implied threat of aggression towards unwanted visitors). Whilst it can often be belligerent, a hedgehog does none of these things in defence of a defined space. They do not establish and hold a territory the way that robins do in a garden. Why should they bother? Their food is plentiful and widely distributed and they are not restricted to one particular type of food or place where it might be found. They have no need to keep other hedgehogs away from their home range or nests, so what would be the benefit of spending time and energy in territorial defence? All the studies of hedgehog movements so far reported, here and abroad, show that individual hedgehog home ranges overlap considerably, even in New Zealand where hedgehog population densities are much greater than in Britain and hedgehogs might therefore have a reason for defending resources within their home range. In Finland too, hedgehog home ranges overlap despite living in very different habitat and climate (Rautio *et al.*, 2013a).

Male home ranges often encompass those of two or three females, for understandable reasons, but there is no attempt made to guard mates or repel alternative suitors. Male home ranges also overlap the ranges of other males, sometimes completely. Instead of defending a personal territory, hedgehogs appear to have a different form of social organisation in which they may sometimes defend the space that immediately surrounds them at any one time, but not an extensive area of habitat. Adult males change their daytime resting place frequently, allowing them to range over the largest area possible in search of females, and simply avoid contacting each other. Mutual avoidance allows non-simultaneous use of the same areas by several individual hedgehogs as they forage and behave in a sexually promiscuous manner (see Chapter 7). Despite not defending a territory, some hedgehogs do show a marked tendency to remain in the same general locality year to year, and the same recognisable individual may be a faithful visitor to the same garden for many weeks or even years. Conversely, every attempt to mark hedgehogs and keep a record of which ones are found again has identified a significant proportion, perhaps 20 per cent that are seen once and never again. They are often young males. It is as though the population includes nomads of no fixed abode or maybe they are the ones that engage in long-distance dispersal movements. We still have much to learn.

MOVEMENTS: DISTANCES TRAVELLED

Home range is a concept not a definitive entity and a quest for accuracy is beguiling but perhaps futile. Moreover comparisons between habitats and different studies will not be valid unless time is taken into account and a robust protocol adopted governing the minimum number of location fixes used in subsequent analyses. But in our Isle of Wight study, estimated sizes of home ranges were strongly correlated with the total distance travelled per night, offering the prospect of using these calculations as another measure of activity. Over three weeks, the females generally and consistently travelled about 1 km per night (Fig. 123). The very active adult male managed more than 3.14 km on one occasion, taking him nearly seven hours, almost the entire period of darkness (Fig. 124). The following night he did almost the same distance again, but over a slightly different area (Fig. 125). Again a comparison may be made with the woodland hedgehogs, where females averaged about 630 m per night and the male 868 m (and a maximum of 1,138 m). Comparable figures for hedgehogs in Regent's Park (London) in 2014 and 2015 were 892 m per night in males and 821 m per night for females (Nigel Reeve, pers comm.).

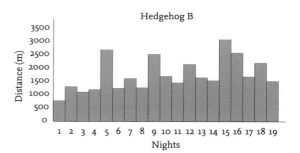

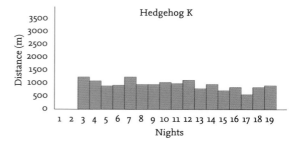

FIG 123. Distances travelled by male 'B' varied each night between about 600 m and 3,000 m. Typically, for female hedgehogs, 'K' travelled between 600 m and about 1,200 m each night.

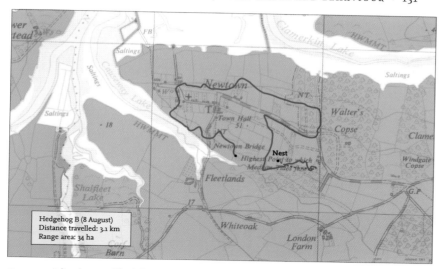

Hedgehog B (8 August)
Distance travelled: 3.1 km
Range area: 34 ha

FIG 124. A 'trackogram' for 'B' on his most energetic night out, travelling a distance of over 3 km and ending at a different nest to where he started out. (the dotted line represents his track between the known site of his daytime nest and the first point where we managed to catch up with him after he set out from it before it was fully dark).

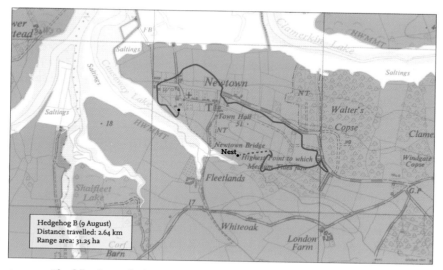

Hedgehog B (9 August)
Distance travelled: 2.64 km
Range area: 31.25 ha

FIG 125. The following night, he set off early from his nest and travelled almost as far again, ending at yet another nest on the outskirts of Newtown village.

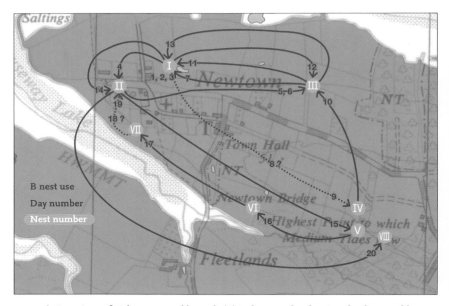

FIG 126. Locations of eight nests used by male 'B' in three weeks, showing that he was able to roam more widely in search of females than if he had returned to the same nest at the end of every night. It is also clear that he was able to find again nests he had used previously.

These figures and the consistent difference between males and females are in line with what Nigel had found on the golf course, suggesting that there is nothing particularly misleading about his data despite the artificial nature of the habitat (Fig. 127). Many subsequent studies have also confirmed that males move around more widely than females, especially adult males during the height of the breeding season. The distances travelled reported in the literature are generally similar, but always with a lot of individual variation among the hedgehogs. At Hawkes Bay in New Zealand, distances travelled averaged 908 m per night (ranging between 477 and 2,264 m) and in England Hans Kruuk found hedgehog footprints on sand exposed at low tide, indicating travel of over 3 km during a tide cycle lasting probably less than eight hours. So hedgehogs do move about a lot. We could even compare their efforts with human activity. If a hedgehog 20 cm long covers 3 km in a night, it has travelled 15,000 times its own length, equivalent to a human journey of 22 km or 14 miles.

However, calculations of how far hedgehogs travel in a night are based on adding the straight line distances between consecutive position fixes. But hedgehogs don't walk in straight lines for very long. They wander and dither about in their search for food. So if an animal is only located six times in a night, its total distance travelled will appear to be one figure, but if it is located 20 times, that figure will be greatly increased owing to all the extra data points that are included as they zig zag about. More position fixes mean more accuracy in defining what the animal is doing. But following one animal closely to achieve this accuracy means a sample size of only one, as it becomes difficult or impossible to get comparable data from following additional animals at the same time. One of my students attempted to clarify this by using a spool of very fine thread attached to a hedgehog's back. As it wandered about, the line snagged in grass tussocks and twigs so the actual track followed could be measured in daylight next morning, a technique known as 'spooling'. This showed that the actual distance travelled by the animal was 40 per cent greater than computed as a straight line between position fixes, even when these were taken at only five-minute intervals. But a reasonable-sized spool will not contain enough thread to leave a trail for the whole night, only for a short sample of the activity period.

So, even figures for distance travelled per night have to be taken as indications rather than definitive statements. These limitations apply to all similar studies of animal movements of course, although they are rarely spelt out when numerical

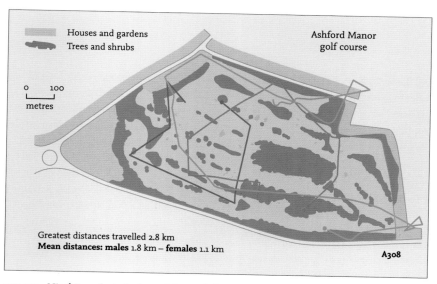

FIG 127. Nigel Reeve's study showed that male hedgehogs (three examples shown here) travel further each night than females, and further than anyone had previously imagined likely.

data are published. Nevertheless, computed distances travelled are useful as they do indicate the minimum journey length and they are closely correlated with spooling distances, providing a useful index of distance travelled for comparative purposes. Distance travelled will closely reflect energy expenditure, a parameter that is grounded in biological reality. The calculated size of a notional home range will be affected by the geometry of the position fixes used and may be distorted by inclusion of habitat patches that are never visited (a lake, for example). Nevertheless, estimations of home range are useful, especially when comparing behaviour in different habitats, and vital when we start to discuss how large an area is needed to sustain a secure hedgehog population.

With so much variation between different habitats and among individual animals, perhaps 'precision' has little meaning. What we need to know is approximately how big an area does a hedgehog need and how far does it normally travel in a night. It turns out that hedgehogs require much larger areas, and travel far further, than anyone had previously imagined. We also need to know how the hedgehog uses that habitat in order to improve its suitability, as suggested in Chapter 13, or at least to avoid compromising the way that the animals can move about to feed and mix with each other (Baaker *et al.*, 2014). Without these studies, imperfect though they may be, we can have no idea how to set about helping hedgehogs to survive in an increasingly challenging world.

GPS TECHNOLOGY

All these studies of hedgehog movements and activity relied on conventional radio-tracking, with people following the animals in the field at night. During the past 30 years, huge improvements in computers and software have enabled far more sophisticated forms of data analysis which help to identify key areas within a home range, but there have been few attempts to apply new analytical techniques to the study of hedgehogs. This is partly because the old problems still remain, crucially including the difficulties and cost of people doing fieldwork at night (Fig. 128). A solution seems to lie in the employment of of modern Global Positioning Satellite (GPS) tags that store geographical positions computed utilising signals from the satellites used by satnav machines in cars. Periodically, data from the tag can be downloaded (or transmitted) containing a summary of locations together with the times those position fixes were obtained. The animals can go on about their business day and night and the investigator can work more normal hours in a nice, comfortable office. These devices have been used very successfully on birds to map migratory flights, so maybe this is a way forward for the study of hedgehogs?

FIG 128. The radio-tracking methods we used required long, lonely and uncomfortable hours of stumbling about in the dark, matching hedgehog time with our own. This is difficult to reconcile with the need for daytime activities too. The alternative of automated tracking using GPS technology has considerable appeal!

GPS tags on hedgehogs were first tried in New Zealand in a study of potential predators of rare ground-nesting birds (Recio *et al.*, 2011). They eliminated the need for observers to follow animals closely in the dark or triangulate them to establish their locations. Position fixes could be gathered every five minutes, not just 'once an hour with a bit of luck', allowing a much more precise analysis of an animal's movements. The study used 27 hedgehogs, but each was followed for only four to eight days because of limited battery life in the GPS tag. Despite their rather large backpacks, the hedgehogs seemed to behave normally and many of them put on weight during the study, suggesting that they were not impeded by the additional burden of their tag.

The main problem with GPS tracking, especially with hedgehogs, is that if the animal goes behind a building, down into a ditch or even under wet vegetation, they can lose the signal from one or more of the vital GPS satellites, resulting in a false position fix. It may then appear that the animal makes an occasional long detour and then quickly seems to come back again as normal contact is resumed, having apparently made a lengthy excursion at high speed. Without 'ground truthing' to check exactly where the animal really is in comparison with what the GPS satellites suggest, one cannot be fully confident of the results obtained. This New Zealand study, for example, suggested that some hedgehogs had surprisingly large home ranges, up to 95 ha, but had they really been to every point that the system said? One way to avoid this problem is to use an algorithm in the analysis software that rejects any position fix that is an improbable distance from the previous one, based on normal speeds of travel.

For birds and mammals that live in open habitats, this technique undoubtedly works well and yields massive amounts of valuable information, but hedgehogs are a different matter. A brief test of GPS tracking tags on hedgehogs in Norfolk generated unsatisfactory results, partly as a result of the animals losing contact with the satellites. A more thorough test was carried out by Lee Glasby and Richard Yarnell in Nottinghamshire. Despite some technical difficulties, most of their position fixes were successful, the failures being mainly around dawn and dusk when the hedgehogs were probably hidden away in their nests, screened from the satellites. After five days or so, the cumulative home range for each of nine hedgehogs was not significantly different from the results obtained using conventional radio-tracking (See Table 11).

TABLE 11. Comparison of average cumulative home range after a few days revealed by GPS tracking and conventional radio-tracking (from Glasby & Yarnell, 2013).

Study	Female cumulative home range after 5 days (hectares)	Male cumulative home range after 5 days (hectares)
GPS Nottinghamshire in pastoral farmland, up to 215 position fixes	12.58	38.4
Conventional radio-tracking in pastoral farmland, Nottinghamshire, up to 98 position fixes	11.85	31

None of this comes cheap, but the GPS technology offers more detail at lower cost, without disturbing the animal's activity and without the problems of working at night. However, the duration of such studies is limited by battery life, less than eight days in the Nottinghamshire study. GPS tags can be made to operate for longer by gathering less information or having larger batteries, but battery life may improve with advances in technology. Habitat type has a significant influence too. Performance and accuracy of the GPS tags was reduced in vegetated and built-up habitats and also when the tags were placed within hedgerows to see the effect of screening vegetation. Further use and field-testing of GPS tags should enable a protocol to be developed that identifies the likely 'rogue position fixes' to eliminate most of them. It appears that this technique would still have limited value for a study of nesting behaviour or activity in urban gardens, for example, because of all the obstructions that might screen or reflect signals from satellites. Maybe other forms of automatic tracking will be developed for use in difficult habitats.

A WIDER RELEVANCE: THE REGENT'S PARK STUDY

Investigating hedgehog movements is not just a matter of academic curiosity. Regent's Park supports the last surviving hedgehog population in central London and GPS tags have been used there by Nigel Reeve, John Gurnell and colleagues to find out how hedgehogs move about within the park (see www.royalparks.org. uk/managing-the-parks/conservation-and-improvement-projects/hedgehogs). They discovered that shrubberies and flower beds are favourite places for nesting and foraging, but the area most popular with the hedgehogs is the car park for London Zoo. More precisely, it is the surrounding rough grassy areas, which are used by a quarter of the hedgehog population for foraging and nesting (Fig. 129). It is also where engineers planning to build HS2 (the high-speed rail link between London and the north) want to create a depot for large equipment,

FIG 129. The excellent hedgehog nesting and foraging habitat adjacent to the car park at London Zoo.

serviced by heavy lorries. This could sound the death knell for the Regent's Park hedgehog population because so many of them use that area. The issue received national attention when a Parliamentary committee debated the future of the HS2 project. To the visible irritation of the HS2 lawyer, hedgehogs seemed to be getting in the way of a key British infrastructure project costing billions of pounds! The use of this area is opposed by the Zoological Society of London (ZSL), whose car park for visitors is likely to be taken over. ZSL also raises funds and campaigns vigorously to help endangered species around the world. It would be embarrassing if hedgehogs became extinct just outside their front door. There ought to be ways to create some similar habitat elsewhere at the edges of the park, but time is short and free space is very limited. Meanwhile, the issue has usefully drawn public attention to the fate of the hedgehog nationally and within Regent's Park. It also shows the value of tracking studies that can tell us what goes on in one of the last hedgehog populations left in central London and, by implication, in many similar urban sites elsewhere.

Another important outcome of the Regent's Park study with wider implications was the revelation that hedgehogs rarely visited the football pitches that constitute nearly a quarter of the total area of the park. Based on previous studies of hedgehog activities, these look like ideal foraging areas with healthy short grass, but GPS fixes show that they are conspicuously ignored by the hedgehogs. Moreover, there is increasing evidence of similar problems elsewhere. Why should that be? One possibility is that the soil (heavy London clay in the case of Regent's Park) has become so compacted that it no longer supports worms, beetle larvae and the many other foods that hedgehogs

FIG 130. The football pitches in Regent's Park, London, appear typical of many across the country, but although they have not been treated with pesticides for many years, the hedgehogs still seem not to use them for feeding.

normally expect to find in short-grass habitats. After all, a footballer thrusts his whole weight into the ground on a few studs under his boot, generating pressures that may exceed 15 kg per cm². Soil compaction is inevitable, especially if the pitch is used multiple times every week for the whole season (Fig. 130). Efforts are made to increase aeration of football pitches by driving spikes into the soil at the end of the season, but this might be making things worse. The spikes leave deep holes, but no soil is actually removed. The particles are simply thrust sideways into the adjacent soil, compacting it further. Air may be able to enter the soil down the holes, but for soil-dwelling larvae and other organisms, the soil particles are rammed so close together in the upper layers of a football pitch that movement and respiration by the soil macrofauna will be impeded. This must severely compromise the abundance and productivity of many invertebrates that hedgehogs need for food – worms and beetle larvae, for example. Treatment of 'sports turf' like this will also often include the use of chemicals to kill the insect larvae that damage grass roots – the very items that are high on the list of prey that hedgehogs need to eat (see Chapter 9) – although this does not appear to be a problem in Regent's Park, where chemical treatments have not been used for many years.

So the Regent's Park study is not just about hedgehogs. It also helps to alert us to wider issues concerning the use and management of urban green spaces. Many studies of hedgehog ecology in the 1990s and earlier, including my own, found they were common on open fields, golf courses and parkland, leading to an assumption that grassy turf was a preferred habitat. That may no longer be the case as a consequence of heavy use and changed management practices that include the introduction of deadly efficient pesticides (see Chapter 10). Studying hedgehog movements may be generating information that has a much wider importance and there is a clear need for more detailed research into the relationship between hedgehog movements and the types and amounts of food potentially available to them, especially in amenity grasslands that are managed in different ways. Perhaps many of the parks and grassy areas of our towns and cities that we presume to be important wildlife reservoirs in built-up areas are becoming less and less viable as refuges without us realising what is happening. Maybe we need to find alternative ways of managing amenity grasslands lest our green spaces become just green deserts, although it may already be too late for some. Isolated areas of urban green space, especially those managed as sports turf, may no longer offer key foraging opportunities for local hedgehog populations and many bird species too. Under a more relaxed and supportive form of management, these habitats might one day recover. The birds could then fly back to recolonise the sites, but not the hedgehogs.

ARABLE FARMLAND

Also important are questions about how hedgehogs use the habitats available in today's countryside because this relates directly to issues of how we might help to conserve them and assist their survival in human-dominated landscapes. Most fieldwork on hedgehogs has been carried out in grazed or mown grasslands for practical reasons and also because it is normally a good habitat for hedgehogs. But what about arable farmland? Is that a good place for hedgehogs or is it a hedgehog desert? The question matters because a quarter of Britain's land area is now managed for arable crops. The land is ploughed and regularly doused with pesticides, both actions being aimed at eliminating the very things upon which hedgehogs feed. Can hedgehogs use this habitat or are they restricted to the field margins? If the latter, then hundreds of square miles of Britain are no use to them. An exploratory study tracking hedgehogs on the fringe of Windsor Park revealed that they used only the margins of maize fields and did not forage in the crop itself. Other attempts to study hedgehogs in arable habitats have been hampered by the difficulty of catching any of them at all, suggesting that arable farmland is not a good place for hedgehogs to be. In two cases, we had to resort to borrowing randy male hedgehogs from animal rescue centres and radio-tracking them on arable land as they sought prospective mates on our behalf, fortunately with some success.

One of those studies (Hof & Bright, 2010) investigated hedgehog use of arable fields in Norfolk and found that they kept very much to the edges, rarely more than five metres from the field boundary. This could be due to hedgehogs being unwilling to venture too far out into open areas for fear of being attacked by a predator. In this study, and others, they appeared to be very wary of using areas frequented by badgers. But this may not be the only explanation. Sampling the soil for invertebrates showed that worms and beetles were more abundant around the field margins than out in the crop area. The best fields had a strip of rough grassland between the crop and hedge offering better foraging prospects (Fig. 131). Moreover, there are no suitable nesting sites or materials out in the crop. Altogether, this suggests that large areas of Britain's arable farmland are sub-optimal habitat at best and even perhaps no use to hedgehogs at all. When choice of habitat was measured (including woodland and amenity grassland), hedges and field margins scored best and cropped areas worst. In fact, only 6.5 per cent of position fixes in the Norfolk study were on the cultivated land. A study at two sites in Norfolk and two others in Yorkshire (Pettett et al., 2017a) found arable land and woodlands were the least-used of the available habitats by a sample of

FIG 131. Radio-tracking studies show the importance for hedgehogs of 'wild' field margins in arable landscapes.

78 hedgehogs. In the first such study in Ireland (Haigh, 2011), arable land proved rather more attractive to hedgehogs, possibly linked to an abundance of molluscs not seen elsewhere. This may reflect a difference in farming methods, differential use of molluscicides, for example, or seed drilling instead of deep ploughing (affecting slug survival rates). But in Britain, it does appear that the major historical change from pastoral farming to arable during the twentieth century is likely to have rendered much of the countryside unsuitable for hedgehogs, causing a reduction in their overall numbers. The radio-tracking studies show that agri-environment subsidies for farmers that encourage wide grassy margins and thick hedgerows can do a lot to stop the hedgehog's decline and will benefit many other species too.

URBAN HEDGEHOG ECOLOGY

Suburban gardens are an important habitat for hedgehogs and may become even more so in the future, both as a refuge from badgers and as an alternative to trying to live in arable farmland, which is one of the largest available habitat types in the countryside. Householders who have marked their hedgehogs often report that ten or more visit their garden, implying a high local population density. This may in part be due to the attractive and supportive effects of bowls of food, often set out specially to attract hedgehogs. In France, the population of hedgehogs in towns is said to be up to nine times greater than in the French countryside (Hubert *et al.*, 2011).

FIG 132. Recent studies suggest that gardens are becoming a vital refuge for future hedgehog populations, given the intensification of farming and prevalence of badgers in the countryside.

Although hedgehogs are a familiar sight in many of our town gardens, we know surprisingly little about their ecology in this type of habitat. For example, several people have written to me with details of their 'attendance register', recording which marked animals come each night to a food bowl in the garden. Sometimes as many as 20 individual hedgehogs will be seen during a single summer. One of my correspondents, a Mrs Margaret Larkman, recorded the visits of about 30 different hedgehogs to her garden in a single year, but none stayed as 'regulars' for more than about two months. Her animals showed a 1:1 sex ratio and a general indifference regarding time of day, rain and temperature. Another correspondent, Mrs Anne Ursell, experienced a similar visiting pattern, with some hedgehogs coming regularly, then being absent for long periods before returning. Three of the 18 hedgehogs visiting my friend Brian Barton's garden in 2012 continued to do so until well into November and one was still coming in January the following year. This helps confirm the principle explained in Chapter 6 that hibernation is flexible and need not necessarily happen if food is still available.

TABLE 12. An analysis of the attendance records of 18 animals visiting a garden in 2012, at least 5 of whom did so for more than 3 months (data kindly provided by Brian Barton). Many individuals came night after night, but then were not recorded for several nights before reappearing. Regular visitors first seen in the spring seemed to disappear and were largely replaced by apparently new arrivals from July onwards. Three animals came 7 times or less, 6 others were recorded on 40 or more occasions. Records like this are of course 'minimal', in the sense that the observer normally goes to bed by midnight! So some animals that are apparently absent may simply have arrived later, adding to their number of nights in attendance. Nevertheless, some seem to discover the food and come on more than 75 per cent of the nights during the period of their visits; others arrive for less than 50 per cent of the feeding opportunities on offer.

Hedgehog No.	Date of first visit	Date of last visit	Duration visiting period (days)	Number of visits made	Per cent of nights visiting	Longest absence before returning (nights)
1	25/3	16/4	23	17	74	2
2	28/3	27/4	31	26	84	2
3	30/3	7/7	101	51	50	11
4	31/3	21/7	114	66	58	10
5	22/4	31/5	39	7	18	21
6	02/5	31/5	30	4	13	25
7	12/5	28/7	78	67	86	2
8	14/5	20/8	99	64	65	7
9	21/5	20/8	92	40	43	8
10	16/6	8/9	85	41	48	9
11	27/7	27/7	1	1	—	0
12	04/8	02/10	60	18	30	22
13	20/8	13/9	25	19	76	2
14	16/8	14/9	30	22	73	6
15	26/8	09/10	45	23	51	7
16	18/9	13/11	57	15	26	21
17	23/8	08/1	106	91	86	19
18	10/10	17/11	39	25	64	2

A general pattern in many of these observational studies is that as the season progresses, more new animals turn up, but the 'regulars' stop coming. Why, having discovered a food bowl put out specially for hedgehogs, do they visit every night and then abandon the habit of coming to a good food source? Maybe they were killed, but some of them actually reappear after an absence of a few days or weeks. Where have they been meanwhile? Why go elsewhere? Why come back? A significant proportion of marked animals are seen once or twice and never again. Why? Where do they go? Are there permanent nomads in the population that just keep moving from one place to another. If so, why does this happen?

We need to know much more about urban hedgehogs, but (as usual!) studies are fraught with difficulty. Householders don't like to have people creeping about their garden in the middle of the night, numerous fences get in the way, dogs become excited and start to bark, the police are called out. Worse still, radio transmitter signals are screened or confusingly deflected by walls and fences. Gardens harbour countless nooks and crannies into which a hedgehog can vanish, hiding both itself and its radio signals. Nevertheless, there have been a few investigations of urban hedgehogs in Britain.

One of mine (Morris, 1985) addressed the obvious question: To what extent do food bowls put out to encourage hedgehogs influence their behaviour? Food availability is likely to affect territory, home range, social behaviour and other key aspects of an animal's life. One might expect a regular, localised supplementation of natural food to result in higher population density and reduced home range size, since the animals will no longer need to travel so far in order to get enough to eat. They will surely seek to minimise the effort of foraging and travel no further than necessary, but this may disrupt natural spacing behaviour. The hedgehogs might remain in a small garden because there is no need to go anywhere else, just as the good people who put out this extra food hope and imagine, but do they stay or commute? There are important welfare issues involved too. Maybe hedgehogs will become reliant on the extra, easy food and suffer when people go away on holiday. Perhaps the animals will forsake natural foraging in favour of easy and unnatural food, then suffer from dietary deficiencies. In other words, this well-meaning attempt to help hedgehogs may do more harm than good, hence the need for a study.

During our investigation, at least 11 different hedgehogs visited the study garden where bread and milk had been put out regularly for seven years by the kindly owners, Mr. and Mrs. Wall (Fig. 133). Six of the animals were radio-tracked closely, two of whom regularly travelled to the garden from more than 500 m away, even though they did not need to, and none actually nested in the garden itself, to the dismay of the kind people who had been putting out the food for so long. One might expect that the hedgehogs would head for the food

FIG 133. Mr and Mrs Wall's ideal hedgehog garden with lawn, flowerbeds, compost heaps and a regularly filled food bowl on the patio that we monitored in a study of hedgehog behaviour and supplementary feeding.

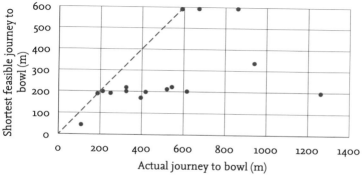

FIG 134. The dotted line represents the shortest straight line distance from several hedgehog nests to the food bowl. The dots indicate the actual distance covered before the animals arrived there. Clearly they knew where it was, but did not abandon natural foraging to go there immediately.

as soon as possible in order to get there before it was all eaten, but they often took nearly twice as long as necessary to reach the garden and sometimes did not come at all. One that needed to travel 196 m from its nest to the food bowl actually travelled over 1.2 km before arriving. Another hedgehog spent four hours getting to the garden which could have been reached in fifteen minutes (Fig. 134). These animals were feeding normally on the way and again later in the night, after visiting the food bowl. They foraged widely in nearby gardens and on the adjacent golf course, seeking natural food (Fig. 135). So the food bowl was only providing a supplement to their natural diet and did not apparently deter

FIG 135. A typical 'trackogram' showing how a hedgehog would forage on the golf course, then detour into the garden to feed at the bowl, before returning to normal foraging back on the grassy areas of the golf course.

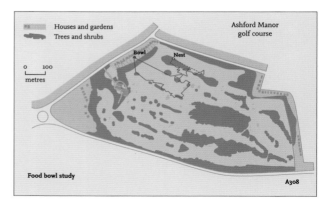

FIG 136. The trackogram for 'Number 28', a blind hedgehog that travelled across the golf course to feed at the bowl before returning to forage in the grassy areas.

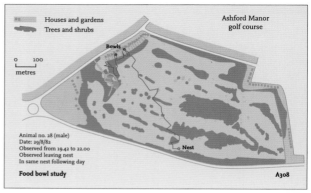

them from feeding normally, even the blind animal 'Number 28'. They ate a lot. The maximum amount taken by one hedgehog in one continuous feed was 94 g, and even the average meal was 54 g. Sometimes a hedgehog would return for additional feeds later in the night. If it is typical, this level of consumption must represent a huge dietary benefit for urban hedgehogs in areas where supplementary food is offered.

Each garden did not have its own exclusive group of visitors, a disappointment to the householders concerned. The hedgehogs certainly did not defend their territory or the precious food bowl that lay within it; instead, they wandered widely and freely, criss-crossing each other's paths. Few disputes were observed, even at the food. Hedgehogs entered and left gardens by the same shared routes and there were often three or more present simultaneously in one garden within 10–15 m of each other. A regularly filled food bowl would appear to be a valuable resource, well worth defending, yet two or more hedgehogs often fed simultaneously or in quick succession. Male hedgehogs still travelled substantially further than the females, confirming that their greater activity is not food-driven. The difference in behaviour between males and females was not disrupted by the presence of supplementary food. Nor was there evidence that the presence of extra food diminished hedgehog wanderings to any significant degree. Minimum distances covered in a night ranged up to 2.3 km, exceeding 1 km on at least 12 animal-nights. The hedgehogs sometimes went on to other gardens with food bowls available or they may have been there first. The nightly consumption of natural food may explain why only a small meal was sometimes taken, and also suggests that the hedgehogs had not become addicted to the bread and milk that was on offer, nor even heavily dependent upon it (and certainly not killed by it after seven years!). Average speeds were lower after visiting the bowl, probably as a result of more and longer resting periods. The bowl was usually empty by about midnight, allowing plenty of time for the hedgehogs to continue feeding naturally somewhere else. Leaving the bowl empty for a few nights, simulating our absence on holiday, revealed that the hedgehogs were not totally dependent upon it. They did not sit about waiting for it to be filled and they readily fed elsewhere. Even the blind one, 'No. 28', managed well, coming in from the far side of the golf course each evening to visit the food bowl (Fig. 136). A short study in my own garden a few weeks later confirmed similar patterns of behaviour towards the provision of extra food (Table 13).

Independently of this study, a lady who had marked her hedgehogs elsewhere reported that she had several hedgehogs coming regularly before she went on holiday. She left the food bowl empty for two holiday periods lasting a week each. Five of the animals came again afterwards and three that did not had only been rare visitors anyway. At least ten different hedgehogs came to her food bowl between May and September. Some were very regular visitors, including one who came frequently over a period of 5½ months, but was often not seen for up to ten nights before reappearing. Two animals who knew the food was available and had eaten it more than once before, were absent for 33 and 40 nights respectively before coming again. These observations provide further evidence of non-addiction and non-dependency. Altogether, it seems that natural hedgehog behaviour is not disrupted by the provision of extra food. They appear to accept it as a useful supplement to their normal diet and in periods of dry summer weather, access to moist food may be a valuable aid to survival, especially for females attempting to raise young. The extra food put out in gardens for pets and wildlife may be a contributory factor in sustaining high population densities of hedgehogs in urban areas.

TABLE 13. An 'attendance register' recording the occasions when six radio-tagged hedgehogs visited a garden food bowl: before, during and after a period when it was left empty. The food was watched from dusk until about midnight on 17 nights (Morris, 1985).

Night No.	Food put out?	Hedgehog no. 1	Hedgehog no. 2	Hedgehog no. 3	Hedgehog no. 4	Hedgehog no. 5	Hedgehog no. 6
1	yes	×		×	×	×	
2	yes			×*		×	
3	yes		×		×	×	
4	yes	×	×		×		
5	yes	×*	×	×	×		
6	yes	×					
7	yes	×*	×	×			
8	no	×*	×	×			
9	no	×*					
10	no	×*			×*		×
11	no	×			×		
12	yes	×*					
13	yes				×		
14	yes						
15	yes	×*					
16	yes	×*	×		×*		
17	yes						

* Known to have gone to another garden food bowl as well as the one under observation.

Roads are another issue for urban hedgehogs. One radio-tracking study (Rondinini & Doncaster, 2002) found that they avoided crossing large roads, especially motorways, and the only road casualty hedgehog I have ever seen on a motorway was actually on a slip road, not the main carriageway. This raises the prospect that major roads may be dividing up hedgehog habitats, with consequent threat to the survival of the small, fragmentary populations that remain. Information gained from radio-tracking studies has been used as the basis for generating computer models that predict likely hedgehog behaviour in respect of roads. The simulations suggested that large and small roads would be treated the same by hedgehogs, but in reality they avoid crossing large roads more often than predicted, indicating that bigger roads are treated as barriers

during their nocturnal activities.
Barriers that fragment habitats,
especially in urban areas, may be one
of the key problems for population
integrity and survival (see Chapter 8).
Road verges were the lowest-ranking
habitat in preference analyses, while
playing fields and urban gardens
were preferred habitats (Rondinini
& Doncaster, 2002). But what if
hedgehogs are prevented from
reaching those preferred sites by roads,
garden fences and other barriers?

A radio-tracking study of urban
hedgehog ecology in Bristol (Dowding
et al., 2010a) also suggested road
traffic was a threat to urban hedgehog
populations. The Bristol hedgehogs
frequently crossed roads, an obviously
hazardous activity, but avoided
actively foraging beside them or along
their verges. Unlike their behaviour
in quieter habitats, the hedgehogs
were significantly more active after

FIG 137. A marked hedgehog, one of at least
seven, feeding at a food bowl on the patio while
my father watches TV.

midnight, when there was a substantial reduction in road traffic and in the
number of pedestrians walking about. The hedgehogs liked to use the large
gardens of semi-detached and terraced houses, but then faced the threat of attack
by badgers. Females seemed to stay out of the larger gardens where badgers were
more likely to occur, although the males were bolder.

This and other studies of urban hedgehogs, including my own, confirm that
the average garden is of inadequate size to support a hedgehog population and that
they need to have access to a number of them, or to larger areas such as recreation
grounds, cemeteries and allotments. In Denmark, Sophie Rasmussen found
individual hedgehogs visited ten or more gardens, highlighting the need for them
to be connected by accessible routes and not isolated by hedgehog-proof fences.
This issue is explored further in Chapter 13. Studies of urban hedgehogs have
drawn attention to the importance of green spaces in suburbia as reservoirs for
many animal species, but also highlight the need to consider how those sites are
used and managed if they are to continue to provide vital support for wildlife.

CONCLUSION

The hedgehog is normally active after dark and appears not to indulge in typical mammalian behaviour such as play, social activities or territoriality. Almost all of its time is spent in routine systematic foraging, which makes it all the more peculiar that occasional bizarre actions occur, including self-anointing and manic running in circles. Radio-tracking has generated much essential information about hedgehog movements, although the results may not be comparable between studies and their interpretation is open to discussion. When describing 'home range' for this and other species, it is important to distinguish between the area used in a typical activity period, the larger area with which the animal is familiar, and the total range area used in an entire year (including winter). This is frequently not done and figures given in print may not be directly comparable and need to be accepted with caution. Hedgehog activity differs according to local conditions and it appears that arable farmland is a challenging habitat for hedgehogs that now covers large parts of Britain. Radio-tracking studies have established that hedgehogs range more widely than expected, raising concerns about habitat continuity and also about the possible unsuitability of intensively managed sports turf, amenity grassland and other urban green space for this species and many others. Suburban habitats are becoming increasingly important as refuge areas for hedgehogs, especially where extra food is put out for wildlife in many people's gardens. This does no harm and may be very supportive of urban hedgehog populations, but we need to know more about hedgehog ecology in built-up areas as urbanisation expands inexorably.

CHAPTER 6

Inactivity: Hibernation

P EOPLE HAVE KNOWN ABOUT HIBERNATION for centuries, of course. It has been a matter of ongoing curiosity that some animals can appear to die in winter, going cold and stiff, and yet come back to life within an hour or so when handled or disturbed. Hibernation is a familiar, but mysterious natural miracle. The eighteenth-century medic and naturalist John Hunter (1728–93) was one of the pioneer investigators of this phenomenon. Apparently he had difficulty in getting and keeping hedgehogs, so he sought help from fellow scientist Edward Jenner (1749–1823), the man who developed the first vaccine for smallpox. They investigated temperatures in hedgehogs, using a thermometer on animals for the first time. They attempted to insert one into the hedgehog's anus and also opened the belly and thorax in order to find out how cold the animal was inside the different parts of its body during hibernation. They observed the fluidity of the blood by comparing it with another animal that had been kept warm. The idea of all this was to discover the lowest temperature at which a hedgehog could survive. Hunter went on to request that his friend should examine hedgehog stomachs and intestines to see what they contained. Presciently, Hunter also wrote to Jenner saying:

> I want you to get a Hedge Hog in the beginning of the winter and weigh him, put in your garden and let him have some leaves, Hay or straw to cover himself with, which he will do; then weigh him in the spring to see what he has lost. Secondly I want you to kill one at the beginning of the winter to see how fat he is and another in the spring to see what he has lost of his fat.

After more than two centuries, those topics remain key issues in discussions about hibernation (see below).

The basic anomaly of a warm-blooded animal that goes cold, but without dying, encouraged many later scientists to study the phenomenon, often in great detail. From the late nineteenth century onwards, these studies became increasingly sophisticated, with a large volume of resulting observations. However, different methods of study and the use of equipment with limited capabilities are bound to deliver variable results. A further complication is that any attempt to study a hibernating animal almost inevitably means disturbing it, and even the tiniest interference alters body processes in hibernation and results in inconsistent experimental results. Unfortunately, as a result, the welter of published scientific information that has been generated in the last 80 years is confusing and often contradictory or inconclusive. Basically we still don't fully understand how hibernation works, although we do know a lot about the many changes that take place during the process.

Mammals are warm-blooded creatures, a condition more properly described as 'endothermic' because their body heat is generated internally. They are also homeotherms, able to maintain a high and constant body temperature. This contrasts with reptiles, which are ectothermic. They bask in the sunshine to gain heat from an external source to raise their body temperature, often to the same levels as mammals, although they cool off overnight or when the sun goes in. They are termed poikilotherms, their body temperature fluctuating in accordance with their surroundings, whereas homeotherms are independent of the surrounding temperatures because they generate their own body warmth. Hibernators like the hedgehog inhabit both worlds so to speak, being warm blooded when active, but behaving as poikilotherms during hibernation. Having a warm body conveys many biological advantages. Nerves and muscles work faster at higher temperatures (within a range up to about 35–40°C), enabling more rapid movements and faster responses. Food digestion is also faster, making the energy it contains more rapidly available to the body tissues. This is all down to basic physical chemistry in which one of the universal principles is that the speed at which chemical reactions proceed will double for every 10°C rise in temperature. All biological activity, including digestion, muscle contraction and the function of nerves, consists of various kinds of chemical reactions. So, when cold-blooded animals cool off, they cannot avoid becoming more sluggish, quite literally because slugs (and other invertebrates like worms and insects) are cold-blooded too. Homeotherms can do what they like, largely irrespective of the temperature of their surroundings, because they use food energy to generate their own heat internally.

But the advantages of being warm blooded come at a high cost. Endotherms use a lot of energy to maintain their body temperature and this means they have to be efficient feeders and eat frequently in order to acquire the energy in their food that serves to pay their central heating bill. For hedgehogs, that becomes a problem in winter when there is less food available and sometimes none at all. This is where hibernation comes into its own. Hedgehogs cannot fly away like swallows, they have to stick it out through the winter, but they cannot afford the cost of homeothermy because there is not enough of their natural food available to yield the necessary energy to maintain their body temperature. Lowering their body temperature, effectively giving up the advantages of being warm-blooded, saves about 90 per cent of this energy cost, but at the price of becoming incapable of normal activity. That is what hibernation is all about.

A 'PRIMITIVE' FEATURE?

Hibernation has often been considered one of the more primitive aspects of the hedgehog, as though it was not quite a fully developed mammal. It seemed to hover between being a poikilotherm and a respectable homeotherm fully in control of its body temperature. But this overlooks the many studies that show that hibernation is really a very complex physiological adjustment. In fact the hedgehog's capacity for physiological control is similar to that of other placental mammals and for a wide range of ambient temperatures it is capable of maintaining its body temperature constant, although often at a level a few degrees lower than is typical of other mammals. Oxygen is consumed in a process known as oxidative phosphorylation and increased metabolism can be directed towards the generation of heat rather than production of ATP (adenosine triphosphate), the 'energy chemical' needed for muscles to contract. This represents a rather specialised development, suggesting that hibernation in the hedgehog is not simply a failure to keep warm in a primitive mammal. Moreover there are complex control issues involved: for example, managing the change between normal carbohydrate-based metabolism to release energy from food and switching to fat-based metabolism to maintain the body during hibernation, and then switching back again during periods of arousal and subsequent normal activity. There is also the fact that a hedgehog's nerves continue to function even at very low temperatures and the ability of its heart to experience substantial cooling without suffering from fibrillation. These are very specialised modifications of normal mammalian physiology and perhaps it is inappropriate to consider hibernation as a primitive feature at all. Instead, we should think of it as a highly successful strategy for dealing with the problem of overwinter food shortage. Actually, the strategy may be so successful that it has evolved more than once, becoming a key part of the lives of such widely differing animals as bats, ground squirrels, hamsters and dormice as well as hedgehogs. This could cause confusion when results from studying one species are assumed to apply to others, when their actual mechanisms may differ, having evolved independently.

A beguiling hypothesis is that, because hibernation involves an almost complete shutdown of an animal's body functions, it wears itself out more slowly and consequently enjoys a longer lifespan. For example, the edible dormouse, the *Siebenschläfer* ('seven sleeper') that hibernates for a long time, often lives more than five years and some exceed ten (Morris & Morris, 2010). Most non-hibernating mammals of comparable size are lucky to live that many months. Hibernating bats also live a long time compared with other small mammals, sometimes more than 20 years, corresponding to Max Rubner's 1908 hypothesis that metabolic rate is a major factor in determining longevity (Herreid, 1964). Large animals have lower metabolic rates per gram of tissue, interpreted as living at a slower rate, and these too are expected to have a longer lifespan than smaller animals. The suggestion is often made that longevity is linked to the total number of an animal's heartbeats and slowing down in hibernation will lead to a longer life. This may apply to hedgehogs as they can live to be at least seven years old, longer than a rabbit of similar size.

ONGOING SCIENTIFIC INTEREST

Some experiments at the University of Missouri back in the 1960s suggested that hibernation in hamsters may be at least partly genetically controlled. Half of the experimental animals would hibernate readily, while their litter mates did not do so, even after two years under identical conditions. Selective breeding generated two populations, one in which only 22 per cent of the hamsters hibernated and another in which 74 per cent did. The small number of generations within which this change was achieved suggests that the capacity to hibernate might be controlled by a very small number of genes, possibly only one. Genes control production of enzymes and these regulate chemical synthesis, so it is reasonable to suggest that hibernation might be caused by a specific substance. If this could be identified and isolated, it might then be possible to initiate hibernation using a pill or an injection.

This is one reason why hibernation research has been funded by space agencies and the military. It would be helpful if astronauts on long journeys could be induced to hibernate, reducing their food requirements by about 80 per cent.

FIG 138. Improbable though it may seem, studies of hibernation physiology have been funded by the military and space exploration programmes. There would be many practical benefits if ways could be found to enable astronauts to hibernate during long journeys in space. Launch of Apollo 15 in 1971.

Now that we understand more about the problems of bone resorption during the long periods of weightlessness involved in space travel, this idea seems less straightforward. By a similar argument, it has been suggested that in times of famine, whole populations could be put into hibernation, to be roused again when normal food supplies resumed. The financial and political costs of doing this make that a rather impractical idea too, but the mere suggestion encourages further research interest in hibernation as a natural phenomenon. More down to earth, the physiological principles of hibernation have been applied to the development of surgery. For example, reducing a patient's body temperature to 20°C allows a heart surgeon about seven times as much time to complete his procedure. Cooling also lessens the traumatic effects on tissues that are cut or bruised during the operation and reduces the immediate effects of injury (to soldiers in a war, for example). A lowered body temperature also conveys a degree of resistance to the effects of radiation. This too could be useful in space travel, but more immediately in the treatment of cancer, where the nasty side effects of radiotherapy might be reduced, allowing more opportunity for other treatments to be effective. If we humans spend a few days ill in bed, we feel very 'weak at the knees' when we get up. But after many weeks inactive in hibernation, hedgehogs wake up fully 'fit for purpose' and can soon walk about in the normal way. How do they do that? Maybe if we knew the answer, it might help treatment for muscle-wasting diseases or at least speed our recovery after being confined to bed for a while. So much for the general background and why there is ongoing interest in hibernation research – but what does it all mean for the hedgehog?

WHAT CAUSES HEDGEHOGS TO GO INTO HIBERNATION?

There has been much discussion about what causes hedgehogs to hibernate. It is not simply because 'it is time to do so', although it has been suggested that some form of biological clock might be involved. According to Konrad Herter, hibernators will go into hibernation if there is a readiness to do it (their *Winterschlafbereitschaft*), but what is the actual trigger? We need to remember that hibernation is a strategy to overcome the challenge of remaining warm-blooded when there is insufficient food energy available to meet the metabolic cost. If hedgehogs are kept properly fed, they don't need to hibernate and many will not do so, even if subjected to low temperatures. On the other hand, if they are deprived of food for even a short time, some may go into a torpid condition even in the summer. So neither temperature nor food supply alone triggers hibernation, but it is a combination of the two that matters. There seems to be a critical temperature below which most hedgehogs will respond by hibernating if they are short of food, but there is considerable flexibility and individual variation. It is also important that the cold conditions persist if hibernation is to continue.

FIG 139. 'Is it time to hibernate yet?' Actually it's not time that determines the onset of hibernation, but a combination of falling temperatures and diminishing food supplies.

Central to this concept of 'readiness to hibernate' is a critical temperature below which the animals will go into hibernation and Herter suggested it was about 17°C for hedgehogs; and rises above about 10–12°C will cause one that is hibernating to wake up. However, there is much variability between individuals and geographical regions, and in experimental conditions it also depends on how quickly the surrounding temperature changes. If the ambient temperature approaches freezing, hibernators will increase their metabolic rate, without actually waking, in order to keep the body above freezing point. This response occurs below about 3°C and certainly by 1°C, and will result in using up fat reserves. Metabolism also increases progressively at higher ambient temperatures, also consuming fat. It appears that the optimum temperature for hibernation in hedgehogs is about +4°C, the temperature at which metabolic consumption of fat will be at its minimum (Kristofferson & Soivio, 1964b). This is a key fact to recall when discussing the nature of winter nests and also what to do about keeping captive hedgehogs over winter.

In general terms, timing, control and duration of hibernation seem to be governed by a complex of environmental and hormonal factors. Secretion of melatonin, a hormone produced by the pineal gland in response to the ratio between daylight and darkness ('photoperiod'), seems to be important. It is also associated with reduced levels of testosterone, crucial to regulating reproductive activity. In male hedgehogs, melatonin levels increase in the autumn, with maximal levels in January. As the photoperiod increases in the spring, melatonin declines and gonadal activity recommences so that animals are fully sexually active as soon as hibernation ends. In females, hibernation seems to be less affected by hormonal changes. Photoperiod, melatonin secretion in the pineal and sex hormones are all closely linked and very important to mammals in general, but it is difficult to see how changes in photoperiod can easily be detected by a nocturnal animal hibernating inside a dark nest or down a rabbit hole.

EFFECTS OF HIBERNATION AND CHANGES IN THE BODY

Hibernation is often described as a form of deep sleep, but the two processes are very different. Sleep normally occurs in a daily pattern, but hibernation lasts for weeks or months (although it is usually not continuous throughout that time). While sleep is essential, hibernation is an optional energy-saving strategy and if the animal is kept warm and properly fed, it will not need to hibernate and often will not do so. During sleep, the body temperature may fall by a few degrees, heart rate and breathing may also be slowed to some extent. In hibernation, the changes are much more profound. The body temperature falls drastically to match that of the environment; breathing and heartbeats almost stop. Basically sleep is a regular and relatively minor adjustment to normal activity, but hibernation involves major changes in an animal's physiology.

The most obvious, and most studied, change in the hibernating hedgehog is its reduced body temperature. In normal activity, this will hover around 35°C, falling a degree or two in the middle of the day when the animal is fully asleep, in just the same way that a human's body temperature is lowest around three or four in the morning. In hibernation, the hedgehog effectively abandons the maintenance of its warm body and allows its temperature to fall and match that of its immediate surroundings, often only a few degrees above freezing.

In midwinter, metabolic rate is reduced to only about 2 per cent of the levels in active animals. Confronted by severe cold, as the body approaches freezing, metabolic heat production begins again in order to prevent freezing of the tissues. Metabolic rate and energy consumption will rise at sub-zero temperatures, fuelled by the consumption of fat. Under experimental conditions, hedgehogs subjected to a temperature of –5°C, risking frostbite, consumed 22 times as much oxygen as they did when hibernating normally (Dickman *et al.*, 1968), reflecting metabolic attempts to keep the animals from suffering severe damage. But if the hibernating animal is warmed too much, its chemical reactions will increase, burning up fat twice as fast for every 10° rise in temperature. This is why it is important that hibernators kept in captivity over winter should remain cool and not be kept 'nice and warm' in the greenhouse or the kitchen. A body temperature of say 15°C is not warm enough to be fully and properly active and able to feed and digest properly, yet at that temperature the hedgehog will use up stored fat twice as fast as if it were being kept cool at 5°. This is also why the hedgehog's winter nest is so important in protecting the hibernating animal from becoming too warm.

CHANGES IN RESPIRATORY PATTERN AND HEART RATE

While it is awake, but not moving about, a hedgehog normally breathes about 25 times per minute. Breathing is at regular intervals, contrasting with the respiratory pattern observed during deep hibernation. In this situation, the animal often spends an hour or so without breathing at all and then engages in a series of 40–50 rapid breaths which gradually tail off into little pants before sinking into another long period of apnoea (the 'Cheyne–Stokes' respiratory pattern). The longest periods without breathing may exceed two hours (150 minutes has been recorded). Cheyne–Stokes breathing seems to be a general feature of hibernation, having been reported from other species too, such as marmots (*Marmota* spp.) and dormice. Oxygen deficiency caused by long periods of low breathing rates is tolerated without permanent damage to the body. Restricted breathing causes carbon dioxide to accumulate in the blood, raising its acidity, which in turn raises the affinity for oxygen in the haemoglobin of red blood corpuscles (Clausen & Ersland, 1968). Increased acidity also inhibits glycolysis, the metabolism of glucose, so the acidity is actually helping to reduce the metabolic rate. Periodic apnoea is therefore part of the strategy to save energy.

As long ago as 1815, a hedgehog's pulse rate was measured and found to be 75 heartbeats per minute, but only 25 in hibernation. Many subsequent studies have come up with figures ranging from 110–520 heartbeats per minute during periods of activity, with estimates in hibernation ranging between about 5 and 70. The variation is probably due to varied experimental techniques and the fact that even in deep hibernation, the animal is very sensitive to disturbance, which is difficult to avoid under study conditions. Nevertheless, at normal summer temperatures, a hedgehog's heart rate is about 200–215 beats per minute at rest. In hibernation, its heartbeats generally fall to about 5 per minute.

A drastic drop in a mammal's body temperature often causes fibrillation in the heart (a fluttering of rapid and shallow contractions that pump little blood). The heart may stop working altogether at 15–20°C (Johansson, 1985), but one of the special adjustments we find in hibernators is that the heart is resistant to hypothermia. This seems to be linked to the fact that the reduced heart rate exhibited by mammals entering hibernation begins before there is any noticeable fall in body temperature and is probably controlled by changing the balance between activity in the sympathetic and parasympathetic nervous systems. This results in periods of irregular cardiac activity. Conversely, the elevation of pulse rate that accompanies the onset of arousal is the result of a dramatic rise in sympathetic activation that precedes any increases in body temperature. As the animal wakes up, the influence of the sympathetic nervous system is slowly withdrawn (Milsom et al., 1999).

CHANGES IN BLOOD CHEMISTRY AND OTHER PARAMETERS

During the 1960s, there was a long series of research papers published by Kristofferson, Soivio and Suomalainen at the University of Helsinki, describing physiological changes within a hibernating hedgehog's body. The details lie beyond the scope of this book, but these and other authors have documented the numerous and major physiological adjustments that take place during a hedgehog's hibernation (reviewed by Reeve, 1979; most of the more recent research on this phenomenon has focused on other species). Large seasonal changes occur in concentrations of sodium, potassium and calcium in the blood. There are low levels of blood coagulation factors such as prothrombin, and increased quantities of heparin and other anticoagulants in the slowly circulating blood, reducing the tendency for it to clot. The number of white corpuscles in the blood, normally 18–20,000 per mm^3 falls to less than 3,000. Hibernating hedgehogs rely on their fat reserves and carbohydrate metabolism virtually ceases, so the blood contains very low levels of the pancreatic hormones glucagon and insulin. Normal blood sugar concentrations in active animals are around 125 mg per 100 ml of blood, falling to around 50 mg in hibernation. The reduced heart rate results in diminished renal blood flow, causing a decrease in the efficiency of glomerular filtration in the kidneys. As a result, urea levels in the blood and tissues may become up to 26 per cent higher than normal, but the body seems able to adjust to what are normally damaging levels of urea and also avoids developing harmful crystals of it in the blood.

Reduced blood pressure and flow to the kidneys also reduces their high metabolic demand and the consequent drain on fat reserves. Metabolism of fat generates water, but diminished kidney function means that this does not rapidly accumulate in the bladder, so the hedgehog does not need to wake up and leave the nest to urinate. Any surplus can be urinated during the brief periods of natural arousal. Hibernation continues regardless of whether the bladder is full or not … unlike sleeping humans!

In hibernating hedgehogs, the weight of the spleen decreases and the reproductive organs are quiescent. In males, there is little sign of activity in the testes, which are smallest in the autumn, and the accessory reproductive organs are also much reduced. But after five months' hibernation, the first signs appear of preparation for breeding, with enlarging accessory glands and histological changes in the testes. In females, there is a thickening of the endometrium and the vagina and ovaries enlarge, with the appearance of some maturing follicles, all changes that are somehow stimulated to begin before the end of hibernation.

CONTROL OF HIBERNATION

With a body that is more or less switched off, how does the hedgehog control itself during hibernation, even to a minimal extent? Despite the massive reduction in metabolic rate, it appears that the important homeostatic control centres in the hypothalamus remain responsive and functional in deep hibernation, even though many other parts of the brain become inactive. Biologists have long wondered how the nerve cells in the hypothalamus continue their electrical activity while the rest of the brain sleeps. It seems that these special cells grow extra dendrites, reaching out to adjacent nerve cells, enabling them to detect the faintest neural activity (Sanchez-Toscano *et al.*, 1989). The hypothalamus can then control fundamental body functions like blood circulation, body temperature and the regulation of water. The ordinary nerves of a hibernating hedgehog also remain functional at much lower temperatures than in other mammals. Somehow memory seems to survive the brain's hibernal shutdown as hedgehogs seem to remember from one year to the next where to find plates of food that people put out in the garden.

WINTER NESTING

Whilst a lot of effort has gone into studying hibernating hedgehogs in the laboratory, little attempt has been made to consider what happens in the wild. Published descriptions of hedgehog nests rarely described them in any detail, with little distinction made between those built for use in summer and those specifically intended as hibernation nests (hibernacula) in winter. There was no suggestion that hedgehogs actually took care over the siting and construction

FIG 140. My study site, where hedgehogs congregated to build their winter nests among the log piles and sprawling brambles in the small enclosures along the south wall of Bushy Park, west London.

of their nests. This lack of detail is probably because few hedgehog winter nests are ever found, except by chance. I was lucky in the early 1960s to discover that significant numbers of hedgehogs congregated for the winter in two narrow strips of mixed woodland fenced off along the southern edge of Bushy Park in west London (Fig. 140). Presumably the hedgehogs gathered there because the main area of the park was heavily grazed and provided little suitable nesting habitat. This discovery enabled me to make over 700 visits to 185 different winter nests to study their construction and use in successive winters (Morris, 1973).

The nests were checked every six weeks; more frequent visits were avoided in case this resulted in too much disturbance. A note was made of the condition of each nest and its occupant (if any) and the nest record was terminated when it had decayed beyond recognition. Subsequently, I found many similar hedgehog nests in parts of Surrey and Norfolk, all of which conformed to the same general pattern as in Bushy Park, providing reassurance that my observations were likely to be of general relevance (Fig. 141). Captive hedgehogs have been observed to build nests when the temperature fell below 16°C (Dimelow, 1963) and in Bushy Park there was also a close correlation between air temperature and the number of wild hedgehogs occupying their hibernacula, the maximum number being present during the coldest months (Fig. 142). Typical winter nests began to appear in September and the number of hedgehogs present in the plantations increased as the autumn progressed and they left the more exposed parts of the park for a sheltered hibernation site. In March, the hedgehogs became fewer as they left their nests in the plantations and went to live somewhere else (Fig. 143).

Winter nests are not simply random heaps of leaves as implied by authors in the older literature. Instead, they form compact structures 30–60 cm in diameter,

FIG 141. I visited other sites like this one at Wisley Gardens in Surrey and found hedgehog winter nests just like those in Bushy Park and sited in similar places.

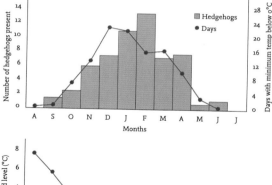

FIG 142. As the average number of cold nights increased, more hedgehogs arrived in their winter quarters, departing with warmer weather in the spring.

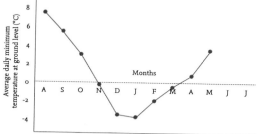

TABLE 14. Numbers of hedgehogs and nests present per month in the enclosures where hedgehogs spent the winter, combined data from five winters 1962–67. (Based on Morris, 1969)

Month	Total number of hedgehogs present	Average number of hedgehogs per month	Total number of nests present	Average number of nests present	Average per cent of new nests built each month
September	3	1.5	28	14.0	4.4
October	7	2.3	57	19.0	16.8
November	30	6.0	104	20.8	22.6
December	44	8.8	128	25.6	16.6
January	44	11.0	108	27.0	14.1
February	53	13.2	136	34.0	11.8
March	29	7.2	132	33.0	7.1
April	31	7.7	126	31.5	6.6
May	3	0.8	70	17.5	0.0
June	1	1.0	20	20.0	—
July	0	0.0	15	15.0	—
August	Not checked	—	—	—	—

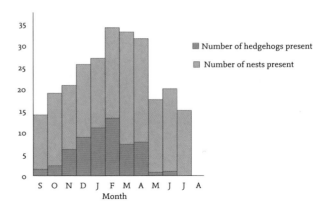

FIG 143. As the winter progressed there were more hedgehogs present, but always more empty nests than animals, as though each hedgehog had several spare hibernacula available for use if necessary.

commonly sited below a small bramble bush, under a pile of logs, at the base of a hedge or underneath a garden shed. The nest walls are of dead leaves closely packed to form a laminated mass up to 20 cm thick. This flat-packing rather than random arrangement of the leaf litter is often the only external indication of the nest and the secret of its success. Hedgehogs may also occasionally use the base of a hollow tree or go down a rabbit burrow. The prime concern in siting a nest seems to be the structural support offered by surrounding fixed objects. In Bushy Park, low bramble bushes that formed a sprawling lattice of horizontally aligned stems were especially favoured nest sites (Fig. 144). There was no statistically significant tendency for the nest to face any particular compass direction, nor was the nest sited with regard to shelter from the sun. This was to be expected in a nocturnal animal, but resulted in unsheltered nests being noticeably warm during sunny weather, potentially triggering premature arousal of a hibernating occupant. A burst of new nest-building immediately followed a warm sunny period in February one year, pointing to the fact that hibernators need to be

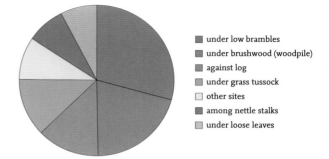

FIG 144. About half of the winter nests were sited under the low, sprawling bramble bushes or below wood piles made of branches pruned from the trees.

FIG 145. There were numerous places where the hedgehogs could find support for their winter nest and they congregated here presumably because the more open areas of the park offered less secure hibernation sites.

FIG 146. Nests built out in the open and made of grass were uncommon and never found occupied, as though the hedgehog that made it realised the unsuitability of this type of nest construction for winter use.

protected from being too warm as much as from getting too cold. Of the four nests whose occupants did not move during that sunny period, three were shaded by a wall and the fourth was screened by dense bushes.

Leaves from deciduous trees were the prime nest constituent; only a few nests contained no leaves and were made wholly of grass (Fig. 146). These were never found occupied. A variety of deciduous trees provided a generous selection of leaves, but the hedgehogs appeared to exercise no strong preference. They used the most readily available types such as oak leaves, although they seemed to avoid trying to use the very large and unwieldly leaves of sycamore, turkey oak and horse chestnut (Fig. 147). Away from Bushy Park, hedgehogs also make frequent use of litter such as rags, bits of soft plastic and paper. Sometimes moss may be incorporated into the structure (Jensen, 2004), although I never found that to be common.

A hedgehog collects its leaves at night, and when it has a small bunch held in its mouth it carries them off to make a heap under brambles or some other

FIG 147. A typical well-constructed leafy winter nest, distinctive without being conspicuous.

FIG 148. Two nests close together, one under bramble strands at bottom left, the other against the log near my friend's hand.

supportive structure. More leaves are collected and thrust inside the heap, which enlarges outwards and upwards against the restraint of the supporting vegetation. The hedgehog then burrows into the heap and shuffles around inside, creating a centrifugal agitation from within which is countered by the constraining pressure of the external support (Fig. 149). Shuffling about inside the heap would normally result in scattering the leaves, but the surrounding support provided by brushwood, brambles or other structure holds the pile of leaves in place. The shuffling then causes the leaves to lie flat against one another and the heap of randomly arranged leaves now takes on its characteristic layered structure, like the pages of a book. This is a fundamental feature of the hedgehog's nest. The whole structure becomes sufficiently firm that when the animal departs, its nest chamber does not collapse, but may remain intact for several months. The choice of site and materials, and the method of construction all determine the physical properties of the nest upon which the hedgehog depends so much.

FIG 149. First a hedgehog will gather a pile of leaves tucked under some supportive structure, then it burrows inside and shuffles about until the leaves form a thick wall around it.

Although my study involved a total of 185 nests, completed life histories were only available for 167 of them because observations were terminated after five winters. Nest histories were analysed on a monthly basis. The rate of deterioration was very variable: some new nests collapsed within a month, others remained functional for 5 months and 30 nests persisted for 12 months or more. Those that remained in good condition the longest were also the most persistently occupied, perhaps because they were of sound construction and the occupant had no reason to leave, although some nests were actually repaired by the hedgehogs using fresh material during the winter. Many nests were very insubstantial and were found occupied only once, as though they were built by inexperienced young animals and then abandoned. On average, nests survived for 6.4 months, with melting snow or wet weather hastening their collapse. The longest recorded lifespan was a minimum of 18 months for a nest sited under some brambles. Fewer than half of the nests lasted more than five months, the minimum time necessary to provide shelter throughout the whole winter, which means that many hedgehogs were obliged to wake up and make at least one new nest sometime during the winter. Survival of a nest was very dependent upon its relationship with fixed objects around it; those built with no additional support were readily broken up by repeated occupation and lasted about three and a half months, only two of them remained recognisable for more than five months. Well-supported nests, sited under nettles, tucked against logs and especially those built under strands of bramble, survived more than seven months on average (Fig. 150).

FIG 150. Firm support for the nest is vital, as the hedgehog shuffles around inside, otherwise the leaves form a loose structure that soon disintegrates. The nests that lasted longest were always those that were best supported under brambles or brushwood piles.

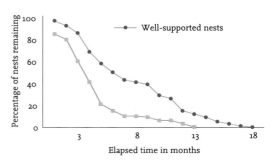

TABLE 15. The longevity of winter nests in different situations (from Morris, 1969)

Nest site	Number of nests	Average lifespan (months)
Well supported		
Under bramble	47	7.9
Against tree or log	21	7.1
Under nettles	12	7.9
Under woodpile	36	5.5
Poorly supported		
In grass	22	5.0
In loose leaves	12	3.4
Others (not recorded etc.)	17	5.0
Total number of nests	**167**	**6.4**

The longest period of continuous occupation was six months. Over 60 per cent of all the nests built were occupied for less than two months, and of these half were never found occupied at all. Grass nests were particularly prone to desertion, suggesting that leaves are very important for successful nesting. Ten nests were occupied on one occasion, then empty for up to four months before being reoccupied, but without breaking the nest open it was impossible to know if this was the original animal coming back or a different hedgehog moving into a convenient ready-made hibernaculum. Other nests were empty when first found, but subsequently occupied, suggesting that hedgehogs may build spare nests early in the winter that are not used unless they are needed later, perhaps because the original became wet or had begun to fall apart. Clearly the animals were moving about quite a lot during the winter and not remaining solidly in hibernation. This has been confirmed in more recent studies, using radio-tagged animals. Amy Haigh found that her Irish hedgehogs used an average of 1.8 hibernacula in a winter, with a maximum of three, and they changed their nest up to five times during the hibernation period (Haigh *et al.*, 2012b). A new study by Lucy Bearman-Brown has also confirmed that most hedgehogs change their nest at least once during the winter. Radio-tagged hedgehogs in Denmark used up to four winter nests (Jensen, 2004) and some moved up to eight times during the winter (Sophie Rasmussen, pers comm.).

In my study, new nests were constructed in every winter month, even in the coldest period. Most of the new nests that were built late in the winter were immediately occupied, but up to 80 per cent of those built during October and November were abandoned, again suggesting that while fresh dry leaves were available, spare nests were being created in case of later need. Three nests had double nesting chambers, implying that there had once been two occupants, and two others were found briefly in dual occupation. This is remarkable, since hedgehogs are normally solitary and often act aggressively towards each other. It would also have been difficult to create the nest by shuffling around inside with two animals present. It is likely that this kind of nest sharing involves newly weaned young of an incompletely dispersed litter staying on in their mother's maternity nest. In contrast to the situation in the wild, nest sharing was regularly observed among my captive animals in summer and also during hibernation. In each case, a single nest box was occupied by two animals for days or weeks, whilst

TABLE 16. Length of time that hibernation nests were occupied. The majority were used for three months or less, indicating that a hedgehog changes its nest at least once during the winter. The average length of time for a nest to be occupied was 1.4 months (From Morris, 1969).

Time occupied (months)	Number of nests
0	56
1	57
2	19
3	14
4	14
5	5
6	2
Total number of nests studied	**167**

FIG 151. Leaves normally decay within a few months at most, but in well-constructed nest they may persist for much longer. Some nests survived into a second winter, but were rarely occupied after the first.

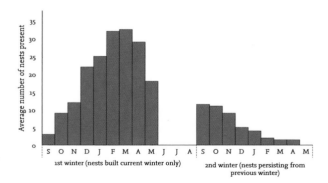

S O N D J F M A M J J A | S O N D J F M A M

1st winter (nests built current winter only)   2nd winter (nests persisting from previous winter)

an identical nest box nearby remained empty. Returning individuals to separate boxes had little lasting effect and one hedgehog continued to cohabit despite its mate being dead and decomposing. Non-simultaneous nest sharing occurs in the wild (where an animal moves into a ready-made winter nest sometime after the original occupant has left), but this is difficult to detect owing to the problem of identifying individual hedgehogs without breaking open the nest.

During April and May, increased hedgehog activity probably loosens the nest structure, hastening its disintegration. Nevertheless some nests persisted for more than a year despite being constructed of dead leaves that are subject to the normal processes of decay. Under natural conditions, 92 per cent of dead leaf material disappears completely within 12 months, but it seems that the special way in which a hedgehog makes its nest with tightly packed leaves successfully excludes the worms and other agents of decay (Fig. 151). About a third of the nests which were present at the end of one winter were still present at the start of the next, but only 3 out of 50 were re-occupied during the second winter, and again it was not possible to know if this was the original owner coming back or an opportunist animal taking over a convenient existing nest.

New nests were dry inside and almost completely waterproof. Their condition often remained unchanged for several months, but after dampness penetrated or the structure was loosened, the whole nest decayed rapidly. Once the roof collapsed, disintegration was usually complete within a few weeks. Some of my study nests disappeared abruptly and five of them were broken open and scattered about, presumably by a fox or an unruly dog that had somehow managed to get into the fenced-off plantations.

Second-hand hedgehog nests were evidently a useful resource for other creatures. Six deserted hibernacula were taken over by field voles, who lined the chamber with grass and were resident for up to two months. Another old nest

FIG 152. Other animals like these bumble bees (*Bombus pratorum* (left) and *B. agrorum*) would use hedgehog hibernacula once their original owner had left. (Gordon Riley)

was relined with finely chewed leaves and occupied by three torpid wood mice (*Apodemus sylvaticus*), a non-hibernating species. They were huddled together and felt quite cold. Their body temperature had fallen to about 16°C and they seemed incapable of more than very sluggish movement, although they became fully active after being warmed up in my pocket. This turned out to be the first time that hypothermia had been observed in that species (Morris, 1969) and later prompted studies of winter torpor in Japanese mice. Other disused hedgehog hibernation nests were taken over by three species of ground-nesting bees (*Bombus pratorum*, *B. hortorum* and *B. agrorum*), which apparently seek out old mammal nests to raise their own larvae. A colony of wasps (*Vespa* sp.) took over another nest and built a series of combs inside. Hedgehog nests, winter and summer, may also play a significant role in the life history of various parasites (see Chapter 11).

Within its nest, the hedgehog lies on its side, eyes closed and partially rolled up with its face and legs tucked away, shrouded by the spiny skin. As the animal is cold to the touch, it is not obvious whether it is alive or dead, but just gently tickling the spines causes them to bristle in response if the hedgehog is alive. One should be careful doing this because even a small disturbance and agitation of the spines can result in arousal from hibernation. This must be avoided because of the high drain on fat reserves resulting from temporary awakening. If the hedgehog is already dead, then the spines will not react to gentle tickling and remain floppy in the skin. One's fingers also become noticeably smelly if the animal has been dead for very long.

The winter nest plays a vital part in protecting the hibernating hedgehog from the worst weather of the year and it also serves to hide the animal from predators. Moreover, the insulating effect of the nest protects its occupant from

FIG 153. The layers of dead leaves forming the hibernaculum wall were very resistant to decay and remarkably effective insulation for the hibernating hedgehog, which needs to avoid the effects of warm weather as much as being protected from the cold.

rapid changes in ambient temperature and from extreme cold or becoming too warm when the sun shines. This is particularly helpful, given the poor insulation properties of the hedgehog's spines and sparse hair. I monitored the temperature inside several empty nests over one winter and for more than three quarters of the time, the nest interior remained between between 0°C and 5°C. Even during the extremes of warmth and cold that winter, the nest chamber never became as warm or as cold as outside (Fig. 154). In Denmark, Helge Walhovd (1979b) recorded ambient temperatures ranging from –11°C to +13°C, but nest temperatures remained between 0°C and 4°C for up to 99 per cent of the total time. So the winter nest helps to maximise energy efficiency during hibernation by maintaining the animal at a temperature that laboratory experiments show is most efficient for hibernation, allowing the animal to consume minimal amounts of precious stored fat.

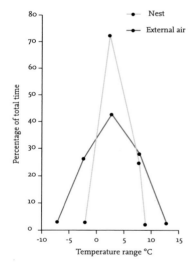

FIG 154. Temperature records from an empty nest during the warmest and coldest periods in winter showed that the interior never became as warm as the air outside, nor as cold. Most of the time, the nest remained between 0–5 °C inside, the optimum temperature for hibernating revealed by laboratory studies.

It is also important to remember that a hibernating hedgehog is still breathing, albeit at a much reduced rate. This means that it will continue to lose water by evaporation from its lungs and it will also lose small amounts via the kidneys. During hibernation, water lost from the body will not be replaced by normal drinking and feeding behaviour, although the metabolism of stored fat will compensate and make some water available in the tissues. The risk of dehydration after several weeks is reduced by the absence of sweat glands in the spiny skin that surrounds the rolled-up hibernating animal like a cloak. Its thin, highly vascularised belly skin will be tucked away inside the curled-up ball, reducing the amount of water that might be lost through it. Nevertheless, it is important that hibernating animals should lose as little water as possible and in hedgehogs (and dormice) there is benefit from having their hibernaculum in contact with the cool soil and preferably sheltered among damp leaves and moss or inside a rotting tree stump. Low and stable ambient temperatures are most likely to be found there too. Bats like to hibernate in caves for similar reasons. Hibernating in dry air risks losing water faster than it is being produced in the body, a point worth remembering when considering where to keep captive hedgehogs over winter. If the hedgehog choses to hibernate in a very dry place (or is kept in a dry building by a well-meaning carer), dehydration may result. In natural circumstances, winter nests are often partially sunk into the ground, under tree roots or down a burrow, ensuring contact with cool, damp soil. The thick layers of leaves forming the walls of the hibernaculum will also hold moisture. This enables the animal to hibernate in a humid atmosphere, but not be actually wet. Breathing damp air will minimise evaporation from the body because the air is already saturated with water vapour. So choosing a suitable nesting place in the autumn becomes another important aspect of the hedgehog's preparation for hibernation.

All of this implies that the winter nest, its materials and siting are vital aspects of the hedgehog's ecology. It is perhaps no coincidence that the northern limit of distribution for this species in Europe generally follows the limit of the deciduous trees that provide shelter and important nesting material in the form of fallen leaves. The same applies in New Zealand, where a shortage of overwintering nest sites is considered to be a major factor limiting the abundance of hedgehogs in the uplands and other areas (Brockie, 1974a).

Hedgehogs are scarce or absent in habitats (and at altitudes) where the essentials for hibernation are lacking. It follows that the survival of hedgehog populations in towns and farmland depends on having access to suitable places in which to build a nest and also the continuing availability of suitable nesting materials. These are important issues to consider in connection with hedgehog protection and conservation (see Chapter 13). Nevertheless, hedgehogs do survive

FIG 155. Secure winter nests are a vital part of the hedgehog's ecological needs. Artificial 'next boxes' may help support them where natural facilities are lacking. (Duncan Usher/Ardea)

in some places that appear unpromising – on Scottish islands, for example, where there are few trees, if any. But rabbits are often abundant and their burrows will provide sheltered hibernation sites. There is usually plenty of grass and this appears to be the main nesting material used by hedgehogs in that type of habitat. They seem to overcome its disadvantages (not being very weatherproof) by nesting in burrows, dry stone walls and other sheltered spots. The gardens also often have dense hedges as windbreaks, offering shelter below. One of my correspondents in Shetland suggested that mild winters reduced the challenge of hibernation and all of the winter nests found there were made of grass, even where a few fallen leaves were available (willow or perhaps sycamore). Hibernacula were also found in haystacks and dry stone walls (John McKee, pers. comm. 1989).

The importance of secure and protective winter nests has led to the suggestion that artificial nesting boxes would be helpful in supporting hedgehogs. A variety of designs are available, some of them quite elaborate and expensive. They range from a simple tent-like shelter made from stiff plastic sheeting that can be slid under a hedge or shed, to massive wooden or ceramic structures that cost a substantial amount. Unfortunately nobody has yet purchased sufficient nest boxes to do a properly arranged comparative study of their effectiveness. They will certainly do no harm and they do help get the message across that winter nesting opportunities are a key ecological requirement for hedgehogs wherever they live. They are even used by hedgehogs, sometimes as breeding nests, but also during the winter. It is important to realise the way that a natural nest is made, shuffling around inside a pile of loose leaves, otherwise there is a danger of providing a nesting chamber that is too large and its roof too high to hold down the leaves and prevent them being scattered loosely. It is also not really necessary to buy an expensive structure. The hedgehog will build its own for free provided that suitable leaves and support are available, and both can be easily provided at minimal cost.

AROUSAL FROM HIBERNATION

Although wild hedgehogs are less often found outside the nest during the winter, activity has been recorded in freezing conditions, even at –7°C, so hibernation is not a continuous, unbroken event. They normally wake up several times during the winter, generally about every 7 to 11 days, even if they are not disturbed. During these periodic arousals, they may leave their nest and move to another one, but usually they remain in the same nest before drifting back into hibernation. Even under controlled conditions and optimum ambient temperatures (4–5°C) in the laboratory, they wake up periodically and spend only 80 per cent of the winter in deep hibernation; even less if they are made to hibernate at 10°C. During the arousal periods, hedgehogs may take some food and water, but they don't necessarily have to do so. It is not clear why these periodic arousals occur, although they seem to be a common feature of all hibernating species. Waking up for only three or four hours consumes the energy equivalent of several days in undisturbed hibernation, a significant cost in terms of fat consumption, so there must be some sort of benefit. Periodic arousals occur even in conditions of constant darkness and constant temperature, so maybe there is a kind of internal biological clock that triggers arousal. But why? It might be that the accumulation of waste products (urea, for example) or metabolic water in the blood creates a need to regenerate the circulation briefly and restore equilibrium (Fig. 156).

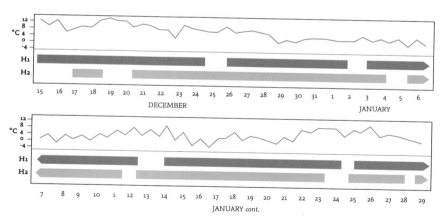

FIG 156. Hibernation is not an unbroken event, but comprised of bouts of physiological inactivity separated by brief periods of normal body temperature that become shorter during the depths of winter. Patterns of hibernation in two hedgehogs (H1 and H2, coloured bars), with arousal gaps in between bouts of inactivity. Red line indicates ambient temperature.

Full arousal takes two to five hours in the laboratory, longer in natural outdoor conditions. During the arousal periods, the hedgehog usually remains inactive with its eyes still closed and with a low body temperature. Initial warming is by heat produced from the metabolism of brown fat, but once the heart begins to speed up, this too generates heat and the blood become warmer and less viscous and is more easily pumped around the body. As the body temperature rises above 15°C, glucose turnover increases as carbohydrate metabolism is re-established. The hedgehog slowly warms up, the thorax and anterior regions first, its eyes begin to open and it starts shivering. When its temperature reaches about 28–30°C, the animal may start to walk about in an unsteady fashion, but most arousal incidents end with the hedgehog going back into hibernation without moving from its hibernaculum. Helge Walhovd (1979b) detected 54 over-winter arousals, none of which involved departure from the nest. Individuals had 12–18 arousals overwinter, at intervals of 3–15 days. Each period of arousal lasted an average of 34–48 hours, with the longest bouts of deep hibernation in January and February. Arousals did not occur at any particular time of day and appeared to be triggered by some kind of endogenous factor, although it is not clear what that might have been. Periodic arousals draw heavily on stored fat reserves and about 85 per cent of all the energy consumed during the whole hibernation period will be used during these short periods of awakening. A single arousal incident lasting only a few hours uses about the same amount of stored energy as several days in hibernation (Tähti & Soivio, 1977), so it is important that hedgehogs should not be disturbed unnecessarily during the winter.

People expect hedgehogs to be hibernating in the winter and so when they are seen active, it results in excited stories in the newspapers or on TV. For example, November 1994 was the mildest since records had begun, a full 3°C above average, and sure enough during that month there were claims made on television about hedgehogs being spotted wandering about instead of being fast asleep in hibernation. This winter behaviour was assumed to be harmful and abnormal. Some asserted that the animals would be a risk later because they had not hibernated at the proper time. Sundry experts happy to court publicity warned that something nasty was afoot, although no evidence was offered in support of these ideas. Reporters who telephoned me were reluctant to accept that there was no story here because to them it seemed there must be (because it was on TV!). Activity in winter is perfectly normal. A quarter of a century previously, I had analysed some 992 sightings and records of hedgehogs killed on the roads in London. This revealed that hedgehogs are active throughout the year with no less than 11.3 per cent of the total records coming from November and December, even as late as Christmas Day. In the three coldest months, January to March inclusive,

32 animals (more than 3 per cent) were recorded. These data were collected between 1956 and 1964, long before the widespread concern about global warming. Hedgehogs were out and about in the cold regardless. (See Fig. 101, p. 98). An almost identical pattern of records has been found in Carmarthenshire (Lucas, 1997) and several other counties for which details have been published (Essex: Dobson, 1999; Derbyshire: Mallon *et al.*, 2012; Wiltshire: Dillon, 1997). The same pattern was also evident in the first atlas of British mammals (Arnold, 1993), which shows from 1960 to 1992 inclusive that approximately 6 per cent of the 1,688 recorded hedgehog road casualties were from the last ten weeks of the year (i.e. after late October) and a few records came even from January and February. Winter activity is not freakish at all. Laboratory studies in Germany and Scandinavia show that hedgehogs wake up regularly during hibernation about once every week or so even when the temperature is kept constant. There is nothing exceptional about hedgehogs being sporadically active in winter; it's normal, and perhaps necessary, behaviour.

HIBERNATION DATES AND DURATION

The length of a hedgehog's hibernation varies according to its size, the climate and to some extent on its sex and condition. In northern Europe, they may hibernate for more than 200 days, from October to April (Rautio *et al.*, 2013b), even up to eight months (240 days) in eastern Finland, leaving little time to do very much else. In Denmark, the period spent in hibernation can range from 129 to 178 days, with ambient temperatures ranging from –11 to +13°C. In Britain, hedgehogs may well remain fully active in October and even into November, and those that survive hibernation are usually up and about by the end of April. So hibernation in Britain normally lasts about 150 to 180 days. The period of winter inactivity is progressively reduced and more variable further south in Europe. In the mild climate of North Island, New Zealand, three quarters of the hedgehogs may not hibernate at all, although more than half do so in the harsher climate of South Island. So hibernation is a flexible form of behaviour, not a deterministic one.

Some of my hedgehogs in Bushy Park had emerged from their winter nests by mid-April, but most did not do so until later that month. Up in the Hebrides, Digger Jackson found that sub-adult animals (previous year's young) emerged from hibernation before the adults and suffered a high mortality rate. Half of them (10 out of 20) were found dead within the month or were never seen again, as though they had barely survived hibernation and then died soon after emergence, physiologically exhausted (Jackson, 2006). Perhaps the losses were caused by shortage of food early in the season. Certainly, the overwintered sub-adults often appear skinny and weak at this time of year. In Denmark, a similar situation was reported where young animals emerged first, but they enjoyed a high survival rate and fed voraciously with rapid gains in body mass, presumably aided by abundant food (Jensen, 2004).

There was evidence that Digger Jackson's Uist hedgehogs had responded not so much to reaching a particular temperature on one day, but to exceeding a threshold temperature for several consecutive days and it was this that initiated emergence from hibernation (Jackson, 2006). Two hedgehogs returned to a torpid state in their nest during a bout of cold weather (i.e. 'went back into hibernation'), confirming that this can occur, with all that this implies for disrupting gestation as speculated in Chapter 7. Jensen found a similar situation with her Danish hedgehogs.

A large number of careful scientific studies, and even just casual observations, make it clear that hibernation is not the simple, inflexible interlude in a hedgehog's life that is often supposed. Mild weather may delay entry into hibernation and can also elicit premature arousal. Moreover young animals (particularly those born in the late litters of September and October) may remain fully active into December, no doubt seeking to accumulate sufficient fat reserves to ensure survival during the rest of the winter. Meanwhile the adult hedgehogs will have begun to hibernate. While the sex ratio among juveniles in the autumn is almost 1:1 (46 per cent males), among the adults 75 per cent are females, probably because activity among the males declines as they become more predisposed to hibernate and do so earlier than the females. Males would have had several months since the peak of the breeding season in which to accumulate fat reserves. In September, the average body weight for adult males is already over 900 g (females average about 100 g less). They are thus fully prepared for hibernation quite early in the autumn. By contrast, the females have had a strenuous time producing and weaning at least one litter and will have had little opportunity to build up fat reserves. In particular, females that have had late litters in particular may still be lactating, even as late as October or November (i.e. actually *losing* fat). Consequently, one expects proportionately greater activity among the adult females during autumn as they strive to feed intensively before hibernating and this probably accounts for their dominating the autumn sample and will cause them to enter hibernation, on average, somewhat later than the adult males. Again, this emphasises the fact that the onset of hibernation is not a sudden and precisely timed event, but consists of more and more animals spending a smaller and smaller proportion of their time active, until most of the population spend most of their time hypothermic in their hibernacula.

Age, sex and the weather all appear to influence the timing of these events, so climatic differences between different parts of Britain could modify the hibernation cycle and make generalisations regarding the hibernation period inappropriate for the country as a whole. To test this idea, I compared the monthly distribution of dated records from different parts of Britain, on the assumption that the number of hedgehogs recorded by observers (including animals seen alive or killed on the road) is roughly proportional to the size of the active hedgehog population at a given time.

Four sets of records were used from clearly separate regions:

1. East Anglia: 445 dated observations made by members of the Norfolk and Norwich Naturalists' Society. Most relate to Norfolk and Suffolk.
2. South West England: 144 records collected from Somerset, Dorset, Devon and Cornwall for use in the Mammal Society's Distribution Scheme of the 1970s.
3. Scotland: 122 similar Mammal Society records from many areas north of the border.
4. London: 992 records from the files of the London Natural History Society, covering a 20-mile radius based upon St. Paul's Cathedral.

Taking monthly totals and expressing them as cumulative percentages of the year's records (i.e. what percentage of the total number of hedgehogs has been recorded by a particular month), a general trend became clear (Table 17). Whereas 42 per cent of the year's hedgehogs had been seen by June in the mild South West of England, only 34 per cent had been recorded by then in London and 32 per cent in East Anglia. It was a further month before Scotland's hedgehog population seemed to achieve a comparable level of activity. Apparently, Scottish hedgehogs do not end their hibernation period until about a month later than elsewhere, and the level of activity in the southwestern population is well in advance of the rest of the country. Although individual hedgehogs may be out of hibernation at any time in any of the regions, the general trend seemed to be for inactivity to be prolonged in proportion to latitude and the coldness of the winter. The same principle appears to apply across northern Europe, with hibernation beginning earlier and lasting longer in the more northerly regions. A similar principle also applies to first flowering dates for many plants, with Scotland being about a month behind southern England.

This little study was sufficiently encouraging that large numbers of volunteers were asked to send in dated records for early sightings of hedgehogs

TABLE 17. Comparison of cumulative percentages of hedgehog records for four regions of Britain. Unfortunately larger samples of observations failed to substantiate the regional differences.

	Scotland (per cent)	East Anglia (per cent)	London (per cent)	South West (per cent)
January	0	1.3	0.5	0.7
February	0.8	2.0	1.4	2.8
March	0.8	3.6	3.3	5.6
April	5.7	7.0	8.8	23.4
May	15.5	18.4	21.6	36.2
June	26.2	32.2	33.8	41.7
July	39.2	46.9	49.9	56.3
August	56.7	59.9	67.6	75.7
September	85.2	74.3	78.8	83.3
October	92.4	83.0	88.6	92.3
November	98.2	93.8	95.3	95.8
December	100.0	100.0	100.0	100.0
Total no. of records	122	445	992	144

in order to boost the sample size and perhaps get a more definitive description of the effects of latitude and climate. Unfortunately, that achieved the exact opposite result! Despite having a much larger sample of observations, spread across three years (2012–14 inclusive), no statistically significant difference was found between the north and south of Britain. Maybe those were just three strange years, unusually warm everywhere. Maybe we should try once more. Maybe the hedgehogs were just being perverse (again!). Anyway it does mean that there is no satisfactory evidence-based answer to the question of how climate affects the timing of hibernation in British hedgehogs.

HIBERNATION IS A LIFE FOCUSED ON FAT

Even though it is not active, the hibernating hedgehog still needs energy to keep its metabolism ticking over at a minimal level. Energy is stored in the form of fat and some hedgehogs may double their weight as they fatten up during a few weeks in the autumn, at least in captivity, representing an average daily weight

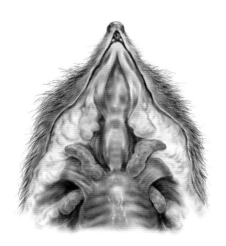

FIG 157. During the autumn, hedgehogs build up large reserves of white fat to keep them going over winter. They also need the lobes of brown fat around their shoulders to generate the necessary heat to restore normal levels of body warmth and activity. (Guy Troughton)

gain of more than 5 g. White fat (actually often rather yellowish) is the main storage tissue that supplies the energy needed for general body maintenance. It is principally deposited under the skin and around the mesenteries of the gut. A well-provisioned adult hedgehog may have a massive layer of fat under its spiny skin that can be over a centimetre thick, a long-term energy supply that is enough to keep it going for many weeks in hibernation. White fat cells contain large droplets of fat and little else. It is these fat droplets that form an efficient and compact store, yielding large amounts of energy for every gram of tissue. The fat globules displace the cell nucleus to one side so that under the microscope white fat cells look like empty frothy bubbles.

Unlike white fat, which occurs among many species of animals, brown fat is a special adipose tissue found particularly in hibernators, and whereas white fat is widely dispersed in the body, most of the brown fat forms two large lobes alongside the chest and over the shoulders. These lobes used to be described as the 'hibernating gland' because they were so prominent in species that hibernate. In a well-stocked hedgehog at the onset of hibernation, its brown fat lobes will be at their largest size and may constitute up to 3 per cent of the animal's total body weight. Their mass will have reduced by half in January and the lobes are virtually invisible in mid-summer. Actually the brown fat lobes are not glands at all, but their cells are crammed full of tiny orange-coloured mitochondria which give the lobes their distinctive colour. The orange colour gradually darkens as the fat is used up.

Mitochondria are the powerhouse of the cell, responsible for metabolising stored fat, and in the brown fat lobes this serves to generate heat. Here, the cells store fat in the form of tiny droplets which can be quickly metabolised, making the energy they contain more rapidly accessible than would be possible from the larger droplets present in white fat. The 'furnaces' of the brown fat lobes seem to be controlled by the sympathetic nervous system, responding to sensors in the hypothalamus of the brain. Anatomically, the lobes of brown fat are located in exactly the area that needs to be warmed first and fast during arousal from hibernation. Heat production in the brown fat lobes lying alongside the thorax warms the nearby heart and enables it to speed up its action, generating more heat by its own activity and pumping blood more forcibly to distribute warmth around the body.

Although it is the brown fat that fires up first, it is the subsequent contraction of limb and body muscles that generates most of the additional warmth needed to get the animal working again. The main purpose of skeletal muscle contraction is of course to make the limbs move, but muscular contraction always generates a lot of heat as a by-product, one of the principal reasons why warm-blooded mammals having such a high body temperature. When the limb muscles contract repeatedly, but without causing the animal to move about, we call it 'shivering' and it is this non-locomotory muscle action that generates most of the heat needed to raise the hibernating hedgehog's body temperature to normal active levels. During arousal, fat is mobilised quickly to raise the body's temperature from about 5°C to the normal working level of around 35°C. As the tissues warm, the muscles become less viscous and can operate more easily. At that stage, the hedgehog might begin to move about in a cautious, staggering gait, but it will take ten minutes or more to be capable of even unsteady movement, and normal activity may not resume for well over an hour.

WEIGHT LOSS DURING HIBERNATION

Fat is a vital component of the hedgehog's body, but fat reserves are depleted during hibernation and the animals usually lose a lot of weight over winter. Estimates vary at around 25 per cent of its total body mass in England and 20–40 per cent in Sweden. An average weight loss of 40 per cent or more was reported in Finland, but this was after 160–170 days of hibernation, rather longer than hedgehogs normally hibernate in Britain, and also under captive conditions (Kristoffersson & Suomalainen, 1964). In southern Ireland, Amy Haigh found a mean hibernation duration of 148.9 days, during which her wild hedgehogs had lost an average of 17 per cent of their autumn mass by the time they emerged in March (Haigh et al., 2012b).

Measures of daily weight loss by captive hibernating hedgehogs are fairly consistent at around 0.2–0.3 per cent of body weight. This would be equivalent to consuming 1.2–1.8 g per day or 180–270 g in five months of hibernation for a hedgehog weighing 600 g (about 35–40 per cent of its autumnal mass). But this is in captive conditions where fat consumption may be higher than in the wild, depending upon ambient temperatures and levels of disturbance.

How much fat do hedgehogs need over winter?

Before commencing hibernation, the hedgehog's body must contain sufficient white and brown fat to support it throughout the likely period of hibernation that it faces. This usually means about four to five months in Britain, at least from December until the end of March. There is a clear implication that the animal must reach a critical minimum body mass before hibernating or risk death by starvation during the oncoming winter as its fat reserves become depleted. This is not just a subject of academic interest, but also a matter of considerable anxiety to the many people concerned about hedgehog welfare and survival. Small hedgehogs are often found in the autumn, many of them wandering about in daylight, leading to a worry that they may be too small to survive the increasingly cold nights and the challenges of several months in hibernation. Many hundreds of these animals, even thousands, are taken to the RSPCA and other wildlife hospitals so that they may be fed well during the winter and released when the weather improves in the spring.

The actual amount of weight loss in a full winter will vary with body size, ambient temperature and the number of times the animal wakes up. Andy Wroot's studies of hedgehog energetics revealed that an adult hibernating hedgehog might consume an average of about 1 g of fat per day. A decent sized adult hedgehog weighing about 600 g or so therefore might need about 130–150 g to keep it going over winter roughly equivalent to nearly a quarter of its body mass the previous autumn. Clearly a juvenile weighing only 200 g or so in October is unlikely to last the winter. But how fat is fat enough?

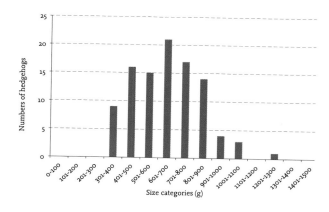

FIG 158. Distribution of actual body weights of 105 hedgehogs in March–April after they have survived the winter.

One way to answer this question is to look at the body weights of hedgehogs that actually do survive the winter. I weighed a sample of 105 hedgehogs obtained in March and April, at the end of the hibernation period and before significant weight gains were likely (Morris, 1984). They included some when they were first seen active and others that had been killed by gamekeepers or road traffic (Fig. 158). A few found dead in their hibernacula were also included because they had at least survived until March. They also provide some, though not all, of the smallest body weights in the sample. It is possible to estimate what all of these animals had weighed the previous autumn by allowing for the percentage of their body weight that would have been lost over winter as their fat reserves were used up. Studies of hibernating ground squirrels suggests that these lose about 28 per cent after 132 days of hibernation, and losses of 30–49 per cent have been reported for bats and small rodents hibernating for four to six months. Among several species of British bats, the weight loss in hibernation was 22–29 per cent (Stebbings, 1970). Comparable observations on wild hedgehogs are few, but average 20–25 per cent. A new study (still in progress) of free-living wild hedgehogs in Britain suggests a weight loss of around 27 per cent over winter (Lucy Bearman-Brown, pers comm.). It seems reasonable to conclude that British hedgehogs are likely to lose about a quarter of their autumnal body weight over winter. This also corresponds to Andy Wroot's energetics calculation mentioned above for an average adult hedgehog under captive conditions.

Based on the assumption that 20 per cent of body mass is lost over winter, the individual weights of those hedgehogs that survived until March or April can be multiplied by 100/75 to obtain an estimate of what their weight would have been before they began hibernating (Fig. 159). There were no survivors whose weight would have been less than 400 g in the autumn, so any hedgehogs that

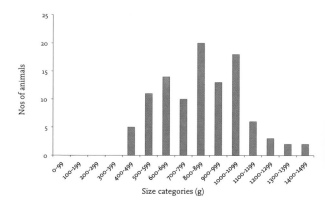

FIG 159. Estimated weights of that sample of 'survivors' the previous autumn, assuming a 25 per cent weight loss over winter. Notice that none of those that survived the winter had weighed less than 400 g before hibernating.

commence hibernation at less than this weight would not be expected to survive until the following season. As British winters vary in severity and duration, this figure represents a minimum and perhaps should be raised to about 450 g in order to guarantee sufficient fat reserves are available to enable survival under adverse conditions. This higher figure was widely publicised in the media as being both precautionary and also convenient as it corresponds to about 1 lb avoirdupois, the size of a jar of jam and an easy amount to imagine for those who were more familiar with pounds and ounces than newfangled decimal units. In reality, there will be considerable flexibility as both body weights and winters are highly variable. Basic principles suggest that large individuals should lose a lower percentage of body weight than small ones. Clearly there can be no single definitive figure, which will apply equally well to all hedgehogs in all years. Nevertheless, a figure of 450 g seems a reasonable estimate for the threshold below which survival is unlikely and above which there is a good chance of getting through a British winter. Many juvenile hedgehogs can grow to 500 g or more within eight to ten weeks, but those born after September probably have insufficient time to do so in the face of declining food availability as nights get colder. They will be at greatest risk and it is likely that comparatively few of these late-born young reach the necessary weight to survive the winter.

In the longer winters of Denmark, ten radio-tagged hedgehogs were monitored over winter (Jensen, 2004). Juveniles lost an average of 22.1 per cent of their weight, adult females 30.2 per cent and the minimum pre-hibernation body mass sufficient for survival was estimated to be 513 g. In southern Ireland, the climate is so mild that late-born juveniles were able to survive with a pre-hibernation body mass of only 175 g, perhaps because they were able to continue normal active life longer into the year, thereby reducing the length of time they needed to rely on fat in hibernation (Haigh et al., 2012b).

In New Zealand, hibernation begins when the ground temperature falls to about 10°C and juveniles need to reach 300 g for successful hibernation, at least in North Island. This would be fat enough for three months hibernation at 5°C. In the warmer frost-free areas they hibernate for only brief periods and sometimes not at all (Brockie, 1974a).

This matter became highly contentious when a paper was published which included the suggestion that a minimum weight of 600–650 g might be necessary for overwinter survival in Britain (Bunnell, 2002). This figure was widely publicised and discussed on social media, sometimes in rather intemperate terms. My figure of 450 g was described as 'not a valid figure', 'informed guesswork' (despite the evidence supplied) and 'out of date', and therefore implicitly wrong. Relying on this figure as the threshold above which hedgehogs would probably survive was criticised as being liable to condemn the many animals that weigh around 500 g to a needless death if they were not rescued. Many well-meaning hedgehog supporters went on to interpret the higher figure as a minimum, rather than optimum. They sought to 'rescue' hedgehogs weighing up to 700 g 'just to be on the safe side', thereby encouraging the capture of many animals that would survive perfectly well and removing adults from the population as well as juveniles. At least one public campaign was launched aimed at getting people to actively search for hedgehogs in the autumn and take in virtually all of them.

This controversy is important because if animals weighing more than 450 g are taken into captivity when they do not actually need to be rescued, they will use up resources at animal rescue centres. There will also be needless disruption to the animals' lives and in captivity there are unfamiliar stress factors and perhaps a risk of infection from animals kept nearby that may have contagious conditions. Rescuing larger animals than necessary is highly undesirable. So how did it come about that these two estimates of the minimum weight necessary to survive differed by so much? Close inspection of Toni Bunnell's paper suggests that her information was based on a study of about 25 animals kept in semi-captive conditions in a private garden and subject to varied conditions and levels of disturbance. At least some of them appear to have been supplied with food for at least some of the time, and some of them were kept indoors. If food is available, hedgehogs will often not hibernate properly, but remain at least partially active, even in cold weather. They are not in continuous hibernation, but active in ambient temperatures that are well below what they experience in the non-hibernation season. The result is 'partial hibernation', an unnatural and unhealthy state that probably involves loss of body heat and an inability to digest properly. In these unnatural circumstances hedgehogs often do not thrive.

More importantly, it is very evident from my studies of rehabilitated animals released into the wild (see Chapter 11) that hedgehogs in captivity are usually generously fed and get little exercise, so they put on large amounts of weight and become bigger than is normal for their age. They lose this excess weight very quickly when they are released into more natural conditions. Moreover disturbance during hibernation results in arousals and the consumption of fat. Many of Bunnell's animals were disturbed at least once during the winter. So all in all, it is not surprising that her semi-captive hedgehogs lost more weight than would be expected in normal wild animals.

It is possible to test the hypothesis that hedgehogs need to weigh 650 g in order to survive hibernation. If a hedgehog loses 20 per cent of its mass over winter, its weight will reduce by 130 g as fat reserves are consumed. This means

FIG 160. Large numbers of juvenile hedgehogs weighing less than 450 g are now being rescued and fed in captivity before being released, enhancing their chances of survival. Without such support, they would almost certainly have died before the end of winter.

that there should be no animals alive in March/April that weigh less than 520 g. That is simply not the case. I used data for animals collected in March, April and May (i.e. after hibernation), trapped or killed on the roads (to eliminate sick animals brought into care), and separated adults and juveniles, determined by one or both of two independent age determination methods (see Chapter 8). This identified a sample of 55 hedgehogs that had successfully overwintered for the first time and 68 adults that had hibernated at least twice.

Of the 19 juveniles ending their first winter in March/April, 10 (52 per cent) weighed less than 520g. They should have been dead according to Bunnell's prediction. Eight of those animals were still alive despite weighing over 100 g less than Bunnell's suggested minimum. Even in May, after a few weeks to fatten up, 16 of the 36 juveniles found that month (44 per cent) still weighed less than 520 g. Among the *adults* that had hibernated at least twice, 21 per cent were below the critical weight of 520 g in March/April and 11 per cent even in May, yet they had still survived. Assuming that hedgehogs lose 25 per cent of their weight, instead of 20 per cent, makes little difference to these figures. At this higher rate of estimated weight loss, a 650 g hedgehog would lose 162.5 g and none should be alive next spring weighing less than 488 g. In fact, more than half the surviving juveniles in my sample were smaller than that. (See also size data in Chapter 3, p. 61, Fig. 69; also Fig. 158).

Samples of hedgehogs weighed in spring include many that are quite tiny, well under 500 g, and some successfully reach the end of winter and are still alive, even though they weigh less than 350 g. No single universal figure can be calculated that will fit every year, every animal and every place. It will vary anyway, not least because of variable ambient temperatures and the frequency of arousal during the winter, so there cannot be a definitive figure, only an estimate that can serve as a guide. But however you view these figures, it is clear that a substantial number of animals (perhaps even 52 per cent of juveniles!) weighing well below 650 g before hibernation can and do survive the winter. The prediction that they must weigh at least that amount is demonstrably incorrect. We are speaking here only of the minimum weights below which survival is unlikely (although still not impossible). It must also not be forgotten that reaching a threshold weight in autumn, whatever it is, will not guarantee survival. Some will die anyway.

This issue remains a matter of contention and is of considerable concern to hedgehog carers and also to the RSPCA and managers of animal hospitals. To clarify the debate and reduce the confusion, in 2015 a meeting was held with the BHPS, the British Wildlife Rehabilitation Council, the RSPCA and one of the larger wildlife hospitals (Vale, in Gloucestershire). They put their names to a joint statement on this matter, making the key points (see Box 2).

Another way of looking at this whole question is to mark some animals in the autumn and record their weight, then see which of them are still alive the following spring. The survivors can be weighed to see how much weight they had lost and what proportion managed to survive the winter. Although this idea seems sensible enough, it is beset with a number of practical difficulties. Nevertheless, with the help of some volunteers recruited through the BHPS, I had a total of 17 garden hedgehogs marked in the autumn. Eleven of these were seen again after the winter, suggesting a minimum survival rate of 65 per cent, which is pretty good. About half of those that died had weighed less than 450 g in the autumn, although one survived to March even though it had weighed only 370 g the previous November before it hibernated.

At 35 per cent, the overall mortality rate among these 17 garden hedgehogs is about what I would have expected. It is also similar to the mortality rate observed in a study of garden hedgehogs in Sweden and very close to the 28 per cent mortality rate among a sample of hedgehogs kept from October until May

BOX 2. Some basic facts and principles agreed in discussion with the BHPS, BWRC, RSPCA, and wildlife carers

People were actively looking for healthy hedgehogs and collecting any that were under 600 g to take into care before the onset of hibernation. Acting with best intentions, people can sometimes cause welfare problems. Actions should be based on scientific evidence, not personal hunches, no matter how experienced a hedgehog carer might be.

- It is important to distinguish between wild hedgehogs and captive-reared animals, particularly with respect to body weights in the autumn.
- Most wild hedgehogs that hibernate at less than 450 g will probably not survive, although some occasionally do.
- Greater weight will probably reduce the likelihood of dying, but it is not essential. Hedgehogs can, and mostly do, survive winter weighing substantially less than 600 g.
- They should normally be rescued at weights less than 450 g in October to February; 'rescue' at 500+ g is unnecessary and potentially harmful.
- 'Rescue' at weights above 600 g in the autumn, based on weight alone, is counter-productive and strongly discouraged. Bringing a healthy hedgehog in to a rescue centre will be stressful to the animal and carries additional survival risks.
- Hedgehogs held in captivity put on weight quickly compared to their wild counterparts of similar age, sometimes reaching double their natural weight. They shed this excess on release and thus lose weight faster than wild hedgehogs. To allow for this, captive-reared hedgehogs should not be released at weights below 500 g in the early autumn, 600 g in very late autumn. Excessive weight is probably not beneficial and may be harmful.
- Body weight is not the only criterion of health. If a hedgehog is active during the day or it appears ill or injured at any time of year, it should be given veterinary care.
- No specific weight will guarantee survival for hibernating hedgehogs.

in outdoor cages in Denmark. The survival rate of those Danish hedgehogs was highest among adult-sized hedgehogs; smaller specimens with initial body weights between 200 g and 440 g all died (Walhovd, 1979a).

The evidence suggests that British hedgehogs need to weigh 450 g to enjoy a reasonable chance of surviving hibernation. They might be better off if they were fatter, but it is not essential. Clearly there are also other factors to consider, including injury and disease, that will compromise survival whatever an animal's weight. Relatively few hedgehogs reach 650 g in their first year and the species has survived for millions of years without having most of its juveniles 'rescued' because they had not reached that weight by October. Using an excessively high cut-off weight will result in taking large numbers of animals into captivity that would probably have survived anyway. This has serious welfare and cost implications and could be considered irresponsible.

CONCLUSION

Hibernation is a major event in the hedgehog's calendar. It involves substantial seasonal physiological changes, whereas typical mammals like guinea pigs and humans are physiologically constant all year round. Hibernation is not simply a failure to maintain a warm-blooded state by a primitive mammal, but a profound physiological adjustment to minimise energy consumption in the face of a restricted food supply during the winter. Despite a drastically lowered body temperature, the hedgehog's heart and nerves remain functional. Normal metabolic processes for releasing energy from carbohydrates are replaced by systems based on the metabolism of fat, large reserves of which need to accumulate in the body during the autumn. Hedgehogs lose about a quarter of their body mass as these reserves are consumed over winter and normally need to weigh 450 g in order to be fat enough to survive. The onset of hibernation is triggered by a combination of low temperatures and limited food supply, but there are frequent periods of arousal over winter during which the animal may leave its hibernaculum and construct another nest. Many published statements relating to the hibernation period of the hedgehog convey the impression that hibernation in this species is unbroken, of fixed duration, and has relatively consistent dates of commencement and termination, but the whole process is highly flexible and arousal in winter is both frequent and normal. Hedgehogs are critically dependent upon their winter nest to provide physical protection and also as a buffer against temperature changes, so that the hibernating animal is kept at around 4°C, the optimum at which metabolism and fat consumption are minimised. The availability of suitable sites and materials for the vital hibernaculum may be an important factor limiting the hedgehog's geographical distribution and its success in some habitats. This implies that conservation measures need to focus not just on behaviour and activity during the summer months, but also take account of the hedgehog's needs in hibernation, which may occupy one third of its entire life.

CHAPTER 7

More Activity: Reproduction

THE HEDGEHOG HAS 48 CHROMOSOMES (Searle & Erskine, 1985) and the sex ratio, as in other mammals, is genetically determined, so there are normally equal numbers of males and females. This is the case with nestlings and juveniles that have not yet bred for the first time. However, among the adults, there is often a significant preponderance of males among those found in the spring and early summer, but the observed sex ratio changes to a preponderance of females in the autumn. This is due to seasonal changes in behaviour that affect the probability of being caught or found dead (See Chapter 5). Unusually, Digger Jackson found 1.8 males per female in late summer among hedgehogs in the Uists and attributed the relative scarcity of females to a higher mortality rate associated with many of them attempting to rear two litters in the season (Jackson, 2007).

Male and female hedgehogs look much the same, although many 'experts' will insist that they can tell the difference by the animal's bulk, head shape or another similarly subjective feature. This has some appeal because it allows gender recognition without the need to disturb the animal by catching it and picking it up. However, unless you actually check, you cannot be certain because the only reliable way of telling the sexes apart is by inspection of their underside. The animals will rarely permit this without rolling up, so sexing hedgehogs requires them to be caught and then persuaded to uncurl. Most will do so if they are held in gloved hands and gently bounced and shuffled so that the animal puts out its nose and forefeet to steady itself. With those on one hand and gently getting the hind feet extended on to the other, it is then possible to stretch the animal with its back pressed against your chest. Doing this will get most hedgehogs to unroll sufficiently to allow their belly to be examined. The

FIG 161. The difficulty with sexing hedgehogs lies in getting them to unroll sufficiently to inspect their underside. Females have two openings (anus and vagina) lying close together.

female's vagina opens just in front of the anus, with less than a centimetre separating the two (Fig. 161). The male has a conspicuous penis sheath that opens in the middle of the belly, several centimetres in front of the anus and about where one might expect to see a navel (Fig. 162). There is no scrotum in the male as primitive mammals like the hedgehog retain their testes within the abdomen throughout life; they do not become conspicuous in the breeding season as they do in rodents, for example. Nor do they reside in an external scrotum all year round like those of many more evolutionarily advanced mammals in which an external pouch for the testes is often said to be a special adaptation, keeping them cool and ensuring more efficient sperm production. Both sexes may have up to five pairs of nipples visible among the coarse hair of the belly, but they are often rather inconspicuous in the male. In females, especially those that are lactating to feed their young, the nipples are more prominent and often the surrounding skin is pinkish in colour.

The female reproductive system is anatomically similar to that of most other eutherian (placental) mammals. There is a marked seasonal cycle in the development of the reproductive tract, which doubles in weight during the breeding season (and becomes bigger still during pregnancy, of course), then shrinks rapidly in the autumn. Similarly the mammary glands reduce to insignificance during the winter, but enlarge again in late pregnancy the following season. Unlike some mammals, hedgehogs do not ovulate in response to copulation and giving birth does not stimulate a post-partum oestrous. Instead, they are spontaneous ovulators, experiencing a succession of oestrous cycles as the breeding season progresses, each lasting about seven to ten days. This means that the male has to identify females and try to mate with those that are 'in season' at the

FIG 162. In males, the penis is where you would expect the navel to be, normally at least 2–3 cm in front of the anus.

right stage in one of those cycles. That may be the purpose of the extended courtship rituals discussed below.

The structure of the male reproductive system is also similar to other mammals except that the hedgehog's accessory reproductive organs can reach a state of flamboyant development unrivalled by any other species. A normal pair of hedgehog testes generally weighs barely 5 g. Whilst these and the penis remain more or less the same size all year round, a massive increase in the size of the male accessory glands takes place in the spring, dwarfing the testes (Allanson, 1934). The most prominent structures are a pair of huge pinkish seminal vesicles that lie either side of the bladder, with an orange prostate gland alongside and a pair of white Cowper's glands beside the urethra at the base of the penis. Even these are larger than the actual testes in an adult male that is fully sexually active (Fig. 163).

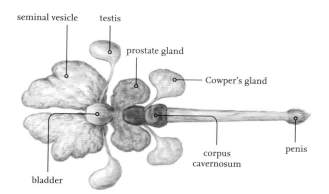

seminal vesicle testis
prostate gland
Cowper's gland
corpus cavernosum
penis
bladder

FIG 163. The male reproductive organs become extraordinarily enlarged in the spring, especially the pink seminal vesicles. (Guy Troughton)

Spermatogenesis continues from April until late August, when the testes rapidly regress until they begin showing signs of activity again early in the new year. The seminal vesicles undergo a tenfold increase in size within a few weeks of ending hibernation. They secrete a fluid with crystalline inclusions consisting of glycolipids and mucoproteins that show intense acid phosphatase activity, but it is unclear what significance this has. The whole assemblage of reproductive apparatus may reach 10 per cent of the total body weight in some of the older males (yearling males are less well endowed), all the more remarkable, since the function of this complex apparatus is obscure. It has been suggested that at least some of these glands might secrete fluids containing pheromones (chemical stimulants) which are liberated during the lengthy courtship process and serve to make the female more receptive to a male's advances (Poduschka, 1977). Even if that is true, it is hard to see why they need to be so big. Some mammals have large accessory glands that produce fluids which congeal inside the female to form a vaginal plug after mating, effectively sealing in a male's sperm so that subsequent matings by rival males are prevented from achieving successful fertilisation of the female's eggs. Vaginal plugs are not found in hedgehogs, although the copious gooey secretions from a male's glands may serve a similar purpose. It has been suggested that another possible function of these secretions from the male's massive accessory reproductive glands might be to deposit scent on the female to signify that she has already mated and deter other males from doing so, thereby achieving a genetic monopoly of the female's subsequent litter. If that is the idea, then it doesn't seem to work. A study of the DNA in mothers and their young found evidence of multiple paternity: in two out of only five litters examined, the family had more than one father (Moran *et al.*, 2009). This shows that whatever the accessory glands may do to seal off access to a female's eggs after mating is not very effective. By late August, all of the male hedgehog's accessory reproductive organ complex has regressed, almost to the point of invisibility, and remains quiescent over winter.

THE BREEDING SEASON

Some young hedgehogs might reach sexual maturity at an age of nine months, and in captivity both sexes are sometimes capable of breeding within their first summer. This is unlikely to happen in the wild, where nine months old is too late to breed successfully in that season, even for one born as early as April. Reproductive organs regress over winter so nothing useful can be done until the following year. This means that a wild hedgehog will not normally breed for the first time until it is about eleven months old or more, but it can then continue seasonally for the rest of its life, even at an age of five or six years old. On South Uist, all the females attempted to breed and at least 96 per cent of those adults that were found early in the season became pregnant, leading to births from late May into June. However, most sub-adults (i.e. those born the previous year) did not breed until later in the season and more than a third of them did not breed at all until their third calendar year (Jackson, 2006). That could also be the norm elsewhere, overlooked because previous studies had used different methods to arrive at their conclusions. One Uist female that did not breed in her second calendar year as a sub-adult went on to have two litters in her third summer and another two litters in her fourth. On the mainland of Britain, older females also appear able to breed well into their fifth or sixth year. In captivity, the majority of breeding females seem to weigh 700 g or more, but wild hedgehogs will certainly breed at a smaller size, although few will do so at a body weight less than about 500 g. Even under captive conditions, hedgehogs were said not to breed in their second calendar year unless they had been very well fed during the previous winter instead of hibernating (Edwards, 1957). In both sexes, the mean weights of reproductive organs increase seasonally and regress over winter, but cumulatively become larger with increasing age (Morris, 1969). This is in line with the suggestion that successful breeding is mostly accomplished by animals in their third summer or older.

With wild hedgehogs, there are signs of activity in the sexual organs of both males and females even during the late winter whilst hibernation is still in progress. The active breeding season then begins more or less as soon as hibernation ends, but that is not a fixed date and varies a lot depending on the weather. Well fed in

TABLE 18. Weights (g) of the male reproductive complex during the spring (April–June inclusive) in young and old male hedgehogs showing a progressive increase in size (From Morris, 1969).

Age	Mean weight (g)	Range (g)
1st summer (juveniles) Collected July–November inclusive.	1.9	0.45–3.56
2nd summer	16.3	4.0–38.9
3rd summer	23.9	6.9–44.3
4th summer	24.0	8.1–42.3
5th summer	25.9	25.0–26.6
6th summer	34.0	33.7–34.5
7th summer	42.3	42.3

captivity, they may become sexually active weeks earlier than they would in the wild, especially when confronted by inclement weather. There is much flexibility, but active production of sperm in the males can start as early as March and is normally fully under way in April. It continues until about August, after which males cease to be sexually active. The presence of sperm inside females in April shows that they commence breeding activities as soon as possible after emerging from hibernation. Some hedgehogs must be capable of breeding very early as there are occasional records of babies being born in April, but the main birth season is May and June.

With some animals, particularly colonially nesting birds, social stimulation among the colony ensures that matings are synchronised, so that the breeding season begins and ends for the majority of individuals within a very tightly defined period of time. Among some mammals, synchrony among breeding females can be brought about by pheromones wafted on the air (the 'Bruce effect'), and a German biologist, Walter Poduschka, claimed to have observed this phenomenon in his captive colony of hedgehogs. But captives live in close proximity and there are generally several in the same room. There is no evidence of pheromone-induced interactions like this among hedgehogs in the wild. Each one does its own thing at a time determined by its own individual inclination and state of reproductive development.

The most detailed analysis of the reproductive organs in female hedgehogs was carried out by Ruth Deanesly in the 1930s. She was able to confirm that some females are pregnant as late as September. Nestling young are occasionally reported as late as October and these late litters may represent a second family for those mothers who have lost an earlier one due to an accident or predation (Deanesly, 1934). After a litter is removed from a female in captivity, she is highly fertile and mates again almost immediately (Morris & Steel, 1967). Second litters are also possible where a female gave birth and reared a family early in the season and is now breeding again, but only one of Deanesly's 18 pregnant animals had actually given birth to a previous litter that season, confirming that two litters per season is possible but infrequent. Second litters were also found among females on the Uists (Jackson, 2006). Oestrous is suppressed during lactation, so we do not find hedgehogs shortening the time between births by raising a family whilst also being pregnant with the next litter.

Baby hedgehogs born in second litters are likely to leave the nest so late in the season that few will survive anyway, being unable to grow sufficiently fat before being overtaken by winter and the need for hibernation. In the course of my study of hibernacula in Bushy Park, I found 20 hedgehogs dead in their winter nest. Of these, 18 (90 per cent) still had their last lower deciduous premolar present, so they were only a few weeks old (see Chapter 8) and were evidence of failure to survive hibernation by late-born young. Late litters must therefore be regarded as potential rather than actual additions to the population. Their contribution to boosting numbers is likely to be minimal except when the autumn is very mild and extends well into October and November, allowing more time to fatten up before hibernating.

Late litters may also result from some of the previous year's young females entering hibernation at a low body weight and needing part of the following summer to build up sufficient body condition before they can breed. Deanesly found several animals that had not mated for the first time until as late as June. Late-born litters face the difficulty of growing and fattening sufficiently to survive the winter, but in the mild climate of North Island, New Zealand, where hibernation is brief or dispensed with altogether, the breeding season is effectively extended and allows time for some females to have two or even three litters in a year. A third litter is also possible in the benign conditions of captivity. By contrast, in Scandinavia, winters are longer and the brief summer allows time for only a single litter each year. In Denmark and Sweden, second litters are unknown. This conforms to a principle that where higher latitudes mean a shorter breeding season, animals will produce bigger litters but less frequently. Swedish hedgehogs have an average litter size at six weeks old of 5.2, compared with 3.7 in Britain, a difference that is statistically significant. In effect, Scandinavian hedgehogs have given up the possible advantage of having a second litter in favour of breeding later with a larger family. Abandoning the second litter by ceasing to breed as early as June in favour of the offspring being better prepared for northern winters may be a decisive factor in allowing this species to spread so far north in the Baltic countries. All of which again shows how flexible the hedgehog can be and also how variable are its reproductive arrangements.

Although some British hedgehogs may come into breeding condition in April, pregnancies are not normally recorded before May and rarely as late as October (Table 19). Nestlings are therefore to be expected between May and the end of October. A nest with five young was found in London in April, implying successful mating in March, and an actual litter found in March has also been reported (Taylor-Page, 1964), but these are obviously exceptional and may even have been incorrectly recorded.

Hedgehogs need to get their breeding season started as soon as possible in order to allow their offspring enough time to grow and fatten up in advance of the next winter, but it is hard to know exactly what it is that triggers the necessary physiological preparations for reproduction or hibernation, a topic also discussed in Chapter 6. Many species are stimulated to breed by increasing daylength as the season progresses, but it is puzzling to see how this would work for nocturnal hedgehogs, especially as they are still in hibernation during the weeks leading up

TABLE 19. The number of pregnancies found per month in samples of wild hedgehogs totalling 73 pregnant females, all taken from Wales and southern England. A different pattern might be found further north. There is some evidence of second/late litters (see text). (* the figure in brackets is the number of females examined)

Source	May	June	July	Aug.	Sept.	Oct.
Deanesly (1934)	7	6	3	2	0	1
Morris, B. (1961)	11 (21)*	6 (15)	11 (27)	1 (4)	13 (25)	—
Morris, P. (1960s, unpublished data)	2	7	2	0	1	—
Total no. pregnancies	20	19	16	3	14	1
Per cent of 73 pregnant females	27	26	22	4	19	2

to the breeding season. On the other hand, hedgehogs experimentally subjected to additional illumination towards the end of winter showed some increase in gonadal development (Allanson & Deanesly, 1934), but that was under artificial conditions. Hormone levels (including melatonin) in the blood of hedgehogs kept in outdoor enclosures responded to changes in photoperiod (Fowler, 1988), although experimentally blinded male hedgehogs will complete hibernation and come into breeding condition in the following season in the normal way (Saboureau & Dutorné, 1981). It seems unlikely that changes in daylength, useful cues for many other animals, are the signal for the breeding season to begin in wild hedgehogs. Preparation for reproduction can occur as early as January, and it has been reported in other hibernators too, when they are inactive and inside a nest or burrow, making it difficult for them to monitor changes outside. Hibernation itself is not the trigger either, as hedgehogs kept warm and well fed over winter do not hibernate, but they still come into breeding condition at the normal time, or even a little earlier. This is further confirmation of flexibility in the hedgehog's behaviour in response to environmental conditions, contributing to its success over a wide geographical range of habitats.

COURTSHIP BEHAVIOUR

There is a well-worn joke which goes: Question: 'With all those spines, how do hedgehogs mate?' Answer: 'Carefully'. Actually this is not far from the truth. The pre-mating behaviour of hedgehogs is a long-drawn-out and noisy nocturnal ritual that takes place on warm summer evenings. It is often referred to as

FIG 164. A male hedgehog energetically pursuing a mate, into shallow water in this instance.

'courtship', although perhaps this is technically not a correct use of the word. Courtship in birds and mammals usually consists of a ritualised sequence of events often involving the deliberate display of conspicuous identity marks on the fur or feathers. Hedgehogs do not attempt a display, nor do they conform to a standardised sequence of behaviours. The whole procedure involves none of the complexity seen in the courtship rituals of more highly evolved mammals and the whole procedure is singularly lacking in apparent affection or sensitivity. It basically consists of the male attempting to mate with a female rather cautiously, being met with a general lack of cooperation on her part. As the male tries to get behind the female, she keeps turning to face him, more or less pivoting on the spot instead of running away (Fig. 164).

How they actually achieve copulation is a fundamental problem with such a spiny mammal and a matter that has occupied the minds of savants down the ages. Normal procedures were so obviously out of the question that the Greek philosopher Aristotle said that mating took place standing upright, belly to belly, an assertion that was repeated by the widely respected Roman author Pliny 2,000 years ago. It was so obvious that this must be true that Topsel's 1658 book reiterated the same misinformation in English, adding the helpful (but

FIG 165. A female rebuffs an approaching male by using her skin musculature to move more of her spiny skin towards him.

unverified) comment that 'they are a very little while in copulation because they cannot stand long on their hinder legs'. Others claimed to have seen a female lying obligingly on her back to facilitate the proceedings and to avoid her mate enduring unnecessary discomfort.

Actually, the male mounts the female from behind, just as in most quadrupeds, but to achieve successful mating she has to help out by extending her hind legs and pelvic region rearwards and perhaps not bristling her spines too much. Her nose points to the sky as she flattens her body against the ground in a submissive posture known as 'lordosis' (Fig. 166). So the purpose of the male's courtship behaviour is to get the female to cooperate in doing what appears to be otherwise impossible. He constantly circles her, snorting loudly and attempting to approach her from the rear. Sometimes he will bite at her legs or dorsal spines, which does not appear to be a very promising gambit! The female responds aggressively and, with dogged perversity, continually turns to keep facing him. The male persists, with more enthusiasm than might be expected, given the spiky drawbacks that confront him, and the female may rebuff his advances with some vigour. Both animals snort loudly and persistently, perhaps suggesting a role for pheromones here. Indeed, Walter Poduschka

FIG 166. A compliant female needs to flatten her body and spines, then extend her hind quarters in order for the male to mate successfully. Much can go wrong at this delicate stage and many mating attempts are unsuccessful. (Mary Morgan/BHPS)

suggested exactly that. Based on observations of captive animals, he postulated that the smell of secretions from the male's accessory sexual organs deposited on the female's spines during courtship helped to make her more compliant by inhibiting her tendency to run away or shake him off (Poduschka, 1977). He may be right, but the evidence is unclear and observations in the wild suggest it doesn't work very well with most mating attempts ending in failure.

The whole process often continues for 20 minutes or more, sometimes even an hour with a few breaks. There is apparent wariness on the part of both animals and they do a lot of puffing and snorting. The noise may well attract other males too and fights can then break out, allowing the female to make her escape. Even if she is compliant, the slightest mishap with bristling spines can easily result in a failed mating. Nigel Reeve witnessed 76 courtships, of which only 5 resulted in successful mating (7 per cent), and Digger Jackson recorded 260 hedgehog courtship events (Jackson, 2006), only 10 of which resulted in copulations (4 per cent). Amy Haigh's Irish hedgehogs were even less successful and none of the 39 courtship events that she witnessed ended in copulation (Haigh *et al.*, 2012b). Even when consummation was successful, Deanesly's detailed study of female hedgehog reproductive organs suggests that a significant proportion of matings may not actually result in a pregnancy. None of her females appeared to have become pregnant at their first mating and several had mated more than once without conceiving.

It seems that reproduction in hedgehogs is a very chancy business, made worse by the fact that it is possible for eggs to be fertilised in the normal way then fail to implant in the uterine wall, perhaps because the female has entered a state of torpor brought on by bad weather. It is quite likely that periods of cold weather in spring induce a temporary return to a hibernation state and this could affect hormonal balances and their target tissues, disrupting the normal control systems that initiate pregnancy. This sort of eventuality could account for the fact that although ovulation begins in April, there are few pregnancies recorded in that month. The whole system seems rather haphazard and inefficient. It would not be surprising if some females failed to become pregnant early in the breeding season and perhaps not at all. This contrasts with the mole (another member of the Insectivora) where the females may mate only once, during a single very brief oestrous occurring just once a year, and yet all of them get pregnant each season.

Promiscuity is the norm among hedgehogs. In Nigel Reeve's study, spread over 3 summer seasons, courtship events were witnessed 69 times, in which both partners were individually identifiable by their unique pattern of clipped spines. Female No. 111 was courted by at least 16 different males, 8 of whom were known to have consorted with at least one other female. One female engaged in courtship behaviour with at least seven different males in a fortnight. Males also had many partners: at least 12 of them in the case of male No. 106 and No. 117 had 14 or more partners, and both of these males were found at least once each with females 107, 111 and 180 (Reeve & Morris, 1986). Digger Jackson found hedgehogs had at least five partners of the opposite sex, corresponding to what might be expected given the number of home ranges that each individual overlaps. Amy Haigh also recorded promiscuous behaviour in Irish hedgehogs, where females consorted with up to seven different males in a season, and those were only the occasions when the animals were caught in the act. In all of these studies, there may have been other encounters that escaped observation.

One advantage of this apparent free-for-all, coupled with the prolonged and arduous courtship ritual, is that the female does have an element of choice which may allow her to reject less persistent suitors and only mate with the strongest and fittest males. A female may encounter more than one male in a night, leading to the possibility that some of her eggs will be fertilised by sperm from different males, and siblings born to the same mother can thus have different fathers (Moran *et al.*, 2009). This too may be advantageous in that the female is then not relying on the fitness of just one male to provide the genetic heritage of her offspring.

There is no pair bond in hedgehogs. After mating, the male makes no attempt to guard the female or remain with her to defend the nest that will later contain his own offspring, nor does he play any part in raising them. In terms of evolutionary biology, he is better off chasing more mates than sticking with just one, so long as she is able to raise his offspring successfully on her own. That way he can maximise the proportion of the next generation that will be carrying his genes. It is therefore possible that one or two males in a small population might sire a disproportionate number of the young born in a given season. This could tally with the increasing size of reproductive organs in older hedgehogs and Digger Jackson's observation that matings among the Uist hedgehogs mainly involved older and larger males. It also suggests that small populations may rely heavily on perhaps only one or two males and if anything happens to them, the viability of the whole population suffers. This needs to be taken into account when considering the fragility of small populations (see Chapter 10).

In contrast with the apparent inefficiency of the hedgehog's mating behaviour, there appears to be a high success rate among fertilised eggs that implant into the lining of the female's uterus. The developing embryos are subject to an unusually low mortality rate and barely 3 per cent of them die before birth and are resorbed into the mother's blood stream. Hedgehogs follow the normal pattern of having their embryos evenly divided between the left and right horns of the uterus. In a sample of 32 pregnant hedgehogs, only two had more than one embryo difference between the left and right sides.

There has long been uncertainty regarding the duration of pregnancy in hedgehogs. Human pregnancies usually last for about nine months, but estimates of the gestation period in hedgehogs range from four to seven weeks, a variation of over 70 per cent. This is an inevitable result of not necessarily knowing when successful mating had taken place (even in captivity) and the difficulty of establishing when births occurred without opening a nest and causing the mother to eat or desert her young. Moreover, there have been no large-scale studies of hedgehog reproductive behaviour. The most detailed and precise observations mostly come from an experimental colony kept in captivity at the University of Nottingham by Bryn Morris. To make matters worse, hedgehogs are often rather reluctant to breed in captivity, much to the chagrin of a film cameraman I met who spent three years trying unsuccessfully to film births for the BBC.

The consensus appears to be that pregnancy usually lasts about 34 days, but with considerable variation between 30 and 39 days. That variation may be due to pregnant females going torpid for a few days if they are confronted by adverse weather conditions in the early spring. This can certainly happen with bats and may even be artificially induced by subjecting pregnant females to lowered ambient temperatures. Their pregnancy can then be extended by a fortnight or however long they spend in experimentally enforced torpor (Racey, 1969). Like bats, hedgehogs depend on invertebrate prey, which becomes less active and less available in inclement weather. Maybe pregnant hedgehogs do also become torpid during bouts of bad weather, not an uncommon feature of our climate, and effectively impose torpor upon their own developing foetuses. That would mean the hedgehog has no definite gestation period and would account for the highly variable estimates of its duration that have been published. Likely though this scenario is, there seems to be little evidence that it actually happens in hedgehogs.

Few females will allow exploratory fingers to determine by palpation how many embryos are present in the uterus; instant rolling up is likely to be the response if anyone tries. Palpation is also likely to be misled by feeling the bladder. The largest number of embryos reported in the hedgehog literature is seven, but at least one of the older accounts said that nine may be found in a single litter. Dissection of 53 dead animals (Morris, 1961) showed an average litter size *in utero* of 4.6 and Ruth Deanesly reported an average of 4.7 foetuses in 10 pregnant females that she dissected. A sample of 15 pregnant animals that I examined gave a mean litter size of 4.5. This is the basis for saying that the normal family size in Britain is four or five. Three of those fifteen had six embryos, suggesting that perhaps 20 per cent of females have these larger litters. Elsewhere in northern Europe, the average family size may be slightly higher, and litters of six or seven are said to be more common. In Sweden, mean litter size is certainly larger, perhaps compensating for the fact that the shorter summer season at higher latitudes allows insufficient time to raise a second litter, as mentioned above (Kristiansson, 1990). This could also reflect the fact that Continental hedgehogs tend to be larger animals, and females might therefore be able to accommodate more babies. A German hedgehog gave birth to 11 offspring (Neumeier, 2016), although the largest litter size reported from Britain in any of my literature surveys was 10 and this appears to be exceptional.

In preparation for births, which are said to occur only at night, the female will build a large nursery nest rather like the one used for hibernation. It is made of leaves, grass, paper and anything else that can be pressed into service. Like the hibernaculum, a nursery nest will be tucked away under some supportive structure such as a garden shed or pile of brushwood. As the time of birth approaches, the female becomes fidgety and very sensitive to disturbance, which may result in her eating her newborn young. For this reason there have been very few direct observations of the actual birth process, even in captivity. The female will lick herself and tremble during birthing contractions, which can last for several seconds. She may also pause and move about in between births. It can take minutes or even hours for the whole litter to be born. Topsel's quaint account of hedgehog natural history says that the female may become so distressed by the pain of parturition that she will poke her own belly with her spines as a form of distraction. Anatomically, that would be difficult, but there is also little reason to believe the tale because the newborns are small in proportion to their mother, only about 2 per cent of her body weight, somewhat smaller than a human baby in relative terms. Even the whole litter is only about 10–12 per cent of the female's mass. On the other hand, stillbirths can occur and a baby may even become stuck during birth, with fatal consequences to both mother and young.

The new babies are up to 70 mm long and can weigh 25 g, although they are normally about half this size, depending upon how many of them there are. Soon after birth, each hoglet attaches to a teat and begins suckling, rhythmically nuzzling the mammary gland to stimulate the flow of milk. There are five pairs of nipples, enough to go round even for the largest litters. However, it is likely that they will not all be equally functional, so smaller or less pushy hoglets may begin life at a disadvantage, especially in larger litters. The mother lies on her side to allow access to her belly, just like a sow with piglets. The young depend entirely on milk for about four weeks, during which time they will more than quadruple their birth weight. They begin to eat solid food (at least in captivity) at an age of about 25 days. The hoglets can crawl about in the nest and if one becomes isolated and detached from its mother, it will emit a piping call which stimulates her to retrieve it.

Newborn hedgehogs have no hair, but their claws are already formed. They have no spines either, although tiny raised tubercles on the skin show where they will later appear (Fig. 167). The neonates are covered by membranes, including

FIG 167. Baby hedgehogs are born without spines, but soon afterwards these begin to sprout from raised tubercles on the skin. (Elizabeth Bomford/ Ardea)

FIG **168.** The first coat of about 100 white spines is soon supplemented by spines with normal brown colouration.

the placenta, which swiftly rupture and are eaten by the mother, who also licks her new babies clean. The young are born blind, pink and helpless, with droopy ears. By about a week old they will begin growing hair on the face and flanks; their ears cease to be floppy and become more upright. The young hedgehogs begin to be capable of defending themselves by butting with their head lowered. The skin darkens after a week or so, but the eyes do not open until an age of 14–16 days, sometimes later. From eleven days old they will show signs of being able to partially roll up, but they will not be capable of rolling up tightly until their skin muscles have fully developed, and that will take at least another three months.

The first coat of spines appears remarkably quickly, too fast for such structures to grow. In fact they are already there, but embedded in rather bloated

FIG **169.** By about ten days old, there are plenty of dark-coloured spines appearing, although the original white spines are still present. The hoglet's eyes open soon after this stage.

FIG 170. Two hoglets at about ten days old. The eyes will open soon and the drooping ears begin to assume a more upright stance.

skin, and as fluid is withdrawn from it the skin puckers, taking on a more wrinkled appearance. The shrinking skin accelerates emergence of the embedded spines, allowing them to make their rapid appearance, and they are already a few millimetres long within hours of birth. These first spines are white and there are about 90–100 of them (Fig. 168). They grow in two strips, on either side of a 'parting' down the middle of the hoglet's back. At this stage, the skin is still pale in colour. The white spines are soft at first and never go brown. Instead, a set of thin brown spines grows up among them, followed by another wave of spines that are thicker and adult-coloured (Fig. 169). All three sets of spines are present by the age of about ten days and the new spines that grow are larger and stiffer as the baby gets older (Fig. 170). By the time it leaves the nest, some of the first spines will be falling out (although the full-sized adults spines last much longer, often more than a year). Once fully independent, a juvenile hedgehog has about 3,000 spines, adding more as it grows. It has about 5,000 spines as an adult, based on counts I made on a small sample of dead animals (see Chapter 3).

Years ago, there was a report of a litter consisting of six young hedgehogs that were two different sizes. I have seen this myself, but only in dormice where some females create a crèche that includes the young from two different mothers, although only one of them is actually present. At the time of the hedgehog story, it was suggested that the two sets of young could have been the result of superfoetation, where extra fertilised eggs had become implanted among a set of developing embryos within the mother. An alternative speculation was that some eggs had been subject to delayed fertilisation, but there is no supporting evidence that either process occurs in hedgehogs. A much more likely explanation is that a second female brought her young into the shelter of another female's nest, especially as the report mentioned that there were two adults as well as the six babies present in the nest. I doubt if hedgehogs form crèches even if dormice think it is a good idea and I have never heard it reported in wild hedgehogs.

Like other mammals, the first milk a mother hedgehog produces (called 'colostrum') contains large quantities of antibodies. These enable the mother to provide a gift of immunity, helping to protect the hoglet from future infections by many of the pathogens that she has herself encountered. In hedgehogs, this type of passive immunity is conveyed through the colostrum and absorbed by the stomach and intestine, not transmitted via the placenta (another 'primitive' feature). That requires the digestive system to refrain from digesting these precious proteins by not becoming fully competent for a while. What happens is that the stomach wall develops the cells that secrete pepsin, but this protein-digesting enzyme only becomes properly active in an acid environment with a pH of less than 4. In the hedgehog, the acid-secreting cells necessary to achieve this do not become fully active until the age of four weeks or more. The nestling's digestive system retains a neutral acidity (pH 5–7) until it is about a month old and even at six weeks the number of acid-secreting cells is less than 75 per cent of what is found in the adult. This means that the babies do not have a fully functional acidic protein-digesting system until they are old enough to leave the nest and need it to cope with worms, beetles and all the other normal hedgehog foods. By that time, the inhibition of acidic digestion will have allowed the young hoglet to have absorbed valuable proteins from its mother to boost its own immune system. A similar arrangement is found in lambs, but suppression of acid secretions persists for much longer in the hedgehog.

The first teeth begin to erupt after about 12 days. These are premolars; the incisors appear much later, perhaps making it easier to suckle, both for mother and offspring. Nestling hedgehogs can begin to eat solid food at about 25 days, but they continue to take milk from their mother until they are up to 40 days old. A female hedgehog's normal milk is rather watery and contains less fat than some other species, but it does the job. By the time her offspring are ready to leave the nest, a mother may have raised up to half a kilogram of babies, often nearly equivalent to her own body weight. Large litters of five or six babies may all die if she is not able to supply enough milk for the whole family, and this may well happen if a prolonged drought or series of cold nights coincides with the period following the birth of her young. There is some statistically robust evidence to suggest that larger litters face a higher probability of loss. This is not surprising given the very high energy cost to the female of raising even three babies, never mind six.

In the wild, the mother probably remains with her new litter for the first night after they are born but later she will go out foraging, sometimes returning during the night to feed the family. She will keep the nest and babies clean by eating their waste and licking their skin. Once they are about five days old and the young have begun to grow spines, they are safe from being eaten by their mother if she is disturbed. Instead, she will use her teeth to grip each baby in turn by the scruff of its neck, lift it high off the ground and carry it away to another nest. This frequently happens in daylight and has been reported surprisingly often (Fig. 171). In one case, four young were transported, one at a time, to a new nest 70 m away in the space of an hour. Such dedication and determination contrasts with a mother's readiness to sacrifice her whole family at an earlier age by eating them all if she is disturbed. Gruesome though it may seem, at least that helps to recycle the investment she has made in providing food for them.

No solid food is brought back to the nest before the babies venture out to feed for themselves on a normal adult diet of invertebrates and other materials. This

FIG 171. If a mother is disturbed when the nestlings are at an early stage, she is likely to eat them. But once they have begun growing spines, she will rescue them one at a time and carry them off to another nest. (Alan Lochhead/Hedgehog Street)

they do at about four weeks. The young hedgehogs leave the nest, following their mother as she seeks out places to feed. The spiky procession of female and family makes a charming sight as the youngsters become familiar with the great outdoors, but there is no evidence that the mother actually teaches her offspring what to eat. They must just find out as they go along. The young hedgehogs do not engage in playful activity or in grooming each other, but the family returns to the nest at the end of each night. This pattern of activity continues until, one after another, the youngsters grow large and bold enough to wander off on their own at about six weeks of age. A few may remain with their mother for a while longer.

By now they each weigh 120–200 g, but they are very vulnerable at this stage. They are no longer kept warm by their mother and siblings, their fur and spines are ineffective insulation and the nights are cold, especially if they emerge towards the end of summer. Instead of feeding, they need to spend time building their first nests and as food becomes scarcer, they face the challenge of having to more than double their weight ready for hibernation, which may be forced upon them at any time by the first frosts. It is not uncommon to find these newly weaned juveniles active in daylight, often with evidence of sickness and a heavy burden of parasites. In these circumstances, they usually become incapable of keeping themselves warm and begin to suffer from hypothermia, with the body temperature falling below 20°C (when it should be 35°C or more). This severely reduces their ability to digest food properly and also results in muscles not working as they should, leading to a hesitant staggering gait. They begin a downward spiral, eating less, digesting less, getting colder, eating even less. Few of those affected will survive, but rescued animals often recover very quickly, just by being given a hot water bottle and some food.

Provided that they survive their first winter, yearling hedgehogs normally weigh about 400–500 g and continue to grow, although at a slower rate than in their first season. By age two or three years, many will weigh 600 g or more, but weights are extremely variable between individuals and fluctuate greatly according to the seasons. Lucky (and well-fed) hedgehogs can occasionally grow to more than 1.5 kg in the wild and may exceed 2 kg in captivity.

As with other species, a mother's task finishes with the independence of her young and it is interesting to assess her success. This has been done for very few other mammals, apart from those like deer whose young are visible above ground from birth onwards. With species whose family life takes place underground or in a well-hidden nest, it is difficult to gather the necessary information. However, hedgehog breeding nests are often found accidently during normal operations in the garden. Hedgehogs are unlikely to be misidentified and the young are few

FIG 172. When the young are about four weeks old, they are ready to leave the nest and begin following their mother on nocturnal foraging excursions. The family then progressively splits up as individuals break away to live their own independent life. (Hedgehog Street)

in number, so they are easily counted. Hedgehog nests are found sufficiently frequently by the public to accumulate enough one-off observations to see a pattern emerge based on accurate counts and reliable identification. A survey carried out via a BBC Radio programme, together with many casually acquired observations, generated a sample of 223 reports of hedgehog family size, of which 105 were sufficiently detailed to permit further analysis (Morris, 1977). This revealed that early nestlings – at this stage pale, blind and helpless (i.e. probably less than a week or so old) – averaged 4.4 per litter (30 litters). That is almost the same as the average litter size among foetuses described above (4.6), suggesting a low perinatal mortality. Family size for late young (described as having dark skin with brown spines) averaged 3.7. The average number of young seen out foraging with their mother was also 3.7 (Fig. 172). This little survey had revealed a drop in average family size from birth to independence, from 4.4 to 3.7, representing a 16 per cent mortality rate among nestlings. This study was extended to Germany and the Netherlands, with similar figures being obtained for litter sizes and mortality rates among nestlings (Table 20).

In Sweden, Kristiansson (1990) also noted the discrepancy between estimated litter size at birth (6.5) and the number of juveniles actually recruited to the population per adult (2.8), representing a mortality rate of over half. Clearly, the first few weeks of a hedgehog's life are among its most challenging.

These figures exclude cases where whole litters had been lost, so it is reasonable to estimate that overall pre-weaning mortality is about 20 per cent. Moreover, nearly half of the 'early young' litters (43 per cent) were of five or six young, but by the 'late young' stage that had fallen to 21 per cent. This

TABLE 20. Mean family size at different ages, showing an apparent mortality as the hoglets get older (based on questionnaire returns describing 506 litters and including the 105 British litters described in Morris (1977). Total number of litters in brackets.

	'Early young' (*pink body, eyes closed, white spines*) Age stage 1	'Late young' (*body dark, eyes open, brown spines*) Age stage 2	'Seen out of the nest with mother' (*probably almost weaned*) Age stage 3	Percentage loss between age stage 1 and 3
Britain	4.28 (70)	3.83 (78)	3.65 (43)	15 per cent
Netherlands	4.15 (20)	4.34 (23)	3.60 (5)	13 per cent
Germany	5.05 (83)	4.82 (140)	4.50 (44)	11 per cent

suggests that a higher mortality rate occurs in the larger litters. It is likely that the one (or two) lost from the average family will be the smallest individuals and it is commonly observed that litter mates differ in size even though all are the same age. The biggest ones are likely to get the best teats and most food and consequently get bigger still, leaving 'Tail-end Charlie' to be left behind and probably die if there is any shortage of food, as may well happen in a dry spell during the summer. Overall, a 20 per cent loss before weaning may seem a lot, but put another way, hedgehog mothers seem to raise successfully to independence 80 per cent of the young that they produce.

For many mammals, the energy demands on the male during the breeding season are considerable, especially for those species that need to become hyper-active in search of a mate or to defend territory, even to the extent of reducing their average lifespan. Male hedgehogs have no need to defend territory, but are nevertheless very active and travel at least twice as far as females each night as they search for mates. Reproduction is very demanding for the females too, of course, especially during pregnancy, but the energy requirements during lactation are even greater. Imagine a mother who rears three offspring that weighed a total of 15 g when they were born. By the time they are big enough to leave the nest, their combined weight will be about 350 g, maybe more, all of it built on a foundation of their mother's milk. The energy cost of such copious milk production is about four times greater than the female's requirement outside of the breeding season when she is at rest and not raising young (Król, 1985).

The information above is based upon relatively small studies of hedgehogs on the mainland of Britain. Digger Jackson's major study of hedgehogs introduced to South Uist in the Hebrides (see Chapter 1) has provided some more details. Despite the higher latitude, a few animals had already emerged from hibernation

FIG 173. On average, a female manages to rear only about three of her offspring to independence. The family does not normally remain together for more than a few days once the young begin to leave the nest. (Elizabeth Bomford/Ardea)

by mid-April, and peak occurrence of courting behaviour was later that month and into May, somewhat earlier than is usually reported from the mainland. After that, things quietened down but courtship continued to be observed into early August. Sub-adult males (i.e. last year's young) were less sexually active and none were seen to engage in successful copulation, confirming that it is the older males that do best in this respect. Two hedgehogs were found to have returned to a torpid state in their nest during a bout of cold weather (i.e. 'gone back into hibernation'), confirming that this really can occur, with all that it implies for disrupting gestation as speculated earlier.

Almost all the females that gave birth early in the season engaged in sexual activity soon after their litter was born, confirming the observation that females who lost their family early would rapidly begin another. On South Uist, these replacement litters were born from July to early September. At least 81 per cent (26 animals) of females on South Uist attempted to have a second family in late summer, having reared or lost an earlier litter. Second litters were born between early August and mid-September. For the first time, this confirmed unequivocally that British hedgehogs can and (on South Uist at least) often do have second litters in the wild. Most adult females on South Uist became pregnant within two weeks of emerging from hibernation, perhaps enabled by an early start to breeding that may not be normal elsewhere or might just have been made possible by winters being mild in the Hebrides or ending early in the study years. There was evidence that the young hedgehogs born early in the season were weaned at a younger age. There is probably no great disadvantage being left to fend for themselves at the height of summer and it does give the female more time to raise a second family. Having a high proportion of females raise two

FIG 174. The male hedgehog plays no part in raising the young or defending his family. He is busy seeking additional matings.

litters in a season might help to explain the rapid increase in hedgehog numbers that took place within 20 years of their introduction to the island. The principal drawback to having second litters was the cost to the mothers themselves. At least 3 out of 19 that reared later litters died in an emaciated condition soon after their young emerged from the nursery nest, and several of the others were sufficiently weakened that they did not survive the ensuing winter. Having a second litter is evidently possible in the environmental conditions of the Hebrides, but is nevertheless a severe challenge. This is not surprising, given the high energy cost of pregnancy and especially lactation.

On South Uist, the gestation period was recorded as lasting for between 31–39 days, the uncertainty and variability being a result of the same issues that have led to a similar range of estimates in other studies. To avoid disturbance to mothers and their offspring, the number of young in nursery nests was not determined, but when they emerged at about seven weeks old the average family size was 2.85 in a sample of 34 litters. This is similar to my estimates of family size given above for mainland hedgehogs when they leave the nest. The success of female hedgehogs was calculated by taking account of the proportion of females attempting to breed, the proportion of breeding attempts that were successful and the mean litter size at emergence from the nest. The average productivity per adult female was 4.04 young per year among adults compared to only 0.82 per female among the sub-adults (because so few of the younger animals had actually bred). Taking into account the fact that the spring population was 35 per cent sub-adults, barely one year old, and 65 per cent adults, productivity in the population as a whole was calculated to be 2.91 young per female, which is probably close to the annual productivity on the mainland when calculated in the same way.

In the Uists, male hedgehogs did not reach full sexual maturity in their second calendar year and only 15 of the sub-adults were seen to attempt breeding. Again this suggests that, like females, full sexual maturity is often not reached by the time males are about 11 months old and most defer breeding until their third calendar year. The implication is that most fathering in the hedgehog population is by older males and returns us to the possibility that the 'inefficiency' of courtship behaviour could well be a form of mate selection on the part of females, rejecting younger animals as being a waste of time.

CONCLUSION

To summarise, hedgehogs do not breed in the year of their birth and many probably do not succeed in their second year either. Successful reproduction in hedgehog populations relies heavily on older animals, not yearlings. The breeding season typically lasts from April until September and normal family size ranges from four to six young born. Some females could produce a second litter in the same summer, although relatively few are successful in doing so. Breeding late leaves too little time to raise offspring before the onset of hibernation and also compromises the female's own chance of surviving the winter. In theory, the potential annual production could be as much as ten young per female (i.e. two litters of five babies), but in reality the actual number reared successfully per female in a season is only about two or three. These still have to face the rigours of their first winter before attaining maturity and may not breed successfully until their third calendar year. Deferral of successful breeding like this is what hedgehogs have evolved to do over the course of millions of years, but in the modern world they face a great many new hazards that have arisen in only the past century or so. Their breeding strategy may not fully compensate for this, resulting in a chronic decline in population size.

CHAPTER 8

Population Issues

CCURATE DETERMINATION OF AGE IS an essential prerequisite for
understanding many aspects of an animal's life. We can appreciate
this best by reference to our fellow humans, as there is hardly any part
of our lives which is not closely tied to age. Our learning ability, social behaviour,
legal status, reproductive capabilities and probability of death, for example, all
change as we get older. We can also appreciate how difficult it is to be sure of an
individual's age, even in our own species, because it is obvious just by looking
around at our friends and family that some people develop and age faster than
others. We should remember this when trying to guess the age of hedgehogs.
Some look old, others don't, but we might be wrong about both of them (Fig. 175).
With people, if it is essential to know their age, it is relatively simple to check

FIG 175. How old is
this hedgehog? Who
knows? How can you
tell? How can anyone
be sure?

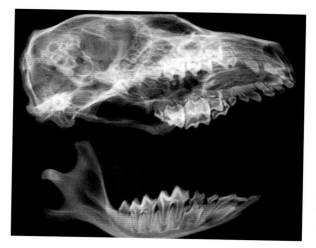

FIG 176. This juvenile hedgehog has its posterior premolar milk tooth still in place in the lower jaw, with the permanent tooth developing below, ready to replace it at an age of about three to four months. Other milk teeth are also about to be replaced, indicating that this is a young animal in its first summer of life. The permanent molars are already in place.

because registration of births has been compulsory in Britain since 1837. This provides an ultimate and accurate way to determine someone's age because everyone born here and still alive has a birth certificate.

Some animals may have the equivalent, especially pedigree domestic species where genealogical records are officially kept, but hedgehogs have no records of when they were born. Instead, we must look within their own structure for signs of age – some sort of biological record of the passage of time. Biologists have devised an ingenious variety of age determination techniques, based upon an animal getting bigger with increasing age or losing material through wear and tear as it gets older (Morris, 1972). One of the most ancient ways of estimating age in mammals is to look at their teeth and the expression 'never look a gift horse in the mouth' (to ascertain its age) is attributed to Saint Jerome in the fifth century AD. Experience with humans also highlights the importance and practical usefulness of teeth for establishing approximate age where this is in doubt. In the early nineteenth century, children under seven years old were not legally responsible for crimes committed and their teeth were used as the most reliable guide to eligibility for legal immunity. The Factories Act of 1833 restricted the employment of children below a certain age and again dentition became the final arbiter. More recently, refugees from Africa and the Middle East were allowed into Britain if they were 'children' and, in the absence of any paperwork, teeth may have been used as a means of separating them from adults. Teeth are also still used for estimating age in archaeological and forensic investigations. We know that in humans the last milk teeth are usually lost in childhood and

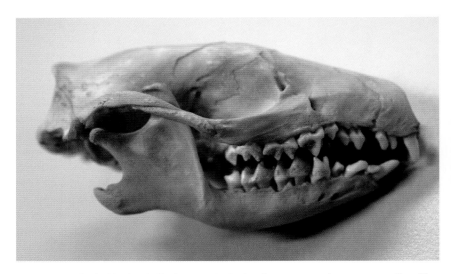

FIG 177. This looks like the skull of a young hedgehog because cranial sutures are still visible and most of the teeth are relatively unworn, but that could be because it fed mainly on dog food in captivity. Despite being the same age, another animal could have its pointed tooth cusps much more heavily worn as a result of feeding on a more natural diet, including gritty worms. Either way, we still cannot say how old it is in terms of years or months.

the posterior molars ('wisdom teeth') erupt in our late teens. Unfortunately, in hedgehogs the last milk tooth (a lower premolar) is lost at about three months old (Fig. 176). This means that the presence of milk teeth is only any use for identifying very young animals, so tiny that they are obviously barely out of the nest. The molars are all fully erupted and in place within a few months, eliminating those too as a useful indicator of age in the population.

Tooth wear is another sign of age frequently used by wildlife biologists. As the animal gets older, the tooth crowns become smoother and worn down. Many adult hedgehogs have almost flat teeth, but this is a very unreliable guide to age in a species that has such a varied diet. Obviously if the molars still have sharp-pointed cusps, the animal is likely to be fairly young, but molars could be worn smooth early in life as a result of feeding mainly on gritty earthworms (Fig. 177). Conversely, another animal that fed mainly on pet food could retain unworn teeth until a later age and be mistaken for a youngster. Nevertheless, Jan Skoudlin collected a sample of 215 *E. europaeus* from around Prague in early summer and used a tooth abrasion index to assign them to one of five age groups. It was concluded that hedgehogs older than six years occur rarely in nature (3.5 per cent) and that juveniles suffer a first summer mortality rate in the region of 44 per cent (Skoudlin, 1981). This turns out to be fairly near the truth despite the limitations of the technique.

Body size changes with age too. Big hedgehogs are often (but not always) older animals. But weight varies enormously with the seasons and a 700 g animal found in October could easily be only 500 g in the following April, despite being six months older, simply as a result of seasonal weight changes associated with hibernation. Measuring changes in size such as head and body length is hard to do consistently even with dead hedgehogs and impossible with live ones. Whilst claws might be measured (assuming they grow longer with the passage of time as our fingernails do), they also get worn down, so claw length cannot be a reliable indicator of a specific age group. Hedgehogs also change shape as they get older. Young mammals have a short rounded face with a muzzle that elongates as it gets older. The changes are reflected in skull measurements such as condylobasal length and zygomatic width, and in the ratios between them. Skull measurements are so closely correlated that almost any one of the standard skull dimensions may offer a guide to increasing age. The most reliable measurement is that of the hedgehog's lower jaw, which increases in length from about 30 mm to 40 mm in the first year, but after that, growth begins to slow and barely any change occurs in later life. Unlike body weight, the jaw does not undergo confusing seasonal variation in size, but how old it actually is remains a mystery.

The most reliable measurement for age determination, in hedgehogs and many other species, is the dry weight of the eye lens. This seems a highly obscure thing to study, but the lens develops from embryonic ectodermal tissue (like skin) and continues to grow throughout life, but its special position inside the eye means that it is not worn away in the course of normal activity. Nor is it affected by seasonal changes in body mass. Increasing eye lens weights are consistently related to increased age, although the animal's actual age in terms of months or years remains elusive. Like other methods of assessing relative age, this measurement, suggesting greater age in one animal compared to another one, can only be converted into actual age by comparison with some known-age specimens. These are normally available in the form of captive animals whose growth is probably faster and more regular than in wild animals, so they do not make for a reliable comparison. Moreover, lens weights and skull measurements can only be obtained from dead animals, yet we want to know the age of living ones too.

In young mammals, growth takes place in a cartilaginous region near the end of the each limb bone. Once adult size is attained, this growth zone ossifies and the terminal part of the bone, the epiphysis, becomes solidly fused to the main shaft of the bone. X-rays can reveal whether this has happened or if the epiphyseal

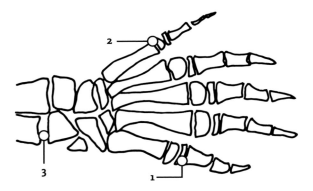

FIG 178. Epiphyseal cartilages in the hedgehog's forefoot. 1–proximal phalangeal; 2–distal metacarpal; 3–wrist (radius and ulna). As the animal gets older, the cartilages ossify, closing the epiphyseal gap in that sequence.

cartilage is still present as an indication of continuing growth. Some epiphyses close at an earlier age than others and the sequence in different bones will serve as a guide to an individual's age. Using x-rays this method can be applied to live animals and not just dead ones, a big advantage. I used x-rays of hedgehog paws because they were easy to work with. The hand has three sets of epiphyses and the developmental stage of each allowed animals to be assigned to one of seven age-related categories (Morris, 1971). The epiphyses in the hedgehog's forefoot ossify sequentially: proximal phalangeal ('fingers') at about three to four months old and distal metacarpal ('palm') epiphyses at about one year. The forearm (radius and ulna) epiphyses do not fuse for at least one and a half years and may still just be open at five or six years old. This method was particularly useful for distinguishing sub-adult animals that were one year old (in their second calendar year) from juveniles less than one year old and from older adults (Table 21).

The results were checked against the growth of 11 animals in captivity and it appears that the latter were able to reach development category 5 sooner than in the wild. Older hedgehogs showed a slower rate of skeletal maturation, taking over a year to progress from category 4 to category 6. A small sample of nine wild hedgehogs was marked, x-rayed before release and again at recapture after a long interval. One animal (No. 122) assigned to category 5 showed no change during four winter months, but grew to category 6 in two summer months. No. 134, about ten months old (category 4) in March, reached category 6 the following year in its third summer of life. These results help to underpin the ages given in Table 21. The technique is particularly valuable because it can be used on live animals as well as dead ones.

Estimating relative age is essentially a comparative exercise relating to growth. An animal's measurements (lens weight, jaw length or whatever) are compared to a growth curve or regression line previously prepared from known-age material. But these methods provide increasingly inaccurate results

TABLE 21. Age categories based on fusion of epiphyses in the forefoot (From Morris, 1971). O=open and very distinct; I=nearly closed and indistinct; F=solidly fused to the main part of the bone.

X-ray cat.	Phalangeal epiphyses	Metacarpal epiphyses	Forearm epiphyses	Age in months	
1	O	O	O	1–2	
2	O	O	O	2–4	
3	F	O	O	>6	
4	F	I	O	5–6, 10+ if after hibernation period	
5	F	F	O	12+, at least in second summer	
6	F	F	I	Adult 18+	
7	F	F	F	Old Adult 18+	

in the older animals. Once a hedgehog has grown beyond the stage of being recognisably juvenile, there is usually little reliable indication that one animal is much older than another and nothing at all to show exactly how old either of them is in terms of years or months. As growth slows with age, there is minimal difference between a hedgehog that is four years old and one that is five. It is often only possible to classify the members of a population as 'young', 'adult' and 'very old' and even then not with much confidence. What we really need is a method for determining absolute age, measured in terms of actual units of time. Normally this is betrayed by the presence of incremental lines in teeth or bones ('growth rings') that reflect regular seasonal changes in growth. Their number tells us fairly precisely how long an animal has lived. These lines represent interruptions to normal regular growth, recording a period of quiescence such as during hibernation. Age determination based on this principle suffers less from individual variation and is unaffected by seasonal gain or loss in body mass. Growth lines provide an important check on other age criteria that are easier to apply, but subject to varying degrees of uncertainty.

The familiar example of this principle is seen in cross sections of trees where seasonal differences in the nature of wood growth result in annual rings. Similar rings occur in fish scales. In mammals, growth lines will only be persistent and clearly demarcated in dense hard tissues like teeth and bones, not in muscles, for example. In some mammals, they show up well in tooth cement that is continuously formed around pre-existing tooth material. Cement is laid down around the outside of the tooth roots and environmental effects cause variations in the rate of its deposition and the nature of the cement itself. This is manifest as 'growth lines' around tooth roots and has been widely used as a method of age determination in carnivores and marine mammals. Unfortunately it doesn't work with hedgehogs because the layer of tooth cement is too thin, and its texture too granular, for distinct annual lines to be distinguished.

A better method is to examine the new bone tissue that is laid down around existing bones to make them thicker and stronger with increasing size and age. This appositional bone is secreted by the inner layer of the periosteum, a membrane that encloses the main shaft of a bone, and because of differential seasonal growth rates it may assume a layered structure in the same way as teeth. The thickest layers of periosteal bone are found where stresses are greatest – for example, just below the molar region of the dentary (lower jaw). That bone needs to become more robust as it lengthens with age otherwise the animal would be unable to chew properly. This is the function of the extra layers of dense bone added to its surface and growth lines can be seen within it under the microscope in stained thin sections of the jaw (Morris, 1970) and clearly visible in Fig. 179. This

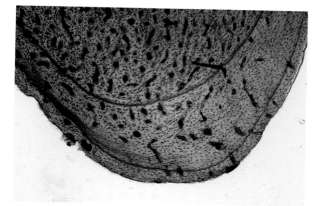

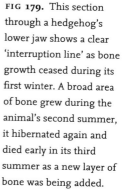

FIG 179. This section through a hedgehog's lower jaw shows a clear 'interruption line' as bone growth ceased during its first winter. A broad area of bone grew during the animal's second summer, it hibernated again and died early in its third summer as a new layer of bone was being added.

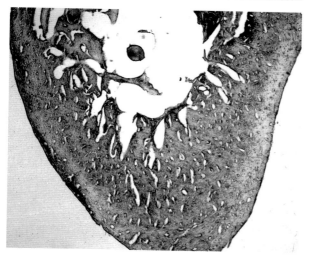

FIG 180. This jaw section from an adult hedgehog in New Zealand shows no interruption lines, corresponding to having experienced minimal reduction in bone growth as a result of having hibernated for only a short time, if at all. Captive-reared hedgehogs that were well fed during the winter also showed little or no sign of 'growth lines' in their bone.

method of assessing age is particularly suitable for hedgehogs, as the number of growth lines tells us how many winter hibernation episodes the animal has lived through, but obviously the technique can only be used on dead animals whose jaw can be extracted and made into thin sections for inspection under a microscope. The real value of this technique lies in helping to validate methods that can be used on live hedgehogs, but do not indicate actual age. It can also be used to calibrate other age determination methods where no known-age animals are available for comparisons to be made.

Using growth lines in jaws extracted from 244 dead hedgehogs (mostly road casualties and bodies collected from gamekeepers) enabled me to separate the

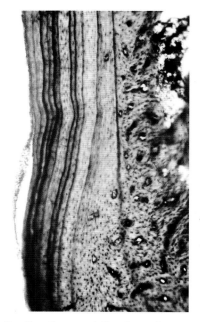

FIG 181. Counting growth lines is not always straightforward. Some very old animals showed complex patterns of bone growth, but very old animals represent only a small proportion of the population. Occasional anomalies do not seriously affect the overall picture. Multiple periosteal growth lines like this do at least confirm that the animal is probably at least four or five years old.

sample into year groups and calibrate growth curves derived from eye lens weights and jaw lengths. It was then possible to confirm the ages indicated by the age-related categories revealed in x-rays showing epiphyseal fusion. Eight captive animals whose age was known to within three months were available and in every case the age estimated from the lens weight/jaw length combination was very close to their true age, and jaw growth lines always accurately indicated their actual age. This form of cross-checking between methods meant that age could be assigned with a fair degree of certainty to almost all of the animals available, making a total sample size of 244. As that sample was fairly large and also randomly obtained, it is reasonable to assume that the proportion of animals in each age group represents the age structure of the hedgehog population as a whole (Table 22).

Juveniles (in their first summer) are under-represented because they would not appear in the population until nearly half way through the collecting period. Nevertheless, the general pattern of population structure and survival is clear. It also points to the maximum likely lifespan in wild hedgehogs. Several authors, including Konrad Herter (1938), have described individual hedgehogs that survived seven years in captivity, but clearly that is rare in the wild. These results can also be compared with those from other field studies. Hedgehogs from the cull in the Uists showed a roughly similar age structure in a sample of 66 animals (Lindesay Scott-Hayward, pers comm.), although a higher proportion appear to have survived to their fifth summer or beyond (13.6 per cent compared to 6.6 per cent in Table 22), but that is because her sample excluded the young of the year (Table 23). Jan

TABLE 22. Age structure in a sample of 244 hedgehogs from southern England collected in summer (April–November), from Morris (1969).

Age (years)	Number	Per cent of total sample
<1 (=first summer): 'juveniles'	36	14.7
1 (=2nd summer): 'subadults'	90	36.9
2 (=3rd summer): 'adults'	61	25.0
3 (=4th summer)	41	16.8
4 (=5th summer)	8	3.3
5 (=6th summer)	7	2.9
6 (=7th summer)	1	0.4
7 (=8th summer)	0	0
Total	**244**	**100**

TABLE 23. Age structure in a sample of 66 hedgehogs from the Uists, Outer Hebrides. They were collected in April and May, so only adult animals are included because no young of the year were available that early in the season. Animals recorded here as one year old are therefore in their second calendar year. (Lindsay Scott-Hayward, pers comm.).

Age (years)	Number collected	Per cent of total sample
0 (year of birth)	None collected	0
1 (=2nd summer)	22	33 per cent
2 (=3rd summer)	12	18 per cent
3 (=4th summer)	15	23 per cent
4 (=5th summer)	8	12 per cent
5 (=6th summer)	4	6 per cent
6 (=7th summer)	5	7.6 per cent
7 (=8th summer)	0	0 per cent

Skoudlin, using a different method of age determination, found only 3.5 per cent reached age six or more in the wild. In Switzerland, the hedgehog population appeared to renew itself in about 6.6 years, with the oldest individual surviving 7 years. In the former Czechoslovakia, hedgehogs that had hibernated once (i.e. were in their second summer of life) were the most abundant adult age group, with progressively fewer in older categories, and those that had hibernated five or six

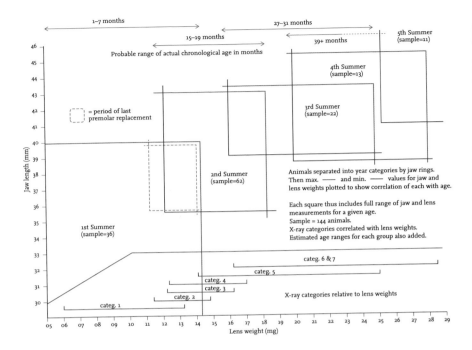

FIG 182. No wild hedgehogs of known age were available to make comparisons, but by linking several different age determination criteria it was possible to assign the majority of hedgehog specimens to an age class with a reasonable degree of confidence.

times were very scarce (Kratochvil, 1975). In Finland, one hedgehog in a sample of 67 adults had survived into its seventh year (1.5 per cent), despite the harsh winter conditions there (Kristoffersson, 1971). One of my correspondents claimed to have a distinctively coloured hedgehog that visited her garden for eight years (Hilda Purtell, pers comm.), but I have no way of verifying this. In Ireland, two eight-year-old males were reported and two females that were nine (Haigh et al., 2014b), but the majority (87 per cent) of the animals sampled there were three years old or less. These figures are all in broad agreement, suggesting that the age determination methods used were valid. The picture they reveal is of a population that has a high mortality among juveniles, with diminishing numbers of animals surviving until a maximum age is normally reached at about seven years old.

SURVIVAL OF JUVENILES IN THEIR FIRST SUMMER

It is customary to calculate survival rates from the time that young become independent of their mother, although in the hedgehog it is possible to demonstrate that nearly 20 per cent of hedgehogs born will die before leaving the nest (see Chapter 7). In order to estimate the proportion of young that died during their first year after becoming independent, we need to compare the number of juveniles present in the population before and after their first winter and hence estimate the loss over the first year. The problem with this is that we don't know what the juvenile population size is. Simply using the number of juvenile (i.e. first-summer) animals found in my sample of dead hedgehogs gives an incomplete picture because juveniles are only available to be sampled after about July, whereas the adults will be sampled for at least three months longer. Juveniles will therefore be under-represented in the sample and give a misleading impression of their abundance and survival rate.

A better way of estimating survival would be to make a 'longitudinal study' in which a sample of animals is marked and then subsequently recaptured, allowing an estimate of how many had been lost by the following year(s). This is exactly the sort of valuable insight that can be gained by studies of marked hedgehogs that visit gardens. One of my correspondents, Pat Lorber, was disappointed to report that only a quarter of her adult hedgehogs marked in one season had reappeared by April after overwintering, plus a few new arrivals. That could suggest a very high mortality rate, but there could easily be other survivors that did not return to the same garden, so survival rates calculated from mark and recapture studies must be regarded as the minimum likely level, while actual mortality rates remain uncertain. Hans Kristiansson carried out one of the few such studies, monitoring the survival of 220 hedgehogs for eight years (1972–79) around a village in southern Sweden (Kristiansson, 1990). He found a mortality rate of about 33 per cent among juveniles in their first year, a similar figure to adults, which seems rather low, but may be due to not taking account of young animals that dispersed or died before being found and marked. The number of juveniles actually captured was consistently less than the number estimated to have been added to the population using a Jolly-Seber analysis of the recapture data. So there must be some uncertainties here and mortality rates among young animals are likely to be somewhat higher than Kristiansson's figure. There was no difference in survival rates between males and females. The survival rate during the first year of life among British and Swedish hedgehogs was approximately half that of hedgehogs in New Zealand, where winters are shorter and less severe.

If we accept that first-year mortality is at least 30 per cent and probably double that given the number dying before being weaned, the general shape of the hedgehog's survival curve is similar to that for many other mammals that have been studied. There is a high mortality rate among the juveniles, including those that die before leaving the nest, but hedgehogs that survive their first winter stand a good chance of living another two or three years. The mortality rate among adults is about 30 per cent per year, but this increases in old age until the chances of further survival reduce to nil.

LIFESPAN

Assuming a juvenile mortality rate of up to 65 per cent in the first 12 months of life, including first winter losses, the average lifespan is about two years. A similar calculation in New Zealand suggests that average life expectancy there lies between 1.97 and 2.67 years (King, 2005), with a maximum of seven years. If 1 animal in my sample of 244 lived long enough to reach its seventh summer, then perhaps 4 or 5 in a thousand might live to that age, implying that a very few, maybe 1 in 10,000, might live to be 10 years old. It is unlikely that this age would be reached very often, if at all, because the gritty diet of wild hedgehogs wears down their teeth, compromising the ability to feed properly.

There is a beguiling idea that mammals have a finite number of breaths and heartbeats in their lifetime, reflecting differences in metabolic rate, and this is related to an animal's size. Small mammals breathe and metabolise faster than large ones and die younger. It is alleged that all mammals end up breathing about 200 million times in their life, one standard lifespan. If that is true, then a hibernating hedgehog that reduces its respiration rate by 90 per cent by hibernating for a third of the year should lengthen its lifespan by at least a couple of years compared to say a rabbit of similar body size. This appears to be true, in that it is very rare for a rabbit to live to be five years old, but that may be less to do with physiological limitations than heavy predation rates, something that has not been a threat to hedgehogs (at least until recently).

Using age-related data for modelling populations
It is possible to bring all this information together in order to create a survival curve that indicates the relationship between life expectancy and the passage of time (Fig. 182). But few actual studies have been made of living populations and only one (Kristiansson, 1990) that lasted more than five years, following animals as they lived from year to year. We might even use the data on population

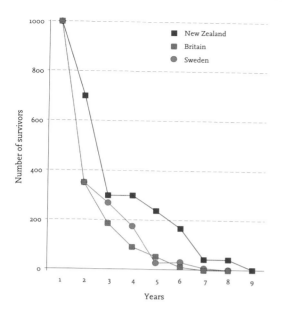

FIG 182. Comparative survival curves from Britain, Sweden and New Zealand show a broadly similar pattern, suggesting that they are probably fairly close to the truth. (Based on Brockie, in King, 1990)

structure to draw up a life table, attaching actual figures to numbers surviving year to year, mortality rates and life expectancy, but for an animal like the hedgehog where sample sizes tend to be small, there is considerable variation in data simply because of chance effects. Nevertheless, information about age structure and survival rates within a population is not just a matter of academic interest. Using this information for modelling populations is of considerable practical value. By including data about reproductive output, a 'virtual population' can be developed to predict population growth (or its decline to extinction) under various circumstances. Although one needs to take the figures with a pinch of salt and accept that they are likely to be approximations from which real life will frequently deviate, predictions based on population modelling are better than having no idea at all.

The power of modern computers is such that key population parameters can be applied in various combinations and changed randomly to represent stochastic events in real life. Knowing the sex ratio, number of young produced annually per female, likely lifespans and mortality rates, it is possible to predict the population size after a selected time interval like ten years. The predictions can be recalculated thousands of times with varying values for key parameters to end up with an average estimated population size and an expected range for maximum and minimum likely numbers. This was the approach used by

Tom Moorhouse for the People's Trust for Endangered Species to estimate the minimum viable population size for the hedgehog – in other words how few is too few for long-term survival, a vital issue with isolated populations such as those in urban areas. The derived estimates ranged from 32 to 60, depending on what figures were assumed for factors such as mortality rates and productivity per female. Below this number, the population could be expected to die out within 100 years. The minimum size of rural populations needed to be larger (up to 250) to counteract the added mortality caused by predation in the countryside and exposure to harsher weather that would result in greater variation in survival rates. These estimates are critical when discussing habitat size and accessibility for effective conservation of hedgehog populations.

Using the key parameters such as reproduction and survival rates, modelling a hypothetical population in a simplistic way could be used to test the feasibility of the bold claim that a few hedgehogs introduced to South Uist could have generated a population of 5,000 within 30 years. It turns out that it would just about be possible, but only with very high survival rates. Modelling can also be used to explore issues to do with removing the hedgehogs from the island in order to eliminate their predation on nesting birds. A simple model would suggest that catching 500 per year for 10 years would eliminate a population of 5,000, assuming that they did not breed. But if the model takes account of data on reproduction like that given in Chapter 7, it becomes clear that more time or an increased annual capture rate would be necessary to render the Uist hedgehogs extinct. Using published data for key parameters, a more sophisticated population model was devised (Shirley *et al.*, 2010) to estimate the time and effort it would take to remove all those Uist hedgehogs within one to six years. This was important because of the need to budget for the considerable cost of prolonging such an exercise if staff must be employed to catch the animals. Independently, my colleague Steve Carter developed another model to address the same practical issues, taking into account that hedgehogs would breed and die during the removal period. That model predicted removal of 1,000 per year would be necessary to enable eradication within 15 years, but would cost upwards of £500,000. Removing 2,000 each year would reduce the time to extinction by two thirds but require hugely increased effort. The model also indicated the severe cost penalty of pursuing a policy of not culling hedgehogs during the breeding season (to avoid the welfare problem of removing females and leaving dependent young to starve). In reality, barely 500 hedgehogs were removed from the Uists each year. The implication of these models is that eradication would be unlikely without a change in strategy involving a major increase in capture effort (and cost) and abandoning the principle of not removing lactating females.

CONCLUSION

It is possible to estimate the age of wild hedgehogs, with a fair degree of confidence, to generate data on population structure and survival rates. This is not just a matter of academic interest or idle curiosity. The data derived from such studies can become the inputs needed to create computer-based population models which have important predictive and practical uses. Population modelling is a valuable tool, but ultimately relies on data gathered from just a few studies, many of them carried out a quarter of a century ago. Even the most sophisticated models are like a house built on sand. Greater accuracy and reliability would be achieved if there were more replicates of the old investigations, gathering more data from a wider range of sites and influenced by different weather conditions. We could have more confidence in present-day population models if more research funding had been channelled into hedgehog studies in the past, but that's history. Meanwhile, hedgehog population models enable important questions to be identified and addressed. The answers may not be completely reliable, but they are better than pure guesswork and are considered further in Chapter 10.

CHAPTER 9

Death on the Roads and Other Dangers

L IKE A LOT OF OTHER species, the hedgehog has survived for millions of years in the face of many natural hazards. The problem now is that it is being confronted with serious threats that are the result of comparatively recent human activity, to which it is not adapted and which require rapid responses if the species is to thrive. However, although these may be the most pressing issues of today, we should not overlook the natural processes that also impact on the hedgehog population. Foremost among these is the challenge of hibernation, a major physiological readjustment that is needed every year to cope with food shortages in winter, but it also renders the animal helpless in the face of flooding or an inquisitive dog. Whilst relatively few hedgehogs probably die during hibernation itself, there is a critical time when they arouse in the spring. Food may be short and cold nights often resume, restricting the availability of many of the hedgehog's natural prey. Those that do successfully survive the winter will have depleted fat reserves and little to help tide them over until better weather resumes. They will be very vulnerable when metabolising what fat remains and any harmful chemicals that may have accumulated within it. Another period of extreme vulnerability occurs when young hedgehogs depart from their maternal nest. They leave behind the protection of the nest itself and the warmth of their mother and siblings. Poorly insulated and with little or no fat, survival can be very precarious, especially if the weather turns cold or dry. Parasites represent another natural challenge, with some of them posing a real risk to survival (see Chapter 11). However, these are all normal challenges and the hedgehog has had plenty of time for natural selection to adjust its population dynamics to cope with the inevitable mortality. It is the newly arrived dangers that threaten its long-term survival.

DEATH BY MISADVENTURE

Hedgehogs do seem rather prone to falling into things, and they may die simply because of their inability to climb out. However, many of those hazards are created by humans, such as trenches on building sites, and I once found the remains of several hedgehogs that had fallen into the underground explosives store of a wartime blockhouse. Cattle grids certainly claim numerous hedgehog victims, with as many as 52 being reported when one was cleaned out. I have several times seen hedgehogs drowned in cattle grids that had filled with water and a campaign to get escape ramps fitted was begun by Willie Euman after he had found ten of them in the pit below a cattle grid (Euman, 1979) (Fig. 183). This idea was later carried forward to great effect by Adrian Coles (see Chapter 13), who succeeded in getting the British Standards Institute to include an escape ramp in

cattle grids built in conformity with a new official British Standard 4008. Despite this, a countywide survey in 1990 by the Lancashire Wildlife Trust found that 80 per cent of installed grids lacked an escape ramp. I have noticed a similar lack of escape routes, even among some of the cattle grids on National Trust properties. The trouble is that new cattle grids are built infrequently and many were installed long ago without any escape route for animals that fall in. A retro-fitted ramp is not expensive and a small pile of bricks will do instead, but it needs an army of volunteers and a campaign among landowners to make all existing cattle grids safe, not just for hedgehogs but also for toads, shrews, newts and many other creatures that must be trapped in them, year in, year out.

FIG 183. There are thousands of cattle grids installed in the British countryside, permanently open pitfall traps for a wide range of animals that fall in and drown or starve if they cannot get out. Hedgehogs appear to be a frequent victim.

Garden ponds (and swimming pools) are another danger. One correspondent told me that six were

FIG 184. Hedgehogs easily become entangled in garden netting and will die if not soon discovered and released.

drowned in a neighbour's pond within a short time and four others rescued from it alive. Hedgehogs can swim, but they cannot get out if the pond has a smooth fibreglass or plastic lining unless there is a shallow escape route or some other structure that allows them to climb free. There are many other hazards around the garden too. Strawberries and peas are often protected by covering the plants with netting, cricket and tennis nets are frequently set out for a game in the summer, but not put away afterwards. Baggy piles or lines of netting are a threat because hedgehogs will push underneath, perhaps to hide there during the day, and their legs and spines become entangled (Fig. 184). There is no escape and they will die a slow death. These dangers can be easily mitigated (see Chapter 13).

Hedgehogs also seem to be rather prone to accidents. A few years ago, it was reported that some of them had been feeding on the dregs in plastic coffee cups discarded by staff outside the Rutherford and Appleton Laboratories. Backing out, the animals jammed their spines into the soft plastic and ended up unable to feed or move about owing to the large container covering their head. A similar problem affected the polystyrene packaging used for 'McFlurry', and the BHPS launched a successful campaign to have McDonald's modify them or take them off the market.

There is a problem with mowing machines too. Unlike other animals the hedgehog's natural response to the approaching noise and disturbance is to roll up and sit tight, not run away, so they do not flee to safety as a mowing machine approaches. Domestic lawnmowers pose no threat but gardeners, park managers and farmers often use strimmers to cut back weedy growth that intrudes into places meant for flowers or mown turf (Fig. 185). Following radio-tagged hedgehogs reveals that they often chose exactly this type of rank vegetation in which to lie up on warm summer days. There may be no visible sign of the animals, making it hard to avoid them when using these machines. Strimmers have a whirling cord that cuts

FIG 185. Hedgehogs often nest in rank vegetation, exactly the type of growth that is cleared away by gardeners and maintenance workers using a strimmer. The whirling cord in one of these machines inflicts appalling damage on any hedgehogs that are resting there.

back plant stalks, removing the cover and nesting material that hedgehogs need. They also inflict terrible injuries on the animals, severing limbs and noses or cutting deeply into the skin. Such damage may well be fatal, but traumatised survivors are now one of the most frequent arrivals at the door of wildlife hospitals and rescue centres.

Larger mowing machines are a common sight in the summer, cutting back the grass and wildflowers along road verges. These are usually flails towed by a tractor, the cutting blade being invisible as it is covered by a protective metal hood about 1.5 m wide (Fig. 186). It simply smashes anything in its path, leaving a mulch of mangled vegetation. This will bury the remains of any hedgehogs that are encountered, so we have no way of knowing how many animals might be killed by these machines and what effect that might have on their population as a whole. Roadside

FIG 186. Flail mowers are used to keep areas of long grass under control, especially road verges. Hedgehogs often lie up in such habitats during summer days. It is impossible to know how many are killed by these mowers, as they will leave little in the way of conspicuous evidence.

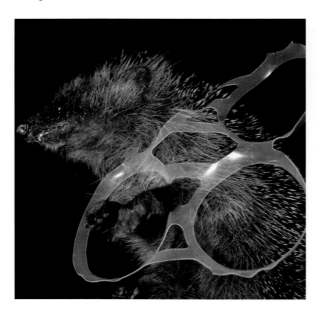

FIG 187. Foraging hedgehogs often fall foul of litter like this plastic six-pack holder or the thousands of elastic bands discarded by postmen.

vegetation has to be managed for safety and amenity reasons, so there must be some hedgehogs lost in this way, perhaps quite a lot. Hedgehogs will be among the many creatures that benefit from campaigns to protect insects, wild flowers and nesting birds that also inhabit roadside vegetation. These campaigns have mainly focused on delaying the onset of mowing in early summer and reducing its frequency, but increasing fuel and labour costs also mean that road verges seem to be mown less often now than in the past. This is a welcome development, but we still have no idea of how big an impact mowing machines make on the national population of hedgehogs.

Fires, natural and otherwise, also result in hedgehog casualties and this is a particular problem around Guy Fawkes' night. Shortly before 5 November each year, the BHPS issues a warning about the threat posed by bonfires and urges care over lighting them or the piles of garden refuse in which hedgehogs may have chosen to hibernate. The danger was even mentioned in Parliament in 2015. Flooding probably accounts for a few more deaths each year, but this is likely to be a relatively minor issue and anyway hard to quantify, just like the victims of fires and mowing machines. However, there are several other clear and distinctive threats to hedgehogs that pose a serious challenge to survival, killing hedgehogs both directly and also indirectly in ways that may not always be immediately obvious.

ROADKILL

Flattened hedgehogs are one of the more distinctive forms of road casualty and the animal's remains are easily recognised, so people are very conscious of having seen them. Most other species would go unrecognised and without comment. In the past, whenever anyone made lists of species killed on the roads, hedgehogs were usually one of the two or three commonest casualties recorded, but this could simply be because their tough skin and robust spines mean the carcass persists for longer than those of say rabbits or rats. It is possible that the ease of detection and recognition exaggerates the apparent importance of road traffic accidents for this species. Nevertheless, roadkill is a matter of high public awareness and also prompts obvious questions about the numbers killed and what threat it poses to the population as a whole (Fig. 188).

It is popularly supposed that the apparent high numbers of dead hedgehogs seen on roads is a consequence of their natural habit of rolling up when confronted by danger, in this case an approaching vehicle. Actually, unless they are physically touched, hedgehogs do not roll up completely when threatened, but lower the head and hunch the body whilst still remaining on their feet. Either way, rolled up or not, they are no match for an approaching vehicle. A beguiling theory has been aired suggesting that some hedgehogs might be learning to run away instead of staying still. Natural selection would then favour them and we may see the evolution of a race of speedy hedgehogs that take avoiding action when confronted by approaching danger, the way that other mammals do, rather than standing their ground. This idea has an appealing Darwinian flavour, but

FIG 188. In the past, the hedgehog has been one of the top three mammal casualties killed by road traffic (rabbit and brown rat being the other two). Many are still killed on the roads, but badgers and foxes are often more numerous victims these days.

is basically flawed on two counts. Firstly, we have no data on what hedgehogs did before the invention of fast cars and lorries, so that proving an evolutionary trend by making 'before and after' comparisons is not possible. Secondly, if an animal runs away obliquely in the path of the vehicle, it actually spends longer in the track of the oncoming wheels. If it runs off to one side, at right angles to the approaching danger, it could easily cross the path of a tyre which would otherwise have missed it had the animal stayed still.

Nevertheless, this story gained a lot of press attention and remains a favourite source of conjecture when the issue of roadkill is discussed. My colleague Steve Carter carried out some experiments (carefully!) to observe how hedgehogs behave when confronted by an approaching vehicle at night. His hedgehogs often did not attempt to avoid roads, but on the road itself they tended to move faster than when on the grassy verge. When a slow-moving car approached, about half of the experimental animals reacted by running off, while the rest adopted the typical 'freeze' reaction, waiting for the threat to recede. Those that ran away reacted when the car was so close that under normal circumstances they would probably have been run over anyway. These observations suggest that when a vehicle approaches a hedgehog, it makes little difference whether the animal freezes or runs – they are likely to become traffic victims either way. There is no evidence that we are observing natural selection promoting an evolutionary trend towards fleet-footed hedgehogs.

Why should they get killed on roads at all? Why would a hedgehog set out to cross a road, especially a wide one? The road surface is inherently hostile, being smelly with oil and rubber residues and also very rough on the hedgehog's soft feet. It is unlikely it can see anything attractive on the far side, in the dark and with eyes barely 2 cm off the ground. In fact there is evidence that they will frequently turn away from a road and refrain from crossing it (Rondinini & Doncaster, 2002). It is rare to see a dead hedgehog on a British motorway, with its wide carriageways and heavy traffic. Hedgehogs are far more commonly killed on our smaller roads, but even these may act as a disincentive to dispersal, with animals being able to cross but reluctant to do so. This is certainly the case with other small mammals (MacPherson et al., 2011) and there are significant implications for fragmenting existing populations. Hedgehogs may cross roads less often than we think, in spite of the numbers we see dead. Nevertheless many get killed doing so. Maybe traffic density reaches a level at which it becomes a deterrent and will cause a hedgehog to turn back rather than venture forth. In New Zealand, it is asserted that roads carrying more than 3,000 vehicles per day form barriers to larger mammals, and it is the less busy roads that claim the most victims (Brockie et al., 2009). However, an analysis

FIG 189. Roads are smelly, noisy and often have approaching vehicles, so hedgehogs often turn away rather than cross. Many are killed there nevertheless, with much debate about whether they would be better off running away rather than curling up in a defensive posture.

of roadkill in Britain showed no correlation between traffic flow and counts of dead hedgehogs or rabbits (Bright *et al.*, 2015) (Fig. 189).

Driving a regular route does create the impression that hedgehogs are run over more often in certain places than along the route as a whole and this has been confirmed by statistical analysis in Ireland (Haigh *et al.*, 2014a). That might suggest hedgehogs are using their own regular pathways, but it might also be because fences and other obstacles prevent access elsewhere and funnel the animals into crossing at particular places. The numbers we see dead on the road do vary seasonally, often with peaks in April and May, which is when the males are especially active seeking mates. There is another peak in late summer as the population reaches its maximum before winter begins (a pattern also observed in Ireland and other countries).

HOW MANY HEDGEHOGS ARE KILLED ON THE ROADS?

Regular counts following a standard protocol can provide data from which conclusions may be drawn regarding comparative abundance of hedgehogs at different times and in different parts of the country (see Chapter 2), but trying to estimate the total number killed in Britain each year is not easy. It is important because we need to assess whether roads represent a serious threat to the population or merely kill a small proportion of the total numbers, with no long-term impact on the population as a whole.

The obvious way to estimate the total number killed in this country is to count how many are seen dead on a sample of roads and scale up that number to take account of the total mileage of roads in the country as a whole. The problem here is that if the original sample count happened to be in an area where hedgehogs were unusually abundant, scaling it up will result in an excessively large estimate for the country overall. This is why the figure of 1 million killed on the roads each year, published in a Sunday newspaper in the 1960s and widely publicised since, is likely to be a significant overestimate. In an attempt to approach this and other hedgehog questions more rigorously, the People's Trust for Endangered Species (PTES) instigated regular counts of road casualties by volunteers, the Mammals on Roads (MoR) surveys. In the four years 2001 to 2004, there were 6,411 dead hedgehogs counted on a total of 270,000 miles of roads surveyed. This works out at an average of about one hedgehog per 42 miles of road. Since there are about 245,000 miles of roads in Britain, one might estimate an annual mortality of about 5,900 during the three months that the survey was undertaken annually (July–September inclusive). Scaling this up to take account of hedgehogs being active for at least six months of the year, the annual mortality seems likely to be a minimum of 12,000 animals, probably nearer 15,000 and more still because the survey counts excluded any killed on motorways and also the large numbers that are killed in urban areas (because these were excluded from MoR surveys). By this line of reasoning, the annual toll on the hedgehog population would be between 15,000 and 20,000, perhaps more. A survey on the roads of Suffolk, conducted between January and October, found 1,488 hedgehogs. Suffolk is about 3 per cent of England, so scaled up to take account of the rest of Britain, there would be over 50,000 deaths on roads. But Suffolk is not typical of the country as a whole. It has also been suggested that the density of roads is a key factor; more roads means more chance that a hedgehog will get run over, so comparisons between different parts of the country with different densities of roads is unreliable. If so, then scaling up from any local survey to a national level will give invalid estimates for total roadkill.

However, it is important to take account of the practical and methodological details of the MoR surveys. For example, when driving on dual carriageways, observers were told to count only the hedgehogs seen on the carriageway they were using and, for safety reasons, not to attempt to scan the other half of the road at the same time (which anyway might be the other side of a wide central reservation). Thus, an unknown fraction of the hedgehogs killed on dual carriageways remained uncounted, perhaps as many as half. Since dual carriageways account for about 17 per cent of all major roads, this omission could represent a significant number of animals. The MoR surveys also instructed participants not to count in the rain because of reduced visibility and because wet, flattened hedgehogs are less conspicuous than dry ones. This 'detection factor' is another of the methodological problems with counting roadkills. It reflects the proportion of hedgehogs that escape notice, perhaps also because observers are driving too fast or they are distracted by more important things around them. Yet another issue is the 'carcass persistence time'. This too is an unknown quantity. If the tough and durable remains of a dead hedgehog continue to be recognisable for a week, they are more likely to be noticed and counted than say a frog whose body might be obliterated by passing traffic within a day. Sometimes a squashed hedgehog can actually remain recognisable for up to a month, its skin baked hard on the road by hot summer sunshine. However, only a small amount of rain will soften up a flattened body and traffic will pulverise the remains sufficiently that it will soon become difficult to spot from a moving vehicle. In wet conditions, a body may be lost within a few days. There is also the possibility that local authority street cleaners or scavenging foxes will remove a proportion, again unknown, before they are seen and counted by MoR volunteers.

So there are several key factors that affect the arithmetic when estimating total roadkill numbers. All of them will have a significant effect if taken into account, but all of them are also unquantified and perhaps impossible to estimate accurately. However, if some of these issues are added into the calculations, the total hedgehog roadkill may be as many as 167,000–350,000! (Wembridge et al., 2016). This is an order of magnitude greater than suggested earlier, but the extent of the variation in that estimate is itself an indication of the uncertainties involved in its calculation. In the Netherlands, it is estimated that between 113,000 and 340,000 hedgehogs are killed on the roads annually; in Belgium, the annual mortality is said to be 230,000–350,000 (Holsbeek et al., 1999). These figures are higher than estimates for Britain, but suggest that road traffic could be killing enough hedgehogs to make a significant contribution to a decline in the size of the hedgehog population.

The question remains as to the extent of the threat to the British hedgehog population as a whole. Assuming that there are about 1.55 million hedgehogs in Britain (Harris et al., 1995), then 15,000–20,000 deaths per year represents a minor loss of around 1–2 per cent killed by traffic annually. If roads really did account for as many as 350,000 hedgehogs each year, that would be a massive 23 per cent loss every year. This seems both unsustainable and improbable, but it could be even worse, since the estimate for the total population size used here (1.55 million) is based on dodgy data from long ago (see Chapter 10) and there are now also considerably fewer hedgehogs about.

Another way of assessing the severity of roadkill at the population level would be to consider a more limited area than the whole of the country. For example, a survey of road casualties on Jersey in the Channel Islands recorded more than

600 hedgehogs killed in a year. This implies a major loss to what is a limited island population (Morris & Burdon, 2008), possibly in the region of 10 per cent.

One way of quantifying the significance of roadkill on the population as a whole would be to estimate population densities by capture-mark-recapture methods (see Chapter 10) in areas of the countryside with differing levels of traffic flow. But those methods are subject to many uncertainties and there would also probably be other factors affecting hedgehog numbers, including habitat type or the presence of badgers. However, in the Netherlands, an index of abundance (the frequency of finding hedgehog footprints in feeding tunnels) was used to compare areas where there were many roads with locations where there were few roads. On that basis, it is claimed that roadkill may reduce hedgehog population densities by up to 30 per cent (Huijser & Bergers, 2000).

Although they represent only small samples, we can also look at the numbers killed during studies of marked populations of hedgehogs. Of the 80 or so marked animals on a golf course in west London, very few were found dead on the road that runs alongside most of its length despite its fast and heavy traffic load, but they comprised 18 per cent of all known deaths (Reeve, 1994). Traffic accounted for 33 per cent (12 known deaths) of the 30 hedgehogs translocated in Oxfordshire (Doncaster, 1992), a mortality rate that may have been exacerbated by transferring the animals to an unfamiliar place, resulting in increased activity on their part. At a study site in New Zealand, only 4 per cent of marked hedgehogs ended up dead on adjacent roads, but traffic densities there are low. In the Netherlands, the comparable figure was 12 per cent within two years. A detailed four-year study of road casualties on a 16.5 km section of road in southern Sweden (Göransson et al., 1976) found 18–39 (17–22 per cent) of the local hedgehogs were killed on that road annually, although this appeared not to result in a dwindling population. Hans Kristiansson monitored the survival of 220 hedgehogs in a Swedish village for eight years, during which road traffic accounted for between 2 per cent and 22 per cent (average about 8–10 per cent) of the population each year. In a Finnish study, three quarters of known deaths were caused by human activity, 97 per cent of which were due to road traffic (Rautio et al., 2016), and in Poland, 24 per cent of a population of 78 hedgehog were run over in a single year (Orlowski & Nowak, 2004). In one of my own studies, 2 out of 12 animals (17 per cent) were killed on local roads in just a couple of months, but in special circumstances that were different from other studies and in a habitat that was not typical of the country as a whole.

The upshot of all this is that we simply do not know how serious road traffic is as a mortality factor for hedgehogs, but in terms of percentage loss the figure is not inconsiderable. Having evolved for millions of years into an animal that is largely unaffected by predators, the sudden onslaught of road traffic is an additional form of 'predation' to which the hedgehog's population dynamics have not had time to adjust. The numbers killed this way certainly cannot be doing the species any good and may be a serious threat to small and isolated populations like those that occur in many urban areas. Some evidence in support of this was published in Bavaria, where the possible loss of entire village populations of hedgehogs was attributed to roadkill (Reichholf, 1983). Ironically, road verges can be important foraging sites and dispersal corridors for hedgehogs, despite the hazard they represent.

PREDATION

Bristling spines present an impenetrable panoply to any would-be predator and a hedgehog can remain in a spiky rolled-up condition almost indefinitely. If a paw (or finger) is trapped when it curls up, the combination of sharp spines and powerful rolling-up muscles can create a very painful experience for any attacker. Rolling up might also result in squeezing and emptying a full bladder, giving rise to the suggestion by Pliny (and copied down the ages by many other authors) that a hedgehog will do this deliberately as a form of defence, increasing its unattractiveness for a meal. Most predators leave hedgehogs alone.

Eagle owls seem to take them occasionally (Andrews, 1990); in Germany, the remains of 160 hedgehogs were found among 2,211 vertebrate prey taken by eagle owls and I once found the bones of a young hedgehog in a disintegrated pellet regurgitated by a large predatory bird in Turkey. But eagle owls are not a problem for British hedgehogs, nor would they be much troubled by buzzards or golden eagles, which are active during the day, although red kites probably take a few scavenged off the roads. There were no hedgehog remains among the thousands of prey items I have identified in barn owl pellets, but I have seen an eyewitness account of a tawny owl that attacked a hedgehog in Lancashire and probably carried it away, but this is likely to be a highly unusual occurrence. A short video clip was posted on YouTube in 2014 showing a tawny owl swooping down beside a moving hedgehog, which flinched and then scuttled away to hide, but the owl made no attempt to attack it. Magpies will often go for sickly hedgehogs that wander about in daylight and they may sometimes inflict serious wounds, perhaps even resulting in death. In New Zealand, hedgehog fur was found in 3 out of 358 cat droppings and once in the gut of 45 cats, but this could represent scavenging rather than direct predation. British cats are unlikely to kill many hedgehogs.

If your dog is
likely to attack
a hedgehog...

...for both of their
sakes, keep the dog on
a lead for garden runs,
especially after dark.

HEDGEHOG HOUSE, DHUSTONE, LUDLOW,
SHROPSHIRE, SY8 3PL
Tel: 01584 890801
E-mail: info@britishhedgehogs.org.uk
www.britishhedgehogs.org.uk
Registered Charity Number 1164542
(formerly 326885)

British Hedgehog
Preservation Society

FIG 190. Dogs, especially the larger breeds, will often interfere with hedgehogs, perhaps just lifting them in the mouth, but sometimes actively biting and causing injury. With so many dog owners often taking their dog for a walk after dark, dogs have become a significant threat to hedgehogs.

Dogs may be more of a problem, but hedgehogs are able to defend themselves and incidents involving dogs probably more often result in injuries (to both species) rather than death (Fig. 190). Dog bites are a common reason for hedgehogs to end up in rescue centres and dogs off the lead will endanger any defenceless young that are found in a hedgehog's nest. The BHPS issues periodic warnings about the need to keep dogs under control and just their presence in gardens may deter hedgehogs from visiting.

It is likely that the majority of predated hedgehogs are in fact juveniles, in which the spines are not only thin and relatively soft, but the skin musculature is also incompletely developed. These younger animals are less able to resist determined efforts to attack them by rolling up tightly. Their skin is also insufficiently voluminous to allow the animal to be fully enclosed by its spiny skin and a determined predator could exploit this weakness, but we have few wild species that could tackle a hedgehog successfully. Over the centuries, bears and wolves were heavily persecuted and their extinction removed them as a threat to hedgehogs.

There are occasional old records of hedgehogs in the diet of polecats (see Macpherson, 1892, for example), and humans might also be added to the list of occasional predators (see Chapter 12). Foxes can and do eat hedgehogs, but these are probably mainly road casualties, the fox acting simply as an opportunistic scavenger. However, foxes have been seen to attack live hedgehogs (Harris, 1986) and they have been accused of depleting hedgehog numbers in urban areas, especially through their predation on nestlings. There are also persistent folk tales of foxes taking a hedgehog to water or urinating on it to provoke the animal into uncurling (Fig. 191). Foxes might kill the odd one or

FIG 191. Many of the old accounts of hedgehogs tell tales of foxes rolling them into water or urinating on them. Allegedly, this causes the creature to unroll, thereby becoming less well defended against being killed and eaten.

two occasionally, but generally it is not worth the effort, especially in urban areas with abundant pet food and bird tables. Some hedgehogs brought in to care centres show injuries to their hind legs which are attributed to foxes, but dogs and other hedgehogs will often snap at the protruding hind legs of a hedgehog as it runs away, causing at least superficial injury. In many cases, the damage is far more serious and must be due to a large animal. It would be difficult to attribute the wound to foxes with certainty, but there is abundant direct evidence that foxes (and dogs) do attack hedgehogs and both are now very abundant in many urban areas where hedgehogs ought to be safe from predation. Nevertheless, observers who have kept careful records of the wildlife in their gardens through the PTES Living with Mammals Project showed no significant increase in fox numbers at around 3,000 sites, so it is unlikely that

FIG 192. Regular surveys of householders by the PTES reveal hedgehogs and foxes often coexisting in gardens, suggesting that the latter are not a widespread or serious threat. (Angie Davidson/ Hedgehog Street)

foxes are exerting greater pressure on hedgehog populations than they did in the past and they are probably not responsible for a chronic decline in hedgehog numbers (Fig. 192). By contrast badgers are increasing and there is more and more evidence accruing that this species is having a serious impact on the hedgehog (Pettett *et al.*, 2017a)

THE BADGER AS A PREDATOR

The badger is undoubtedly the most important predator of hedgehogs. It is the one carnivore that has claws long enough to reach down to the hedgehog's skin among a mass of its bristling spines. Its forelimbs are also powerfully developed for digging, enabling a hapless hedgehog to be easily torn apart. The badger is supremely well equipped to prey upon any unfortunate hedgehogs that it comes across and its attacks have been well chronicled in the literature. Topsel (1658) recorded it as a killer and most wildlife authors since have done so too, sometimes mentioning the victim's 'hideous cries' while being caught and devoured. Usually, the hedgehog is ripped open and its body torn away from the dorsal part of the skin and eaten. Only the spiny skin remains, a fairly unequivocal indication of who the predator was (Fig. 193). Some keen supporters of the badger have sought to deny its sins, but I have seen these pathetic remains and also viewed several gruesome video sequences obtained using trail cameras. Despite this, and much of what I have written in this book, I like badgers and still clearly recall the thrill of seeing them for the first time, even though that is now more than half a century ago. Nevertheless, it has become increasingly clear that interactions between badgers and hedgehogs are an issue that cannot be ignored.

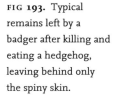

FIG 193. Typical remains left by a badger after killing and eating a hedgehog, leaving behind only the spiny skin.

Badgers are omnivores, but also predators. They feed on animals including worms, beetles, insect larvae and occasionally on mammals, birds and eggs. In fact they eat many of the things that sustain hedgehogs and that also form part of the diet for shrews, moles, fox and polecat. These are all species that do much the same thing: prey upon macroinvertebrates. In this way, badgers and hedgehogs belong to the same feeding 'guild' and compete with each other for some of the same resources. In addition, badgers will kill and eat hedgehogs. This is referred to as 'intraguild predation' and is much discussed as an ecological principle in the literature. Eating a hedgehog has the double advantage (to the badger) of not only getting a useful meal, but also eliminating a competitor for food. This may seem like a good idea from the point of view of the top predator, but if such predation becomes too successful it may disrupt a long-standing natural balance. If one layer of a food pyramid is removed in this way, then the top predators may need to expand their diet, perhaps to include unexpected and valuable alternative prey such as chickens or domestic stock. If the middle-ranking predator is severely reduced or eliminated, perhaps its erstwhile prey will become embarrassingly abundant. These are interesting issues, but perhaps not of pressing concern in relation to hedgehogs. What matters is that badgers kill hedgehogs and also compete with them for certain forms of macroinvertebrate food such as earthworms.

So long as badgers remained relatively scarce, they would have had only a minor impact on hedgehogs at the population level, but in recent times their numbers have hugely increased. In the late 1980s, it is thought there were roughly a quarter of a million badgers in Britain living in about 45,000 'social groups'. The badger population of England and Wales was put at 225,000 (Cresswell et al., 1990). Within in a decade, there had been a 24 per cent increase in the number of badger social groups in Britain, rising further to 81,000 by 2013. The actual total population of badgers that this represents depends upon the average number in a social group. If it is still 5.9, as in the 1980s, the total number of badgers may have doubled, in England at least. The most recent estimates, taking account of several factors that may vary across the country (including social group size), suggest the total population of badgers in England and Wales is approximately 485,000, at an average density of between 0.26–5.98 badgers per km^2 (Judge et al., 2017). The reason for this big increase in numbers is unclear, but it may be a consequence of changes in habitat quality. Another possibility is better survival among cubs during warmer, wetter summers, leading to a larger number of breeding animals the following year, repeated for several years in succession. Some would argue that the increase is a welcome confirmation that legal protection given to the badger since the 1970s has had the beneficial effect of allowing the population to

FIG 194. Badgers forage for earthworms and other food items that support hedgehogs. In this way, as competitors, they can suppress hedgehog populations. Preying on hedgehogs exacerbates the threat they pose.

bounce back to its proper level, having been previously suppressed by excessive levels of persecution, especially by badger diggers. However, there is no indication as to what the population size might have been in the distant past. Records of bounty payments made by churchwardens prior to the 1830s (Lovegrove, 2007) show remarkably few badgers (called 'greys') being killed despite a generous bounty payment of one shilling each, more than many men earned in a whole day. Despite this incentive, few parishes where badgers were killed averaged even three per year. This suggests that badgers were uncommon animals for centuries, and that modern numbers are way above the historical norm (Fig. 194).

Further evidence comes from studies of the relationship between the size and abundance of mammals. Across the world and covering many species, there is a direct correlation between an animal's size and its population density. Small mammals are more abundant than big ones. In this respect, badgers are out of line, with far more of them present than would be predicted from their body size. The total biomass of badgers in this country is 36 per cent greater than that of all our other terrestrial carnivores put together (Harris & Yalden, 2008). Put another way, there is a far greater tonnage of badgers in the British countryside than would be expected based on both logic and biological principles. One could argue endlessly and fruitlessly about whether there are 'too many badgers' (as Prince Charles once told me very firmly!), but just being numerous is the problem. Badgers are large animals. Each one eats about the same amount as five hedgehogs. Every extra badger eats the food that would otherwise be there to support other wildlife, including thrushes and starlings, whose numbers are also declining. More badgers has to mean fewer of something else, even without actually preying on them. The hedgehog loses out twice over: badgers compete

FIG 195. Badgers are sometimes recorded feeding in the same gardens as hedgehogs. Perhaps the additional food put out by people means there is sufficient for the badger not to bother the hedgehogs. It is also possible that predation on hedgehogs is limited to particular individual badgers, and not all of them are guilty. (Angie Davidson/Hedgehog Street)

with it for the same foods and badgers also eat hedgehogs directly. A survey carried out by the Central Science Laboratory in 2006 found a negative correlation between numbers of hedgehogs and badgers – where there were more badgers, there were fewer hedgehogs, a pattern that has been confirmed by several other radio-tracking studies and independent surveys. Indeed, almost all the recent field studies of hedgehogs conclude that badgers are a significant threat and their presence affects both hedgehog behaviour and distribution (Fig. 195).

As with road casualties, it is difficult to know the extent to which badgers threaten the hedgehog population as a whole, but again we can consider the fate of individuals that were followed in the course of particular studies. In one of mine, 3 out of 12 (25 per cent) were killed by badgers within two months (compared with only 2 run over on local roads). Beate Johansen experienced similar losses in Norway – 6 out of 17 eaten by badgers (35 per cent), but only 3 run over. Patrick Doncaster found badgers ate 3 of his 12 adult hedgehogs (25 per cent) within two months of starting a study in Oxfordshire. Similarly when he introduced 30 radio-tagged hedgehogs into Wytham Woods near Oxford, 7 (23 per cent) were eaten by badgers. There is also abundant evidence that the presence and number of badgers affect the nightly movements of hedgehogs, with avoidance behaviour perhaps keeping them away from good feeding areas. Even just the smell of badgers is sufficient to elicit avoidance behaviour on the part of hedgehogs (Ward *et al.*, 1997). Clearly, badgers have become an important issue in modifying the ecology, behaviour and survival of British hedgehogs (Doncaster, 1993; Hof *et al.*, 2012) and a similar situation is found in the Netherlands (van de Poel *et al.*, 2015). Principal component analysis suggests that the combination of badger presence and food availability is the main determinant of hedgehog abundance, and local extinction

FIG 196. Data from the first national badger survey showing numbers present in the late 1980s. Studies in Oxfordshire suggested that hedgehogs faced the likelihood of extinction once badger numbers exceeded about 13 per 10 km², a figure already exceeded in some areas 30 years ago. Badger numbers have greatly increased since then.

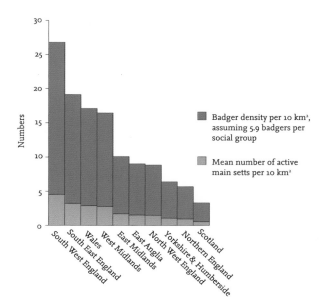

was predicted to occur when the density of badgers exceeded about 2.27 setts per 10 km² (Micol et al., 1994). That density of badgers had already been exceeded by the time of the first national badger survey in the 1980s (Table 24). Over England and Wales, the average density of badger setts is now almost double that (Judge et al., 2017), with a probable increase in social group size as well. This does not bode well for the hedgehog (Fig. 196).

It has been widely assumed that urban areas were a refuge from badgers and this is why hedgehogs are often more numerous in and around towns than in the countryside. Several studies of hedgehogs in rural areas have found them gravitating towards villages, farm buildings and gardens. Again this is often presumed to be evidence of avoidance behaviour and assumes that such places are safe from badgers. However, as our urban fringe relentlessly extends into the countryside, and as badger numbers continue to increase, we find them living commensally with humans increasingly often. The urban refuge is no longer safe and the probability of hedgehogs surviving in urban areas declines towards zero in places where there is a high density of badgers (Young et al., 2006). We might reasonably assume that the badger population will continue to exert a downward pressure on hedgehog numbers.

In the early 1970s, bovine tuberculosis (bTB) was found in wild badgers. This country had been almost free of the disease, but since then there has been

TABLE 24. Regional densities of badgers. Data from the National Badger Survey of 1985–88 (Cresswell *et al.*, 1990). Studies in Oxfordshire suggested that once the density of badger setts exceeds 2.27 per 10 km², equivalent to a population of about 13 badgers, the local hedgehogs face extinction (Micol *et al.*, 1994). This figure had already been exceeded in several parts of Britain by the 1990s (marked * in the table) and badger numbers have risen substantially since that time, perhaps even doubled.

Region	Mean no. of active main setts per 10 km²	Badger density per 10 km², assuming 5.9 badgers per social group
Northern England	0.96	5.66
Northwest England	1.49	8.79
Yorkshire & Humberside	1.08	6.37
West Midlands	2.77	16.34*
East Midlands	1.70	10.03
East Anglia	1.52	8.97
South West England	4.51	26.61*
Southeast England	3.20	19.00*
Wales	2.88	16.99*
Scotland	0.56	3.30

a significant increase in the incidence of bTB in dairy herds. The cost to the taxpayer was estimated to be about £100 million per year in 2015, with around 30,000 cattle having to be slaughtered annually. Badgers are a reservoir for the causative bacteria, although their role in actually transmitting it to cattle has been endlessly disputed. Culling badgers might help reduce the problem, or might make it worse by causing the established territorial systems of badger clans to break down, leading to more dispersal movements and greater risk of spreading the disease. Years of heavily criticised badger culling strategies failed to resolve that issue or result in controlling bTB. Culling is very unpopular with the public, but politically necessary given the devastation that the disease has caused in the dairy industry. For several years, badgers were culled in a large and structured experiment to measure the effects of doing so in relation to controlling the disease. They were removed from a selection of specially chosen areas in the Randomised Badger Culling Trials of 1998–2008, often called the 'Krebs trial' after Sir John Krebs who designed the experimental protocol for the cull. Five years after badger culling began, it was found that in areas of amenity grassland, a preferred hedgehog habitat (at least in those days), their numbers had more than doubled, from 0.9 per ha to 2.4 per ha. Hedgehogs remained fewer (0.3 per ha) and unchanged where no badgers were killed (Trewby *et al.*, 2014). The apparent increase in numbers seen after removal of badgers was perhaps an illusion resulting from the same number of hedgehogs being bold enough to range more widely once the threat posed by badgers had gone. However, radio-tracking showed no major changes in hedgehog behaviour after badgers had been removed, so the observed increase in their numbers was probably real.

The Krebs trials had indicated that culling could exacerbate the bTB problem by causing the badgers to move about more. Despite this, a political decision was taken to instigate further badger culls. About 10,000 were killed in the autumn of 2016, making a total of more than 14,800 in three years. For political and economic reasons, badger culls may be extended in the future, in spite of widespread protests. Ideally, we should have a 'before and after' survey of hedgehogs at more than one culling site to measure the effects, but the cull locations were kept secret beforehand because the protesters were becoming seriously threatening. The PTES and BHPS jointly rejected the proposal to cull badgers mainly on the grounds that it would not solve the disease problem and that culling might make it worse.

This is a difficult issue. On the one hand, killing small groups of badgers results in others moving into the vacated territory, potentially spreading disease further. On the other hand, if enough badgers are killed over a big enough area, it could at least remove them as a reservoir of bTB. This was the approach recommended by the Government's Chief Scientist Sir David King and led to the recent culls. Farmers are desperate to see the bTB problem resolved and they can put pressure on their MPs, but culling alone will not solve the problem because there are other factors involved. There needs to be an integrated approach that includes much greater control of cattle movements and better cattle management, perhaps even a reappraisal of the farming industry, including the genetics of dairy cattle and more accurate methods of testing for bTB. Where badger culls have taken place, hedgehog numbers have increased, but few people want to kill badgers and nobody should advocate killing them just to help hedgehogs. Belatedly, extensive trials are in operation deploying vaccines to control the disease, and from 2018 the policy in Eire will change from culling badgers to a strategy based on their use. If vaccination proves to be successful, British badgers will not need to be killed to control or eradicate bovine TB. Their numbers will then remain high, an ongoing threat to rural populations of hedgehogs. If culling proves to be a more cost-effective solution to the bTB problem than vaccines, culling will probably resume on a larger scale. Local increases in the number of hedgehogs could be that cloud's silver lining.

POISONS

As a rather generalist feeder, the hedgehog is vulnerable to a wide range of poisons and contaminants that are released into the environment for different reasons. These will include heavy metals from a variety of sources, consumed via the hedgehog's prey. Cadmium, for example, accumulates with increasing age in an animal's liver (Rautio *et al.*, 2016), although there is no evidence to suggest that this or other industrial contaminants pose a significant threat to hedgehogs. Agricultural chemicals appear to be more of a problem, especially where efforts to increase the yield from arable farming include elimination of invertebrates that eat or damage crops. In the past, crops were sprayed with organochlorine compounds (like DDT and Dieldrin), killing weevils, aphids, caterpillars and anything else that compromised plant viability. Seeds were coated with Aldrin to kill insects that invade seed stores or have larvae that damaged the seeds after they have been sown. These agricultural insecticides proved to be extremely harmful because they are bioaccumulators. Tiny amounts consumed from each contaminated insect built up in a predator's tissues. Carnivores further along the food chain would accumulate small sub-lethal quantities from each

FIG 197. Some crops receive repeated doses of chemicals whose purpose is to eliminate the very wildlife that hedgehogs need for food. Ploughing also reduces soil invertebrates.

of their prey until a toxic level had accumulated internally. Widespread deaths and reproductive failures among birds and bats in the 1960s highlighted the problem posed by these toxic organochlorine compounds and their physiological and ecological effects were intensively studied. Little attempt was made to establish the effects on hedgehogs, either as individuals or at the population level. However, the use of agricultural pesticides cannot have been benign, if only because their purpose was to reduce or eliminate the very prey that hedgehogs rely on for most of their food (Fig. 197). At the individual level, small non-lethal doses of organochlorine compounds would also have accumulated in the hedgehog's fat, to be released as reserves were consumed over winter, especially in a burst at the end of hibernation as the last dregs of fat were used up. This could have led to an increased mortality rate among hedgehogs at that critical time of the year, especially the smaller ones with lower fat reserves. These harmful chemicals were mostly banned in the 1970s, so they have not therefore been responsible for reducing hedgehog numbers in the past 30 years, but they may well have contributed significantly to earlier losses.

Just as insecticides could easily be assumed to be harmless to hedgehogs, because they were aimed at insects, one might be forgiven for assuming that hedgehogs were safe from weedkillers. These kill grass and weeds, so what's

FIG 198. There is increasing evidence that hedgehogs can only thrive around the uncultivated margins of arable fields, leaving large areas of the countryside devoid of them.

the problem? In fact one of the most commonly used herbicides, paraquat, was actually highly toxic to animals and a foraging hedgehog pushing through rank vegetation that had recently been sprayed would easily pick up such a substance and then ingest it when licking its fur during a session of grooming. The sale and use of paraquat has been banned, and now the future of glyphosate is under review. This has become the universally used herbicide, but turns out to have more widespread effects, including causing liver damage in mammals at very low levels. As one ecological villain is removed, another comes along, including endocrine disruptors. These are often polychlorinated biphenyls (PCBs), which act by blocking hormone receptors in an animal's tissues, resulting in reduced fertility. These chemicals are components of a vast variety of modern substances ranging from plastics and flame retardants to printing inks. PCBs can be biologically active at much lower concentrations than the older organochlorines. Endocrine disruptors mostly seem to be an issue with aquatic species, which have to live in water contaminated by factory effluent or treated sewage outflows, but terrestrial species are not immune. Hedgehogs frequently forage around accumulations of waste and will lick or eat things that could easily be contaminated, especially as so much litter and other refuse is nowadays discarded in the places where they live. Endocrine disruptors and the bioaccumulators are not directly toxic, the way we normally think of 'poisons'. Their effects are at the population level not just on the odd unlucky individual.

The need to protect food and horticultural plants from insect pests is real and requires fresh substances to be deployed as soon as those with undesirable side effects are removed from the market. Since the 1990s, new synthetic pesticides have been available in the form of organophosphorus compounds called neonicotinoids. These prevent the nervous system from working properly (and not just in insects!) by blocking the connection between nerves and muscles, resulting in paralysis. They also have a cumulative toxic effect, so multiple exposures to the chemicals amplify the toxicity for anything that eats contaminated insects. In recent years, it has become common practice to use such chemicals to control leatherjackets (Tipulid fly larvae) and 'chafer grubs', which damage turf by eating away at the grass roots. This is necessary, not just to maintain an attractively uniform green sward without patches of dying grass, but also to retain a tight root mat in order to support the increasingly heavy demands placed on it by rising numbers of human users. Pesticides that are used to sustain 'sports turf' such as football pitches, golf courses and general recreation grounds may have resulted in eliminating most of the invertebrates that live there. The chemicals used to control the 'pests' were usually chloropyrifos and imidacloprid. These have trade names that imply a

FIG 199. An adult cockchafer beetle, whose larvae live in the soil for several years before emergence. The larvae eat grass roots and are deemed a pest as they damage lawns and sports pitches. They are eliminated by using poisons that kill them and many other soil invertebrates that are important food items for hedgehogs.

direct enhancement of the grass plant or suggest they have a specific target like the large larvae of the cockchafer beetle ('Maybug', *Melolontha melolontha*) (Fig. 199). But they kill other insect larvae too, including leatherjackets, a favourite food of the hedgehog. Serious concern about the unintended effects of neonicotinoids on bees, worms and ecosystems has resulted in at least a temporary ban on the use of these chemicals across the whole of the European Union, as from October 2016, but the ban is only partial (effectively to protect bees that visit flowering plants) and poisonous seed dressings appear to be still allowed. Chemical treatments for 'grubs' will probably also continue, at least for now. But 'grubs' are among the key items of a hedgehog's diet.

The problem with all pesticides is that the chemicals do not confine their effects to pest species. Neonicotinoids kill insects, and that includes bees. They have been blamed for the rapid and ecologically disastrous collapse in honey bee colonies and bumble bee populations. Bees are vital pollinators, of valuable agricultural crops, not just wild flowers and garden plants. But it turns out that these substances are also very harmful to earthworms, more so than other modern synthetic insecticides (Wang *et al.*, 2012). Earthworms, like bees, are ecologically vital animals. They are key elements of the hedgehog's diet too. Plant sprays and pesticides appear to be remote from hedgehogs, but when it rains, sprays get washed off into the soil. Neonicotinoids are absorbed by plants, which later die or may be eaten by caterpillars, slugs, herbivorous mammals; who knows where they might end up?

Pesticides that appear safe and irrelevant to hedgehogs are potentially implicated in declining hedgehog populations even if there are no direct effects on the individual animals as a result of eating contaminated prey. The purpose of pesticides is to reduce or eliminate many species of invertebrates upon which hedgehogs (and many other creatures) depend for food. Neonicotinoids and other pesticides are usually not species-specific; they tend to kill a wide range of creatures, including most of the prey upon which hedgehogs normally depend (see Chapter 4).

Molluscicides

Since 1937, metaldehyde has been recognised as an effective poison for killing molluscs and mixed with bran it was widely marketed in the form of small pellets. Over 350 tons of slug pellets were deployed on almost a million hectares of land in 2000 (Bourne, 2017). The pellets are highly visible and very good at killing slugs and snails, giving rise to a widespread belief that they might also pose a threat to hedgehogs. The pellets are normally dyed blue, as this is thought to be an unattractive colour to birds and should minimise the risk of being eaten by them. But this is irrelevant to hedgehogs, as they lack colour vision and anyway colours are not distinguishable to a nocturnal animal in the dark. Toxicity to molluscs does not mean that it is safe for other things to eat slug pellets containing metaldehyde, only that they are particularly lethal to slugs and snails. These will be killed by a dose of between 5 and 20 micrograms per gram of body weight, whereas dogs, cats and guinea pigs require 40 to 50 times as much to kill them (200–1,000 micrograms per gram of body weight). Dose rates like this are obtained experimentally by seeing how much poison is needed to kill 50 per cent of a sample of luckless laboratory animals. The four- or fivefold difference in what is needed to kill them suggests that there is plenty of variation in the threat posed to individuals and some (maybe even half) might not be killed at all.

Moreover, hedgehogs may be more susceptible (or more resistant?) than the types of experimental animals used for testing. But the little evidence available does suggest that hedgehogs are neither more nor less vulnerable to metaldehyde poisoning and that this substance will cause sickness and perhaps death if enough slug pellets are eaten directly. That is probably an infrequent event because hedgehogs do not normally like to eat dry pellets, but these can become soft in the rain and might then be eaten more readily. In the last 30 years, there have been plenty of post-mortems carried out on hedgehogs confirming that they can and do ingest slug pellets, although that might not always have been the main cause of their death. In 1991, a report describing results from 74 hedgehog autopsies identified 3 that had eaten slug pellets. In one case, the animal had absorbed the poison, not just swallowed it, and in sufficient quantity for it to be hazardous to its health.

FIG 200. Slug pellets can be deployed safely by covering them with a heavy slab raised on sticks or small pebbles and perhaps baited with orange peel. The slugs seek out cool shady places and can get under the slab, but hedgehogs and pets cannot. The poisoned slugs die there, but if they crawl away first, their bodies contain only harmless residues of metaldehyde.

Metaldehyde, intended to kill slugs and snails, kills dogs too and can now be found in some of our drinking water, despite its passage through purification processes (Bourne, 2017). It appears not to harm plants or non-molluscan invertebrates, but there remains a fear that hedgehogs might still be at risk from eating poisoned slugs. Happily, that appears not to be a serious problem. If a poisoned slug retained in its body all of the dose needed to kill it, an animal the size of a hedgehog would probably need to eat hundreds of contaminated slugs, perhaps more than a thousand, to be in danger of dying. Metaldehyde is not a cumulative poison, unlike DDT and the organochlorines, so those slugs would have to be eaten all at once. What actually happens is that the metaldehyde in a dead slug rapidly decomposes to acetaldehyde (a natural substance anyway) and this swiftly breaks down into carbon dioxide and water, neither of which will harm the hedgehog. A visiting researcher agreed to analyses some poisoned slugs for me and found no toxic residues in them shortly after their death. Independently of that, two studies in Switzerland fed poisoned slugs to hedgehogs with no discernible ill effects, even though each consumed up to 200 of them. It seems safe to conclude that eating poisoned slugs is not dangerous and that slug pellets are less of a threat than is often imagined. Nevertheless, it is important to deploy slug pellets in such a way that they cannot easily be ingested by hedgehogs or by any other non-target species, including pets and children (see Chapter 13).

This all relates to using the type of slug pellets that are normally available in shops and garden centres. Pellets containing a different molluscicide, methiocarb, were widely deployed for agricultural use with apparently little interest in what effect they might have on wildlife. Hedgehogs were said to eat methiocarb pellets, which seemed to be three times more palatable than metaldehyde-based pellets (Gemmeke, 1995). The recommended rate of application on farmland was equivalent to about 30 pellets per square metre and a foraging hedgehog would encounter sufficient to have a 50 per cent chance of death in just two square metres if it ate all the pellets available. Such incidents would probably be infrequent as the main areas where these pellets were used, in extensive wheat fields for example, would be rarely used by hedgehogs. Our limited experiments suggested that methiocarb did not decompose within the poisoned slugs, so their consumption would be harmful. If hedgehogs ate pellets or contaminated prey it could lead to physical symptoms such as diarrhoea and weight loss, but also potentially affect crucial behaviour patterns. However, our hedgehogs appeared to avoid eating contaminated slugs, suggesting a reduced risk in the wild. Happily, methiocarb is no longer an issue since the European Commission withdrew permission for it to be used anywhere in the EU, giving farmers until mid-2015 to use up their stocks of it.

The risks associated with controlling slugs and snails will be further reduced if biological control methods become more widely adopted. For example, *Phasmarhabditis hermaphrodita* is a nematode parasite that is lethal to slugs and appears not to attack other things (not even snails). It works by transmitting a deadly bacterium to the slug host. This prevents the slug from feeding, leading to its demise. Meanwhile the nematode can continue to multiply, allowing a build-up of the parasites in the soil, reducing slug numbers at least as efficiently long-term as conventional slug pellets (Rae *et al.*, 2006). The nematodes are harmless to hedgehogs and can be supplied in a form suitable for horticultural applications and for use in protecting high value crops. Organic slug pellets based on iron phosphate are also available along with various forms of slug repellent (see Chapter 13 on creating safer gardens).

Rodenticides

Several studies in recent years have found traces of 'rat poison' in dead hedgehogs, often in a high proportion of those examined: two thirds of 120 sick animals brought in to the RSPCA for example. Clare Dowding found rodenticide residues in a majority of the hedgehogs she analysed, with 22.5 per cent of her animals carrying residues of more than one compound, suggesting multiple exposures to rodenticides (Dowding *et al.*, 2010). Although the rodenticide may not be an immediate cause of death (if it is found in a road casualty for example) nobody knows what might be the effect of sub-lethal amounts of these poisons in hedgehogs. Rodenticides may well weaken an animal, slowing its movements or compromising reproduction or in some way reducing its potential lifespan.

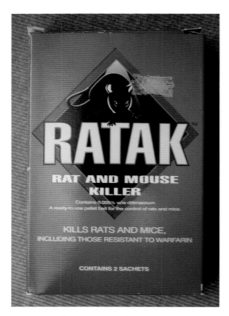

FIG 201. Slow-acting rodenticides allow poisoned rats and mice to disperse and be eaten by scavengers and invertebrates. The poison in the dead animals can then kill a wide variety of unintended victims, including hedgehogs. Limiting sale and use of rodenticides to trained operatives makes little difference; the poisoned rodents are still a threat no matter who was responsible for poisoning them.

Small quantities might reduce blood clotting and cause injured animals to die that might otherwise have survived. Whatever else, the poison certainly would not be doing the hedgehog any good. Higher doses will be fatal, but the body is unlikely to be found and submitted for toxicological analysis, so we can never know how many hedgehogs die in this way and therefore how serious a threat rodenticides might be to the population as a whole. What we do know is that a high proportion of dead hedgehogs are found to contain rodenticide residues. The question is, where is this stuff coming from, and how do hedgehogs end up eating it?

Normal rat poisons are dispensed in grain baits, wax blocks or some other material that is attractive to rodents but unlikely to be gnawed by hedgehogs and many other wild animals. So it is regarded as safe to use these poisons to kill rats and mice in places where they are not wanted. In the past, that has meant dispensing the poisons indoors, such as in houses, chicken sheds and food stores. Inside a building, most wildlife species will not be directly at risk. However, in recent times it has become commonplace to deploy powerful rodenticides out of doors, not just around farms, but in towns and gardens too. Metal shelters containing the poison can often be seen outside supermarkets and in their car parks, even around garages where the 'rat problem', if it ever existed, is likely to have been minimal. If undesirable rodents are attracted to rubbish bins and other debris, then the best way to solve the problem is to tidy up! Waste food and empty food containers can be disposed of in rodent-proof bins. Putting out poison is less like hard work, but should be a last resort. What actually happens is that poison dispensers are deployed 'just in case', even when there is

FIG 202. Poison bait stations are now commonly installed as permanent fixtures, albeit not always with poison inside. Although intended to control rodent numbers, they have implications for other wildlife, including hedgehogs.

not a rodent issue. The manufacturers and corporate users will say that the metal shelters protect dogs, cats and birds (and hedgehogs) from gaining access to the poison, so they are safe. However, the entrance hole is 60 mm in diameter, a bit of a squeeze for an adult rat, but easily accessible to harmless species of wild mice and voles that rarely, if ever, venture indoors (Fig. 202). One of the most frequent autumn visitors to buildings around my home is the yellow-necked mouse (*Apodemus flaviciollis*), a nationally rare species, maybe getting rarer still thanks to the six poison dispensers in the yard at my local supermarket. Who knows?

The reason why this is important to hedgehogs is that the poisons used are anticoagulants. These are not acute poisons that suddenly kill a victim, often painfully. Instead, after being ingested, they prevent mammalian blood from clotting so that wounds or minor leakages continue to bleed indefinitely, especially from the blood vessels around the intestines. The animal dies slowly, becoming weaker over several days and is unaware of its fate. This helps to prevent the rats from learning to avoid poison baits because they do not know what is happening. A single dose is not intended to cause death immediately and the poisoning strategy relies on animals living long enough to eat some more of the poison. Meanwhile, the poisoned rodent continues to walk about for up to 12 days with one or more doses of anticoagulant in its body. Small doses, insufficient to cause death to a rat or mouse, accumulate in the animal's liver.

The contaminated animal is now a hazard for any predator or scavenger that might catch and eat it. This is especially easy in its weakened state, and easier still for any mammal or bird to feed on its carcass after death or for a hedgehog that eats the invertebrates that have been assisting with the poisoned animal's decomposition. Poisoned rats can be found up to a hundred metres away from a bait station and it is likely that more wide-ranging species such as wood mice could carry the poisons even further away. This is how larger animals can be at risk, even though the poison is not intended for them and they cannot get at the actual poisoned bait inside the metal or plastic dispenser. Predators and scavengers get the poison second-hand so to speak, a process known as 'secondary poisoning'. This is often a threat to predatory birds that feed on rodents weakened by anticoagulants. Rodenticide residues have been found in 92 per cent of British red kites, up to 91 per cent of barn owls and 80 per cent of kestrels, for example. Polecats are another proven victim of secondary poisoning, as a result of feeding on rats and mice around farmyards (Shore *et al.*, 1999). Dogs and cats are at risk too, although few of their owners appear to realise this. Modern rodenticides appear not to be metabolised within animals, so they remain as active molecules in faeces and dead bodies, easily picked up by worms, beetles, maggots and other decomposers, the very things that hedgehogs eat. Like many other modern chemicals released into the environment, it is hard to know where they will end up. In the USA, thousands of children have apparently been found contaminated with rodenticides after showing signs of poisoning. Secondary poisoning is a serious issue and not just for hedgehogs. Like the fabled genie, once poisons are released, they are difficult to get back into the bottle and you never know where they will turn up next.

It is illegal to leave poisons about without using devices to exclude larger animals, and although hedgehogs cannot get into rat poison dispensers, they are very vulnerable to secondary poisoning, an unintended consequence of making sure there isn't a rat problem. Hedgehogs will readily consume dead mice, voles and rats along with any rodenticide residues they may contain. Moreover, slugs and other invertebrates that feed on poison baits or dead rodents can do so with impunity as they have a different blood chemistry, but crawling about with anticoagulant in their gut, they offer another way for a hungry hedgehog to become an unintended victim.

Poisons are supposed to be a last resort, but it is quite normal to see bait stations set out with no attempt made to clear away attractive food waste nearby in spite of good practice recommendations. The rat poisons used today are referred to as SGARs ('second generation anticoagulant rodenticides') because they largely replace the anticoagulants used in the past such as warfarin. The new ones are much more potent and the danger they pose is obvious, so there are regulations that limit their use. For example, brodifacoum is supposed to be restricted to indoor use only (although poisoned rats and mice could still wander away and be eaten outside). Only a couple of SGARs are permitted to be used out of doors, the usual one being bromadiolone. Officially, this must only be deployed in dispensers that prevent access by non-target species, but there is no way of controlling secondary poisoning as a result of rodents (including non-target species) wandering away carrying a dose of rodenticide within their body. That could be a particular danger where farmers use rodenticides around cowsheds or chicken pens, remembering that studies show farmland hedgehogs (particularly in arable areas) tend to gravitate towards farm buildings. Another obvious focus would be in woodland areas where gamekeepers rear pheasants and use rodenticides to reduce losses of feed meant for the birds. The intended targets may be rats or grey squirrels, but large numbers of wood mice and bank voles (*Clethrionymus glareolus*) will be killed along with any rats that might (or might not) be living there. Their contaminated bodies will be available for consumption by hedgehogs, foxes, badgers and dogs too. It is small wonder that rodenticide residues are now turning up in all manner of wild animals.

To reduce risks to wildlife (and humans), there are rules about who may buy and use rat poisons, and penalties for misuse. One of the rules is that bait stations should not be used continuously for more than 35 days. But 'better to be on the safe side' and they often seem to be permanently in place. Who checks whether they are baited or not? When I checked a few of them near my local shops, one still had the poison inside, evidently forgotten when the last poisoning episode had ended. When poison baits are being deployed, users are required to search regularly for dead rats so as to remove them and prevent a hazard to pets and wildlife. Despite the fact that people have been prosecuted for not doing this, a survey reported by The Barn Owl Trust showed that this regulation was ignored by 98 per cent of users, probably because poisoned animals could have hidden themselves away almost anywhere and looking for them was considered to be a waste of time.

The risks associated with outdoor use of SGARs represent a higher level of threat than would normally be regarded as acceptable. Recognising this and under pressure from the EU, new rules mean that after mid-2016 SGARs would only be available to professional pest controllers and others (such as farmers) who have been appropriately trained in proper procedures. That did not prevent me buying packets of poison pellets in early 2017, with a cheery assurance from the shopkeeper that all was well. This tightening up should prevent casual use by gardeners and householders and place more emphasis on controlling an actual rat problem, rather than using poisons 'just in case'. However, a poisoned rodent is a danger to any hedgehog or other animal that eats it, regardless of whether or not the poison was put out by a properly certified and regulated operator. Better regulation might reduce the risks to wildlife, but will not eliminate them. In particular, it will be impossible to prevent secondary poisoning, of hedgehogs and anything else, so the danger will remain. Poisons kill things, that's what they are for, but maybe our modern, highly efficient poisons such as SGARs and neonicotinoids are just too efficient in what they do and the collateral damage they cause to wildlife is too high a price to pay for what they achieve. Perhaps the more potent anticoagulant rodenticides will be banned, just like DDT and the other ecologically dangerous cumulative organochlorine poisons of the 1960s. Meanwhile, rodenticides seem to be a likely contributor to recent declines in hedgehog numbers, adding to the modern dangers that confront this ancient species.

The basic message here is that if we want to increase food production, as we must in view of the rising human population, then we have to consider the law of unintended consequences. Whenever a new chemical is added to the tools of farmers and gardeners, we don't necessarily know where it will end up or what other unexpected effects it might have. Ivermectin is another example. It is used as a 'de-wormer', for the desirable purpose of ridding pets and other animals of intestinal parasites such as tapeworms and nematodes. It is routinely given to cattle (and hospitalised hedgehogs!), but cows then create contaminated cow pats that cannot support the usual crop of flies and insect larvae that are important foods for many birds, bats, small mammals and hedgehogs. Using poisons of any kind is like releasing a mad dog – you never know where they might go or what they might do.

CONCLUSION

For millions of years, the hedgehog has only needed to cope with natural hazards and its population dynamics have evolved to ensure continued survival of the species. Suddenly, within a few decades it faced an unprecedented increase in the numbers of its most significant predator, the badger. Numerous other novel threats have also emerged, including road traffic, and even more abruptly it has been confronted with highly effective pesticides that reduce or eliminate many of its main prey. The most efficient of these chemicals are so dangerous that their use has been banned throughout the European Union, a situation that hopefully will survive Britain's departure from that political entity. But the disruption that they have wrought among invertebrate populations may persist for decades. Hedgehogs also face a threat posed by insidious poisons intended to kill rats and mice. These substances are actually a hazard to any other species that may consume the poisoned rodents. They are widely distributed and regardless of measures to control their use, they continue to spread into the environment, creating an almost universal threat of secondary poisoning for hedgehogs and many other predators and scavenging species. Curiously, most people appear unaware of this, despite the danger to wildlife, their pets and perhaps even their own children. There is a widespread assumption that weedkillers kill weeds, rat poisons kill rats and insecticides aren't a worry either. Hedgehogs pay the price for this ignorance.

CHAPTER 10

Hedgehog Numbers and Population Biology

OW MANY HEDGEHOGS ARE THERE and what controls their numbers? Why aren't there more of them? Is it true that there are fewer these days? These are important and legitimate questions that are frequently asked and in recent years there has been some progress in addressing them, albeit with the usual problem of uncertainty due to the limited number of studies.

POPULATION REGULATION

Bearing in mind that animals add offspring to their population each year, why don't we end up with too many of them or indeed too few given that animals also die, sometimes in large numbers. The natural mechanism by which populations are regulated was at one time a hot topic for discussion by academic ecologists. It was suggested that there were two basic ways in which animal populations could be held in check, by density-dependent factors and density-independent ones. The latter include extraneous influences that are there anyway, irrespective of how many animals are present. That would include the weather, for example, 'good' and 'bad' years would cancel each other out and maintain numbers that fluctuated around a normal, long-term average population density. In the case of the hedgehog, a prolonged winter might mean fewer animals surviving and a reduced population until this was offset by a warm, moist summer with plenty of food about and enhanced survival of the young, allowing numbers to pick up again. During his studies of hedgehogs in the Outer Hebrides, Digger Jackson gathered data which showed that the weather did indeed have a strong effect on breeding success in the local hedgehogs. The population density was strongly correlated with temperatures during the previous winter and preceding summer, with warmer conditions boosting both breeding success and survival rates (Jackson, 2007).

Another density-independent factor affecting hedgehogs might be the availability of nest sites. This is certainly something that limits the local abundance of hole-nesting birds, whose numbers can be boosted by providing tree-hole substitutes in the form of nest boxes. The same applies to dormice and putting up nest boxes, as a substitute for tree holes increases their population density. But hedgehogs are not constrained by having to nest in only one type of site, and it is hard to think of another factor that might limit their numbers in a similar way. However, they do need special facilities for winter nesting which will not be available out in open fields, for example, but there is little to stop them congregating in locations that do have the necessary attributes. In my study of hedgehog hibernacula in Bushy Park (see Chapter 6), there could be a dozen hedgehog nests within a 100 metres or so on some occasions, with plenty of room for more if there had been greater demand.

Density-dependent factors are those that act directly in response to the number of animals already present. Too many animals eating worms or grazing a field will mean that any additional feeders will reduce the food available for everyone and cause some individuals not to thrive. This way the population is prevented from becoming too large. If it is reduced for some reason, there will be fewer animals competing for the food and the population increases in response to greater availability of food, perhaps through enhanced breeding success or better survival of the young. The increase continues until the habitat reaches 'carrying capacity', beyond which density-dependent control will step in to keep the numbers in check.

This is obviously a simplistic description and in reality the regulation of hedgehog numbers is bound to be brought about by a complex mixture of different factors. The academic issue need not concern us very much except that it became a serious financial and public relations matter when action was taken to deal with the hedgehogs that had been introduced to South Uist (see Chapter 12). A policy of killing the animals was adopted, assuming that translocating them to the mainland would be harmful if the numbers there were density-dependent. The logic was that if the mainland of Scotland could support more hedgehogs, then their numbers would already have increased until carrying capacity was reached. In other words it was assumed that the mainland was already 'full up'. Taking hedgehogs from the Uists to the mainland would then displace others already there, to the likely detriment of their welfare. It was therefore deemed appropriate to kill the Uist hedgehogs rather than remove them for release elsewhere. The logic is clear, but there is no actual evidence to support the assumption that the size of the hedgehog population is density-dependent. Like the Emperor who had no clothes, the policy lacked a sound foundation. In fact one of the few hedgehog population studies available at that time explicitly said, 'It is argued that the population size appears to be more influenced by environmental factors such as food availability, winter nest sites and winter climate than by density-dependent factors' (Kristiansson, 1990). Ignoring, or overlooking, that study cost the lives of over a thousand hedgehogs before the policy was changed to one of translocation rather than killing.

Actually it is hard to see how the presence of too many hedgehogs would result in a natural suppression of their numbers. They do not appear to have social behavioural mechanisms that might achieve some sort of population control. For example, they do not defend exclusive territories or feeding areas and they will often feed together at a food bowl or in a good feeding area with little sign of one animal attempting to monopolise the resource, even in times of food shortage. Running short of food because of excessive numbers might cause more to starve and thus reduce the population, except that hedgehogs are highly omnivorous. If they were short of worms, for instance, the evidence suggests that they would switch to something else. Any situation where all the many and varied potential food types became dangerously scarce as a result of hedgehogs eating themselves out of house and home would hit a lot of other creatures too, such as blackbirds, weasels, polecats and frogs. A situation like that might arise as a result of prolonged drought or ongoing use of pesticides, but not because hedgehog numbers had doubled.

In practice, of course, it turns out that population regulation mechanisms are highly complex, not just a matter of one type of control or another. In the case of hedgehogs, it is likely that factors such as weather and the duration of winter will play a key part in some years, but not in others. Density-dependent factors might become important in localised areas, especially in dry weather, but predation could also be an increasingly significant issue. Patrick Doncaster artificially increased the local hedgehog population density by importing some from elsewhere. Subsequent dispersal, especially by males, and predation by badgers reduced the population close to its original level within one month. After that, the number of hedgehogs remained relatively stable for a further two months of the study (Doncaster, 1994). As for the many threats posed by pesticides described in Chapter 9, while these will undoubtedly reduce numbers of hedgehogs, they can hardly be said to control them because they do not act to support or build up the population, only reduce it. Similarly, when gamekeepers

FIG 203. Hedgehog numbers vary between habitats and from year to year, probably in response to a wide variety of influences.

seek to control hedgehogs, they are aiming at a population size of zero rather than an optimum level.

Another topic that has excited interest among academic ecologists is the occurrence and possible causes of population cycles. There is a possibility that regular fluctuations in hedgehog numbers will be reflected in the vermin bag records kept by gamekeepers on large estates. This prompted a small study which looked at numbers of hedgehogs that had been killed across two decades, between 1943 and 1965, on an estate in Hertfordshire and another in Hampshire (Jefferies & Pendlebury, 1968). There were major differences in the numbers killed per 1,000 acres on the two estates, but no regular pattern in the numbers taken each year that might reflect a cyclic population. The problem with this study and other analyses of vermin records, including amounts paid out by churchwardens (see Chapter 12), is that the number killed is not simply a reflection of population size. It also depends on the amount of effort (e.g. the number of active gamekeepers) put into killing the hedgehogs. There is no way of measuring the effort that was spent catching them each year long ago. If it was not constant year to year, any apparent fluctuation in numbers of hedgehogs might simply be due to the greater or lesser number of people or traps being used to catch them. Similarly one cannot compare one place with another unless the catching effort was the same at both. As a result, there is no reliable evidence that hedgehog populations are cyclic like those of certain rodent species such as lemmings. However, numbers do appear to fluctuate from year to year, probably as a result of variations in breeding success and food availability, but not in the form of regular cycles of abundance.

Repeat surveys using the same methods and amount of effort have certainly shown that a hedgehog population can collapse. Hedgehogs were introduced to the island of North Ronaldsay in 1972 and by 1984 they were said to number 1,000 or more. A survey in 1987 by Hugh Warwick estimated the population at roughly 514, which appeared to have fallen to barely 100 when he surveyed the same sites using the same methods a few years later. More recently, the numbers are said to have increased again (Hugh Warwick, pers comm). Other populations established on islands have flourished for a while, but then dwindled to extinction (see Chapter 2). In New Zealand, Bob Brockie counted the number of hedgehogs killed on the roads that he drove regularly and found a severe reduction in 30 years, but no evidence of cyclic fluctuations.

POPULATION DENSITY

With large animals that live out in the open, a telescope or aerial photographs might be used to count all those seen in a given area and thus calculate a population density in terms of numbers per hectare or square kilometre. Obviously that cannot work with small mammals such as mice and voles and for them we rely on a procedure known as 'capture-mark-recapture' (CMR). The standard technique is to set out a grid of traps that catch a sample of the animals alive overnight. These would then be marked in some way and released for the traps to catch another sample on the next night. The proportion of marked animals in the second sample (60 per cent, for example) is deemed to be the same proportion as the full second sample forms of the population as a whole. There are more sophisticated variants on this procedure (which is known as the 'Lincoln Index') that use multiple sampling to increase the accuracy of the estimate. CMR works well for species that live at high densities, such as insects or voles, but with hedgehogs many more traps would be needed, spread over an impractically large area, in order to obtain sufficient animals for the calculations to generate consistent results. In practice, traps are not used and instead most hedgehog studies have been based on walking about finding the animals by torchlight. Suppose you catch five hedgehogs on the first night and the second sample is only four, of which one is marked. That would imply a population size of 16 animals. But if the second sample was five, with one marked, the estimate would be 25. In other words, with a low-density population a single extra animal (or one less) makes a big difference to the calculated population size. Stumbling upon a mother with her three offspring, just once, would generate a completely different population estimate. I calculated that the population density during one of my studies lasting about three weeks (Morris, 1988) was 1 per 4.5 ha (0.22 per ha), although shortly afterwards four newly weaned young appeared, making it about 1 per 3 ha (0.33 per ha).

More reliable perhaps are population figures based on catching and marking all the animals present, although this will take some time and may miss a few. This is known as a Minimum Number Alive (MNA) estimate. Using this approach, Nigel Reeve had about 50 different hedgehogs present each summer on the golf course he studied, an area of 40 ha (equivalent to 1.25 hedgehogs per ha) in a whole season. But this included animals seen only once which, arguably, were not residents there. In a three-week period (to compare the estimate with mine above), many of these transient animals would not have been seen and the estimated population density would have been lower. On a golf course in

FIG 204. Population estimates have almost all been based on searching for hedgehogs by torchlight in open grassland, but many hedgehogs live in areas of scrub or gardens, where they remain hidden. Estimates are likely to be inaccurate, variable and not applicable everywhere. In turn, this adds to the problem of estimating the total British population of hedgehogs.

FIG 205. Hedgehogs may cluster in gardens or other favoured feeding areas, making a very high population density locally, which creates a misleading impression of abundance when scaled up to take account of a wider area.

New Zealand, Bob Brockie marked 207 hedgehogs on 56 ha in two years and 150 on 16 hectares of farmland in 17 months. At any one time, the farm population density was never above 2.5 per ha or above 1.75 per ha on the golf course. But such estimates are strongly affected by hedgehogs clustering around good places to feed. Pitfall traps around a dotterel colony in New Zealand caught 400 hedgehogs in two years.

To translate a 'population figure' into an actual density as numbers per ha, it is necessary to know how large was the area being sampled. With grid trapping for small mammals, that is easy because the traps can be set out to cover a known area of say 0.5 ha. Hedgehogs sampled by torchlight are normally assumed to be living in the area searched, usually open grassland (Fig. 204).

Actually many of them will be nesting somewhere else, but where else? In other words it is hard to know how large is the total area being used by the estimated number of hedgehogs. The problem is particularly clear when hedgehogs are marked as they visit a food bowl in a garden (Fig. 205). Over a few weeks a dozen or more may visit a garden of 100 m², but they don't all live there. Our radio-tracking revealed that such a garden might not have any resident hedgehogs at all! So the population density is not 12 in 100 m² (equals 120 per ha). It is 12 in who knows how many hectares. This may be an extreme example, but it illustrates the principle that the population density estimate is affected by the size of the sampling area. The smaller the sampling area (e.g. a garden), the greater the number of animal 'passers-by' that will be seen only once or twice. This creates an impression that the hedgehog population includes many nomadic animals, which may actually be true. According to Bob Brockie, about 20 per cent of the population in a given area may be 'transients'; Nigel Reeve found a similar proportion on a west London golf course (Reeve, 1981).

A similar effect is seen with hedgehogs that come to gardens, where a significant proportion of marked animals are seen once and do not reappear. If these transient animals are included in CMR calculations, it results in improbably high population estimates. Despite all of these drawbacks, most of the published estimates of hedgehog population density have relied upon CMR methods often using different analytical methods, making direct comparisons problematic.

Using powerful lamps, a team of searchers and a sophisticated version of CMR, Digger Jackson estimated that there were about 57 adult hedgehogs per square kilometre (0.57 per ha) in the machair grasslands of South Uist (Jackson & Green, 2000). No formal surveys were conducted in other habitats, but he considered that hedgehogs were less abundant on the peaty 'blacklands' and scarcer still on the upland areas of moorland, although they were still present there. Searching with lamps, a comparison of hedgehogs found on pasture and amenity grassland in four different English counties and two different seasons found an average of 0.47 hedgehogs per ha in the latter, but barely a tenth of that in pastureland (Parrott et al., 2014). In such studies, it is assumed that the size of the area used by the hedgehogs is the same as the area being searched by the observers, even though some of the hedgehogs will be living some of the time somewhere else.

'Distance Sampling' (DS) is a different way of estimating numbers that has been devised to overcome the problem of not knowing the size of the area being sampled. It involves walking along a transect route, counting animals seen on either side, together with their distance from the path being followed by the observer. The subsequent calculations will define retrospectively the area that has been sampled and express the population in terms of numbers per hectare (see, for example, Buckland et al., 1993; Hoodless & Morris, 1993). It is a method ideally suited to counting hedgehogs by torchlight, but suffers when too few are seen. That results in such variable population estimates that they become statistically unacceptable. Longer transects would find more animals and reduce the problem, but it is hard to find areas that are big enough to accommodate these within a fairly uniform habitat. It also means more hours need to be spent walking and searching.

One of my students, Alison Tutt, tried using both the DS method and various types of CMR on the hedgehogs of Alderney in the Channel Islands (Fig. 205). Transects were searched in areas of grassy habitat in order to estimate numbers of hedgehogs there and compare the results obtained by different methods. Eleven transects were chosen ranging from 175–2,750 m in length and sampled for up to 17 nights each. All of the hedgehogs were marked and data collected for analysis using CMR and DS methods. Averaged over several

FIG 205. Alison Tutt compared population density estimates using different methods among the blonde hedgehogs of Alderney. There were plenty of open areas to search at night, with few obstructions and little disturbance. Even the island's airstrip was available as a sampling site.

nights, the DS technique gave population estimates ranging from 0.42 to 0.63 hedgehogs per ha (a close match to the average reported elsewhere by Parrott *et al.*, 2014), but the two shortest transects generated figures of 1.34 and 4.37 per ha (the latter being on the cricket pitch), highlighting the problem of variable results, depending on how the study is conducted, and the need to use the longest possible transects. Using five different versions of the basic CMR techniques generated density estimates in grassland areas ranging from 0.64 to 1.83 hedgehogs per ha. Again the cricket pitch, site of the shortest transect, generated much higher figures of 3.6 to 17.38 hedgehogs per ha, depending upon which CMR method was used.

Sampling the worms on the different transect sites showed that the cricket pitch had more than three times the density of worms (172 per m²) than on

TABLE 25. Population densities per ha in various grassland sites, estimated by different methods (based on Tutt, 1993).

Site	Distance sampling (DT) per ha	Lincoln Index (CMR)	Jolly-Seber method (multiple CMR)
Golf course	0.63	1.1	1.08
Airport grassland	0.49	1.02	1.25
Cricket pitch	4.37	6.75	13.15
Rough grassland A	0.42		
Rough grassland B	1.34		

the other grassy habitats, with hardly any of them available (6 per m²) in an area dominated by bracken. That explains why the hedgehogs were actually preferentially feeding on the cricket pitch, aggregating at a higher density there and seriously skewing the results of the study. Another sampling study in France (Hubert *et al.*, 2011) used distance sampling (43 transects, 127 hedgehogs) to estimate population densities in the Ardennes countryside at 4.4 per km² (0.044 per ha) and 36.5 (0.36 per ha) in an adjacent urban area. The latter figure is similar to many of those reported in the literature for good hedgehog habitat in Britain; the former may be nearer what we might expect in intensively managed farmland. That study compared hedgehog numbers with availability of typical hedgehog food and found 14 per cent of their hedgehogs were on pastureland where there is plenty of food, with no hedgehogs in forest areas, despite an abundance arthropods and worms. But hedgehogs are harder to see in woodland than in pastureland.

In spite of all the drawbacks involved in population estimation, it is obvious that there are not hundreds of hedgehogs per hectare, and most of the published figures offer numbers that seem reasonable (Table 27). However, they are almost all based on 'good hedgehog habitat' suitable for doing research projects where you need to be able to find plenty of animals. This means mostly short grassy turf where hedgehogs are reasonably easy to spot and few will escape detection. We have little data on the numbers of hedgehogs that inhabit woodland areas and population densities in many rural habitats probably vary a lot according to what type of farming predominates locally.

TABLE 26. Comparative numbers of hedgehogs found in rural and urban habitats in France (based on Hubert *et al.*, 2011).

Habitat type	Rural sites Per cent of total study area (3,611 ha)	Urban sites Per cent of total study area (486 ha)	Per cent of 127 hedgehogs found	Mean earthworm biomass (kg/ha)	Mean arthropod biomass (kg/ha)
Pasture	25	0	14	933	852
Arable	20	0	4	284	3325
Meadow	21	1	4	1424	4652
Forest	22	3	0	154	5696
Lawns & paths	12	96	78	1848	188

TABLE 27. Some published estimates of population density. Despite being based on various methods, and for studies lasting varying lengths of time, there appears to be a consensus that hedgehogs generally occur at a density of less than one per hectare, with more in small and particularly favoured areas where there is abundant food.

Source	Population density per ha	Place	Habitat
Parkes, 1975	1.1–2.5	Manawatu, New Zealand	Dairy pasture
Haigh, 2011	3.07	County Cork, Eire	Mixed agricultural landscape
Doncaster, 1992	0.23–0.25	Rural Oxfordshire	Grassy habitats
Morris, 1988	0.33 (adults only)	Isle of Wight	Pasture and hedgerows
Reeve, 1981	0.83 average	West London	Golf course
Jackson & Green, 2000	0.57 (adults only)	South Uist, Outer Hebrides	Machair grassland
Tutt, 1993 (DT) (CMR)	0.42–0.63 0.64–1.83	Alderney, Channel Islands	Various grassy habitats excluding cricket pitch
Hubert et al., 2011	0.04 0.36	Ardennes, France	Rural areas Nearby urban areas
Kristiansson, 1990	0.48	Sweden	Village and surroundings
Brockie, 1974	0.64 (average)	North Island, New Zealand	two years, suburban golf course
Warwick (pers comm.)	0.52	North Ronaldsay	Open habitats
Parrott et al., 2014	0.47 (average)	Various English counties	Amenity grassland
Parrott et al., 2014	0.04 (average)	Various English counties	Pasture

At the time of writing (2017), the Random Encounter Method is being trialled, not used on hedgehogs hitherto. It aims to identify where hedgehogs are present but also estimate their abundance. It is based on the frequency of occurrence of animals, in footprint tunnels in this case (see Appendix), but results are not yet available.

Whatever method is used, hedgehogs may congregate in a small garden or good feeding patch, and create a misleading appearance of abundance. That becomes a serious problem when we try to estimate how many hedgehogs there are in Britain as a whole. This is a somewhat futile exercise, but journalists in particular always seem to want to know 'How many are there?' The first attempt seems to have used a density figure of one per acre (i.e. 2.4 per ha), suggested by Maurice Burton (Burton, 1969). When I asked him about this, he told me that it was based on seeing about ten hedgehogs in ten acres during an evening's stroll in Kew Gardens. Scaling that up to take account of the total size of Great Britain would put the population at some 50 million hedgehogs, but most of Britain is not like Kew Gardens. We could eliminate mountainous areas and make it 30 million, then reduce numbers for arable land and so on. Employing this approach, a group of us (Harris *et al.*, 1995) used different density figures for the various broad habitat types (for example, 1 per 2.5 ha for woodlands and unimproved grasslands, 1 per 10 ha for built-up areas and 1 per 20 ha for coniferous woodland, bracken and arable land), and estimated the pre-breeding population of the hedgehog to be about 1,550,000 in Britain (1.1 million in England, 310,000 in Scotland and 145,000 in Wales). This estimate also took into account the fact that most published population density estimates had been based on studies made during the summer and therefore included juveniles. The adult pre-breeding population would be somewhat smaller than any number based upon density figures obtained later in the summer (when most published studies were undertaken).

A more recent attempt to estimate the size of the national hedgehog population suggests a figure that lies between 731,546 and about 12 million! (Croft *et al*, 2017). But despite the highly sophisticated modelling used, the estimate still relies on the few published estimates of population density from the small sample of sites where relevant fieldwork has been carried out, sometimes long ago. The enormous range in that estimate is itself an indication of just how much we need better data and how ineffectual modelling is without it. We need a more structured approach to studying population densities. For example, the models predict high hedgehog numbers in arable habitats, but that is probably because published studies have (of necessity) focused on the animals that live around the margins of arable fields. As the authors point out, 'the population density over most of an arable landscape may be close to zero'. Yet studies of population density in hedgehogs (or other species that live across a wide range of landscapes in comparatively low numbers) are extremely challenging for practical reasons and also not a fashionable subject for research funding. It's all rather speculative and hard to defend whatever figure is offered as the total number of hedgehogs in Britain. It is so imprecise that it will be no use for monitoring population trends. For this we must fall back on using indices of abundance, which can be more reliably calculated.

INDICES OF ABUNDANCE

One obvious indication of hedgehog abundance is the frequency with which we see them dead on the road. We can count hedgehog road casualties more easily than for many species because they are so conspicuous and also easily recognisable. For most people, the majority of hedgehogs they see are dead and flat. To ignore these seems a waste of an opportunity to learn something about hedgehog numbers, but what do the numbers actually mean? Some have argued, as they have with badger roadkills, that larger numbers dead on the road is an indication of a declining population because so many are being killed, leaving fewer alive (Fig. 206). Others argue the opposite, that more dead ones must indicate a large and healthy population in order to supply so many victims. Yet another line of argument says that the number of animals seen dead on the road is simply a reflection of traffic density and tells us little about the animals themselves (except that they are dead!).

FIG 206. Road casualties are the way we see most hedgehogs most often. They offer an obvious way of counting numbers, but what do those numbers actually mean? Do more roadkills mean more hedgehogs or do they imply fewer because so many have been killed?

Counting dead hedgehogs is relatively easy and likely to be accurate owing to their distinctive appearance, even when squashed. But people kept insisting it was a waste of time because 'everyone knows' that the number killed on roads simply reflects the number of vehicles passing by. It was 'obvious' that counting dead hedgehogs was just a crude way of measuring traffic density. This turns out not to be true. The number of hedgehogs I saw killed per 100 miles driving about in New Zealand in 1987 was much higher than in Britain, despite the far lower traffic densities there (Morris & Morris, 1988).

There are good reasons to believe that the numbers of other mammals that are killed on roads reflect their local abundance in the adjacent habitats. For example, the frequency of badger roadkills that I have seen in Britain has increased enormously in the past 30 years (sometimes I now see more dead badgers than hedgehogs) and is matched by independent estimates of an increasing badger population based on counts of setts, suggesting a link between population size and numbers killed on the roads. A survey of roadkill rabbits showed that the number seen dead was directly proportional to the numbers seen alive nearby (George *et al.*, 2011). In other words, counting animals seen dead on the road could serve as an index of abundance in the living population. It does not say how many animals are alive locally, but it does reflect local population density. The number of hedgehogs killed on the roads does not simply reflect traffic density (Bright *et al.*, 2015), a fact also confirmed by studies carried out in the Netherlands (Huijser & Bergers, 2000). So the scepticism has been refuted and we now have confirmation that counting hedgehog roadkill is a meaningful activity and worth doing.

But it is not a new idea. Sixty years ago, J. L. Davies published details of the number of hedgehogs he had seen killed on roads in Hampshire and the distances that he had driven (Davies, 1957). He suggested that this could form the basis for an index of abundance, the number of casualties per 100 miles. This indicated a greater abundance of hedgehogs in the second year of his observations (1953–54) compared to the previous year (Fig. 207 & Table 28). He further suggested that this form of monitoring could be taken up by the Mammal Society and extended nationwide to monitor the hedgehog population. I deeply regret not pursuing that idea in the 1960s, but everyone said that it wouldn't work and counting road

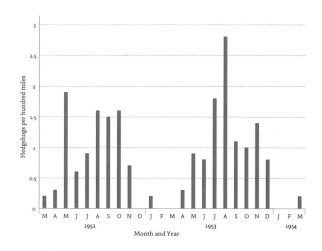

FIG 207. J. L. Davies was the first to suggest monitoring hedgehog numbers by regular roadkill surveys and used numbers killed per 100 miles driven as an index of abundance to compare seasonal mortality between two years in Hampshire. It was 40 years before we tried that idea nationally.

TABLE 28. A roadkill survey from the 1950s by J. L. Davies in Hampshire (Davies, 1957).

Months 1952–3	No. of miles driven	No. of hedgehogs	Hedgehogs per 100 miles	Months 1953–4	No. of miles driven	No. of hedgehogs	Hedgehogs per 100 miles
Mar.	463	1	0.2	Mar.	966	0	0
Apr.	665	2	0.3	Apr.	687	2	0.3
May.	535	10	1.9	May	651	6	0.9
Jun.	840	5	0.6	Jun.	906	7	0.8
Jul.	983	9	0.9	Jul.	706	13	1.8
Aug.	687	11	1.6	Aug.	506	14	2.8
Sep.	411	6	1.5	Sep.	282	3	1.1
Oct.	493	8	1.6	Oct.	295	3	1.0
Nov.	297	2	0.7	Nov.	282	4	1.4
Dec.	302	0	0	Dec.	530	4	0.8
Jan.	558	1	0.2	Jan.	410	0	0
Feb.	1025	0	0	Feb.	424	0	0
Mar.	—	—	—	Mar.	629	1	0.2

casualties was a waste of time. Anyway I could not see how to muster enough volunteers to obtain sufficient data for a robust analysis. In 1990, I nevertheless decided to try this idea and used a radio programme to recruit volunteer counters. Scepticism remained and caused one angry biologist to send a written complaint to the BBC accusing them of promoting pseudoscience. But the roadkill surveys of 1991–94 inclusive turned out to be very instructive and, in retrospect, an important milestone for revealing changes in the hedgehog population.

However, if comparisons are to be valid, the data must be collected in a standardised way. A protocol was therefore established that ensured all my volunteers operated according to a set of rules that included instructions to record the mileage driven on all journeys greater than 20 miles, whether a hedgehog was seen or not. Counts would not be done in the rain, on wet roads, at night or any other time when visibility was impaired. Journeys on motorways and in major cities would be excluded, also the opposite lane on dual carriageways. Observers were urged not to include counts on the same stretch of road if driven a second time within the same month and to count only definite hedgehogs not 'probables' or 'possibles'. The count was limited to three summer months (July–September inclusive) in order to maximise the numbers seen, and reduce

TABLE **29.** Roadkill counts in the early 1990s.

Year	1990	1991	1992	1993	1994
No. of observers	140	58	49	64	52
Total miles driven	35,720	37,977	28,966	30,360	29,020
No. of hedgehogs recorded	1,187	1,305	832	1,244	753
No. of miles per hedgehog	30.1	29.1	34.8	24.4	38.5
No. of hedgehogs per 100 miles	3.32	3.44	2.87	4.09	2.59

the demands made on volunteers. It also avoided the problem of bad weather in the spring or autumn resulting in the effective population size being reduced by some animals being in hibernation and therefore not available to be counted.

For five years (1990–94) observers scanned about 30,000 miles of road annually. The numbers of hedgehogs counted were fairly consistent between the years, with an average of about one per 30 miles driven. The same three regions of the country recorded the highest numbers in all five years (East Anglia, East Midlands and North East England), ranging from 3.3 to 9.75 hedgehogs per 100 miles (Table 30). The lowest counts were also in the same three regions in all five years (South West and South East England, West Midlands). If roadkills were just random numbers, you would not expect such consistency year to year. Nor would you expect this pattern if it were simply a crude measure of traffic density. Despite the greater number of miles driven by observers in the south west, fewer hedgehogs were counted there per 100 miles than in the south east. The southeast consistently scored poorly, despite its very high traffic density. Statistical analyses suggest that there were no major `differences between observers or years, so data from all five years could be combined to create a snapshot of relative abundance for comparison with similar surveys sometime in the future. Overall, observers travelled 162,043 miles and counted a total of 5,321 hedgehogs, giving an abundance index of 3.28 per 100 miles for a sample of five years in the 1990s.

A decade later, the PTES began regular monitoring of mammals killed on British roads, using an almost identical protocol to allow comparisons to be made with the surveys made in the 1990s. In the intervening years, great strides had been made with involving volunteers in 'Citizen Science' projects, especially using the internet (see Chapter 13). In the first four years of the Mammals on Roads (MoR) project, hundreds of volunteers surveyed 433,000 km (269,054 miles)

TABLE 30. Average roadkill index for 1990–94 inclusive, showing regional differences in relative abundance of hedgehogs.

Regions	Hedgehogs per 100 miles
North East	6.66
East Anglia	6.42
East Midlands	4.36
Scotland	2.98
Wales	2.66
North West	2.59
South	2.31
West Midlands	2.01
South East	1.64
South West	1.23
Overall index for five years	3.28

of roads, covering most parts of mainland Britain. They counted 6,411 hedgehogs. That equates to a crude average abundance index of 2.38 per 100 miles, a decrease of nearly a third since the 1990s (Fig. 208). Even within the period 2001–04, the index declined consistently year on year for four years, especially in eastern England (Fig. 209). The regional rank order of the abundance index remained much the same, with hedgehogs apparently more abundant in the east and northeast and least numerous in southwest England. They did seem to

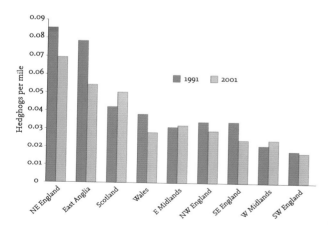

FIG 208. Structured roadkill counts in 2001 and a decade earlier, showing consistency in rank order and also a general decline in hedgehog abundance.

FIG 209. Roadkill counts per 100 km driven in 2001–04 show a similar rank order of regions and a continuing overall decline, even within four years.

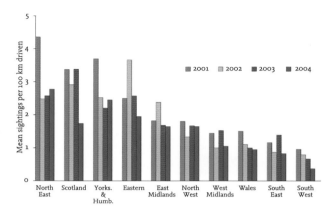

have increased somewhat in Scotland since the 1990s. Evidence of a consistent downward trend also helps finally to nail the argument about traffic density. If more traffic results in more roadkill, then the trend over time in the number of dead hedgehogs counted should have been upwards as numbers of vehicles increased, not the reverse.

The MoR surveys recruited many more observers than in the 1990s, generating very large numbers of survey journeys, leading to results that are more robust than earlier. Statistical analysis indicates that enough data exist from MoR to generate consistent values for the abundance index and also to predict future trends with considerable confidence. These roadkill counts have formed a basis for answering the question of whether or not the hedgehog population is in decline. Yes it is, and numbers appear to have fallen by about a third in a decade. The roadkill counts mainly survey rural areas and numbers may have held up in urban habitats that were excluded from the counts, suggesting that additional survey methods are needed, but see below.

The counts made by Davies in the 1950s during the months of July, August and September can be compared with the more recent figures. He recorded 56 hedgehogs on Hampshire roads in 3,575 miles, equivalent to 1.57 per 100 miles. In 1952–53 it was about 1.33 per 100 miles and 1.9 in 1953–4. These are lower values than recent surveys have found (2.31 for this region) and it is hard to see why, except that he covered only a very limited sample of roads. I did try some counts myself in the 1960s, recording dead hedgehogs each week on my three different routes to work, and found 13 hedgehogs in 400 miles. Using only the numbers for July, August and September to be comparable with later surveys gives an abundance index of 3.25 per 100 miles, a figure comparable with those obtained nationally in the 1990s, but well above what would be expected now on those same routes. Indeed, some sample journeys I made along the same old roads (largely unchanged) 40 years later frequently found no hedgehogs at all.

Roadkill counts in other countries usually do not follow a standard protocol similar to that used in Britain, so direct comparisons are perhaps inappropriate. However, in Ireland 133 casualties were counted in a total of 50,430 km, giving a crude abundance index (i.e. not restricted to July–September) of 0.264 per 100 km, equivalent to 0.42 per 100 miles (Haigh et al., 2014a). In New Zealand's North Island, Bob Brockie's average abundance index was 40.23 hedgehogs in 100 miles (25 per 100 km) in the 1950s, falling to 17.7 (11 per 100 km) in the 1980s and 2.7 per 100 miles (1.7 per 100 km) in 2005, a drastic decline in the same half-century, paralleling that which has occurred in Britain (Brockie et al., 2009). In 1987, my wife and I counted hedgehogs on about 4,600 miles of roads in New Zealand and found an overall average of 17.8 per 100 miles (11.1 per 100 km) in North Island, a comparable figure with Brockie's, and about double the figure for South Island. Dead hedgehogs were also several times more abundant in New Zealand than in England when we counted using the same protocol later that same year.

Badgers are absent from New Zealand and farming there is probably less intensive, so it is hard to account for the changed status of hedgehogs in that country. Brockie suggested that a simultaneous decline in both Britain and New Zealand might indicate a disease being responsible, but offered no evidence for this idea and nobody here has reported a sudden increase in deaths from a mysterious new illness. The one new thing, at least in Britain, has been the widespread release into the environment of seriously effective pesticides (see Chapter 9).

DECLINING NUMBERS OF HEDGEHOGS

There is nothing new in the suggestion that hedgehogs are in decline. As long ago as 1957, Maurice Burton counted 20 freshly killed hedgehogs in 50 miles between London and Salisbury, plus a few older remains (a total of more than 40 hedgehogs per 100 miles!). During the 1950s and 1960s he gained the impression that there was a 'marked falling off in the numbers of casualties. During that period also my impression is that the numbers of hedgehogs has fallen throughout the countryside' (Burton, 1969). In 1990, I sent a questionnaire to members of the National Federation of Women's Institutes and found that more than a third of the 1,200 respondents felt that there were fewer hedgehogs than in the recent past. Only a minority (25 per cent) thought that hedgehogs had become more numerous. The greatest pessimism was expressed by those living in the southeast and southwest of England, the same regions that also had the lowest numbers of hedgehogs killed on the roads. Another survey, launched by the PTES in 2005, resulted in 20,000 people submitting information, nearly half (47 per cent) thought that hedgehogs had been declining over the previous five years, especially in the Greater London area. In 2016, *Gardeners' World* magazine sought the opinions of its readers and 51 per cent of the respondents said they had not seen a hedgehog in the past 12 months, up from 48 per cent the previous year.

The PTES initiated an annual questionnaire-based survey ('Living with Mammals'), adding to its Mammals on Roads surveys, and also a special one specifically directed at gathering observations of hedgehogs ('HogWatch'). Meanwhile, both the RSPB and British Trust for Ornithology (BTO) have been gathering information about hedgehog sightings from more than 2,500 sites as an adjunct to three of their regular surveys of bird abundance. Thus, by 2010 there were several different lines of enquiry generating independent sets of survey data that might reflect changes in hedgehog numbers, including urban areas. All of them seemed to indicate a declining population, but varied in their methods and offered differing estimates of severity. Moreover, some were 'anecdotal', based on impressions rather than actual counts, so were they fully reliable?

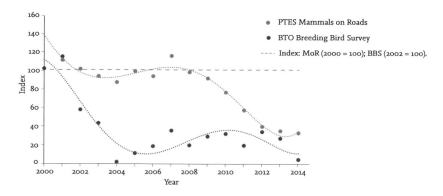

FIG 210. Indices of abundance derived from the PTES 'Mammals on Roads' data and from direct observations of hedgehogs noted in the BTO's annual 'Breeding Bird Survey'. The indices are standardised against the figure for 2000 (MoR) and 2002 (BBS: which began collecting data on hedgehogs a year later) to reveal annual changes. Some years appear to be better than others, probably as a result of the 'noise' often found in data from independent observers, but the overall trend is consistently downwards, despite both sets of data being obtained in a completely different manner.

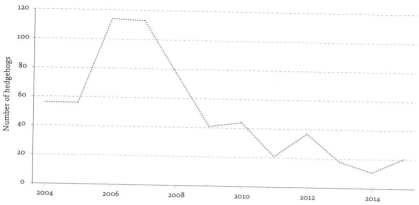

FIG 211. Mavis Righini operated a small hedgehog rescue centre in south east London. The number of hedgehogs brought to her declined steadily for eight years, perhaps another indication of a failing local hedgehog population. However, as with many of these graphs, we have to take account of human behaviour too. In this case, she began to limit her intake, taking only those from her own borough, because of the time and work involved in handling so many animals. But numbers continued to decline.

The PTES commissioned population statisticians at the BTO to review these various approaches to decide whether they confirmed any apparent trends and the extent to which they could be relied upon, given all the many drawbacks involved in gathering such information from so many people who might not all be following their instructions in exactly the same way (one of the drawbacks of using 'Citizen Science' data). The review concluded that all these different approaches clearly indicated a decline in hedgehog numbers. This was despite the surveys being in existence for only a comparatively short time (between 4 and 14 years, 1996–2010). Roadkill counts were the most consistent and reliable and also go back furthest in time. This and the information gathered via the BTO's own 'Garden Birdwatch' survey were sufficiently robust to predict with 80 per cent confidence a population decline of 10 per cent in a decade. In other words, the apparent decline in hedgehog numbers is both real and based on reliable data (Roos *et al.*, 2012). The actual rate of decline varied slightly between the surveys, but given the vagaries of weather, observer effort and other variables, it is unrealistic to expect exact figures or total agreement to the nearest decimal point. Further independent evidence comes from the Game Conservancy Trust, who record that the number of hedgehogs killed by gamekeepers has halved in 50 years (see Chapter 12). The central message is clear – we are losing our hedgehogs!

One slightly confusing factor is a study, by Anouschka Hof and Paul Bright, which used a completely different method of assessment and suggested the rate of loss was less than had been claimed. They compared distribution maps, past and present, recording where people had reported seeing hedgehogs. The idea was to see if there had been a change over time in the number of map squares where hedgehogs were reported to be present. They concluded that there had indeed been a decline: there was a 5–7 per cent reduction in the number of map grid squares where hedgehogs had been recorded between 1960 and 1975 and the distribution in 2000–2015 (Bright & Hof, 2016). This could imply that the hedgehog's demise had been less drastic than previously thought and perhaps the earlier statements about hedgehog losses might be exaggerated and alarmist. However, this is a simplistic approach that takes no account of the actual number of hedgehogs present. A 10-km square on a map will be recorded as 'occupied' even if there is only one hedgehog left! The rest of the population may have gone already, but that will not be evident by counting the reduction in numbers of occupied squares on maps. The result is to overestimate abundance and mask actual decline in population size. What that study did show is that there has been a reduction in geographical coverage. It also adds to the series of investigations, all using different approaches, that combine to indicate a downward trend in the hedgehog's fortunes. Despite the many drawbacks of Citizen Science, the weight of evidence all points in the same direction – hedgehogs are getting scarcer.

At the time of writing (2017), efforts are under way to assess both distribution and abundance of hedgehogs by using 'tracking tunnels'. These record the presence of hedgehogs by registering their footprints within a plastic shelter instead of using much more expensive traps (See Appendix). The idea is to obtain information on hedgehog population density in different habitat types and also in relation to the proximity and local abundance of badgers. The same sampling protocols, using tracking tunnels, could be repeated annually or at longer intervals to gain an index of population density and quantify any apparent increase or decline in the future (Yarnell et al., 2014).

WHY ARE HEDGEHOGS IN DECLINE?

Demonstrating that hedgehogs are becoming fewer invites the obvious question as to what is causing this to happen. Many of the 'likely suspects' are identified in Chapter 9 and reviewed by Hugh Warwick (Warwick, 2016), but these relate to direct causes of death and may not be the reason for long-term losses at the population level. Increasing road traffic is an obvious factor to consider (Fig. 212). Roadkill is a very explicit form of death. We see the bodies and assume a negative

FIG 212. Road traffic is an obvious threat to hedgehogs, but its contribution to population decline is difficult to assess. We see the flattened victims – maybe other threats are more serious, but the effects are not so visible.

effect on populations and it is likely that roadkill is contributing to a reduction in the total hedgehog population, at least to some extent. However, the greatest threat is probably the insidious expansion of both urbanisation and intensive farming. These rarely kill individual hedgehogs outright, but instead prevent them from living successfully. The effect is on the population, not just on the individual. Also we are not reminded of the threat by having regular sightings of dead hedgehogs, so the effects of farming and urbanisation may go unnoticed. One effect of changed farming practices is the increase in field sizes since the 1960s to allow the use of larger and more efficient machinery, especially in arable land. This creates very large areas of open habitat and several recent studies suggest that hedgehogs prefer to avoid wide-open spaces, where they are more vulnerable to predation. Another effect of farming is to reduce the availability of key prey items. Simply ploughing the soil causes the number of earthworms to decline sharply in comparison with land subjected to reduced tillage, an effect that has probably worsened over time, exacerbated by the application of chemical treatments specifically designed to minimise populations of other macroinvertebrates such as slugs and beetle larvae. This may account for the relatively high roadkill counts sometimes seen in landscapes dominated by arable farmland, roadsides being more productive places to feed than the neighbouring fields. But road verges are a dangerous place to be.

Chapter 9 outlined the dangers posed by cumulative organochlorine pesticides, which have now been removed from use and ecosystems should become progressively clear of them and their effects. Nevertheless their use in gardens and on farmland may well have had an impact on hedgehog numbers in the past, from which the species has not recovered. Since then, we have seen the introduction of neonicotinoid poisons, used specifically to eradicate insect larvae from lawns, football pitches and other forms of managed grassland. The emergence of these chemicals exactly coincides with the period of fastest decline

FIG 213. Pastureland offers a good feeding habitat for hedgehogs, with plenty of worms and insects around the cowpats that nutritionally enhance the sward, but the dairy industry is in decline and many farmers have given up keeping cows or other livestock. Much now depends on the nature of future farming subsidies.

in hedgehog numbers. So there is a strong possibility that amenity grasslands, and even many garden lawns that have been treated with these chemicals as part of their normal management, have been abruptly denuded of a substantial proportion of their soil macrofauna, including worms, leatherjackets and beetle larvae. Cockchafer larvae are 30 mm long and are, or at least were, both common and large enough to be useful food for hedgehogs, moles and many species of birds. Eliminating them must have hit some local animal populations very hard. My own house is adjacent to a well-managed

. In early summer, we used to have lots of cockchafer beetles attracted to the lights of our house, but since the management of the football pitch was enhanced by the use of chafer grub control chemicals, we have had none at all. Elsewhere, hedgehogs are reported to have become scarce recently on apparently suitable grassland in urban parks where they had formerly been abundant. Even where pesticides are not used, increased trampling and soil compaction reduce the prospects of foraging successfully for soil invertebrates.

There may be lessons to be learned here, especially if football pitches, parks and recreation grounds turn out not to be useful hedgehog habitat any more. They comprise an important element of many green spaces in our urban areas, but they may have ceased to be supportive of hedgehogs in the recent past and their isolation prevents recolonisation. The problem now is that these chemical treatments were apparently intended to be used for two or three seasons specifically in order to break the insect life cycles. Once the insects are gone, they are likely to stay gone, especially for isolated urban sites, unless by some freak event a few beetles manage to recolonise and survive to breed and begin the slow process of rebuilding a viable population. It will take years and in many places may never happen. Even if the insect populations do recover in time, hedgehogs may be unable to recolonise due to the absence of a source population and difficulty of negotiating the many obstacles to dispersal in the urban environment

Those chemicals were not just for professional managers of sports turf, but were readily available in garden centres. So some people will have sterilised their lawns too. It is sad to think that kindly gardeners may have been encouraging hedgehogs by putting food out for them and making holes in their fences, but at the same time treating their lawn in such a way as to remove, perhaps permanently, the insect larvae that form one of the most important natural foods for hedgehogs. Removing chafers, leatherjackets, worms and who knows what else severely reduces natural food for hedgehogs and has the potential to disrupt soil ecosystems. The use of neonicotinoids has been banned as from late 2016, at least from use on flowering plants, but toxic chemicals will remain available for the management of amenity grassland unless the ban is extended following ongoing assessments. We may heave a sigh of relief once these dangerous chemicals are no longer in use, but the damage has been done and many small populations of hedgehogs may have been eliminated perhaps never to return.

There are safer substitutes becoming available that avoid chemicals altogether. Certain species of nematodes ('roundworms') that are natural parasites in Britain are being cultured and sold as a form of biological control. A packet of nematode larvae sufficient to treat 500 m^2 of turf contains about 250 million worms, enough to boost the natural population sufficiently to wipe out the target pest, but they are minute and no use as hedgehog food. *Heterorhabditis bacteriophora* and *Steinernema feltiae* kill cockchafers and leatherjackets respectively without apparently doing any other damage. But this misses the point: removing large insect larvae might make a nice lawn, smart golf course or robust turf, but it is at the expense of depriving hedgehogs of vital fare. Much of the damage will already have been done and it is likely that many areas of previously suitable habitat will remain devoid of these large insects and the hedgehogs they support. Perhaps we have moved on from the research phase to one of needing to raise

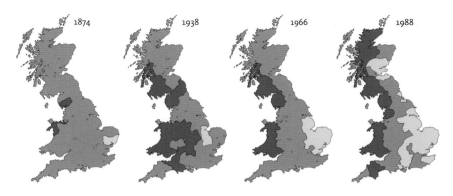

FIG 214. Progressive expansion of cultivated farmland at the expense of pasture. Cultivation involves actions that restrict food availability for hedgehogs (e.g. ploughing and use of pesticides). Enlargement of fields to increase efficiency removes winter nesting places and materials. The result tallies with regional differences in hedgehog roadkill, fewer where arable land predominates and more where non-cultivated land predominates. Dark green = less than 20% of farmland cultivated; Pale green = 20–60% cultivated; Yellow = more than 60% of farmland cultivated. (Based on Tapper, 1992)

public awareness of what has happened and we now need to take some form of action to repair the damage (see Chapter 13). Meanwhile we can be confident in adding grass treatments using neonicotinoids to the list of probable explanations for the recently accelerated decline of hedgehog populations, along with the probable losses from secondary poisoning by widespread use of rodenticides.

A similar situation occurs on farmland. The use of pesticides and the removal of hedgerows to enlarge field sizes for gains in productivity are just two of the more obvious things that will not have benefitted hedgehog numbers. The intensification of farming in response to subsidies and economic need has transformed the British landscape. Before the First World War there were millions of horses in the countryside, creating short turf and piles of dung that provided excellent foraging for hedgehogs. Horses were normally kept in small fields fringed with hedges where the hedgehogs could nest. The horses have been replaced with tractors and hedges removed to accommodate bigger machines and enhance their efficiency. The fields have been regularly ploughed and treated with multiple applications of fertilisers and pesticides. Those changes have greatly increased farmland productivity and given us the countryside that is familiar to us now. These same changes must have contributed to a significant reduction in numbers of hedgehogs, but because we do not see the dead bodies (unlike road casualties), we remain largely unconscious of the massive effects that these changes are likely to have had on hedgehogs at the population level. Radio-tracking studies have shown that large areas of farmland are now sub-optimal habitat for hedgehogs and questionnaire surveys have shown that hedgehogs are more abundant where farmers receive special payments to support wildlife by maintaining hedgerows and uncultivated areas. But those subsidies are at the mercy of political change. Policies that help support farmers are likely to change again with Britain's withdrawal from the European Union, but each policy change, now and in the past, will have its effects on wildlife. Once hedgehogs are squeezed out, it may be a long time before they return, if they ever do, even though more benign agricultural policies might be pursued in the future.

POPULATION GENETICS AND THE EFFECTS OF ISOLATION

According to the Royal Horticultural Society, the equivalent of 15 square miles of town front gardens have been lost nationally, often paved over, in the ten years between 2005 and 2015, and more than 5 million of our urban front gardens now have no vegetation at all. In London, half the front gardens have been paved, often to accommodate a parked car. We have lost a lot of back gardens too, especially the large ones surrounding big Victorian and Edwardian houses, where the whole site has been cleared to make way for several smaller modern dwellings. Often these do have a garden, but it is tiny and fenced off from its neighbours.

In some ways, fencing is even more of a threat than the more obvious loss of flower beds and shrubbery to patios and decking. Roads are another obstacle restricting hedgehog movements. But why does it matter? We know from the principles of island biogeography that two small islands will support fewer species than one large one covering the same total area. Similar principles apply on land, where our countryside is increasingly divided into smaller and smaller parcels by the seemingly relentless construction of roads, fences and other barriers to free movement, in addition to existing natural obstacles like rivers or lakes (Fig. 217). Each time a large area is divided into smaller parts, species that need plenty of space find themselves with less available habitat. Often the barriers are not absolute and can be crossed, but only with difficulty. Studies on mice (*Apodemus* spp.) and voles (*Clethrionomys* spp.) revealed that they would much rather stay on one side of a road, even a narrow country lane barely 5 m wide,

FIG 215. Concrete barriers erected along the central reservation of our motorways now create barriers for many miles that no animals can cross. This divides animal populations into ever-smaller units, raising the risk of their local extinction.

than cross to the other side (MacPherson *et al.*, 2011). A similar study with those species in Germany showed the same effect, even on a forest road with no traffic at night (Mader, 1984). Hedgehogs might be bolder and they will at least attempt to cross roads, but they are generally reluctant to do so, especially wide ones, and many end up dying in the attempt. Hedgehogs will often turn back rather than venture onto a hostile road.

Consequently, the ever-increasing numbers of roads and other barriers results in the national population of hedgehogs becoming divided into smaller and smaller groups. This situation is often termed a 'metapopulation', one in which the total number of animals alive is distributed among many smaller sub-groups whose members can use habitat links to disperse and exchange genes with members of other sub-groups. Gene flow is crucial if genetic diversity is to be maintained, but roads, canals, fences and suchlike all obstruct the process, leaving small groups of animals largely isolated and unable to benefit from the occasional arrival of new animals that reinforce a perilously small sub-population and bring a fresh input of genes.

In small populations, restricted availability of mates means that the animals are likely to experience inbreeding. This increases the probability of individuals acquiring two harmful recessive genes (one from each parent), perhaps directly affecting viability. Inbreeding also reduces the spectrum of genetic attributes, leaving the population less able to evolve in response to changing circumstances. These are theoretical problems, based on established principles of inheritance and supported by laboratory studies. But research on wild bird and mammal populations also suggests 'inbreeding depression' can significantly affect many aspects of an animal's life, including birth weight, survival and resistance to disease. On the other hand, we see natural behaviour that suggests the issue may not be as dire as sometimes suggested. For example, the breeding and territorial behaviour of harem species like fur seals serves to restrict genetic diversity by limiting the gene pool to traits inherited from only a few dominant males. It is also the case that some species like the cheetah continue to survive despite having a very limited gene pool, having passed through some form of genetic bottleneck in the past. All the world's pet gerbils and golden hamsters derive from just a few individuals. With all this conflicting information, it is hard to say definitively that inbreeding is a threat to hedgehog survival, only that it may well be.

There has been little research into the genetic composition of hedgehog populations or the effects of barriers that separate them. A study of hedgehog genetics in Oxfordshire took samples from 160 members of 8 isolated populations within a 15 km radius. Some of those populations may have been as small as 12 animals, others perhaps 25. Overall they showed a high degree of genetic differentiation, implying restricted gene flow between the groups. This was presumably due, at least in part, to natural and man-made barriers in the countryside (Becher & Griffiths, 1998). Other investigations are in progress elsewhere aimed at determining the effect of motorways and roads as barriers to gene flow. A study of wood mice (which can be obtained in larger samples than hedgehogs) has shown genetic richness and heterozygosity is greater in farmland than in urban sites, where there are more barriers to animal movements, resulting in a greater degree of inbreeding (Wilson *et al.*, 2016). On the other hand, there are several robust hedgehog populations that have survived for decades on islands, despite having had only a handful of founder members and with inevitable inbreeding among the early generations in their new home.

FIG 216. Modern garden fencing like this is a barrier to almost everything. Hedgehogs are thereby excluded and their movements are constrained, reducing gene flow. Small groups of hedgehogs (and other species) are left isolated and facing almost inevitable decline.

FIG 217. Thanks to campaigns like 'Hedgehog Street', many gardeners and landowners are now creating special 'hedgehog holes' in their fencing to help reduce this problem. (Hedgehog Street)

Nevertheless, it is evident that population fragmentation caused by barriers and obstructions to free movement is at least as important as simple loss of areas of habitat. That is the principle behind campaigns to make holes in garden fences to facilitate dispersal by hedgehogs and other species (see Chapter 13). A study of habitat connectivity in Switzerland used predictive computer models to establish that there were key pinch points within the habitat that would compromise animal movements and that connectivity and habitat quality were two of the key variables which determine suitability for wildlife. Predictive models that take account of habitat connectivity are a new tool that may allow evaluation of the impact of future landscape changes or management scenarios and might assist in designing wildlife-friendly designs of new housing or factory estates, for example (Baaker *et al.*, 2014).

Whatever the genetic implications of isolation, it is certainly the case that small populations are more vulnerable to random events, such as flooding or shortage of food in a drought. Small populations could also fluctuate strongly from year to year depending on minor variations in sex ratio, reproductive success or survival rates. Modelling the effect of these changes indicates that small, fluctuating populations suffer an enhanced risk of extinction (Soulé, 1987). It may be pertinent to note that small numbers were introduced to certain islands around the British coast (see Chapter 2), but in many cases the population collapsed, and sometimes died out, following a 'boom and bust' population increase. Even the much larger North Island of New Zealand appears to have suffered a collapse in its population of introduced hedgehogs. Small populations need to have links to other groups of the same species which can then stage a kind of rescue effect through the periodic arrival of animals dispersing from elsewhere.

The issue of population viability can be explored by using software such as 'Vortex', written by Robert Lacy of the Chicago Zoological Society and published in 1993. This simulates wildlife population dynamics and how they alter through time in response to changes in the environment or variations in birth and death rates. It is the most frequently used tool for population viability analysis (PVA) and allows predictions to be made about what happens if numbers decline below a critical level. In 2013, the PTES commissioned Tom Moorhouse at the University of Oxford to perform a hedgehog population viability analysis, using the available data on reproduction and mortality rates. The aim was to get some idea of how small a hedgehog population can be and still remain viable in the long term. How small is too small to have a realistic chance of long-term survival? Also how much space might that minimum viable population need? Answers to these questions would provide some kind of guidance regarding the future prospects of the hedgehog, particularly those living in isolated groups in urban areas. As always, these population models are heavily dependent on the data used, much of which is somewhat uncertain. In real life, there will also be variation in litter sizes and survival rates and unpredictable factors such as food abundance and weather conditions. The outcome of the study would depend very much on how those variables were estimated and incorporated. Multiple runs of the model, with many different combinations of data and chance factors, provided estimates of the minimum viable population that varied between 32 and 250 hedgehogs. This wide range of estimates itself serves to highlight the uncertainties involved and the need for caution in interpreting the predictions. To view this in a broader context, informed opinion elsewhere suggests that a mammal or bird population should not number fewer than 50 in the short term if it is to avoid inbreeding depression, and in the long term should not be below 500 in order to maintain evolutionary potential.

Nevertheless we can take 32 as an approximate minimum number of hedgehogs needed to ensure a reasonable probability of a population's persistence and relate that to figures described earlier for population densities. This suggests that an isolated urban hedgehog population may require at least 90 ha (and perhaps over 200 ha) of suitable habitat. Rural populations may need even more because much of their habitat may be less supportive than urban gardens. This puts into perspective the plight of many town-dwelling hedgehogs that are increasingly hemmed in by roads, walls and garden fences that soon reduce the area available to them to well below 90 ha. They are living precariously on an 'island' that is too small.

We can view these findings in relation to actual hedgehog populations. Nigel Reeve's study area, a golf course in west London, extends to only 40 ha, but it had

FIG 218. Heavy use of amenity grassland reduces its ability to supply hedgehogs with invertebrate prey, even where pesticides are not used.

an apparently thriving hedgehog population in the 1970s, perhaps because the adjacent gardens added a lot of excellent foraging habitat, creating a realistically large area for survival. Regent's Park in London is more than the necessary 90 ha (actually more than 160 ha), but its effective size is reduced because radio-tracking shows that about a quarter of it is shunned by the hedgehogs, perhaps because large areas are too exposed or they offer poor feeding prospects. Hedgehogs have already gone from London's Hyde Park, a slightly smaller area, and also from St James' Park, perhaps also due to a shortage of nesting sites. A broader survey in London highlighted the importance of parks and other urban green spaces for hedgehog survival in urban areas (Hof & Bright, 2009). But many of them are likely to be less than 90 ha in extent, even allowing for access to adjacent gardens, allotments or cemeteries. Those green spaces may also include football pitches and other forms of amenity grassland subject to intensified management practices, highlighting the precarious situation in which those small populations of urban hedgehogs exist, assuming they still do. Hedgehogs might still be present in many town parks and green spaces, at least for now, but maybe not forever unless active attention is paid to free movement between the widest possible range of sites and habitats. Access is crucial; barriers are a threat. Badgers are also a threat (see Chapter 9), especially in small or isolated habitat units where there are few places to hide from them.

CLIMATE CHANGE

As a hibernating species, the hedgehog is likely to be sensitive to possible future climatic changes, but much depends on what actual changes take place. For example, an all-round warming, as seems to be happening now, could extend the active season and allow earlier breeding and enable more of the late-born young to survive. Hedgehogs might then enjoy the sort of success they have had in the North Island of New Zealand, at least in the past. If climate change gives us more sunshine, this will warm the soil and enable beetle larvae and caterpillars to grow faster and probably fatter, making better and more abundant food for hedgehogs. But, if more sunny days also means less rain, we may be confronted with long periods of summer drought, severely restricting the availability of important hedgehog prey. Warmer winters may be shorter, but will also increase metabolic fat consumption during hibernation, requiring hedgehogs to become active sooner or die. If climate change means more torrential rain and less drizzle, that could be a problem too, and if it means less rain altogether, that will certainly create difficulties by making worms harder to get. Climate and weather patterns are bound to change, they always have, but it's hard to predict what the effect will be on hedgehog numbers. Meanwhile, other factors may be even more pressing and take effect sooner.

The possible effects of climate change come on top of where we are already. The 'State of Nature' report published by a coalition of 52 wildlife-oriented groups in 2016 quantified losses and gains among more than 400 British species. This long tale of woe detailed major losses: 54 per cent among farmland birds since 1970, for example. It identified intensification of farming as the greatest single driver of population declines in the countryside and the hedgehog is likely to have been harmfully affected. Departure from the European Union offers opportunities to escape from the restrictions of the Common Agricultural Policy, but cannot free us from reality. Energy from the sun, via plants, becomes our food on the table. The more that wildlife intercepts it on the way, the less there is for humans and the less income there is for farmers. So, to feed our increasing human population with only a limited supply of land, farming has to become more efficient. That means removing weeds (competitors for space and soil nutrients) and also limiting losses due to pests. That's what agricultural intensification is all about. Horrendously effective agricultural and horticultural chemicals may become a thing of the past, but something must take their place. The more we use pesticides or other methods to focus food production on human needs by killing beetles, caterpillars, slugs and the rest, the less there will be for hedgehogs and other wildlife that effectively live as passengers on our farming systems. The larger the farmer's fields, the more efficiently they can be farmed, but the less habitat there is for hedgehogs to nest. Even in our own gardens, pathetically small by standards of the past, areas of decking and elegant paving reduce usable habitat for the hedgehog. The actions we take to manage neat lawns or weed-free flowerbeds and eliminate caterpillars from our vegetable patch will do nothing to improve the prospects for hedgehog survival. More than half of the people surveyed in 2016 had not seen one at all in their garden and only 12 per cent reported them still to be regular visitors.

Viewing this gloomy scenario and the graphs showing population declines has led the popular press to predict the hedgehog's extinction, perhaps within as little as 15 years. This is nonsense, of course. Hedgehogs could not be exterminated in 15 years on the Uists, despite determined efforts to eradicate them and a limited land area to deal with. Hedgehogs will remain a British species for a long time yet, especially in areas of the country not under pressure from housing developments or intensive farming, and there is also much that we can do to help them to survive and prosper where adequate space and resources remain, including in our own private and public gardens (see Chapter 13).

CONCLUSION

Practical difficulties and the limited number of studies mean that we still do not have good figures for hedgehog population densities. Many of those that have been published may now be obsolete owing to changes in land use and farming practices that have occurred since the studies were conducted upon which those estimates were made. There is consequently little confidence in our estimate of the total size of the British hedgehog population. However many hedgehogs there may be in this country, structured counts of hedgehog road casualties suggest that the total population size may have fallen by up to a third during the last quarter of a century and the decline continues. Other methods of monitoring hedgehogs also all point to long-term diminishing numbers. The main causes are likely to be associated with changes in land use, particularly intensification of agriculture, rather than the direct causes of mortality to individuals such as predation or poisoning, although these and other threats such as road traffic will have contributed to reducing the number of hedgehogs and continue to do so. There is little sign of improvement in the hedgehog's abundance and chronic decline is likely, a prospect that it faces along with many other species. Its future will depend a lot on how much help well-meaning people provide and also on the sensitivity of future land use policies to the needs of wildlife in general.

CHAPTER 11

Hedgehogs in Sickness and in Health

M OST OF THE DISEASES THAT hedgehogs carry are of little concern to humans and many of their parasites are host-specific and unlikely to affect people. Hedgehogs have not been strongly implicated in the widespread occurrence of wildlife rabies across Europe; nor have they been an issue in the ongoing problem of bovine tuberculosis in cattle and wildlife. Like many other mammals, they can carry bovine TB but few infected hedgehogs have been found in Britain and a survey of the problem in New Zealand found only a 5 per cent infection rate among 79 wild hedgehogs in an area where the disease is endemic.

In Britain, hedgehogs were reported to carry foot and mouth disease over 70 years ago, developing lesions on the skin of their feet and face and becoming dozy, diurnal and reluctant to roll up. They were apparently able to carry this disease into hibernation and still be infective when they became active again in the following spring. This appears to have been forgotten during both of the major outbreaks of foot and mouth disease in Britain that have occurred since, but there have been no serious claims that hedgehogs were implicated in either of those nationwide disasters. Paramyxoviruses have also been reported in hedgehogs, similar to those that cause canine distemper, but this seems not to be a serious problem, although few surveys of the parasites and infections found in hedgehogs have included checking for viruses. Various bacteria have been isolated from hedgehogs, including one responsible for sore throats, and others, like *Salmonella*, which cause intestinal upsets in both hedgehogs and humans. Evidence of leptospire infections have also been found in British hedgehogs, but not relating to *Leptospira icterohaemorrhagiae*, the dangerous bacterium that is found in rats and causes Weil's disease in humans.

From the hedgehog's point of view, their most important endoparasites are the tiny nematode worms *Capillaria aerophila* and *Crenosoma striatum*, collectively referred to as 'lungworms' or 'threadworms'. Slugs and snails are the secondary hosts for *Crenosoma*, while *Capillaria* occurs in earthworms at one stage of its life cycle. These nematode parasites transfer to the hedgehog when their host is eaten. They invade its lungs, causing a nasal discharge which results in coughing and sneezing. There may also be physical damage to lung tissues, which might then develop bacterial infections. The eggs of these parasites are passed out with the hedgehog's faeces, and thereby gain access to the invertebrate host to complete their life cycle. Lungworm is one of the principal disorders recorded among sick hedgehogs in animal hospitals. The characteristic nematode eggs are typically found in up to half of all faecal samples taken from the wild hedgehogs that are brought in to animal care centres, indicating that these parasites are a common and widespread problem, with *Capillaria* being usually the more prevalent of the two. Infections can be treated fairly easily with a high degree of success, but severe cases that are left untreated will often result in death, especially among the youngest hedgehogs. Both parasites are host-specific and do not infect humans.

Tapeworm and fluke infections are also common, and in Jersey the fluke *Brachylaemus erinacei* was found in about one in seven of the faecal samples collected from 789 hedgehogs (Burdon & Reeve, 1997). This fluke is transmitted via various land snails as intermediate hosts. It causes serious distress to infected hedgehogs, which become agitated and very restless, often with significant loss of weight. But nearly three quarters of all hedgehog faecal samples show no evidence of tapeworm or fluke infestation.

Occasionally concern is expressed regarding 'gum disease' or the accumulation of tartar on teeth in hedgehogs that have been brought into care centres. Gum disease and progressive accumulation of tartar on the teeth are a health problem for humans, but hedgehogs are not people. They do not live long enough for progressive disease conditions to develop to the same extent as in humans and there appears to be little evidence of dental issues being a significant threat to hedgehog survival. Obviously it would be better if every animal had perfect teeth, but in New Zealand nearly half of the wild hedgehogs have some form of dental abnormality, yet populations thrive there with no evidence that defective dentition affects survival. It may be the case that tartar and gum disease are most often noticed among hedgehogs in animal care centres, where they will normally be fed on soft foods that lack the abrasive scouring properties of a diet rich in earthworms and beetles.

FLEAS

Among the hedgehog's various ectoparasites, fleas are the most visible and notorious. They are particularly conspicuous among the sparse spines of the hedgehog's back, creating the impression that hedgehogs have more fleas than other mammals. However, in a sample of 136 hedgehogs, two thirds carried fewer than 20 fleas and many had none at all. In Ireland, 1,063 fleas were collected from 19 hedgehogs, an average of 56 per animal. In Germany, the average was only 6.4 among 76 hedgehogs (Visser *et al.*, 2001). The numbers of fleas (and ticks) may be much greater in certain individuals that are already unhealthy, and several hundred may sometimes be found on one individual sickly hedgehog. Almost all the fleas reported in surveys of hedgehog parasites have been identified as

Archaeopsylla erinacei (Fig. 219). There are at least 60 other species of bird and mammal fleas in Britain, but the hedgehog has this one as its very own, specially adapted to the peculiar circumstances associated with living on it. The spiny skin and coarse hair offer a very open habitat, a completely different environment to what a flea might experience on the skin of another, more furry mammal. Fleas normally need warmth for successful reproduction, which ceases when the temperature falls below about 10°C. Crucially, a hedgehog flea has to overcome what appears to be basic flea behaviour, that of deserting the cooling body of a dead host. Hedgehogs regularly 'die', especially during the cycles of warm bloodedness and hypothermia that characterise hibernation or bouts of hypothermia (see Chapter 6). The low nest temperature during its host's winter inactivity is not the only adverse condition experienced by the

FIG 219. The hedgehog has its own species of flea, *Archaeopsylla erinacei*, specially adapted to living on the peculiar and challenging environment of the hedgehog's skin. It is rarely found on anything else and the special fleas associated with other mammals like cats and dogs do not live on hedgehogs.

hedgehog flea. Food availability is curtailed during hibernation as blood flow in the peripheral circulation is reduced due to the lowered heart rate. Again the flea must not react by deserting its host, as would happen with other mammal fleas when the body cooled after death. So the hedgehog flea is a special species, adapted to the peculiar circumstances of living on this particular host.

Few fleas of other species (cat and vole fleas, for example) ever rise to the challenge of invading a hedgehog. Of 1,158 fleas that I collected from hedgehogs, only one belonged to another species: *Hystricopsylla talpae* (mole flea). Conversely, hedgehog fleas are very rarely found living on anything else; they are highly host-specific. They will occasionally get on to humans, but rarely stay very long (I'm glad to say!). When not on a hedgehog, *Archaeopsylla* is most commonly encountered on dogs and foxes, both of which are known to interact frequently and closely with hedgehogs. But if household cats or dogs have fleas, this should not be automatically blamed on the local hedgehogs. Pets have their own species of fleas, better adapted to life in warm, soft fur, and these are likely to be more numerous than the occasional invading *Archaeopsylla erinacei*, casually acquired whilst muzzling a dead or defensive hedgehog. The hedgehogs that were taken to New Zealand lost their fleas on the way (or had them removed), so *Archaeopsylla* is absent there, although a few rat and cat fleas may sometimes take their place.

Crawling about in the large gaps between the hedgehog's spines, fleas are very exposed and appear to be both numerous and also easily dislodged by even the most perfunctory grooming activities, but the hedgehog will rarely attempt to get rid of them. Actually they seem not to mind their tickly attendants and barely flinch, even when one crawls across the hedgehog's face, one of the most sensitive parts of its anatomy. In winter, fleas remain on the hibernating hedgehog, but feed only during periods of their host's arousal. As the hedgehog lies on its side during hibernation, the fleas cluster on its flank lying underneath against the nest floor. When they do feed, the fleas excrete faeces that are rich in blood constituents, the main source of food for their larvae that develop in the nest lining. Over half of the adult fleas are likely to survive the winter and they start to lay eggs into the nest as soon as winter ends. Fleas take three to four weeks to grow from the egg and young fleas and larvae reach maximum numbers by late summer in the nests of breeding female hedgehogs. They invade baby hedgehogs before the youngsters leave their mother's nest. So the hedgehog's nest acts as a flea nursery and forms an important link in the insect's life cycle (Brinck & Lofqvist, 1973). Hedgehogs that have had their fleas (and ticks) removed, swiftly regain a fresh set of passengers. They can become reinfested with fleas within a week, picked up from visiting other hedgehog nests or from fleas lying in the grass waiting for a new host to pass by (Buckle, 1975).

TICKS AND MITES

Hedgehogs often carry one or more grey, globular ticks attached to the skin, especially behind the ears and on the flanks (Fig. 220). Full-sized, engorged adult ticks are each about 1 cm in diameter, but despite their size they seem not to bother their host unduly. They suck blood from the hedgehog, swell up and then drop off to rest until they encounter a new host. They do not have eyes, but are very sensitive to body warmth, vibrations and to the carbon dioxide in a mammal's breath, all of which signal the proximity of a potential new host. Once aboard, the tick will sink its barbed proboscis into the skin and begin to feed, increasing its weight a hundredfold, before dropping off to moult and invade a new host. In Britain, we have two species of hedgehog tick: *Ixodes ricinus* and *Ixodes hexagonus*. Both occur on other mammals too (particularly *I. ricinus*) and their nymphs (tiny, brown, crablike creatures) will also be seen on hedgehogs, sometimes with 50 on a single host. Several hundred more may be lurking in its nest. As with fleas, hedgehog nests play an important role in the tick's life cycle. *Ixodes hexagonus* is mostly found in the warmer parts of Britain and is the one that is most often associated with the hedgehog. It can be exceedingly abundant in a hedgehog's nest. That will be of particular importance to the male ticks, as they live in the nest lining rather than on the hedgehog, and the ticks mate with their females in the nest, not on the host. Successful completion of the tick's life cycle and transmission to a new host therefore relies heavily on hedgehogs visiting each other's nests. This certainly happens in summer, when male hedgehogs often visit a nest that has been previously occupied by a female (see Chapter 5). Hedgehogs probably visit each other's hibernation nests too and these can accumulate plenty of ticks.

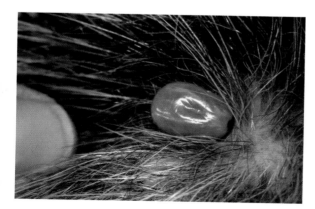

FIG 220. Ticks are small, globular creatures with tiny legs. They attach to the hedgehog, feed on its blood and then drop off and lie about waiting to invade another host. The commonest ones are also found on sheep.

Ticks are likely to be less numerous in the summer nests, as hedgehogs normally only occupy them for relatively short periods.

Ticks are the principal carriers of *Borrelia burgdorferi*, the causative agent of Lyme disease, a serious illness in people. *Borrelia* has been present in British ticks since at least 1897 (Hubbard *et al.*, 1998), but Lyme disease has had a low profile in Britain, although there were 483 confirmed cases in the first half of 2017. However, that is almost double the number seen in the same period of the previous year. In Switzerland, 12 out of a sample of 13 hedgehogs were carrying ticks infected with *Borrelia*, and hedgehogs themselves were also able to carry *Borrelia* in their blood stream, infecting new ticks as they fed. It must be borne in mind that ticks also occur on plenty of other species of mammals (including pets and birds), so the hedgehog should not be regarded as anything more than a bit player in the story of Lyme disease in humans. Tick bites seem to be mainly a problem where deer and sheep are abundant, as the adult ticks prefer to live on these larger mammals. But infections may reach humans via the ticks carried by small rodents. People most often seem to get infected with Lyme disease after walking about in long grass following a period of dry weather. Hedgehogs are not common in long grass or the extensive areas of woodland often frequented by deer, so they and their ticks are less likely than deer, sheep or rodents to be implicated in transmitting Lyme disease to humans.

Mites are tiny spidery creatures related to ticks, but much smaller (pinhead size). The ones found on British hedgehogs, and in their nests, are usually facultative parasites that normally live as scavengers among leaf litter, although they may live on an animal for a while if they get the chance. They are a minor irritation, although one species, *Caparinia tripilis*, causes mange and is probably responsible for the large flaky bald areas seen among the spines of some sickly looking hedgehogs.

This mite is more prevalent in New Zealand, where 37 per cent in a sample of 650 hedgehogs were reported to be infested with them. They can be a threat to a hedgehog's wellbeing and are even said to sometimes endanger its life. In some cases, the mites cause lesions which can be severely incapacitating and occasionally even fatal. The dry, scabby skin associated with mange impedes the hedgehog's ability to roll up and I have seen one whose suppurating skin had clogged the fur with adherent dust to such an extent it could hardly walk. In a case like that, survival may well be threatened and the mite is considered to be one of the few natural factors that might limit the abundance of hedgehogs in New Zealand (Brockie, 1974b). Perhaps *Caparinia tripilis* is more numerous there, and its effects more severe than in Britain, because New Zealand hedgehogs have no fleas. Although fleas are not predators, they might compete for space and blood supplies on the skin, keeping in check the number of mites on British hedgehogs.

RINGWORM

This is not a worm but a form of fungal infection in the skin, similar to 'athlete's foot' in humans. It is a host-specific organism called *Trichophyton erinacei* that causes swollen, crusty ears in older hedgehogs and sometimes results in pale, scurfy patches on the face (Figs. 221 & 222). In young animals, or in the early stages of infection, the fungus can only be detected by plucking out a few hairs and incubating them on a special agar plate. The fungus then generates a very distinctive yellow stain in the jelly (Fig. 223).

Throughout Britain, many hedgehogs are affected. Nearly one fifth of those that were randomly sampled from urban areas were found to carry ringworm, although they were often without visible symptoms (Morris & English, 1969). In New Zealand, the infection rate among hedgehogs is around 47 per cent, more than double the rate in Britain, perhaps reflecting higher population densities there. I found a similar proportion (44 per cent) where hedgehogs congregated to hibernate in Bushy Park. Although common in hedgehogs, *Trichophyton erinacei*

FIG 221. A normal healthy hedgehog's ear has thin, smooth skin.

FIG 222. A chronic ringworm infection causes the ear margin to become swollen and crusty, but it takes a long time, so this condition is normally only seen in old animals.

FIG 223. Ringworm is a fungus, diagnosed by culturing hairs on a special agar jelly plate. Other moulds and fungi will grow there too, but *Trichophyton erinacei* characteristically causes bright yellow patches to develop in the jelly.

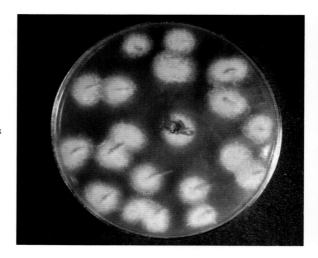

is evidently not highly contagious. Both repeated and prolonged exposure is probably necessary for it to become established in the skin and it takes several months for it to spread to other parts of the hedgehog's body (Morris & English, 1973). The fungus is probably transmitted as a result of fighting, one hedgehog butting another with the sharp spines on its head, injecting fungal material into the skin of an opponent. The head is the area most frequently infected, and males (who probably do most of the fighting) are twice as likely to be infected as females (Fig. 224). Ringworm infections are age-related and about 80 per cent of infected animals are more than one year old. *T. erinacei* is much less often seen among juvenile hedgehogs and never in nestlings, but the older the animals get the more likely they are to develop a chronic infection.

FIG 224. Ringworm is most often found on the head and face; the ventral surface (right) is least often infected. Males are more often infected than females.

TABLE 31. Ringworm infection rates among 203 randomly sampled British hedgehogs.

Habitat	Number sampled			Per cent infected
	Male	Sex unknown	Female	
Urban	31	22	24	16.8
Rural	16	25	16	8.8
Not recorded	25	18	26	—
Per cent infected	25		12.3	

TABLE 32. Ringworm infection rates among 125 hedgehogs whose age could be accurately estimated.

	Juveniles (first year of life)	Adults (>one year old)
Number sampled	66	59
Number infected	5	18
Infection rate	7.6 per cent	30.5 per cent

Another possible route of infection is via the nest (English & Morris, 1969), especially the winter ones that are occupied for longer than those used in summer. Hedgehogs shed infective material into the nest lining, where it may remain viable even over winter. Later visitors might then become infected. This could also explain how people occasionally get hedgehog ringworm (gardeners and children, for example), perhaps after clearing up leaves in the garden, although handling infected animals is the most likely route of infection. Most human ringworm infections, here and in New Zealand, involve other species of dermatophyte that come from pets and farm animals and not from hedgehogs. Hedgehog ringworm in humans is actually very rare, only 0.3–0.5 per cent of the total number of ringworm cases identified in Britain. Normally it is mainly children that are affected: more than two-thirds of 77 hedgehog ringworm cases in New Zealand were in children less than 15 years old. Infections in humans cause itching and mild inflammation, but the hedgehogs seem to be indifferent. They do not spend extra time scratching themselves nor do they show signs of general debilitation or weight loss. They are unlikely ever to rid themselves of the infection once it is established and hibernation certainly does not kill off the fungus, although its growth will be curtailed for the duration. There is no evidence that age confers immunity; on the contrary, it is the oldest animals that are most often and most severely affected. It is these animals that develop the characteristic dry, crusty ears that always seem to be associated with heavy infestations of this parasite.

OTHER MISERIES

Although they are not really parasites, blowfly eggs and larvae ('maggots') can sometimes be seen on hedgehogs that are still alive. Sickly hedgehogs, especially young ones, often become hypothermic and in this condition might easily be mistaken for dead by a blowfly, which selects the wet areas around the eyes and mouth to lay its eggs on the 'corpse'. Most small mammals would die quite soon having reached such a condition, but hedgehogs seem to expire in slow motion and may spend several days in a cold and lethargic state, yet still be able to crawl about. By this time, fly eggs will have hatched, especially in warm weather, generating a cluster of live maggots on a living host. The sight of seething maggots in a hedgehog's eye is particularly revolting, but the stoic hedgehog seems to ignore them, or perhaps it is beyond caring.

Fly eggs and larvae can be swabbed off with disinfectant and many of the other afflictions can be treated fairly easily. Commercially available insecticides (like 'Frontline' products) that are used on pets can rid a hedgehog of its fleas and ticks, although aerosol treatments should be avoided. Ticks can be removed manually with tweezers or by coating them with olive oil or washing up liquid (to block their respiratory openings). Lungworm can be treated with the same substances that are used on domestic animals (with dose rates adjusted to take account of body size). Trauma injuries are more difficult and need professional attention. Detailed advice on caring for sick and injured hedgehogs is available from the BHPS in the form of advisory leaflets and an extensive hedgehog care manual (Bullen, 2010). A treatment summary for professionals has also been published (Robinson & Routh, 1999).

Among some of the other hedgehog literature can be found at least one small book that describes homeopathic treatments for hedgehogs (Sykes & Durrant, 1995). This fashionable way of dealing with human ailments attributes greater effectiveness to increasing dilutions of natural substances. This is intuitively worrying because it implies that undetectably small amounts of something are more potent that a stronger solution. Sceptics find it hard to discover properly structured experimental evidence for success, even with humans, who can be asked if their treatment has been successful or not. Hedgehogs cannot answer that question. They might have recovered anyway without any treatment at all, especially as this species appears to be very robust and shows a remarkable ability to recover from injury without assistance. In 2016, over 3,000 vets signed a petition calling on the Royal College of Veterinary Surgeons to declare homeopathic treatments for animals unethical and ban vets from prescribing them.

The RCVS subsequently agreed a policy statement declaring that 'there is no recognised body of evidence for homeopathy' and that it was 'not based on sound scientific principles' (*The Times*, 20 November 2017). The statement was also supported by the British Veterinary Association. Such treatments will do no harm, but whether they do any real good is problematic. Using them might mean that effective conventional treatments are set aside, raising potentially serious welfare issues. Others suggest hypnosis to avoid using medicines of any kind. There is lively debate in print and on the internet about the ethics of caring for wildlife, but advice and commentaries offered via social media are best treated with the utmost caution or ignored altogether, especially when expressed using intemperate language.

HEDGEHOGS IN HOSPITAL AND AFTERWARDS

Hedgehogs are nocturnal; daytime activity is not normal and is often a sign of ill-health or starvation, causing concern to anyone who finds them. There is especially a problem for young animals in the autumn. They often begin to falter during cool nights, losing body warmth and becoming disorientated and failing to feed properly. They may not actually be ill, just in need of warmth and food. Nevertheless, weakness, prominent hips, a staggering gait are all signs of distress and may be accompanied by infestations of parasites that weaken the animal further. Often keeping them warm for a few days will result in revival.

Hedgehogs also seem to be particularly vulnerable to accidental injury. Seeing distressed hedgehogs and the frequent occurrence of sickly individuals in a sorry state tottering about in daylight elicits widespread sympathy among well-meaning people. Perhaps they feel ashamed of what modern human life does to hedgehogs and want to make up for that. Maybe they just want to help out of common humanity. We also often find injured hedgehogs, which are particularly common as a result of collisions with traffic or contact with dogs or mowing machines. Such violent incidents would kill most mammals, but hedgehogs often survive due to the cushioning effect of their spines. Moreover, slowly pottering about looking for worms, a hedgehog can cope with a broken leg during its normal activities in a way that a squirrel, for example, could not. And whereas most mammals would kick or bite anyone who tried to help, the hedgehog just passively rolls up and waits to see what happens next. It can be picked up easily and safely. These are the reasons why hedgehogs are so frequently rescued by members of the public and have now become the most common wild mammal species taken into veterinary care, typically accounting for about one-quarter of all wildlife casualties, including birds.

FIG 225. Hedgehogs are very resilient animals and also able to heal themselves. This victim of a carelessly operated strimmer was dusted with antibiotic powder and simply released nearby. Six weeks later, there was little sign of this major wound.

Hedgehogs outnumber all the other mammalian wildlife victims put together that are taken to the RSPCA and wildlife rescue centres. These have blossomed since the first dedicated hedgehog hospital, 'St. Tiggywinkles', was established in Aylesbury by Les Stocker in 1985. It is difficult to know how many hedgehogs are rescued and taken into care nationwide, but even a decade ago the annual total exceeded 3,000 according to the British Wildlife Rehabilitation Council, who reported that 54 per cent of all wildlife casualties admitted into care at that time were hedgehogs. In a more recent survey (Barnes, 2017; Barnes & Farnworth, 2017), questionnaires were sent to 1,706 veterinary practices and the 10 per cent that replied reported that they had treated 1,932 hedgehogs. Scaled up to a national level, this suggests that UK vets may treat more than 31,000 hedgehogs in a year.

And that's only the vets: over the last 30 years, there has been a huge expansion in the number of volunteer 'hedgehog carers'; the BHPS lists 800 of them. In many instances, a single person may account for scores of hedgehogs annually. One lady, Mavis

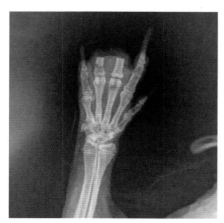

FIG 226. This hedgehog was rescued by Sue Ellis with its foot caught in a mouse trap. It suffered swelling and later lost two toes, but still gave birth to a family of hoglets and survived hibernation the following winter. (Sue Ellis/BHPS)

Righini, in south London, converted her garage into a hedgehog clinic in 1985 and took in 2,338 hedgehogs in 31 years. On an even larger scale, wildlife hospitals and rescue centres often have a 100 or more animals at one time. Vale animal hospital near Tewkesbury, for example, has over 500 hedgehogs per year passing through, including about 300 underweight juveniles being kept over winter before release in the spring. A determined effort by Lucy Bearman-Brown gathered direct evidence that there were more than 20,000 hedgehogs 'in care' nationwide during 2016.

There is a widespread willingness to help hedgehogs, but there may be drawbacks despite the worthy intentions. One carer reported that she was visited by two environmental health officers and a planning officer from the local authority (which claims to be understaffed) who inspected and photographed her property, warning that she may have breached planning permission for her house that only allowed for 'domestic use'.

Rescuing and rehabilitating hedgehogs has become a major activity. There is no legal requirement for sick and injured animals to be taken into care, and apart from anti-cruelty legislation there are also few constraints on what can be done with animals taken into captivity for humanitarian reasons. Much of the care afforded to needy hedgehogs is carried out by well-meaning amateurs with little or no formal veterinary training, although many do have the services of a friendly vet when needed. But the vets themselves rarely specialise in dealing with wild animals, having been mainly trained to deal with pets and farm livestock. The care of sick and injured animals is only very loosely regulated and hardly monitored at all. Sometimes carers without a scientific background will vigorously promote their own ideas, ignoring published facts and data. This can lead to antagonism, when everyone should be on the same side. There is also a problem that people wishing to deal with needy hedgehogs for compassionate

FIG 227. Looking after rescued hedgehogs takes a lot of time and dedication. Nestlings need to be fed by hand and 'toiletted'; older ones are better able to look after themselves. (Graeme Thompson/BHPS)

reasons are unlikely to consider paperwork a high priority. That is why it has been difficult to gather data and assess the scale of this kind of activity or its effectiveness in supporting hedgehog populations. Lack of formal, systematic records also makes it hard to gauge the prevalence of the parasites reviewed above and assess the threat that they and other natural hazards pose to the hedgehog population compared to the injuries that result from human activity (such as roadkill, mowing machines, poisoning and drowning in garden ponds). Fortunately the situation is improving and some of the more responsible hedgehog rescue centres do keep records and are beginning to share them. This allows some assessment, the significance of what the carers are doing and what are the most frequent problems that hedgehogs face (Reeve & Huijser, 1999).

For example, Dru Burdon in Jersey had 9,641 hedgehog admissions in the years 1995–2016, with about 65 per cent being returned to the wild after treatment. About half of the intake suffered from problems originating from natural causes. They were mostly juveniles, reflecting their greater vulnerability, especially in the autumn. The other half were casualties of human activity, including victims of road accidents. However, there would also be many hedgehogs that were killed outright on the road and not taken into care, so Dru's data confirm that anthropogenic hazards probably have a serious impact at the population level and possibly exceed the threats posed by some natural causes such as parasites. Many of those released back into the wild reappeared later with fresh problems to resolve and many others died. However, a significant number of the released animals lived for several more years (over five years in a couple of cases), enabling them to participate in one or more breeding seasons when, but for rescue, they would otherwise have been dead. Similar data from RSPCA rescue centres show 754 hedgehogs were taken in between 2000 and 2004, about half of which were released after being cared for (Grogan & Kelly, 2013). At another reception centre, 168 hedgehogs were taken into care, two thirds of them being nestlings. Subsequently, 74 per cent of those nestlings, plus 55 per cent of juveniles and 58 per cent of adults, were successfully released back into the wild (Bunnell, 2001).

Overall it appears that males more often predominate among casualties taken into care, especially early in the summer when they are most active. Anthropogenic causes are the reason for about half of all admissions to wildlife rescue centres and are in addition to natural threats, justifying current concerns regarding the impact of accidents on the declining numbers of hedgehogs. On the positive side, from the information supplied by a few wildlife carers, their success rate is quite high. A substantial number of hedgehogs that would probably have died are given a second chance at life, helping to compensate in a small way for the many and varied threats that humans pose to the survival of hedgehog populations.

The whole issue of wildlife rescue, in which the hedgehog plays such a prominent part, raises questions about the standards of veterinary care given to wild animals taken into captivity, particularly those kept in domestic homes rather than in purpose-built facilities. The issue is also beset with many ethical problems. It is the policy of the RSPCA to give support to animals that will have a reasonable chance of living a normal life after release back into the wild. Those suffering from injuries that would preclude a normal life later should be euthanased early without wasting resources on them. Other carers have taken a different view and sought to rescue and release as many animals as possible, including those with amputated limbs. In one case I saw, a hedgehog with its snout torn off by a mowing machine was successfully prevented from dying. Its carer was publicly proud of that success, but should it have been kept alive when smell is so important to hedgehogs? Should it have been released back into the wild? If not, then what was the point of 'saving' it? Controversial matters such as these have led to the suggestion that there should be a licensing system for wildlife carers. But many of those people expend considerable amounts of their own time and money on what they do, often to good effect. They might be reluctant to meet the cost of a licence and pay for the associated inspection and accreditation system. There is also the tricky issue of who would judge what is appropriate and what is not when keeping sick and injured hedgehogs or other species, and who would judge the judges? Perhaps it is better to have a slightly muddled system, with occasional unsatisfactory outcomes, rather than attempt more rigorous control that may disincentivise many who have the welfare and survival of hedgehogs high on their list of personal priorities.

On the other hand, because so many carers fail to keep or share their records, we still cannot tell how many hedgehogs are removed from the wild each year for humanitarian reasons. We cannot say how effective this nationwide effort might be, as we do not know how many are released back into the wild. Nor do we know where they are released and under what circumstances, and mostly we have no idea what happens to them. We cannot tell the extent to which the hedgehog population is endangered by anthropogenic factors as opposed to natural hazards, nor whether there is an increase (or otherwise) in the incidence of various parasites. It remains anomalous that this casual system is based entirely on benevolent concerns for the welfare of a popular animal, yet fails to address issues of major concern. The need for more professionalism and some sort of data sharing is obvious, but somehow achieving that has proved elusive.

Many of these carers gain satisfaction from what they do and measure their success by the number of the animals that they release back into the wild. The real question is what happens after that? Do hedgehogs that are released at unfamiliar sites, as is often the case, attempt to 'home' and go back to where they came from? Some other species certainly do, at least occasionally. Are they able to find sufficient to eat and can they build nests and find them again in an unfamiliar place? Is it fair to release young animals raised in captivity that have had no previous experience of life in the wild and leave them to look after themselves in a relatively hostile environment compared to the restricted, warm and well-provisioned environment they have left behind? Maybe they just die slowly over the next few days or weeks. Is 'rehabilitation' simply an illusion with serious negative impact on the welfare of the individual hedgehogs involved?

REHABILITATION: PUTTING HEDGEHOGS BACK INTO THE WILD

When I began to ask these awkward questions publicly, there was reluctance among carers to pursue the matter, apprehensive that the answers might cast doubt on the validity of their activities and prove to be an embarrassing disappointment. But these are important issues, not just for ethical reasons to do with animal welfare. There is also the practical consideration that caring for sick and injured hedgehogs costs time and money that might be better spent on other species if ultimately the 'rehabilitated' hedgehogs cannot cope with being released back into the wild.

With the help of my students, I began a series of investigations to see what happened to hedgehogs after their liberation following a spell in a care centre. In the first pilot study, three were taken from Aylesbury in Buckinghamshire to Malham Tarn in Yorkshire, over 300 km away, and released where they could never possibly have been before (Fig. 228). Fortunately it immediately became clear that they did not attempt to 'home' by heading south every evening. Instead,

FIG 228. In the first follow-up study, we took three hedgehogs from an animal hospital in Buckinghamshire and released them at Malham Tarn, Yorkshire.

FIG 229. Samantha and another of my students monitored the released hedgehogs closely for two weeks to establish whether they would attempt to 'home' and how well they managed to forage.

they remained close to the release site and interacted freely with a dozen or more wild hedgehogs in the locality. They built natural nests and found them again without difficulty, instead of wasting valuable foraging time by having to build a new nest at the end of each night. But after two weeks, they were still losing weight, as though they had been unable to feed adequately (Morris et al., 1992). Insufficient funds meant that this study had to finish before the final outcome of the experiment became clear. We never knew what happened to those three hedgehogs in the end.

So the following year, a larger sample of hedgehogs was supplied by an RSPCA care centre in London and released in a farming area at Flatford Mill in Suffolk. They were monitored closely for three weeks, then checked again some two months after being liberated (Morris et al., 1993). The animals managed surprisingly well and two of them even swam across

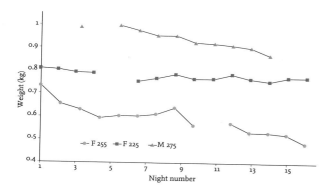

FIG 230. All three animals lost weight after release, suggesting there was a problem, but lack of funds meant we were unable to prolong the study to find out what the outcome would be.

FIG 231. This hedgehog swam across the River Stour after release and found her way to some discarded food packets. She put on 10 per cent body weight within six weeks, but was killed on a local lane – ironically at a village called Dedham.

the River Stour (Fig. 231). Most of our hedgehogs scattered widely from the release site as though they were trying to find a habitat more like the urban environment from which they had originally been rescued. One of the adult males immediately departed and established himself in a nearby village and went back to it after being retrieved and released a second time at the original site (Fig. 232). Perhaps rehabilitated animals should be returned to a familiar kind of habitat wherever possible, although this will often expose them to the same dangers that caused them to be rescued in the first place. There was no evidence of any of these animals becoming emaciated or suffering as a consequence of release. Several of them were never found again, but they and the one that got run over had been given another chance of survival, having been rescued from likely death some months earlier.

FIG 232. 'Baldy' was a strimmer victim and had spent a year in hospital before being released in Suffolk. He concentrated on consorting with the female hedgehogs and then ran off to the local village.

FIG 233. Rescued 'autumn orphans' released after winter would have had no experience of building their own nest, no exercise beyond life in a cage and probably no experience of finding and recognising natural food. Could they cope with being released into the wild? (Graeme Thompson/BHPS)

All of the animals studied so far had been adult hedgehogs who were accustomed to life in the wild before they had been taken into care. What about juveniles, especially the so-called 'autumn orphans', large numbers of which are taken into captivity in the autumn because they are too small to survive hibernation (see Chapter 6). Many will have been rescued as hoglets when a nursery nest had been accidentally destroyed during gardening operations or farming activities. These animals may never have seen a worm and never had to build their own nest. They might never have been out of contact with each other and had always fed on artificial food from a bowl. Kept for months in a cage or small enclosure, they will have only ever walked a few centimetres. Yet every year thousands of these inexperienced young hedgehogs are being released into the countryside after being cared for over winter (Fig. 233). Could they really cope with life in the wild?

At the end of winter, in April 1993, 12 of these inexperienced juveniles were taken from an RSPCA rescue centre in Somerset and released on the farm that had already been designated as their intended future home. They were given a professional veterinary health check and cleared for release (Sainsbury *et al.*, 1996), then monitored closely every night for five weeks to follow their movements and locate their daytime nests. Their body weights were recorded at frequent intervals. Several of the animals travelled more than 500 m in a night, hundreds of times further than they could ever have walked before. They managed to build nests, just as normal wild hedgehogs do, and succeeded in finding them again after a night's activity. We had put out plenty of suitable dogfood for them in an effort to soften the shock of release, but they mostly ignored it. They behaved in every way as fully experienced adult hedgehogs, an astonishingly successful and encouraging

FIG 234. The RSPCA had 12 overwintered juvenile hedgehogs that had never experienced independent life outside a cage. By April, they were due for release on a farm in Devon. Hugh Warwick closely monitored their movements and body weights to discover how well they adjusted to life in the wild, if at all.

outcome (Morris & Warwick, 1994). However they steadily lost weight as though they were starving. One animal lost a third of its weight in a month. But after four weeks, body weights had levelled off and all the hedgehogs remained a relatively constant size thereafter. In fact some of them had become seriously obese during their period in captivity, reaching double the size that would be expected of wild hedgehogs at less than one year old. They were not starving following their release, but simply losing the excess gained in captivity and restoring themselves to a more normal body size for their age (Fig. 235).

By the end of the study, 2 of the 12 hedgehogs had been killed on local roads, despite the fact that few vehicles were seen after dark in the lanes around the farm. Three of the hedgehogs were eaten by badgers five weeks into the study (Fig. 237). It was suggested afterwards that we should

FIG 235. Some of the animals, like these two, lost nearly a third of their body weight following release. This looked very alarming, as though they had been unable to find enough to eat.

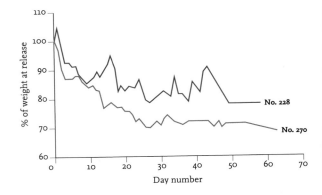

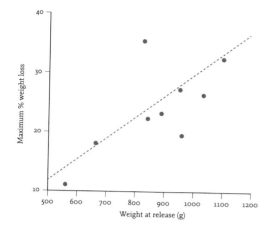

FIG 236. The hedgehogs that lost the most weight were heaviest to begin with, and actually nearly double what would be expected for normal subadults at that time of year. Those that were closest to natural weights lost less. Clearly the animals were mostly overweight after being generously fed in captivity with little exercise. They were simply slimming down to something nearer their natural body size.

not have released hedgehogs where badgers were known to be present, a criticism which was later taken up vigorously by some of the national newspapers. But the release site was the one normally used by the RSPCA and badgers live in high numbers throughout South West England. Avoidance of badgers, like avoidance of roads, was not a realistic option, especially given the distances that these hedgehogs were later shown to travel. The fact that three of our animals were eaten by badgers was unfortunate (see Chapter 9), but at least four survived until the end of the study more than two months after their abrupt release into unfamiliar and challenging circumstances.

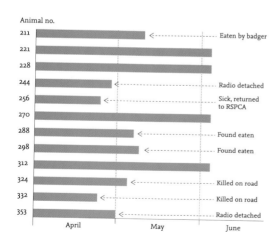

FIG 237. Focussing on the animals that died, as many critics did, overlooks the fact that one third of this sample of completely inexperienced animals did survive. Without their rescue the previous year, all would have been dead. Releasing these animals had given them another chance, offering at least some an opportunity to reach their first breeding season.

This shows that even inexperienced, overwintered juvenile hedgehogs can, and do, survive release into the wild surprisingly well and justifies their rescue and rehabilitation. Nevertheless they are still vulnerable to the same dangers that threaten wild hedgehogs almost everywhere, perhaps more so because they may have become relatively tame in captivity. Criticism of the apparently high mortality rate (42 per cent) among our dozen newly independent hedgehogs overlooks the fact that if these non-viable animals had not been taken into care by the RSPCA the previous autumn, they would all have been dead.

Another follow-up study was later carried out in Jersey, where there are no badgers, again using inexperienced juveniles and several more of my student volunteers. Thirteen of these hedgehogs (six males, seven females) were radio-tracked. Six of them originated from the study garden used as the release point and the others came from different parts of the island. They had all been born in late 1994 and had little or no previous experience of life in the wild, having been taken into care over winter as underweight juveniles. There was no significant difference between the two groups in the way they behaved after release; those from elsewhere in Jersey did not immediately disperse in search of 'home'. The hedgehogs quickly learned to find their way about. They all managed to build nests or find secure daytime resting places, and then found them again on subsequent nights. They even managed to relocate a previously used daytime nest having lived elsewhere for at least a day, sometimes over 200 m away. All the animals showed a marked association with gardens and rarely used the large areas of open crop fields all around. They interacted normally and frequently with the local population of hedgehogs, of which there were at least 30 in the surrounding area, with no sign of territorial aggression. The general pattern of behaviour was for the animals to scatter then settle down within 400 m of the release point as though dispersal is a natural feature among hedgehogs. It was not the result of being displaced by overcrowding at the release site nor did dispersing animals wander widely in an attempt to return home to their place of origin. All 13 of the animals survived at least four weeks and 10 (77 per cent) were known to have survived more than six weeks. There is no reason to believe that the remaining animals were dead or that the mortality rate increased after the study ended. The survival rate was very high despite the animals being inexperienced juveniles (Morris, 1997).

Many of these studies had involved releasing animals into good hedgehog habitat, mainly open pasture and farmland. In spite of that, a few of the freed animals dispersed several kilometres, perhaps because they were 'squeezed out' by the existing hedgehog population, although there was little evidence of this in our Jersey study, where a very high population density existed (exceeding one per hectare in the study site overall), especially in the study garden where extra food was put out.

To investigate further, Nigel Reeve took ten animals that were ready for release from a care centre in Surrey and liberated them in an area of natural woodland not far away. This was the sort of site that could easily be chosen by carers because it is a safe nature reserve and a 'nice place'. But woodland, including that site, generally harbours a low density of hedgehogs. So the question was whether the animals would stay there or rapidly disperse, with consequent exposure to the risks posed by road traffic and other hazards. The hedgehogs were tracked for up to 108 days, during which time all of them lost weight, just as in previous studies. Most dispersed, up to 3 km from the release point, and within barely a fortnight only one animal remained close to where they had been let go. Clearly they were not being displaced by the resident local hedgehogs, as none had ever been recorded in that wood. The departing animals usually ended up close to an urban area, suggesting once again that this habitat was preferred rather than the woodland. So dispersal was not due to 'push' from an overcrowded population, but 'pull' due to the relative attractiveness of a different habitat (urban fringe and gardens in this case). Two other hedgehogs that were released into an urban setting were content to stay there. However, urban areas offer increased risks from human activities. Of the six recorded deaths, only one was the result of a failure to thrive (pneumonia). All the other

FIG 238. Small ear tags were used by Dru Burdon in Jersey to record the long-term survival of hedgehogs released back into the wild.

mortalities were accidental, including three road deaths, while another was injured in a traffic accident and one drowned in a garden pond. Yet another one was killed by a predator, probably badger, although it could have been a large dog. Despite this, overall survival among the ten hedgehogs after two months was 42 per cent and a quarter were still alive after 15 weeks (Reeve, 1998).

For practical and financial reasons, all of these follow-up studies have been limited to a few animals and less than three months' duration. Real long-term survival rates are therefore unknown. At the suggestion of Nigel Reeve, Dru Burdon in Jersey fitted 1,002 of her released animals with ear tags between 1995 and 2003 (Fig. 238). Some of the tags would have been lost from the hedgehogs, but 156 of them were seen again, a 15.6 per cent recovery rate. Some of the animals were encountered active in the wild, 28 were found dead. Many others were brought back into care, 15 were readmitted twice. One of the released hedgehogs returned to hospital three times. Despite all that, more than a third of the animals survived over a year following release. They had been given a second chance at life and another opportunity to participate in at least one breeding season from which they would otherwise have been excluded by an early death. The longest recorded survivor was found again after five years, a genuine fully rehabilitated animal (Fig. 239).

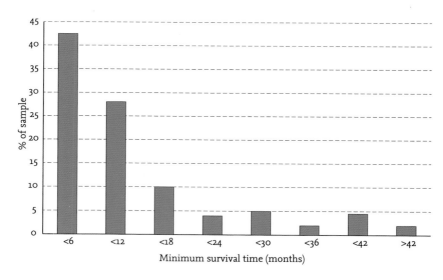

FIG 239. Using ear tags, Dru Burdon was able to show the minimum survival times for rehabilitated hedgehogs released into the wild in Jersey.

A properly structured experimental study, using 109 hedgehogs treated in various ways (some translocated from the Hebrides, others were rehabilitated sick and injured individuals), confirmed all the encouraging findings of previous studies and also suggested that animals directly translocated from the wild to another place benefitted from an intervening period of care during which they could build up body resources (Molony *et al.*, 2006). Those that were taken direct from the Hebrides and released in the suburbs of Bristol fared badly, with a mortality rate of 70 per cent within eight weeks. This is scarcely surprising given the enormous difference in the two environments, including novel exposure to foxes, badgers, traffic and all-night street lighting. The low success rate of that study does emphasise the wisdom of releasing animals into habitats and climatic conditions that are as nearly as possible similar to the animal's original home, as suggested earlier.

It is worth considering further the behaviour of rehabilitated animals in comparison with translocated wild ones. Thirty wild hedgehogs were taken to Wytham Wood in Oxfordshire and released there (Doncaster, 1992). Fourteen of them departed to nearby gardens, leaving only three still present and alive in the wood after 70 days. At least 22 of the 30 animals crossed major roads and one swam across the River Thames, 12 m wide at that point. The 30 animals that were translocated to Wytham Wood dispersed twice as far as another batch of 20 that were taken to Eynsham Park, where there were more worms to be found, perhaps further suggesting that woodlands are not the most supportive habitat for hedgehogs. Others, translocated to different local parks, dispersed up to 3.6 km. It seems that wild hedgehogs may undertake extensive journeys, apparently seeking a better place to live than the one to which they have been transported and liberated. At least some rehabilitated casualties appear to replicate the behaviour of these wild ones, although others (especially sub-adults) seem to prefer staying close to where they were released.

There is now abundant evidence that sick and injured hedgehogs can be rescued and successfully rehabilitated as free-living wild animals. But we have to face up to the fact that many of them will die after release (just as many that already live in the wild will also die). Nevertheless, and despite the losses, putting even a few animals back that would have otherwise been dead does at least offer a small compensation for the many new and fatal dangers that we humans have created for hedgehogs to face. Rescue, care and rehabilitation can give hedgehogs a second chance, but cannot grant immortality. It is important to keep the issue in perspective (Morris, 1998).

These follow-up studies were also important in another context. The troublesome hedgehog population that developed on the Uists from a small number of introduced individuals was destined to be caught and killed (see Chapter 12). The reason given for this was the possibility that they would not thrive if they were taken to the mainland and released there. It was claimed that the animals would suffer in some unspecified way and that their welfare interest would be best served by being euthanased. This unproven assertion lay behind the policy of killing the hedgehogs instead of translocating them, completely disregarding the encouraging results of the studies described above.

CONCLUSION

Hedgehogs are afflicted with various parasites, but these are natural factors to which the species has had plenty of time to adjust. It is unlikely that they have a major impact on the total population size compared to the many man-made threats to which hedgehogs are now exposed. Over the last 30 years or so, there has been increasing activity by 'carers' anxious to help sick and injured animals that are often victims of human activity. The hedgehog has become the principal beneficiary and many thousands are rescued from dire situations and provided with another opportunity to survive. When released back into the wild, these animals (even inexperienced juveniles) appear to cope well. The extent to which the rescue and rehabilitation of non-viable hedgehogs helps to offset the losses from anthropogenic causes of death cannot be assessed as we have little data on the numbers of animals taken into care, the proportion that are later released and their ultimate success. It is to be hoped that the community of carers will become more professional in their approach, both to caring for the animals and to the keeping and sharing of data, so that their contribution can be properly and fully assessed.

CHAPTER 12

The Persecution, Destruction and Use of Hedgehogs

H EDGEHOGS HAVE NEVER BEEN TARGETED as vectors of serious diseases, nor routinely killed to protect crops or other major economic assets. They also escaped the misery of being included among the amazing range of species that have been formally arraigned before the courts. Many other animals have been prosecuted for alleged and bizarre misdemeanours, including witchcraft, with the guilty being subject to capital punishment or excommunication from the Church (Evans, 1987). On the other hand, its fondness for eating eggs and the chicks of ground-nesting birds have got the hedgehog into serious trouble, and not just back in the Middle Ages. It's an ongoing issue.

During the reign of King Henry VIII (1509–47), Britain's rapidly increasing human population was faced with a series of disastrous crop failures. This created a pressing need for greater efficiency in farming methods, particularly in the production of grain. 'Something must be done', even if it was not very effective (or, in the case of the hedgehog's subsequent persecution, not very relevant either). It was this desire for increased agricultural productivity that led to the first Vermin Act of 1532, strengthened by Queen Elizabeth I (1558–1603) passing an 'Acte for Preservation of Grayne' in 1566.

The legislation provided for bounty payments to be made for killing noxious 'Fowles and Vermyn' in an effort to reduce their depredations on the farming economy. Hedgehogs were known to eat eggs and they were also accused of suckling cows, thereby contributing to loss of agricultural output. Despite its relative innocence on both counts, the hedgehog was on the hit list and for nearly 300 years churchwardens were authorised to pay out small sums to local people as a reward for killing hedgehogs (along with all the other designated varmints). The payment set out in 1566 was two pence per hedgehog snout, twice the bounty offered for polecats, stoats and wildcats, a disproportionate sum in relation to their likely depredations. Many parishes raised the bounty to four pence, and it remained so for decades. Trivial though such an amount appears today, it would have represented a day's wages for some and a useful form of extra pocket money for many. As part of their official duties, churchwardens or others who were deputised to make payments were supposed to keep an account of their expenditure, creating a rich legacy of detailed persecution records down the ages. Details survive in local archives of the petty persecution of hedgehogs throughout the land. For example, at Orton parish (then in the county of Westmoreland), the records for 1662 say, 'Disburst by him to Robert Whitehead for 17 hedgoggs £oo-o2s-1od' (Macpherson, 1892), but in some areas the carnage was much more severe.

There was no real strategy or coordination between parishes or the persecution might have been more effective in exterminating some of the target species; it was just haphazard killing (Lovegrove, 2007). In fact, for most species the bounties paid out, reflecting numbers killed, remained fairly constant for decades, suggesting that there had been no real impact on local populations of birds or mammals, just a regular cull. Astonishing numbers were accounted for, like the 6,600 bullfinches killed in one Cheshire parish in 36 years and 696 kites in 8 years. The parish of Sherborne in Dorset paid out on 3,344 hedgehogs in 137 years (1662–1799). Bunbury parish in Cheshire accounted for 8,585 of them in 35 years, an average of 245 annually. This was during the late seventeenth century when the human population density must have been quite low, suggesting a substantial effort was being made by country people. One can easily imagine how local boys or needy farm workers might have spent a summer's evening boosting their wages by trapping or picking up a few hedgehogs, perhaps assisted by their dogs. The accounts from many English parishes show extraordinary numbers of animals killed, year after year, and make interesting comparisons with the relative abundance of hedgehogs and certain other species in modern times. Lovegrove's analysis of parish records suggests that the officially sanctioned killing brought about by the Vermin Acts of 1532 and 1566 may have led to the death of half a million hedgehogs before official persecution ceased. Even before the legislation was repealed in 1863, at least some people must have realised that it was a waste of time and money to continue persecuting such a harmless creature, which anyway was quite useful to have around on account of its ability to catch and eat cockroaches and other undesirables. People must also have recognised the hedgehog's irrelevance to grain production. At least one parish in Sussex granted it an official pardon and their churchwardens were directed to make no further payments for them. In 1703, at Budworth in Cheshire, the vestry announced that 'churchwardens for the time to come shall not pay any moneys out of the Parish Purse for any crow heads, fox heads or urchin (i.e. hedgehog)'. Similar pragmatic decisions were taken at several other parishes too, which may account for the large number of places that recorded no payments for hedgehogs, often for years at a time.

A problem with all wildlife bounty schemes and the analysis of data derived from them is that the payments constituted a useful source of rural pocket money. It is highly likely that the accounts of certain generous and efficient parishes were inflated by people bringing in extra victims from another place where payments were less readily obtained. This practice would surely have been encouraged when certain parishes reprieved the hedgehog and decided they would no longer pay for its destruction, creating a direct incentive to carry on collecting snouts but take them elsewhere to be put on someone else's bill. After all, a few dried hedgehog snouts could be carried about quite easily in one's pocket and might even have been a useful form of rural currency to be exchanged with the local churchwarden, like going to the bank to cash a cheque. This sort of activity could account for the bounty payments being extraordinarily high in some parishes, distorting the official records of local killings.

Relief for the hedgehog came with the repeal of the Vermin Acts in the mid-nineteenth century and it thereby ceased to be a statutory pest. But the reprieve was short-lived because it coincided with the rise in gamekeepers as a new form of predator.

GAMEKEEPERS

When the official killing of hedgehogs and other 'vermin' ceased, much the same suite of species became threatened by the rise in the number of gamekeepers. This came about through the Enclosure Acts of 1750–1850 which conveyed previously open common lands into private ownership, leading to the establishment of sporting estates. There developed a lively interest in shooting game birds following changes in farming and land management. Increasing numbers of wealthy industrialists and businessmen chose to use their wealth to buy country estates. They did not need to focus on food production for an income and instead took to shooting game birds on their land as a recreational pastime, spurred on by improvements in shotgun technology (Tapper, 1992). The passion for shooting was further encouraged as it became a fashionable social activity, led by members of the Royal Family and the higher echelons of

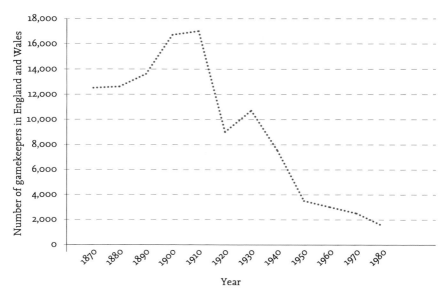

FIG 240. The numbers of gamekeepers employed in England and Wales peaked in 1910 and declined steadily during the twentieth century. A similar pattern occurred in Scotland. (Data from Tapper, 1992)

the gentry. Success, both socially and in terms of demonstrating good estate management, became firmly hitched to the size of the game bag. Large numbers killed would be a source of pride to a landowner who was hosting important guests, but severe embarrassment would occur if numbers fell below expectation. And expectations could be very high – witness the 780 partridges shot in one day at Elveden by the Maharajah Duleep Singh. Any predators, poachers or other threats to game birds would be ruthlessly eliminated on shooting estates. Once again the hedgehog was identified as a pest species because of its liking for eggs and chicks, and its remains joined those of owls, crows and mustelids on numerous gamekeepers' gibbets, where they could be seen by landowners keen to pay close attention to the effectiveness of their employees.

The social and economic importance of shooting and proficient estate management led to increased numbers of gamekeepers that peaked in 1910 at more than 23,000, spread over the whole of Great Britain (Fig. 240). In Norfolk, the most heavily keepered county, there was an average of one per 444 ha (1,100 acres). Gamekeepers took on the job of trapping the hapless hedgehog.

At Sandringham, for example, 5,904 of them were killed between 1938 and 1950; at Holkham (another of the great estates in Norfolk), 5,623 were removed in the six years 1953–59 (Lovegrove, 2007), an average of over 900 per year. The killing of hedgehogs is probably not a very cost-effective activity in terms of boosting game bird numbers and was curtailed somewhat by two world wars that required able-bodied men to be urgently occupied elsewhere. Further relief came with the legal protection afforded to hedgehogs in 1981 by the Wildlife and Countryside Act, but hundreds (perhaps thousands) are still killed by gamekeepers as a consequence of setting non-specific traps for 'ground vermin'. These are intended to remove rats, grey squirrels, stoats and weasels from the land, but they also kill hedgehogs unless special precautions are taken to avoid doing so. In the past, gamekeepers used gin traps whose jaws would slam shut on anything that walked on a triggering treadle. These were banned in 1954, to be replaced by Fenn traps (British Patent No. 763,891). They work the same way, but must be set in small artificial tunnels to prevent accidental injury to unintended victims such as dogs and domestic stock. Fenn traps are very effective. During the 1960s, in nine years on a single estate in Sussex, nearly 400 hedgehogs were killed by traps set in tunnels (Tapper, 1992). Although hedgehogs were given limited legal protection in 1981, they are still caught incidentally by Fenn traps that are set to catch 'ground vermin'. These traps crush their victim around the chest and there is room for concern that death may not be instantaneous for hedgehogs, owing to the cushioning effect of their spines preventing the jaws of the trap closing fully. It is possible to exclude adult hedgehogs and most juveniles just by restricting the tunnel entrance by the addition of a couple of sticks at each end. Gamekeepers are urged to adopt some form of tunnel restriction like this because anyone setting traps is legally required to take precautions that will avoid causing the death of protected species, no matter that it might be unintentional. It is unclear how seriously this recommendation is taken or how many hedgehog lives might be saved by adopting the idea of restricting access to trap tunnels by a change in their design. Hedgehog excluders reduce the efficacy of traps for squirrels and rats, so they have not been made a legal requirement and hedgehogs remain at risk of being trapped inadvertently (Short & Reynolds, 2001).

Nevertheless, I am grateful to the gamekeepers at the Elveden estate, who kindly agreed to preserve dead hedgehogs for me to use in my studies of age determination (see Chapter 8). Their Estate Office had recorded 20,785 hedgehogs killed between 1904 and 1969, an average of 378 per year (allowing for the Game Department being disbanded for a decade during and after World War I), and many other estates also kept meticulous records that have helped chart the

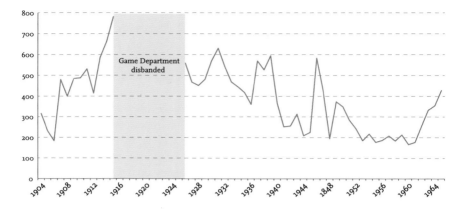

FIG 241. Numbers of hedgehogs killed on an estate in Suffolk in 60 years. As with similar data from elsewhere, the peaks and troughs do not necessarily reflect changes in hedgehog numbers, but may instead be due to employing fewer (or more) gamekeepers.

changing hedgehog population during the twentieth century (Tapper, 1992) (Fig. 241). It is surprising that such large numbers killed on the one estate at Elveden did not cause a steady decline towards extinction; they removed 427 in 1965, almost exactly the same number as in 1907. Instead of a progressive reduction, the number killed remained above 200 for most of the 1960s, as though the population could comfortably withstand that level of loss. When questioned about this, the gamekeepers told me that the trapped animals were from the periphery of the estate and represented only immigrants, as the hedgehog had been eliminated from the rest of the land for which they were responsible.

Perhaps it is unfair to describe the actions of gamekeepers as 'persecution'; after all, they are only doing their job and regard removal of predators as a necessary part of professional game management. For many years, the Game Conservancy (forerunner of today's Game and Wildlife Conservation Trust) gathered data on game bags and predator control from a representative sample of over 400 shooting estates in Britain. The figures reveal that more than 6,000 hedgehogs were killed annually by gamekeepers in the 1960s and 1970s, but this is only the recorded mortality from a selection of estates. The full total would have been much greater, and will have declined significantly over the years as gamekeeper numbers have fallen from a peak of 23,000 to only about one fifth of that by the late twentieth century (Tapper, 1992). This may have taken some of the heat off the hedgehog, which now faces many other and perhaps more pressing problems.

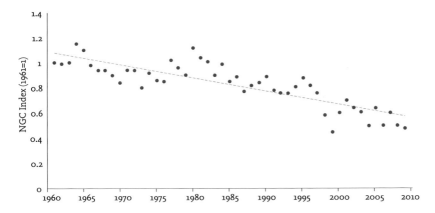

FIG 242. Figures from the Game and Wildlife Conservation Trust show the number of hedgehogs killed on a sample of estates halved in the space of 50 years. This is further evidence of declining hedgehog populations, but probably also reflects fewer gamekeepers and a reducing level of trapping for 'ground vermin'.

THE UIST SAGA

Eggs in the diet of hedgehogs suddenly became highly controversial when evidence was published showing a significant decline in the breeding success of ground-nesting waders like dunlin, redshank, lapwing and ringed plover on South Uist in the Outer Hebrides. South Uist is a 315-km² island about 80 km west of the Scottish mainland, linked by causeways to the neighbouring islands of Benbecula and North Uist (Fig. 243). These islands experience a cool, wet and windy maritime climate and have extensive areas of machair. This is the local term for the flat-dune grassland along the Atlantic coast, enriched by seashells and extensively grazed by sheep and cattle, with small areas of crops. The machair is much favoured by ground-nesting shorebirds and as the islands have historically been free of ground predators, they support one of the largest concentrations of breeding shorebirds in Western Europe. Both the habitat and its birds are protected by national and international conservation designations.

A few hedgehogs were released on South Uist in 1974, with some more the following year, in a misguided attempt to combat garden pests. The islands offered ideal foraging areas for the hedgehogs, with abundant food (which also supports large numbers of birds) and plenty of rabbit holes in which to shelter,

FIG 243. Although much of South Uist is open water, there are extensive areas of grassland and grazing that offer excellent foraging habitat for hedgehogs. There are also patches of dense shrubbery around buildings and many rabbit holes that provide sheltered nesting sites, compensating for the absence of trees.

compensating for the lack of bushes and trees. The hedgehogs also have easy access to the numerous beaches, where large amounts of tideline seaweed support a super-abundance of sandhoppers upon which they can feed. By the 1980s, the hedgehog population was thought to have grown to about 5,000 from the small number of founders, a figure that is just about possible if breeding success had been unusually high and suffered minimal mortality.

The colonies of nesting birds were surveyed in 1983 when hedgehogs were found only in South Uist and surveyed again in 2000, by which time the invaders had spread and occupied all the southern part of the island. They had also become widespread on neighbouring Benbecula, but had not yet colonised much of North Uist. Between the two surveys, the overall numbers of shorebirds in the hedgehog-free northern zone increased by 9 per cent, but in the southern zone where hedgehogs were present, numbers had decreased by 39 per cent. The biggest changes were seen in the numbers of lapwing, dunlin and redshank, which showed large declines in the southern study areas, formerly the home of a significant proportion of the entire British population of these species. Ringed plovers were less badly affected, probably because they normally nest out on expanses of open shingle, a habitat that is not much frequented by hedgehogs. Oystercatchers also suffered less than the smaller waders, perhaps because they are large and robust birds that are capable of vigorously defending their nest.

Losses had been continuous since the release of hedgehogs. This represents a different situation to that on the mainland with predation on game birds. Many Scottish islands like the Uists and Benbecula were naturally free of ground predators. This is precisely why 17,000 pairs of ground-nesting waders congregate there in nesting colonies large enough to be of international importance. The introduction of hedgehogs upset a delicate balance, although there are also predatory gulls and crows present, with plenty of cats, dogs and introduced mink as additional potential predators of ground-nesting birds. Eggshell was found in 13 per cent of 64 hedgehog droppings collected on South Uist during the birds' breeding season and a similar rate of occurrence (11 per cent) in a subsequent sample of 242 droppings (Watt, 1995). Arthropods, molluscs and earthworms were the main prey taken, but nevertheless there was clearly a problem. The EU Birds Directive (2009) requires Britain to keep an eye on declining populations and take action to stop the losses or be subject to heavy fines. This was the responsibility of Scottish Natural Heritage (SNH), the statutory nature conservation body whose remit included these Hebridean islands.

Concern for the birds and the threat of EU fines became the trigger for some of the most thorough recent studies of the hedgehog's ecology (Jackson & Green, 2000; Jackson et al., 2004; Jackson, 2006; Jackson, 2007). Among much else, these revealed that only 10–15 per cent of wader eggs were being successfully reared to independence, implying that the decline in adult bird numbers was due to egg predation on the ground rather than some other effect. Inspection of the nests showed that the majority had been attacked overnight and were therefore probably not the victims of gulls or crows. In addition, the nature of the damaged eggs suggested hedgehogs were responsible for most of the losses. Other likely predators were active in daylight and usually removed an egg intact to eat somewhere else, having been chased off by the parent bird. Hedgehogs stomping about among the broken eggshells characteristically leave a mess of the uneaten egg contents in which is embedded trampled bits of shell and fragments of nesting material waiting to be found next morning. These features were consistent with the damage seen in experiments with captive hedgehogs and also when they were observed directly in the wild at night. Sometimes there was even a hedgehog dropping left nearby. These signs were not seen at 243 nests monitored on North Uist where hedgehogs were absent at that time. Wader numbers continued to decline between 1983 and 1995 (by 81 per cent in the case of the redshank), much of the loss being attributed to hedgehogs.

Overall, predation of wader eggs by hedgehogs accounted for up to 60 per cent of the nesting attempts by the birds, but Digger Jackson estimated that wader eggs only provided between 0.7 and 5.5 per cent of the energy requirements of hedgehogs. He argued that the hedgehogs were probably finding eggs by chance and therefore the intensity of predation was directly linked to the number of hedgehogs present. In other words, he was not suggesting that a few individual 'rogue' hedgehogs were specialising in seeking out eggs during the bird breeding season. This has important implications for any discussion over whether the birds could usefully be protected by setting up hedgehog-proof fencing. If only a few hedgehogs were responsible for most of the damage, then trapping within fenced areas could almost eliminate the problem. If most of the hedgehog population were implicated, then control of total numbers becomes necessary instead. Another of Jackson's important conclusions was that predation on eggs was unlikely to diminish in response to wader population declines. If hedgehogs relied heavily on eggs to support themselves during the early summer, then you would expect hedgehog numbers to fall year after year as they gradually eliminated the birds. Instead, as Jackson pointed out, hedgehogs faced with a diminishing supply of eggs would not starve because they could easily switch to other sources of food. Their population would be maintained, but the birds could spiral into extinction. These studies are extremely important, not just in enhancing our knowledge of hedgehogs, but also in formulating policies for the protection of birds. Nor is this just a local issue. Hedgehogs are regarded as a threat on some mainland nature reserves where the preservation of ground-nesting birds is a priority. Egg predation by hedgehogs has also been blamed for reduced breeding success among redshank and tern populations in the German Waddensee. In New Zealand, the hedgehog's status has changed from being a welcome and benign reminder of Europe to being perceived as a serious threat to the ground-nesting banded dotterel (*Charadrius bicinctus*) and also various rare and endangered species of invertebrates.

There remain some awkward questions about the Uist story, such as some of the inconclusive effects on bird populations that followed local removal of hedgehogs. It is also entirely possible that some of the observed decline in bird numbers was due to something other than predation by hedgehogs, such as food shortages resulting from local changes in cultivation methods (increased use of fertilisers, for example) or habitat loss at other times in the birds' year

FIG 244. Searching for hedgehogs in such a complex mosaic of land and water was never going to be easy, and the eradication of every last one would be problematic. But missing any would allow the population to recover, as the whole problem had begun with the release of fewer than ten animals.

when they have migrated south to estuaries and other distant places. It has also been suggested that predation by gulls may have been underestimated. Another possibility is that the baseline year against which the bird numbers have been compared (1983) was a particularly good one for the waders and the decline has actually been less severe than suggested. Nevertheless, there was clear evidence of substantial consumption of eggs by hedgehogs and a significant decline in the breeding success of several bird species.

SNH formulated a policy to deal with the troublesome Uist hedgehog population. They were destined to be caught and killed, with the aim of reducing or eliminating their impact on nesting birds. The reason given for this, rather than translocating captured animals to the mainland, was based on the contention that Scotland was already fully populated with hedgehogs. It was also claimed that the animals would suffer in some unspecified way and that their welfare interest would be best served by being euthanased. These unproven assertions lay behind the policy of killing, completely disregarding the issues mentioned here in Chapter 8 and ignoring the studies of released rehabilitated hedgehogs described in Chapter 11. Several thousand were killed before the policy was changed, a level of local hedgehog persecution reminiscent of the seventeenth century.

Ironically, some of the islands to which hedgehogs have been taken in the past, including the Uists, may one day form vital refuges for hedgehogs now that their own populations are in decline on the mainland. Nevertheless, it is clear that hedgehogs have been a problem. They should never have been released on islands that were free of them and it should never be done again. Efforts to eliminate the Uist population, and the resultant public outcry, are discussed in Chapter 13. Meanwhile, removal of hedgehogs from the islands continued, amid ongoing concern about funding and in the face of mounting evidence that total elimination of hedgehogs was impossible without substantially increased resources. Incomplete elimination is pointless because the whole problem with the hedgehogs on the Uists began with the import of fewer than ten animals.

Now that EU funding for hedgehog removal on the Uists has ceased, it remains uncertain how the hedgehog/bird conflict will be resolved in the future. Birds have strong public appeal and there is no doubt that hedgehogs should never have been added to the fauna of these islands. It would be a tragedy if the bird populations were devastated, even if the hedgehog population ultimately crashed and some sort of balance was restored. The best way to avoid this scenario would be to use some form of fencing to keep hedgehogs away from nesting birds. This is a policy that has been adopted in New Zealand where hedgehogs have also proved to be a problem. Fencing is used there to protect banded dotterels from predation by hedgehogs; mortalities were eradicated by trapping the birds inside a predator-exclusion electric fence. Within the fenced areas, three times more chicks were fledged from the eggs of ground-nesting birds than outside the fence (Moss & Sanders, 2001). Fencing is also used elsewhere to exclude foxes and even badgers from sensitive nesting areas and the Forestry Commission has enjoyed decades of success using fences to control deer and rabbit damage in conifer plantations. Scottish Natural Heritage has so far consistently rejected the idea of fencing out hedgehogs on the Uists, insisting that some of them were bound to circumvent such barriers. This is true, but surely it is better to fence out the majority of the population and trap those that defeat the barriers each season, rather than allow free access to all of the hedgehogs all of the time? If fencing is ultimately attempted, it will be expensive and now rather late in the day. The Uist hedgehog population seems likely to remain a troublesome problem for many years to come.

Soon after a few hedgehogs were released on the Scottish island of North Ronaldsay, a sharp decline in bird nesting success was recorded and attributed to predation by hedgehogs. Amid a media frenzy, scores of them were deported to the mainland with calls for their complete elimination from the island. However, kittiwakes and fulmars were among the species apparently suffering declining numbers, but their cliff-nesting habits make them improbable victims of hungry hedgehogs. It transpired that there had been a serious collapse in the population of sand eels offshore, a major food source for many of the birds. This was probably the result of changing temperatures and circulation in the surrounding sea. The falling numbers of birds may have had little or nothing to do with hedgehogs and their persecution was probably largely unjustified.

CONCLUSION

Attitudes towards hedgehogs are nowadays generally benign, but it was not always so. For three centuries, the hedgehog was a statutory pest on account of its fondness for eating eggs and alleged thirst for cow's milk. It remains a threat in the eyes of gamekeepers, although its actual depredations are unlikely to be the cause of significant economic losses from reduced game bags on shooting estates. However, hedgehog predation on the eggs of ground-nesting birds can be a serious conservation issue and the costs in both cash and hedgehog lives of releasing a few hedgehogs on South Uist 40 years ago serve to underline that hedgehogs should never be released on predator-free islands. The future resolution of the Uist problem remains in doubt and presents a conundrum: hedgehog populations on the mainland may be declining at least as fast as the birds whose numbers they have depleted in the Hebrides.

CHAPTER 13

Hedgehogs and People

THE EARLIEST SIGNS OF AN association between hedgehogs and humans are in the form of models and wall carvings from ancient Egypt (Fig. 245). They are evidence of a long familiarity with the species that may well extend back beyond any other type of physical record, even perhaps to the Stone Age. The best and earliest wall carvings that show hedgehogs are to be found on the east wall of the mastaba (a kind of tomb) of Ptahhetep and Akhethetep at Saqquara. They date from at least 2,300 BCE and are older than the pyramids. The carvings show two hedgehogs that are just visible among an assortment of antelope that were evidently hunted locally (Davis & Griffith, 1900) (Fig. 246). There is some confusion about the identity of the other animals depicted, but the hedgehogs are unmistakeable (Lydekker, 1904). One of them is shown eating a large locust, plagues of which periodically invaded Egypt

FIG 245. Models of hedgehogs occur among the domestic artefacts of ancient Egypt, often in the form of small bottles that contained perfumes or cosmetic oils – here a jar intended to contain kohl (black eye-paint) from the 6th or 7th century BCE. (© The Trustees of the British Museum. All rights reserved.)

FIG 246. Hedgehogs are shown on an ancient Egyptian wall carving created nearly 5,000 years ago. Various local animals are depicted and the hedgehogs may be the long-eared desert species rather than *Erinaceus europaeus*. One of the hedgehogs is clearly attacking a locust.

and would have been eagerly devoured by the local hedgehogs. Perhaps that is why they were regarded as being of sufficient significance to warrant depiction among the larger mammals. The two animals may be representations of the long-eared desert hedgehog (*Hemiechinus auritus*) rather than our western European species, but they do suggest that these spiky creatures were familiar and perhaps popular animals over 4,500 years ago.

Although we may know what a hedgehog is, what we call it has varied over the ages. The old Anglo Saxon name was 'il', a contraction of the German name 'igel' that is still used there today. The Norman Conquest introduced the British to the hedgehog's old French name 'herichoun', which evolved into 'urchoun', which in turn had become 'urchin' by 1340. Meanwhile, the mediaeval French name 'ireçon' became today's 'hérisson' (also the name of a small village in central France where they sell hedgehog whisky and the houses have small wooden hedgehogs on their front doors!) (Fig. 247). The word 'urchin' is now obsolete (having been somehow transferred to scruffy little boys) and the English name 'hedgehog' has been the norm since the fifteenth century. Shakespeare called it by that name, but also referred to 'hedgepigs' and 'urchins' in various places. Within Britain, there appear to be many local names recorded in the literature, such as 'furze boar' and 'hedgy-pig', which are clearly derived from existing names and probably rarely used these days. The Gaelic name is 'graineog' and the Irish use a similar word which refers to something nasty. In

FIG 247. A village in central France is named for the hedgehog and the local houses have hedgehog-shaped house numbers on their doors.

Welsh, it is 'draened or 'draenog', the spiny thing, and in the Cornish language it is 'sart'. Other old European names often associate the hedgehog with pigs, to which it is not at all related.

As discussed in Chapter 2, many people, especially in less informed times, regard spiny animals as so distinctive that they are probably closely related and there is no real need to distinguish between them. In some languages, the same word may be used to refer to both porcupines and hedgehogs, for example, despite their important zoological differences. Sometimes this makes it difficult to be certain what is being described in the old written accounts of hedgehogs and their relationship with people. As an example of this problem, Figure 248 shows an interesting early engraving by Johannes Stradanus (1523–1605). It depicts some spiny animals being captured and refers to them as 'Echini' in the Latin inscription. That word translates as 'urchins', although in technical zoological terms it refers to spiny sea urchins. But a later handwritten title on the engraving uses the French name 'hérisson'. So what is going on here? Dogs are helping the men in their work, as well they might when searching for hedgehogs, but these could easily be captured without needing nets as depicted. There are plenty of spades and digging tools shown, apparently being used to excavate burrows, perhaps to extract nesting or hibernating hedgehogs. But the rounded face, rather than a pointed snout, and also the long spines might suggest the intended victims are porcupines, which also live in burrows. Hedgehogs were prized as food and might justify an energetic hunt for them, but I can personally vouch for the fact that porcupines are also nice to eat. Both species occur in Italy, where Stradanus worked as a professional artist for at least 25 years. So, can we be sure whether this is a hedgehog hunt or not? Anyway it's a nice picture, but it does highlight the fact that uncertainties can be encountered even in visual representations. It is even

FIG 248. This sixteenth-century engraving highlights the uncertainty involved in the interpretation of old texts. Is this a hunt for hedgehogs (as asserted) or porcupines? If we can't be sure of even a picture, then the ambiguity of archaic words becomes even more problematic.

harder to be certain how to interpret some of the details given in old translations of ancient Latin or Greek texts. This is particularly so when we read what appear to be preposterous claims for the hedgehog's ability to cure all sorts of maladies afflicting a gullible human population.

FOLKLORE AND LITERARY REFERENCES TO HEDGEHOGS

Aristotle promoted the idea that a hedgehog could foretell changing weather and would site the entrance of its nest according to the likely direction of the wind. Despite its improbability, I did test this tale with respect to hibernacula and found nothing to support it. Returning to the Reverend Topsel's statements about the hedgehog in 1658 we learn that:

when the female is to bring forth her young ones and feeleth the natural pain of her delivery, she pricketh her own belly to delay and put off her misery ... whereupon came the proverb (as Erasmus saith) Echinum partum differt, the Hedge-hog putteth off the littering of her young; which also applied against them which put off and defer those necessary works which God and nature hath provided them to undergo as when a poor man defereth the payment of his debt until the value and sum grow to be far more great than the principal.

Since that was a quotation from Erasmus, the philosopher and soothsayer who died in 1536, we can assume that this bit of folklore had been associated with hedgehogs for a long time. However, it is anatomically impossible for a hedgehog to poke its stomach with its own spines and baffling that such a story should have been invented and then persist for so long (Fig. 249).

Aesop is another ancient author who might be expected to write whimsically about the hedgehog, yet his fables include only one brief tale that features this species. Its leading character is a fox that is being plagued by mosquitos. The hedgehog offers some advice on an immediate line of action to reduce the misery suffered by the tormented fox, but the latter rejects the suggestion in favour of a more considered long-term solution to the problem. Aesop's message seems to be about people who possess a broader wisdom like the fox, individuals that we might today term 'lateral thinkers'. They are contrasted with other folk, who like the hedgehog, might automatically think the obvious and act impulsively. It is interesting that Aesop, 2,500 years ago, should be hinting that the hedgehog was an animal of rather fixed and limited behaviour compared with the fox. We would recognise that as fair comment even today.

FIG 249. It is an anatomical impossibility for a hedgehog to prick its own belly, as alleged by Edward Topsel in 1658.

The Bible is another obvious place to look for stories that might show associations between hedgehogs and people. Two species

FIG 250. The popularity of the hedgehog became so great that it began to feature on Christmas cards. Although hedgehogs do occur in the Holy Land, mentions in the Bible are few and somewhat ambiguous.

occur in the Holy Land and in Zephaniah 2:14 it says that 'Flocks and herds will lie down there, [and] all kinds of beasts; even the owl and the hedgehog shall lodge in her capitals'. This does suggest a benign and hospitable attitude towards hedgehogs inhabiting the vicinity of buildings, but in other versions of the Bible, that passage speaks of different species. A similar confusion exists regarding mention of the hedgehog in the book of Isiah. This is because of ambiguity regarding the meaning of an old Hebrew word 'kibbod' or 'quippod' which has been rendered variously as 'hedgehog', 'porcupine' and 'bittern' (Cansdale, 1970). It might actually not refer to any of them. The uncertainty exists owing to differences in the translation used for the Authorised Anglican Version of the Bible and a later translation derived from Hebrew in the official Jewish Bible. The problem was analysed in detail by the Reverend J. G. Wood in his *Bible Animals* (Wood, 1876) (Fig. 251). He seems to have veered towards accepting that the word kibbod did refer to the hedgehog, but without firmly stating that this was his opinion. There are very few other biblical mentions of hedgehogs and they mostly refer to its spiny condition, something that it shares with the porcupine (if not the bittern!). This is another example of how difficult it is to be certain about what writers meant so long ago and in a different language.

One might also look for the hedgehog in more recent literature, but it is not a very fruitful exercise. There is a passage in Shakespeare's *Midsummer Night's Dream*: 'Thorny hedgehogs be not seen; Newts and blind worms do no wrong; Come not near our fairy queen', which some people may find insightful, but I am not one of them. The most famous (and unambiguous!) manifestation of a hedgehog in print is *The Tale of Mrs Tiggy-Winkle* (Potter, 1905), the story of a bustling and business-like hedgehog operating as a washerwoman in the Lake District (Fig. 252). She was created by Beatrix Potter while on holiday at Lingholm

the windows ; desolation shall be in the thresholds ; for he shall uncover the cedar-work."

Now, in the "Jewish School and Family Bible," a new literal translation by Dr. A. Benisch, under the superintendence of the Chief Rabbi, the word Kippôd is translated, not as Bittern, but Hedgehog. As I shall have to refer to this translation repeatedly in the course of the present work, I will give a few remarks made by the translator in the preface.

SYRIAN HEDGEHOG.

"Pelican and hedgehog shall possess it. — ISA. XXXIV. 11 (Jewish Bible)."

FIG 251. The Reverend John George Wood (1827–89) was a prolific nineteenth-century author of natural history books, but despite his keen interest in animals and his ecclesiastical training, he struggled to interpret possible references to hedgehogs in different translations of the Bible.

where she met Lucie Carr, the young daughter of the local vicar and inspiration for the principal human character in the book. A Scottish washerwoman, Kitty MacDonald, formed the model for the role, having worked as a domestic servant for the Potter household at one stage (Taylor et al., 1987). The tale was drafted in 1902 as a children's book suitable for girls, centred around doing useful jobs about the house, all performed by hand without the aid of modern appliances. Thus was created an engaging and timeless story set in a tiny cottage in the Lake District fells, with young Lucie and Mrs Tiggy-Winkle delivering freshly laundered clothing in the neighbourhood.

Beatrix Potter was inspired by one of her own pet hedgehogs called Mrs. Tiggy Winkle. This is curious, as in Potter's day 'winkle' was a euphemism for a boy's penis. Anyway, she was very fond of her hedgehog and carried Tiggy with her in a cardboard box on journeys between London and the Lake District. Potter wrote to her publisher Frederick Warne:

> Mrs. Tiggy as a model is comical; so long as she can go to sleep on my knee she is delighted, but if she is propped up on end for half an hour [to paint her portrait], she first begins to yawn pathetically, and then she does bite!

This is unusual, as hedgehogs rarely bite in anger, but the aggressive act does not appear to have compromised Beatrix Potter's comely watercolour images, nor her fondness for the animal itself. She went on, 'Nevertheless, she is a dear person; just like a very fat rather stupid little dog.'

Soon after the book's publication, Potter's ageing hedgehog began to show signs of failing health and she wrote to a friend:

I am sorry to say I am upset about poor Tiggy. She hasn't seemed well the last fortnight, and has begun to be sick, and she is so thin. I am going to try some physic but I am a little afraid that the long course of unnatural diet and indoor life is beginning to tell on her.

That letter was written in February, so we might suppose that the hapless creature was being kept in relatively cool surroundings, but in a state of non-hibernation. Tiggy would have been frequently disturbed and sometimes too warm to hibernate successfully, but perhaps too cold to feed and digest food adequately. This could account for its indisposition and also be a salutary lesson for many people who think they are helping hedgehogs by keeping them indoors over winter (see Chapter 6). Potter's letter continued, 'It is a wonder she has lasted so long. One gets very fond of a little animal. I hope she will either get well or go quickly' (Taylor, 2012). Soon afterwards, Mrs Tiggy did indeed go quickly, (allegedly) assisted by a bottle of chloroform, and the body was buried in Potter's London garden, now a school playground.

FIG 252. Mrs Tiggy-Winkle, one of the most iconic storybook animals, first made her appearance in 1905. The whimsical tale of a Lake District washerwoman has remained in print ever since and has been translated into more than two dozen languages.

Thirty thousand copies of *The Tale of Mrs Tiggy-Winkle* were produced in late 1905, with thousands more just a few weeks later, reflecting its popular appeal. The book has remained in print ever since and is also available in Braille and as a Kindle version. It has been translated into more than two dozen languages, including Welsh and Russian. Beatrix Potter's charming watercolours show Mrs. T. wearing clothes, including a shawl about her shoulders and a lace-trimmed bonnet, creating a lovable and homely creature whose spiny reality is obscured. The image has immense appeal and Potter was confident that her animal characters would become popular, and so it has transpired, with Mrs T. foremost among them. Her image has been reincarnated as soft toys, china mugs and Beswick porcelain figurines as a profitable form of brand extension. She has also appeared on postage stamps (Fig. 253), fancy

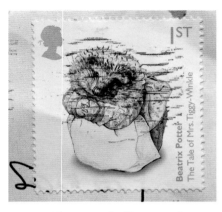

FIG 253. The unmistakeable image of Mrs Tiggy-Winkle on a recent British postage stamp.

biscuit tins, Royal Doulton china and Wedgwood plates. Two American manufacturers used Mrs. Tiggy-Winkle in their products even though hedgehogs are not native to the USA. In 1971, she became a character in a Royal Ballet film, *The Tales of Beatrix Potter*, and in 1993, her story formed an episode of a BBC series about Potter's world of lovable creatures.

Beatrix Potter died in 1943, leaving her home, 'Hilltop', to the National Trust (where it has remained open to visitors since 1946). Meanwhile, her animals live on. In Mrs Tiggy-Winkle, Beatrix Potter left one of the most iconic fictional creatures ever, joining Mickey Mouse, Winnie the Pooh and Rupert Bear as timeless images of childhood engagement with animals and the written word.

THE HEDGEHOG'S MEDICINAL PROPERTIES

Most of the earliest descriptions of hedgehogs included a focus on two issues, food and medical cures, as though those were really the only things that were worth knowing about these animals. Encouraged by the writings of respected authors advocating all manner of promising remedies for common ailments, hedgehogs have for centuries been captured for use as a source of supposed medicinal ingredients. In his *History of Four-footed Beasts and Serpents*, the Reverend Edward Topsel reviewed some of the instructions written by the ancient authorities. Aetius of Antioch, a fourth-century theologian, apparently recommended that

> *Ten sprigs of laurel, seven grains of pepper … the skin and ribs of a Hedge-hog, dried and beaten cast into three cups of water and warmed, as being drunk of one that hath the Colic, and let rest, he shall be in perfect health; but with this exception that for a man it must be the membrane of a male hedgehog, and for a woman a female.*

Topsel also cited other ancient authorities, including one that expounded on the properties of a hedgehog's ashes that 'are used by Physitians for taking down of proud swellings and for the cleansing of Ulcers and Boyles'. Apparently the power of the skin's ashes could be enhanced by being 'roasted with the head and afterwards beat unto powder and anointed on the head with hony, cureth Alopecia'. Topsel quoted a further seven savants who had offered their wisdom regarding the hedgehog's utility, including Pliny, who advocated the use of hedgehog faeces mixed with vinegar and pitch to alleviate hair loss (I have not tried this yet). Salted hedgehog could be eaten by pregnant women to prevent abortions according to Marcellus, who also stated that 'the fat of the Hedge-hog stayeth the flux of the bowels'. The hedgehog's left eye could be made into a potion that would cause sleep if 'infused into the ears with a quill' and there were cures for hoarseness, warts, 'the Bloody flux and the Cough'. The efficacy of some of these preparations could apparently be enhanced by adding a bat's brain and milk from a dog. Topsel also referred to Dioscorides, a Greek physician in the Roman army, whose *Materia Medica* (written between 50 and 70 AD) was widely read for more than 1,500 years and reckoned the hedgehog to have superior curative properties compared to the porcupine.

It is easy to scoff at all this but even now, information is often afforded credibility for no better reason than that it is disseminated via the internet rather than ancient scribes. Manuka honey, colonic irrigation and the alleged benefits of alternative medicine all have prominent and numerous advocates even today in the Age of Science. In a less sophisticated time, such intricate detail as given by the ancient Greek and Roman physicians and contemporary pharmacologists must have imparted an air of authority. Who could possibly gainsay the ancient savants, quotations from whom had been offered as reputable and reliable guidance for more than a millennium? Surely the Reverend Topsel himself could be trusted too, as he was a 'man of the cloth' after all. Their collective words of wisdom regarding the medicinal properties of hedgehogs remained current for centuries, especially in the absence of rigorous testing. Their efficacy on humans is likely to have been minimal, likewise their impact on hedgehog populations.

To be fair, Topsel was merely quoting these historic authorities without offering critical comment himself. Perhaps he was sceptical too, but if he had felt that the inclusion of these preposterous propositions might have undermined the credibility of his book, why would he waste a significant amount of space repeating 'facts' that he did not believe to be true? Perhaps, like everyone else, he was not in a position to question ancient words of wisdom, simply because there was no scientifically reliable information on which to base a challenge. By an interesting irony, several of Topsel's informants mentioned hedgehog derivatives as a cure for leprosy. It turns out that this species, along with armadillos, is very susceptible to *Mycobacterium leprae*, perhaps allowing it to play a part in modern experiments to create a cure for that disease after all (Klingmüller & Sobich, 1977).

Meanwhile, the collection of various hedgehog species continues in North Africa and India, for example (Kumar & Nijman, 2016), evidence that belief in the animal's curative properties is still widespread despite being unproven.

CULINARY ASPECTS OF THE HEDGEHOG

As a slow-moving, unaggressive creature that doesn't bite, the hedgehog has always been a prime target for hungry people wanting an easy meal. One of the most widely known and widely quoted 'facts' about hedgehogs is that gypsies like to encase them in clay to roast in the embers of a hot fire. After a suitable interval, the clay can be broken off, pulling away the spines to leave a tasty snack. It was probably not only gypsies who ate them, but ordinary country folk too, and why not? Hedgehogs do not have strongly smelling skin glands, nor do they eat special prey whose scent might taint the flesh and impart a distasteful flavour to the meat. Hedgehogs caught in the autumn would be very fat and self-basting too, ideal for roasting over a hot fire. It is reported that 'hyrchouns' were served up at a feast in 1425, so their consumption was not restricted to the poor who could not afford a decent diet. Maybe they were quite widely appreciated as something of a delicacy.

When hedgehogs were on the menu, baking in clay was not the only way that they could be prepared for the table. Edward Topsel commented on this, and might be expected to offer reliable information, perhaps based upon some direct personal seventeenth-century observation rather than reliance on centuries-old historic documents. He wrote that they could be roasted on a spit after skinning, but then added inexplicably, 'if the head be not cut off at one blow the flesh is not good'. A more reliable observer was the nineteenth-century naturalist Frank Buckland. He was always keen to pursue good natural history anecdotes and described how he had visited a gypsy woman in Oxfordshire 'who although squalid and dirty was proud of being able to claim relationship with Black Jemmy, the King of the Gypsies'. She obligingly roasted some hedgehogs for him over a fire and told him that they were 'nicest at Michaelmas time when they have been eating the crabs [apples] which fall from the hedges'. Some of them she said, 'have yellow fat and some white fat and we calls 'em mutton and beef hedgehogs and very nice eating they be Sir when the fat is on 'em' (Buckland, 1883). This observation may refer to the difference between white and brown fat (see Chapter 6).

Despite the ease of acquisition and convenience of their preparation for a meal, hedgehog remains do not appear to be common in the household middens of Stone Age settlements or among archaeological deposits accumulated during historical times in this country. It is difficult to understand why hedgehogs were seemingly infrequent food items, but just possible that the name 'hedgepig' and its porcine snuffling and feeding habits served to associate the animal with long-established taboos forbidding the eating of pork. There remains a strong revulsion against eating hedgehogs in Britain, but on the Continent people often ate them in countries where the spectrum of human dietary is wider than in Britain. In Germany, during the dark days of World War II, a local newspaper reported that a gypsy had been fined 10 Reichsmarks for trying to eat one without having an appropriate ration card (Hyde-Parker, 1940). In more recent times, a German chef who offered hedgehog paté at his restaurant in England swiftly removed it from his menu before he was made into paté himself by the press and local critics. It is still regularly asserted that gypsies take and bake them, although this is probably no longer commonplace, given the abundance of more appealing junk food. Nevertheless it does still go on in France, where a local newspaper reported as recently as 2014 that three men were arrested on the outskirts of Paris for collecting hedgehogs for food. Putting the words 'hérisson' and 'food' into Google will find images of a wide selection of dishes inspired by the hedgehog, some of which look delicious. However, if you also incorporate the word 'chasse' into the search, you can visit some French websites with graphic images of butchering hedgehogs that are too gruesome to reproduce here.

OTHER USES FOR HEDGEHOGS

Unlike many other mammals, the hedgehog's skin is unsuitable for making leather and no use at all for furry garments. On the other hand, it does have all those spines and human ingenuity has found plenty of uses for them. When dry, the spiny skin forms a stiff bristling mat that could be stuck to the wooden door of a mediaeval house to keep scavenging dogs at bay. Nailed to a fence, it might stop vandals climbing over to raid an orchard. Fixed to the top rail of a gate, it would deter horses from leaning on it and attached to the shafts of a carriage, it could stop a horse from dozing off and leaning to one side when it was supposed to be at work. Firmly fixed to a pair of boards, two pieces of spiny skin were made into a device for combing wool or flax fibres ready for spinning.
That ingenious idea dates back to at least Roman times, when the Senate apparently became anxious enough to preserve this useful animal and its skin by passing legislation to protect it from destruction (Fairley, 1975). In the laboratory, the spines have been used as pins where tissue samples need to be held down in liquids that would corrode normal metal pins.

HEDGEHOG AS PETS

For millennia, humans have kept animals as useful or entertaining companions and pet-keeping has been fashionable among the wealthy since the Middle Ages. Monks and nuns were repeatedly forbidden to keep pets in mediaeval times. Later, with increasing national prosperity, pets became established as a normal feature of middle-class households. It became possible for ordinary people to afford to support animals that lacked any productive value and were not functional necessities like farm animals. This was especially popular in towns where real live animals were not a normal part of everyday life as they would be for country dwellers. In the nineteenth century, pet-keeping widened and hedgehogs were purchased to release about the house and in kitchens and bakeries in order to harness their expertise in controlling cockroaches, crickets and other undesirable commensals. The hedgehog's utility was enhanced by stories of their rat-catching abilities and also because they required no special food that might otherwise have fed people. Among the notes added to his edition of *The Natural History and Antiquities of Selborne* (White, 1883), Frank Buckland recorded that a Mr. Davy 'has had forty hedgehogs at a time, he sold them to shopkeepers to sell again; the price, wholesale, was from eight shillings to twelve shillings per dozen'. Sales must have been brisk to be dealing in dozens.

Some pet hedgehogs will become very tame and allow themselves to be stroked without rolling up, but this is a very individual trait and others seem never to become tame at all. I knew a hedgehog once ('Georgie') that would come when its name was called and I have read stories about others that were similarly responsive (Fig. 254). It is reported that a Mr. Cocks once tamed a newly caught individual by drenching it with beer as it lay rolled up, stroking it whenever it uncurled. On recovering sobriety, it remained tame for the rest of its life. A story was published in *The Irish Naturalist* in 1899 about a hedgehog that would pull a toy cart, but on the whole, *Erinaceus europaeus* is not well suited to traditional forms of pet keeping in which the animal is allowed to wander freely through the house or kept in a small cage like a canary or hamster. It is evident from earlier chapters here that hedgehogs are surprisingly active animals accustomed to roaming over an area considerably larger than a football pitch. Healthy hedgehogs should not be confined to a small cage. The European species are also rather messy characters in captivity, often mixing their food and water, defaecating profusely and soiling their surroundings. They are mostly not very cuddly and can be quite smelly too. Their natural behaviour takes place after dark, not in daylight when we might want to enjoy their presence. Altogether, European hedgehogs do not make good household pets and probably do not

FIG 254. 'Georgie', a pet hedgehog that would come when it was called. It had a particular fondness for salted peanuts, not an ideal diet but such treats were offered sparingly.

much enjoy the experience either. It is currently not illegal to sell *Erinaceus europaeus* or offer them for sale in the pet trade, but few people do. Instead, there is a lot to be said for adopting hedgehogs as wild, free-ranging pets, a more satisfactory format for them and for us. Putting out supplementary food is a form of pet keeping in which the favoured animals retain their liberty and are able to live normal lives and express their normal behaviour patterns. Although it is not really pet keeping, rescuing sick and injured hedgehogs has also become a widespread activity, motivated by a desire to help and nurture wild animals, especially this particularly distinctive species. The benefits of these activities for wild hedgehogs are described in Chapter 11.

On the other hand, from the early 1990s, African pygmy hedgehogs (*Atelerix albiventris*) became popular and widely available in the USA as 'low maintenance pets' and there is a lengthy instruction manual on their husbandry and welfare (Kelsey-Wood, 1995). These animals are accustomed to living and feeding in dry, semi-desert habitats and have readily adjusted to eating food pellets in captivity. Over the past 30 years, they have been captive-bred for enough generations that tameness has become the normal state. The animal is detached from its natural condition and has become a domestic species just like gerbils and golden hamsters. They have even been selectively bred to generate colour varieties (Fig. 256). They do not deliver a serious bite and can make engaging and interesting companions. These pet animals can bring about extraordinary changes in human behaviour, at least in the USA, with hedgehog conferences, special funerals and a general departure from everyday sanity (Warwick, 2008). Some states have banned their sale, and concern for the animal's welfare has led to controls on removing any more of them from the wild.

Pygmy hedgehogs seen in the pet trade in Britain are animals bred specifically for that way of life and remain available here. They are much smaller than *Erinaceus europaeus* (about the size of an orange) and usually pale fawn or grey. They are a problem because they muddle the distinction between these animals and wild European hedgehogs. The press and social media both disseminate images of cute pygmy hedgehogs to illustrate stories about hedgehog conservation and ecology. Instagram and YouTube create confusion by fostering the impression that 'hedgehogs' are mainstream pets, when this is

FIG 255. African pygmy hedgehogs (*Atelerix* sp.) have become common as novelty pets and adjust to captivity better than European species. This is the natural wild-type colouration.

FIG 256. African pygmy hedgehogs have been selectively bred in captivity for a sufficient number of generations to produce tame individuals and several colour varieties. They are now fully adapted to domestic life, just like hamsters and gerbils, and completely unsuited to life in the British countryside.

not the case with *Erinaceus europaeus*. A further problem arises if these endearing pygmy hedgehogs are no longer wanted and their owners conceive the idea of granting them liberty by releasing them into a garden or the countryside. Pygmy hedgehogs bred for generations in captivity are no better suited for life in the wild than Siamese cats or dachshund dogs. Out of doors, they will be confronted with cold and wet conditions, to which they were never adapted. They will also be required to hibernate during the winter, something that they will not have done before. Pygmy hedgehogs liberated in Britain, far from being granted their freedom, are more likely to be condemned to a drawn-out and miserable death. It is also illegal to release into the wild species that do not already occur in this country. Pet pygmy hedgehogs belong indoors and should stay there.

LEGAL PROTECTION

It was Queen Elizabeth I who enacted legislation that required destruction of hedgehogs as officially designated vermin and it was the second Queen Elizabeth who reversed its status by granting the animal its first legal protection. This is conferred by the Wildlife and Countryside Act of 1981, where the hedgehog is listed on Schedule 6, making it a 'partially protected species'. In reality, this is actually not a lot of help due to the way that the Act is drafted. It is declared unlawful to catch hedgehogs using a snare, use it as a decoy or put out poison to kill it. Its listing on Schedule 6 also means that a hedgehog may not be shot with automatic weapons or caught by using gas, a dazzling light or mirror. Nor may anyone use explosives or a crossbow against it or chase the animals using a vehicle. Banning these activities was intended to protect other species and is all very well, but irrelevant to the hedgehog. There is no protection at all from the very real threats that are reviewed in earlier chapters of this book.

In view of the apparent decline in hedgehog numbers, in 2016 Oliver Colville MP led an energetic campaign to persuade the Government to upgrade the hedgehog's legal status to make it a fully protected species. The campaign was backed by a public petition that gained nearly 60,000 signatures representing all 650 Parliamentary constituencies. In practice, upgrading legal protection would mean adding the hedgehog to Schedule 5 of the Wildlife and Countryside Act, where it would be listed as a fully protected species alongside the otter, dormouse and red squirrel. That too would probably be an empty gesture with little real effect. Amending the law in this way would prevent deliberate killing (although gamekeepers would probably be licensed to continue doing so), but the law would still not, and could not, protect hedgehogs from loss of hedgerows and green spaces, habitat fragmentation, badgers, road traffic, agricultural intensification or secondary poisoning from widespread use of rodenticides. In other words, enhanced legal protection would not help very much, if at all, to address the real causes of decline in hedgehog populations. Pressing for greater legal protection through revision of the Wildlife and Countryside Act might not be the best use of campaigning resources or Parliamentary time. On the other hand, upgrading its legal status would serve to highlight the hedgehog's plight as a declining species and express a national desire to support this popular and inoffensive animal. In this way, full legal protection would be welcome and worth pursuing, in order to draw attention to the various issues involved which threaten our own environment and the survival of other wildlife. Full legal protection would also force developers to carry out survey work before destroying habitats. If evidence of hedgehogs was found, steps would have to be taken to mitigate the ecological damage done by building roads, houses and other major transformations of the countryside. This would be no bad thing, for hedgehogs and many other species. Although political pressures to build more housing are so great that a few hedgehogs would not be allowed to stand in the way of major developments, builders would at least be compelled to think about creating a more wildlife-friendly form of urban land. But rather than just promoting the hedgehog to become a Schedule 5 species, perhaps it would be more effective if Government were to amend planning law to make it a legal requirement in all new residential areas for fencing to be permeable to wildlife, through the inclusion of 'Hedgehog Highways' (Fig. 257). Further encouragement could come from creating a system of points-based awards for new urban green space as used in Sweden and Berlin, an idea that is under

FIG 257. It could be made mandatory (or at least 'good practice') for all new fencing to incorporate a Hedgehog Highway hole to allow free movement between gardens and across a wider range of habitats, especially in suburban areas.

consideration by the Mayor of London for a new London Plan. This seeks to create a more attractive future for necessary urban development, with support for biodiversity as one of its key elements.

Meanwhile, the hedgehog's natural defensive habits make it peculiarly vulnerable to cruel treatment, quite unlike most mammals which run away or bite back when handled. In Grantham, the fire brigade had to be called out one day to rescue a hedgehog from the roof of a house, having apparently been thrown there for amusement. Newspaper reports from elsewhere suggest that vandals may viciously kick a hedgehog about like a football or perhaps set one alight 'just for fun'. That kind of mindless brutality was disappointingly common and it still goes on. In 2017, a Merseyside man pounded a hedgehog to death with a brick in a fit of rage after a dispute with his partner. In the same year, a gang in Cornwall doused a hedgehog with lighter fuel ready to set it ablaze. Legislation to prevent cruelty to animals did not apply to wild species, so prosecutions could not be pursued in the past, but at least that area of legal laxity has been resolved by the Wild Mammals (Protection) Act of 1996. This explicitly makes ill-treatment of wild animals an offence and the hedgehog is probably the biggest beneficiary. Two brothers aged 23 and 31 were given jail sentences in 2016 for kicking a hedgehog to death in County Durham barely a month after another hedgehog had been found impaled on a metal rod in the West Midlands. We might reasonably expect that such bestial behaviour had ceased centuries ago, but clearly it hasn't and legal sanctions are an appropriate response. Separate legislation, creating similar levels of protection, exists for Scotland and Northern Ireland in the form of the Protection of Wild Mammals, Scotland Act, 2002, and the Welfare of Animals Act, Northern Ireland, 2011. Other recent legislation that may be helpful to hedgehogs includes the Hunting Act of 2004. This makes it illegal to use dogs to track down wild mammals. Although it was intended to stop fox hunting and the chasing of hares and deer, the Act might also be used as an additional tool to prosecute in cases where dogs had been implicated in the cruel mistreatment of hedgehogs.

But legislation aimed at specific threats, different for each species, is a scattergun approach to the bigger issue of wildlife conservation at the national and landscape level. A more strategic vision is required and after four years of lengthy consultation, an official UK Biodiversity Action Plan was formulated in 2007 as a statement of concern for more than 1,100 species and as an implied commitment by the United Kingdom to the UN Convention on Biological Diversity. On the strength of the surveys described here in Chapter 10, the hedgehog was listed among the UK BAP priority species for which there was reliable evidence of decline and a clear need for conservation. The BAP process appears to have been abandoned soon afterwards and a revised list of vulnerable species was produced instead. The hedgehog is listed in Section 41 of the Natural Environment and Communities Act of 2006 as a species 'of principal importance for the purpose of conserving biodiversity in England'. This requires that its needs must be taken into consideration by public bodies when performing their proper functions such as when they make decisions about developments that might impact on hedgehog habitats and populations. What this amounts to in practice – for example, when parks or public gardens are due for major improvements – is not easy to see. This is especially so because local authorities are unlikely to have a hedgehog advisor on the staff nor would they necessarily know if or where hedgehogs occurred locally. Presumably they could call upon ecological consultants to carry out the necessary surveys, using the methods described in the Appendix, but that costs money and is easily foregone. The immense political pressures to create thousands of new homes, often by building on greenfield sites, are also likely to sweep hedgehogs and other wildlife to one side. So this is another example of the hedgehog having gained the status of being mentioned in legislation, but probably with little real effect. We cannot rely on the law to save hedgehogs; that will only be achieved through widespread public engagement. Fortunately there are plenty of signs that people are willing to rally round and help.

At the time of writing (2017), Britain has signalled its intention to leave the European Union (EU). This will entail many significant adjustments to our legislation, but the hedgehog is not a 'European Protected Species' (unlike the otter and dormouse, for example) so its legal status is unlikely to change. However, withdrawal from the European Union will mean that EU Directives will no longer apply. The Government plans to enact legislation that transfers all EU agreements (thousands of them!) into UK law, for possible modification later. This could profoundly affect hedgehogs. No doubt the RSPB will see to it that full protection of birds will continue, but one of the reasons why so much effort was put into killing hedgehogs in the Uists was the fear that failure to abide by the EU Birds Directive and protect nesting waders might result in a massive fine being imposed by the European Court of Justice. If we cease to be answerable to the ECJ for lack of action, the Uist hedgehogs could benefit, although culling them has not been cost-effective and will probably not be repeated anyway. Whatever happens, any resumption of culling will not now be funded by the EU and perhaps not by anyone else either. Changes associated with the EU Habitats Directive might also affect hedgehogs. Once the protection of habitats becomes a matter of British law, with no external constraints, the Government may yield to pressures for more land to be released for housing and infrastructure development. Such changes are already being advocated by some and would be unlikely to benefit hedgehogs. However, many conservation organisations see an opportunity to develop a new strategy for managing the British countryside, in particular creating incentives for wildlife-friendly farming to replace the subsidies that currently support farmers through the Common Agricultural Policy of the EU. If that comes about, leading to less intensive farming and financial rewards for maintaining biodiversity, habitat links and ecological integrity, the hedgehog's future prospects could be considerably improved.

Meanwhile there are lesser legal issues that continue to crop up. For example, approval has been sought for use of a new type of trap in Britain. It is marketed in New Zealand as a means of killing small mammal pests, including hedgehogs. That is obviously unacceptable here, but the manufacturers say that the traps can be set high enough off the ground to avoid hedgehog deaths. That is likely to reduce their effectiveness against stoats and rats and it is hard to believe that the traps will not be set lower 'just to make sure' that the intended victims do not escape being killed. Either these traps do catch hedgehogs (as claimed in New Zealand) or they don't. Setting any kind of traps to catch hedgehogs is, and will remain, illegal. But it is easy to claim that hedgehog deaths were accidental and the intention was to catch something else like rats.

THE HEDGEHOG'S POPULARITY

Hedgehogs are rarely far from human affairs, as discussed and illustrated very fully in Hugh Warwick's book *Hedgehog* (Warwick, 2014). They frequently appear in cartoons, often around the themes of prickly defence or being run over (Fig. 258). There are plenty of hedgehog jokes too, usually focused on these same topics. An exception won a prize at the Edinburgh Fringe in 2009 – 'Hedgehogs. Why can't they just share the hedge?' According to the BBC, the judges had sifted through

FIG 258. An example of a hedgehog image being used for a road safety campaign.

thousands of jokes to discover this one by Dan Antopolski. An early computer game, 'Sonic the Hedgehog', gained widespread popularity at the time and a search through the scientific literature reveals technical papers about a 'hedgehog chromosome', apparently named for its appearance, not its origin or effect. An extensive assortment of hedgehog-themed commercial goods has also appeared for sale, ranging from notepaper, slippers, tea towels, mugs and paperweights to less utilitarian items that include a board game and numerous ceramic ornaments (Fig. 259).

Periodically, there have been public opinion surveys to establish Britain's most popular animals. Time and again, the otter, dolphin or badger would top the poll, even though most people had never seen any of them in the flesh. But public awareness has begun to pull the hedgehog to the fore. In 2007, the British people voted the hedgehog as the nation's top 'Icon of the Environment' in a poll conducted by the Government's Environment Agency to celebrate their tenth anniversary. It emerged victorious from 70 nominations that included the Agency's own favourite, the salmon, as well as all the usual suspects like the otter, badger and red squirrel. BBC *Wildlife* magazine reported in 2013 that the hedgehog had gained 42 per cent of the votes in its own survey to find Britain's 'National Species', easily beating everything else, even the badger. It topped the poll again in 2017. In another enquiry, by the Royal Society of Biology in 2016, the hedgehog gained 39 per cent of the votes as Britain's No. 1 favourite mammal.

The hedgehog's popularity seems perverse, given its reputation for being prickly and flea-ridden. It also humanoid features (flat face, forward-facing eyes) that psychologists say make apes and monkeys so endearing. It is not a cuddly creature, yet it behaves in a very agreeable manner, pottering about our gardens eating slugs and not running away (or biting) when disturbed. It appears to be a tolerant and trusting creature, attributes that we welcome and we reciprocate.

FIG 259. A vast range of hedgehog-themed souvenirs and other commercial goods is now available.

FIG 260. Hobson's Brewery in Shropshire made a special brew of hedgehog beer as a one-off stunt to raise funds for the BHPS, with a donation of 5p for every bottle sold. It proved so popular that production continued and over 550,000 pints were drunk, raising £30,000 for hedgehogs. Both the brewing and the drinking continue.

However, the hedgehog also seems particularly vulnerable to many aspects of modern life. Perhaps people feel uncomfortable at the way that humanity storms ahead while harmless creatures like the hedgehog are swept aside or are almost literally downtrodden. Maybe people are simply concerned when they see a sick or injured animal and seek to assist it, leading to the development of hundreds of hedgehog carers and wildlife hospitals (see Chapter 11). Our sympathy for the hedgehog, and its own rather unusual, distinctive appearance, also means that it appears in newspaper stories every month, nationwide. It seems to soldier on stoically despite all the vicissitudes of modern life in human-dominated environments, ranging from the suburbs of Liverpool or Edinburgh, to the South Downs or Romney Marsh. Perhaps we also feel a little respect for the spiny underdog doing its best to survive against the odds.

But popular support is not just a matter of sympathy or publicity and razzmatazz. The public have also provided help in concrete terms by donating money. In 2016, *The Times* newspaper focussed its annual Christmas Appeal on hedgehogs, resulting in a gift to the BHPS totalling more than £62,000. This was sufficient to underwrite the cost of employing a full-time 'Hedgehog Officer' based in Warwickshire with a remit to promote wildlife interest among local children and encourage practical hedgehog conservation measures among gardeners and householders (Fig. 261). Popularity and public support are vital in keeping the hedgehog on the agenda for parliament and local decision-makers. Oliver Colville's parliamentary

FIG 261. Henry Johnson, (in pale blue) was the first full-time 'Hedgehog Officer', funded by the PTES. Simon Thompson and Debbie Wright, attached to Warwickshire Wildlife Trust, and Ali North, attached to Suffolk WT, were all three funded by BHPS. They were charged with the job of raising the profile of hedgehogs and local wildlife conservation.

efforts in 2016 gained widespread publicity and approval for his attempt to promote hedgehogs in the House, no doubt enlivening proceedings in the process. Hansard thus became one of the more improbable publications to feature hedgehogs extensively, at least for a while. In the House of Lords, the Marquis of Lothian asked a bland question about the hedgehog's demise and what was the Government doing about it. The equally bland reply was to the effect that BHPS and PTES were doing a grand job. Such anodyne exchanges may appear to be a waste of time, but they do keep hedgehogs on the agenda in the face of so many other pressures on government. And what's good for hedgehogs is usually good for other wildlife too. Continued public pressure on ministers results in policy commitments promising a better tomorrow. This pressure is vital, with Britain's impending departure from the EU offering unique opportunities to reshape national policy towards integration of farming and wildlife conservation in ways that have not been achieved hitherto except on a local scale.

FIG 262. An early result in Suffolk was a giant mural by 'ATM' in King Street, Ipswich, with the blessing of the Borough Council planning department. (Simone Bullion/ Suffolk Wildlife Trust)

SUPPORT FOR UIST HEDGEHOGS

Public support becomes seriously important when an issue arises like the hedgehog cull on the Uists. As explained in Chapters 1 and 11, hedgehogs were released on the Hebridean island of South Uist in the 1970s and began to have a serious impact on important colonies of ground nesting birds. Scottish Natural Heritage (SNH), the agency responsible for dealing with the problem under international agreements, decided that the hedgehog population should be reduced or eliminated by killing as many of them as possible. Eventually, many hundreds of them were killed at a cost of about £130 each in public money (Lovegrove, 2007). The BHPS was among the leading charities that campaigned hard to gain public support for a policy based upon translocation to the mainland rather than killing by lethal injection.

One of Digger Jackson's conclusions from studying the breeding behaviour of those Hebridean hedgehogs was that removal of adult females would be a priority if the population needed to be significantly reduced, but there was public disquiet about the fate of dependent nestlings if their mothers were removed. It was in response to this concern that the adult females were reprieved during culling operations in order to avoid litters of dependent nestlings starving if their mother was killed. It was not possible to identify with confidence the females that were pregnant or lactating and then release them, because of the difficulty in distinguishing various stages of the female reproductive cycle. To avoid welfare problems, removal of females was therefore confined to the short (two to three weeks) period between coming out of hibernation and getting pregnant. Non-removal of adult females was a very significant concession to public concern, but massively reduced the effectiveness of the cull and increased the probability that it would never be successful in eliminating hedgehogs from the Uists.

SNH were adamant that killing was necessary and hedgehogs could not be simply removed, and to improve catching efficiency, a necessary development if enough animals were to be caught, a plan was drawn up to get dogs to find the hedgehogs and use a shotgun to destroy them. That idea elicited such outrage that the policy lasted barely a week (Fig. 263). People up and down the country were incensed that hedgehogs would be killed, especially when these animals were facing decline on the mainland. The public outcry over the Uist hedgehog cull was enough to fully occupy the SNH Press Officer, with 3,000 protest letters received, but people did not just complain and send emails. They donated £75,000 to support the rescue of doomed hedgehogs (Lovegrove, 2007). This was a very real gesture, made by large numbers of people who felt strongly about the casual

Dogs will be drafted in to help sniff out island's hedgehogs

FIG 263. Using dogs to increase the efficiency of searching for hedgehogs was sensible, but the plan to shoot any that were found was insensitive and lasted barely a week in the face of public opposition.

condemnation of such an iconic animal. Some of that money made it possible to set up a study that confirmed released animals did not suffer unduly. A few hedgehogs rescued from being killed on the Uists were taken to Hessilhead Wildlife Rescue Trust near Glasgow. From among those, we used 20 females for a follow-up study because they would travel less far than males each night and it would be easier to monitor a larger sample than if males had been included. They were released into an area of amenity grassland at Eglinton Country Park, about 50 km southwest of Glasgow, in April 2005 (Fig. 264). They were radio-tracked each night for a month (Warwick *et al.*, 2006). The three hedgehogs that died all did so within a week of release. These, and the one that died of an existing disease and another that disappeared within 48 hours, were all animals right at the end of hibernation in the worst possible body condition and released directly without being given artificial support. They were likely to have died anyway, even if they had not been taken from the Uists. The remaining 15 hedgehogs were monitored regularly. Two were lost to predation and one drowned. Overall, 12 of the 20 animals survived (60 per cent) and maintained their body mass or increased it

FIG 264. Hedgehogs from the Uists were released in Eglington Country Park and their survival monitored. Molehills were an encouraging sign that there were probably enough worms and other invertebrates to support hedgehogs, as well as the moles.

despite the challenge of survival in unpromising habitat so soon after hibernation had ended. One of them was 38 per cent heavier by the end of the study. They also interacted normally with indigenous male hedgehogs and 11 of those released females were seen consorting with wild males at various times. Crucially, there was no evidence of a negative impact on welfare directly attributable to translocation.

In 2007, SNH conceded that translocation to the mainland would replace killing as the means of reducing the impact of hedgehogs on the Uist bird colonies and it was donations from the public that made possible a rescue system which ultimately enabled more than 2,400 hedgehogs to be taken off the islands to the mainland between 2008 and 2016 (Pat Holtham, pers comm). None of this would have been possible without such a massive level of popular support.

HEDGEHOG UNDERPASSES

Another area in which popular support is an important consideration concerns the annual toll on the roads, amounting to tens of thousands of animals (see Chapter 9). Public concern has frequently been expressed over the number of otters that are run over each year and the annual loss of an estimated 50,000 badgers (Harris et al., 1995). There is also an additional monetary cost due to the damage done to cars that are involved in collisions with larger mammals, especially deer. Concern about roadkill is real and justified. In most countries, roadside warning signs inform drivers of the danger of collisions with wildlife, although evidence of their effectiveness in reducing road casualties is lacking (Huijser et al., 2015). Nevertheless, public concern and the need to cater for protected species have led to the construction of special wildlife underpasses when roads are being built. These are meant to allow animals such as otters and badgers to cross the new road without risk of being killed and they represent a relatively minor additional cost for multimillion-pound road construction projects. A similar issue concerns mass mortality among frogs and toads as they migrate to their breeding ponds in the early spring. Large numbers of them splattered on the road is a distressing sight and sometimes threatens the survival of local populations.

Underpasses have been constructed on routes that these animals are known to use regularly, providing an alternative way of crossing the road and reducing the carnage. Wildlife tunnels have met with varying degrees of success and in some cases have been visited by hedgehogs. It could be argued that similar tunnels could be constructed specifically for them, allowing hedgehogs to cross a new road safely. But these animals do not appear to use regular routes in the way that otters, badgers and amphibians do. It is therefore far from obvious where to build an expensive tunnel. The cost of an underpass would be hard to justify and extremely unpopular if it turned out that the hedgehogs never used it. Nor are existing underpasses built for badgers much help to hedgehogs as they are likely to be wary of using them, put off by the smell of their potential enemy (Ward *et al.*, 1997). A survey of 34 mammal underpasses showed badgers used them 2,200 times, but hedgehogs not at all. Work in the UK by Silviu Petrovan at 'Froglife' clearly demonstrates that the responses of species to different wildlife underpass designs are varied and complex and we need to refine our understanding of what might make a tunnel tolerable (or even attractive) for hedgehogs. Their effectiveness might also be enhanced by the judicious addition of low fencing or baffles to deflect the animals from crossing a road and direct them towards a tunnel.

However, as noted earlier, hedgehog traffic victims often seem to be clumped along certain short sections of particular roads, whilst other stretches of road remain free of them. This may be due to physical barriers, but might also reflect unattractive roadside habitat. Creating barriers in the form of fencing would reduce the death toll, but at the expense of exacerbating the problem of fragmenting habitats and populations. There is an extensive literature on the principle of mitigating the effects of road construction through the use of wildlife passages of various kinds, particularly in the Netherlands, but also in Australia and North America. There may also be effective ways of managing the nature of road margins to reduce the number of hedgehogs killed. For example, we know from many radio-tracking studies that they like to follow edges and often forage within 5 m of a hedgerow. If a new road is to be built, then ending a hedge well short of it, or strategically planting another, might indeed guide hedgehogs away from danger. It would be hard to gather statistically robust data to demonstrate the effectiveness of such measures, given the relative infrequency with which hedgehogs cross roads or are run over, but such ideas are worth a try. They can't do any harm and might benefit other species too. The hedgehog's popularity with the public would be key to getting significant money spent on pursuing such ideas and public pressure could encourage more innovative thinking following the lead set by some progressive European governments.

Another way that numbers of hedgehogs and other mammals killed on roads might be reduced could be to modify the road surface. Tyre noise from passing traffic can be altered by changes in the road surface so that the sounds created have an enhanced ultrasonic component. Laying strips of modified surfacing material could allow traffic to generate penetrating noises inaudible to humans, but potentially serving as a powerful warning for wildlife to keep clear. Trials are being conducted in France to see if it works with greater horseshoe bats.

VOLUNTARY ASSOCIATIONS

There is now a widespread groundswell of public support in favour of conserving wildlife or at least preventing its loss as a result of careless indifference. There is a lot of public sympathy for the various conservation organisations involved, and so there should be in a relatively affluent and civilised country like Britain. We spend huge amounts on supporting our historic and artistic heritage in this country; exactly the same justifications should apply to conserving our natural heritage too. We have major organisations devoted to protection of the environment and its associated biodiversity. The National Trust, for example, now has over 5 million members and, despite its focus on stately homes, is actually responsible for more farms and countryside than any other charity or private landowner. Our 47 county wildlife trusts have more members than any political party and the RSPB, with a million members, now embraces a broad approach to wildlife and not just birds. Smaller charities also make an important contribution, both to plant and animal species and to the wider environment. Increasingly, charities are realising that the hedgehog is a near-perfect tool for engaging with the public, resulting in a proliferation of hedgehog-related campaigns and policies. The same applies to businesses: in 2017, the trade newspaper of Waitrose supermarkets advertised their new 'breadhogs' (loaves vaguely resembling hedgehogs), designed to appeal and catch the eye of shoppers sympathetic towards these animals.

Hedgehogs will benefit from all of these developments, but crucially they also have specific support from the British Hedgehog Preservation Society (BHPS), evident in many earlier chapters of this book. The BHPS has its origins in 1982 when Major Adrian Coles, formerly of the SAS and Shropshire County Council, rescued a hedgehog that had become trapped in the cattle grid on his drive. It would never have escaped without help and faced death by starvation. Following this incident, he launched a successful campaign to have ramps installed in every cattle grid in his county, later extended nationwide. The ramps would enable any trapped animals, including hedgehogs, to climb out safely. 'Major Hedgehog' became highly instrumental in raising the profile of hedgehogs. A frequent guest on radio, he was made an MBE and a Freeman of the City of London for services to the community. He died in March 2017, aged 86 (Fig. 265).

Adrian Coles was not the first to suggest fitting escape ramps to cattle grids, but he succeeded in encouraging other county councils to follow suit and generated a massive response via the media. He ran the BHPS initially from his own home to encourage and give advice on the care of hedgehogs and to foster children's interest in these animals. His initiative has been carried forward with endless enthusiasm and ingenuity for more than a decade by Fay Vass, who

FIG 265. Adrian Coles, founder of the BHPS, became a Chelsea Pensioner, here appearing in support of Hedgehog Street at the Royal Horticultural Society's Hampton Court flower show in 2014.

has organised publicity events and two national conferences on the hedgehog. The Society has about 11,000 members and its office supports a sales operation, with a changing stock of inventive and popular hedgehog-themed merchandise. It issues newsletters and also keeps a close watch on hedgehogs in the media, now expanded to include Twitter and Facebook (with nearly 42,000 and 165,000 followers respectively). BHPS provides specialist help for individual hedgehog carers where necessary. It supports education projects and has been hugely effective in raising the profile of this species by creating 'Hedgehog Awareness Week' in early summer. It has pursued campaigns to reduce litter that is harmful to animals and won a long battle with McDonald's to get their packaging changed so that hedgehogs would not get their heads stuck in discarded containers when seeking to benefit from the food remains they contain. In 2015, BHPS pressed successfully for similar changes to the packaging for milkshakes used by Kentucky Fried Chicken outlets, reducing the threat to hedgehogs and including an embossed warning that 'litter harms wildlife'. Another campaign sought to reduce the huge number of elastic bands discarded by postmen on their rounds, creating frequent welfare problems for pets and wildlife that eat them and ugly cases of entanglement involving hedgehogs. Self-adhesive labels have been issued to buyers and users of strimmers and mowing machines, urging their careful use to avoid injury to hedgehogs. The BHPS has also supported several major research projects and many smaller ones, including some of my own.

But newsletters and publicity are not enough. The BHPS Trustees have recognised that there is only so much that can be achieved from an office. What hedgehogs need is a lot of focused support on the ground. In 2015, a decision was taken to fund a full-time 'Hedgehog Officer', Simon Thompson, attached to the Warwickshire Wildlife Trust. The role would entail reaching out to schools to highlight the hedgehog and the strong wildlife conservation messages that go with it. There would also be attempts made to establish 'Hedgehog Improvement Areas', where landowners and householders would be visited personally to encourage hedgehog support on the ground. There were over 150 applicants for the job and the project gained sufficient attention that it was even reported appreciatively in *The Wall Street Journal*. Reaching out to the local people, especially via schools, was sufficiently successful that the project was extended to include funds for a second person. Another full-time employee with a similar brief was funded in 2016 to be based with the Suffolk Wildlife Trust. This too attracted a large number of applicants, from Britain and abroad, although the associated press coverage tended to highlight the salary rather than the human and hedgehog issues involved. Meanwhile, the PTES had engaged Henry Johnson as their first full-time 'Hedgehog Officer', tasked with promoting the hedgehog's interests nationally to considerable effect (see Fig. 261).

It may seem eccentric and perhaps old-fashioned to focus on just one species and many professional ecologists would argue that wildlife conservation needs to have a broader approach. However, the hedgehog is a familiar animal to which many important ecological principles and conservation messages can be attached. It is also a popular creature that elicits sympathy and virtually no hostility. It is an ideal flagship species to carry forward important ecological and conservation principles to a broad public and encourage ordinary people to become involved with wildlife in their own personal environment. Moreover, what is beneficial to hedgehogs on the ground is also good for a wide range of other species to which most people would never give a thought.

Like the hedgehog itself, the BHPS has a slightly quirky feel about it, but membership is not expensive and makes a nice birthday gift for children. Its worthy aims have also struck a chord with many people who have left generous legacies to support hedgehogs and the wildlife conservation principles that are associated with them. Legacies to charities are tax free, so they enable people to give some of their money to support good causes instead of losing it to the Treasury as Inheritance Tax ('death duties'). That way one can steer funds towards worthy projects rather than having it taken as tax and then used for general government expenditure. This principle has been enormously effective in supporting wildlife in recent decades and has inspired many to leave generous legacies for conservation charities that have often achieved far more than the benefactor could ever have imagined in their lifetime.

Among the donors was Dilys Breese, a renowned television and radio producer for the BBC Natural History Unit. She was responsible for many popular radio and TV programmes (some of which involved me too) and in 1982 she made a film called *The Great Hedgehog Mystery* that attracted an extraordinarily large number of viewers, over 12 million when it was first broadcast (more than watched 'Match of the Day', the BBC's leading sports programme at that time). The programme's success boosted both her professional status and her own fondness for hedgehogs. When she died in 2007, Dilys left a substantial legacy which provided the vital foundation for BHPS and PTES to develop the joint project 'Hedgehog Street' which has been so successful in engaging interest in supporting many practical activities that benefit hedgehogs.

HEDGEHOG STREET AND MAKING HEDGEHOG-FRIENDLY NEIGHBOURHOODS

'Hedgehog Street' (www.hedgehogstreet.org) was launched on the BBC's 'Springwatch' broadcast in June 2011 to become a focus for a strategy to help the declining hedgehog population, specifically in gardens and suburban habitats. Hopefully, it would also have community benefits by drawing neighbours together in sharing a street-wide strategy for wildlife. A resource pack was produced that included instructions on what to do to help hedgehogs and within a year 20,000 of these had been distributed.

There are said to be 23 million gardens in Britain, an area equivalent to the size of Suffolk. Gardens are one of the key habitats for hedgehogs, so a

FIG 266. The author, appearing in support of Hedgehog Street at the Royal Horticultural Society's Hampton Court flower show in 2014.

FIG 267. The award-winning hedgehog garden designed by Tracey Foster for the Royal Horticultural Society's Hampton Court flower show in 2014.

strategic focus on them is essential. So it was also decided to invest in having a presence at the Royal Horticultural Society's 2014 Hampton Court Flower Show, a venue second only to the Chelsea Flower Show in national prominence among gardeners. A specialist designer, Tracey Foster, was engaged to create a demonstration garden featuring good things for hedgehogs that could also be aesthetically pleasing (Fig. 267). The result was something novel and appealing. The garden won a Gold Medal and 'best of show' awards, gaining massive publicity for hedgehogs and the practical ways in which gardeners could help them. The idea was also taken up by Harlow Carr Gardens in Yorkshire, where they created a semi-permanent exhibit with a similar theme that is likely to be seen by up to 400,000 visitors a year.

The power of modern communications systems is such that it is now possible to reach out to far more people than in the past. Effective use of this opportunity enabled Hedgehog Street to recruit over 47,000 'Hedgehog Champions' by the end of 2017, all committed to doing something positive to benefit local hedgehog populations. The suggested actions are based upon research and practical experience, with free downloadable resources now available online for registered users, with forums and photo galleries to encourage the sharing of experiences. Many householders already put out food for wildlife, but advice is available on what sort of food is best and what might be the benefits to hedgehogs. It is also essential to create 'Hedgehog Highways', linking gardens and increasing access to wider areas of habitat (Fig. 268). Winter and summer nest sites are important too, and understanding what the hedgehog needs enables gardeners to provide nesting opportunities at minimal cost.

FIG 268. Hedgehog Highways, holes in fences that link gardens and other open spaces, allow access to the larger areas that the animals need. A concrete block, pipe or brick tunnel reduces the headroom so that most longer-legged animals like cats, dogs and foxes are excluded. Over 9,000 gardens have now been linked in this way

Special nest boxes can be purchased or constructed and 4,000 of them were installed in response to encouragement from 'Hedgehog Street'. The dangers of setting light to bonfires can be highlighted and also the need to build an escape route from the garden pond (Fig. 269). There are ideas for the safe control of slugs, where gardeners feel they are a serious problem. These are all practical suggestions for ways of alleviating the threats described in earlier chapters of this book. They can do no harm and might significantly benefit hedgehogs, and probably other species too. An independent survey (conducted by *BBC Gardeners' World* magazine) revealed that 60 per cent of their readers had already done something in their garden to help hedgehogs: 36 per cent avoided using slug

FIG 269. A simple escape ramp in the garden pond (or swimming pool) will save hedgehogs from drowning if they fall in. Cheaper still, a piece of chicken wire will help the animals to climb out.

FIG 270. Offering food to hedgehogs within a wire shelter or underneath a low covering will reduce access for longer-legged animals like foxes and dogs. Hedgehogs access this one via a concrete block tunnel (visible at the back) that excludes cats and magpies.

pellets, 34 per cent retained leaves and twigs for nesting, 26 per cent checked for hedgehogs before using a strimmer and 21 per cent checked before lighting bonfires. The message is getting through!

Particularly important has been getting the message across about habitat continuity. Most gardens are far too small to support even one hedgehog; they need access to others. The campaign to encourage householders to make small openings in their fences to permit hedgehogs to move more freely through a fragmented urban area has been very successful. Over 9,000 gardens have now been linked via these special Hedgehog Highways created by householders. The idea has been met with some wariness because fences are meant to keep things out and maintain exclusivity. Allowing access to hedgehogs might encourage unwanted dogs into the precious flowerbeds or allow the neighbour's cat to enter and threaten one's garden birds. Again, practical advice is available and the use of bricks or a concrete block to convert the hedgehog-sized hole into a tunnel will exclude most unwanted visitors. Food can be offered inside an enclosed feeding station to which animals larger than hedgehogs cannot easily gain access (Fig. 270). These are all direct actions that cost little, do no harm and may go a long way towards helping hedgehogs to survive in an urban setting. Ideas can also make people think and just thinking helps to awaken more ideas and perceptions that enable people to make better gardens, benefitting both themselves and the various creatures that share the same home (Bourne, 2017).

In addition to privately owned gardens, hedgehogs also benefit from access to thousands of hectares of parks, cemeteries, allotments and other forms of public amenity land. The PTES has reached out to the managers of these vital areas by offering courses (21 so far) advising on steps that help support existing hedgehog populations and also avoid accidental loss through unwitting, but harmful, land management practices.

FIG 271. A line of new houses linked with garages prevents hedgehogs travelling between the rear garden, and front gardens or crossing the road to open country on the other side. When planning new housing estates, it would cost little to incorporate more hedgehog-friendly features, especially gaps in fences and between houses.

More strategically, and especially as we begin a massive national increase in housebuilding, developers are being urged to take account of hedgehogs in areas scheduled for new housing by avoiding unnecessary destruction of nesting or foraging areas. Some developers (like Barratt/Kingsbrook) are including in their plans as many supportive features as possible (Fig. 271). Several of the biggest house-builder companies have promised to install and label Hedgehog Highways in new housing developments as they take shape. The challenge is to demonstrate that hedgehog-friendly homes are attractive (or at least have a neutral impact) for prospective buyers. But the power of the 'hedgehog brand' should not be underestimated and these features should also improve the appeal (and value) of the new homes!

Enthusiasm for hedgehogs is not confined to Britain (Fig. 272). In Germany, the volunteer network 'Pro Igel' ('for the hedgehog' – www.pro-igel.de) founded in 1996 continues to publish a regular newsletter for carers and well-wishers in the country. It has a counterpart in Switzerland and, as in Britain, these groups are driven by a concern for hedgehogs among the public and a wide range of non-professional biologists. More formally, there is also a European Hedgehog Research Group (EHRG), a collection of researchers from across Europe. They first met in Arendal, Norway, in 1996 at an event organised by Beate Johansen, with seven subsequent meetings in other countries. The EHRG

FIG 272. Hedgehogs are popular in other countries too, enough to feature on special editions of postage stamps.

is now administered by the PTES via a Google Group. As of April 2017, it included 66 members and will re-form as personnel change, meeting whenever there are enough researchers wanting to do so. These activities and others foster the exchange of ideas about studying and supporting hedgehogs, helping to maintain a high profile for this species and slowly enhance our understanding of its biology and conservation needs.

HEDGEHOGS AND EVERYDAY TECHNOLOGY

One slightly worrying technical development is the availability of devices that emit ultrasonic sound pulses to deter or scare off unwanted animals like rats, cats or moles. It would be a shame if people were to make an effort to ensure their garden was hedgehog-friendly and then deploy a machine to deter cats which also scares away hedgehogs. There is nothing special about ultrasonics, they are simply sounds that are too high-pitched for humans to hear, so they do not trouble us or the neighbours. But they are within the hearing range of certain other mammals (bats, for example) and could be upsetting hedgehogs. Alternatively, animals may learn to ignore them as they often do with other loud sounds. Or the ultrasonic devices may not actually work at all. There used to be a cheap ultrasonic whistle available that could be fitted to car bumpers ostensibly to warn hedgehogs of an approaching vehicle, but cars are noisy and well lit at night, so their approach hardly needs advertising ultrasonically. The one I purchased would not emit any useful sounds at all.

I am sceptical about the efficacy of ultrasonic deterrents. They are widely available, but only one ('Catwatch') is advertised as having been scientifically tested, resulting in endorsement from the RSPB. It emits pulses of sound at 21–25 kHz, a frequency that is probably within the ability of *Erinaceus europaeus* to hear, as other hedgehog species have been reported reacting to much higher frequencies than this (Reeve, 1994). To me, the scientific tests of that machine's effect in deterring cats appear less than compelling, although the results were mostly statistically significant using F-tests of association (Nelson *et al.*, 2006). Maybe 'Catwatch' has no effect on hedgehogs and there is nothing to worry about, but the manufacturers confirm their device has not been tested on hedgehogs to make sure that they are not distressed or put off visiting a garden. However, they do point out that 'Catwatch' does not actually cause harm to anything, merely discomfort. They say that nobody has ever reported adverse effects on hedgehogs, but also admit that nobody has been asked that question either. Thousands of units have been sold in a decade and one person wrote in

2016 to say that hedgehogs appeared to be unaffected. The 'Catwatch' device only operates when it is triggered and the sensor is intended to be set 25 cm off the ground, a height at which a hedgehog should pass by undetected, although it may be picked up if it is further away. However, there are other ultrasonic emitters available on the market, including some that are allegedly tuned to annoy foxes and other mammals. It appears unlikely that their effect on hedgehogs has been fully investigated (Fig. 273).

Trail cameras capable of automatically detecting and photographing or filming hedgehogs in the dark are another technological device that has become sufficiently inexpensive for almost anyone to buy and use. They can be set up to record visits to a food bowl, for example, or study interactions between marked hedgehogs and monitor their dominance hierarchies. They enable simple food choice experiments to be devised and recorded far more efficiently than in the past. People can exchange digital images as email attachments or post video clips (via www.youtube.com/user/HedgehogStreet) showing interactions with owls, badgers or cats, sharing unusual events that have rarely (if ever) been recorded in the formal scientific literature. On that website you can watch a brilliant clip

FIG 273. Various ultrasonic 'scarers' are available on the market. They are intended for use by people who wish to deter cats or other undesirable animals from visiting their garden and posing a threat to birds that are benefitting from the presence of a bird table. Other scarers are supposed to ward off moles that spoil the lawn. It would be a pity if these devices also scared off hedgehogs, undermining efforts to create hedgehog-friendly gardens.

of a hedgehog going upstairs and more observations are bound to be posted as trail cameras become even more widely available. All this not only adds to our knowledge of hedgehogs, but also gives people a lot of fun and engages active interest in ways that could not have been foreseen previously and have not yet been fully explored.

The internet fosters a rapid exchange of ideas in a way that completely dwarfs our efforts to engage with enthusiastic volunteers in the past. Unfortunately it also enables immediate dissemination of muddled thinking and 'fake news', and not just about hedgehogs. We face a tidal wave of information on the internet and there is an evolving social need for us all to become more skilled at assessing it with a critical eye. As an example, for several months in 2017 the hedgehog issue most frequently raised with me was the dire need to stop feeding them mealworms. I would ask why, and the usual answer was 'because it's on the internet'. I would point out that mealworms are actually beetle larvae, one of the main categories of natural food for hedgehogs, so what's the problem? So far as I can make out, the story is to do with the ratio of calcium to phosphorus in an animal's diet. Too much of the latter compromises accumulation of calcium in bones. The experimental evidence (where it exists) seems to be based on racehorses and other species, not hedgehogs. Some circumstantial evidence linking the issue with hedgehogs appears on various internet forums, but without giving sample sizes or providing any data or concrete evidence that mealworms were the problem and not something else (inbreeding or parasite infections, for example). So a whole scare story has been created and retweeted among thousands of people with the hedgehog's welfare at heart, but without anyone questioning its validity. Maybe there is some truth in the story, but we don't actually know. Meanwhile it's all over everywhere as fact.

It is worth remembering that wild hedgehogs feed on a wide variety of things, not just mealworms, so they may still enjoy a balanced diet overall just as we might, despite sneakily eating a cream cake or packet of crisps. Obviously it would be unwise to feed hedgehogs only on mealworms, just as it is unwise for humans to be fed solely on pizzas or Mars bars, no matter how delicious those things are. But what's wrong with a few mealworms being offered? They are not poisonous. If they really did cause some sort of disruption to the normal way that hedgehogs grow their bones, it is unlikely the effects would become evident until after months (maybe years) of excessive consumption. Is that likely if they have access to all the other sources of food locally? Moreover, is it not strange that mealworms are still sold in large quantities by the RSPB? Why are they a danger to hedgehogs but not robins? Why has nobody asked? Maybe there are answers to these questions; maybe there really is a problem. Who knows, but suppose there isn't a problem after all. Thousands of people will have been upset by the thought that they have been wilfully harming their hedgehogs and a perfectly normal element of a hedgehog's natural diet (beetle larvae) will have been needlessly demonised. We all need to be more questioning about information fed to us via the internet and not thoughtlessly pass it on without questioning its validity. We should routinely ignore unsubstantiated information and insist upon supportive data, whether the issue relates to hedgehogs or anything else.

A more positive development is that websites can provide suggestions for hedgehog conservation and ideas for garden improvements, but also reach out to the broader public in ways that were simply not possible in the past. The BHPS website (www.britishhedgehogs.org.uk) had 44,693 visitors in just the first three months of 2017. Websites and the internet now offer opportunities for public engagement, suggesting how people can contribute to the growing bank of information about hedgehogs. One such project is The BIG Hedgehog Map (bighedgehogmap.org) launched in 2014. Over 13,000 hedgehogs were logged on to a distribution map within a few months. This contrasts with the 25 years it took to gather fewer than 7,000 records for the first national atlas of British mammals (Arnold, 1993). Since the RSPB's Big Garden Birdwatch started accepting hedgehog sightings, thousands of new records have been added to our distribution map, which had logged 18,000 records by late 2017. Over 5,000 people have also signed up to help with a study to find out what types of artificial nest boxes are best for hedgehogs and how often they are used. It would be impossible to gather sufficient data by traditional methods, but the internet enables real information to be gathered to answer important questions like these.

The success of these and other web-based projects shows the value of what is now termed 'Citizen Science', where ordinary people can join in wildlife studies and their sheer numbers overwhelm all previous efforts, more than compensating for the relatively low incidence of minor inaccuracies that may get included. It is this kind of public support that has been so important in projects such as the Mammals on Roads and Living with Mammals surveys run by the PTES that have done so much to consolidate anecdotal information and opinions into quantified facts. Another good example is the PTES Hibernation Survey (2013–15), where around 6,000 volunteers recorded hedgehog sightings during the active season for three consecutive years, to investigate potential changes in phenology due to climate change. More than 100,000 individual records were submitted over this period – a volume of data that would have been unthinkable in pre-internet times. But there is much that we still do not know especially about the details of how hedgehogs use different types of habitat, including urban areas, and how best to support them in arable farmland. Effective conservation of hedgehogs needs to be based upon a proper understanding of their ecology and several important new research projects are under way, at the time of writing.

The sheer volume of information gained from Citizen Science projects, and the implied commitment of so many people, has forced politicians and local officials to take hedgehogs much more seriously than they might otherwise have done. There are also many separate lines of discussion in progress on Twitter and Facebook, again testifying to widespread public interest and support. Some of these offer helpful ways of gathering and exchanging useful observations and research data (e.g. www.facebook.com/HedgehogResearch). Sadly, others seem more interested in bickering, but that is a widespread and chronic problem with the modern internet and not confined to hedgehog supporters.

CONCLUSION

Hedgehogs have had a long association with humans, extending back to ancient Egypt and beyond. At times they have been viewed unfavourably, but for most people the hedgehog is an engaging and interesting species. In recent years, it has ousted the badger, dolphin and red squirrel from heading the list of the most popular British mammals. This is important because strong public support makes it an ideal flagship species for encouraging public acceptance of nature conservation principles, particularly in the urban environment. The hedgehog is a valuable bioindicator species, attesting to the viability of ecosystems. Their presence is indicative of sustainable populations of important invertebrates, especially earthworms and the many insects whose larvae and adults perform vital ecological functions. If hedgehogs are present and correct, then all is well. If they are declining or absent, something has gone wrong and we would do well to find out why, for our own sake as well as that of the hedgehog. Through the internet and other modern technology, hedgehogs offer exciting opportunities to engage with Citizen Science projects and practical conservation measures that deepen and broaden public understanding of our precious environment. Hedgehogs have widespread appeal and few detractors, as they do little significant harm and play a useful role in controlling invertebrate pests in gardens and farmland. They are now strongly supported by wildlife charities, especially the BHPS and PTES through the 'Hedgehog Street' initiative, which has successfully engaged the active interest of tens of thousands of ordinary people. This also benefits many less charismatic species and provides a source of interest and satisfaction for the people involved. Public support may be crucial for the long-term survival of the hedgehog, as its declining population faces many modern threats that will need a lot of human assistance to overcome. As *The Times* editorial thundered (29 July 2017), 'Their plight should prick the conscience of the Nation.'

Surveying for Hedgehogs

THE NEED FOR SURVEYS

Gardeners, and perhaps householders moving into a new home, will want to know if hedgehogs are present. Professional ecological surveyors and consultants will also need to know if hedgehogs are living on proposed development sites or in areas scheduled for road widening and other infrastructure construction and improvements. Nationally, we need to have a better idea of exactly where our remaining wildlife lives. We can't protect things if we don't know where they are.

When looking for evidence of hedgehogs, remember that it is a hibernator (at least from October to April). Choose your survey time accordingly. They are also nocturnal and unlikely to be seen during the day. Hedgehogs live at a relatively low population density (about 1 per ha in good habitat), so evidence of their presence will be scarce even in favoured nesting and feeding sites. They are unlikely to be found in extensive conifer woodlands, heathland and moorland, but may well occur around the edges of such sites. Many suitable places are small and cut off by impenetrable fencing or other barriers. Wide roads and expansive arable areas are likely to restrict hedgehog movements and may leave some patches of potential habitat unoccupied. Hedgehogs are most likely to be found in the mosaic of varied habitats around the urban fringe, but also in areas of lowland grassland, woodland margins and mixed farmland. Within urban areas, large gardens (especially of long-established houses) are favoured, with parks, cemeteries, allotments and neglected wasteland often supporting a population nucleus that extends into neighbouring sites. Critically, there needs to be abundant food available (especially macroinvertebrates such as worms and beetles) and undisturbed areas suitable for the construction of winter nests (See Chapter 6). A lack of deciduous trees or sheltering supportive structures (bushes, logpiles or other structures where nests could be made underneath) may mean hedgehogs are absent too, but presence of such features is not proof that hedgehogs live there.

There are various ways of seeking signs of hedgehog presence but experience suggests that no single method can be guaranteed to detect the animals (Haigh *et al.*, 2012a). A combination of techniques should be employed before deciding that hedgehogs are absent from an apparently suitable area of habitat. There are various ways of detecting the presence of hedgehogs:

Asking local people

This is one of the easiest and quickest ways of establishing the presence of hedgehogs, although negative results should not be taken as proof of absence. People take notice when they see road casualties or the animals visit their garden. Unlike with many species, casual observations are generally reliable, as misidentification is unlikely. Asking people if they have seen hedgehogs, dead or alive, can be done verbally face to face or via local newspapers, radio stations and the internet.

Roadkills

These are often the only indication of presence. Flattened, sun-dried corpses are very resilient and can remain identifiable for several weeks, especially in dry weather. Hedgehog remains are visible for longer than in many species, but there is no way of directly relating numbers of hedgehogs killed to actual numbers alive, but the more that are seen dead the more there are likely to be still alive locally. Hedgehog roadkills are not simply a reflection of traffic density.

Searching for hedgehogs at night

Hedgehogs are most numerous in September and especially active during periods of warm, moist weather. Searching with a spotlight is a useful means of confirming their presence and also a method for attempting estimates of abundance. A powerful lamp is needed, scanning the ground to either side as the observer walks slowly forwards, pausing occasionally to listen for rustling noises in leaf litter. However the use of 'dazzling lights' to seek Schedule 6 species (like the hedgehog) may be technically illegal, so it might be wise to obtain a licence (from Natural England or its counterpart in Wales or Scotland) before undertaking lengthy surveys.

Searches are most successful in short grass habitats or along linear features such as rural lanes or woodland rides. Extensive open areas are best surveyed using a line of searchers 10 m apart. Single observers normally walk a straight line transect, which offers the prospect of using Distance Sampling methodology to estimate abundance (numbers per hectare; see Chapter 10). The normal encounter rates (often less than one per hour of searching unless whole families are found) mean that transects need to be replicated and at least 1 km long for consistent or statistically reliable results. Dogs are often good at finding hedgehogs and may be enlisted to considerable benefit. However, professional surveyors should note that anti-hunting legislation prohibits using dogs to trail mammals and may apply to their use for surveys, although that possibility has not been tested in court.

Faeces

Their droppings are often the first indication that nocturnal hedgehogs are present (Fig. 279). Hedgehog's faeces are as thick as a human finger and about 30–50 mm long. They are usually dark in colour, rather crinkly and not straight or smooth. They are studded with fragments of beetles or 'body rings' from millipedes, whereas cat and dog faecal pellets are normally a uniform texture. Fox droppings are usually larger, grey and mostly formed of fur and fragments of bone. They often include pips and seeds from fruits in late summer that hedgehogs are unlikely to have eaten. Fur and bone are not normally present in hedgehog droppings and do not form their main component. Hedgehog droppings are normally found singly, not in latrines or clusters, and are easiest to see in short grass such as garden lawns.

Trapping

Trapping hedgehogs requires a licence (see https://www.gov.uk/guidance/wildlife-licences) and must include checking traps twice daily (dawn and dusk). Cage traps are best set under cover along linear features such as hedges and walls. They are likely to be most effective at gaps where animals pass through. Meat-based dog food, sausage meat or rabbit viscera make the best bait. Catch rate is low, so plenty of traps are needed and incidental capture of rats and birds is frequent, as is disturbance by inquisitive dogs and cattle. Trapping is unlikely to be a cost-effective way of demonstrating presence.

Tracks and trails

Other signs include distinctive five-toed footprints, although these are unlikely to be visible in anything other than very smooth and soft mud. They could easily be confused with tracks of other animals, especially squirrels and perhaps mink or polecats.

Tracking tunnels

These have a specially inked tray and a paper sheet on which animals leave footprints as they pass through (Fig. 279). Details, including specimen footprints to aid identification, are available (see: https://ptes.org/wp-content/uploads/2015/06/Guidance-for-detecting-hedgehogs-using-tracking-tunnels.pdf). Hedgehogs live at low population densities, so there is little point in using only one tunnel. Batches are necessary to ensure a reasonable chance of success, adding to the cost, although they are not expensive to make or buy. Research indicates that if ten baited tunnels are set out in a 1 km line for five consecutive nights, this should be sufficient to offer a 95 per cent probability of detecting hedgehogs if they are present. Some bait may encourage hedgehogs to visit, although it also

FIG 279. Tracking tunnels have a tray that slides inside with some bait added about half way along. Any visiting hedgehog will walk on an ink pad at either end (green in this picture) and leave distinctive footprints on a sheet of paper that is shielded from the rain inside the tunnel. Tunnels are most effective if set along linear features like hedgerows or the borders of garden flower beds.

attracts foxes and badgers that steal the bait and may destroy the tunnel. Footprint tunnels are now used extensively when surveys are needed to establish presence and relative numbers. Tunnels seem to be more effective and reliable than night-time searches by torchlight, as they help to overcome the problem of non-detection, where hedgehogs are actually present but not seen (Yarnell *et al.*, 2014). They also remove the need to work at night, often a significant practical advantage. However, like trapping, there is a considerable element of skill (and luck!) involved in selecting sites for tracking tunnels and failure to detect hedgehogs is not proof of their absence.

Trail cameras

These record images or video sequences in response to movements within their field of view. They are relatively costly and liable to be stolen if left in public places, but are particularly suitable for monitoring baiting points in private gardens or secluded locations. They must be set away from leaves and vegetation that move in the wind, otherwise there will be multiple false triggerings (wasting battery life). Comparison websites such as www.besttrailcamerareviews.org/ or www.trailcameralab.com/ will indicate what features are available. Hedgehogs are best detected using video clips rather than single-shot operation, but the latter will conserve battery life.

Thermal imaging
Heat-sensitive cameras, as used in mountain rescue and in searching for victims after earthquakes, are very expensive. However, costs are falling rapidly and an add-on device for mobile phones is already available (www.wired.com/2014/10/seek-thermal-infrared-camera-iphone-android/ for example).

Nest searches
Summer nests are insubstantial and searching for them is unlikely to be fruitful unless a trained dog is available. Winter nests are more distinctive (See Chapter 6), but a dog is less likely to find one if the hedgehog inside is hibernating owing to the shutdown of its body systems, reducing scent and heat emissions. A visual search of low shrubby vegetation (<1 m high) might be successful, but this will be a time-consuming activity that is unlikely to find all of the animals present except where hedgehogs may congregate (due to lack of alternative nesting sites locally), or in a very small area that can be subjected to a fingertip search.

Environmental DNA
This is a promising new technique for detecting certain species. It is based on locating and identifying traces of species-specific DNA in the environment where they live. This seems to work for great-crested newts, whose DNA can be isolated from samples of the water that they inhabit. The difficulty with using the method for non-aquatic species is to decide where to take the environmental samples. Hedgehogs do not urinate in particular places, and sampling a whole field on the off chance of finding their urine (or scent or other organic residues) seems very hit-and-miss, with a high probability of failing to detect the animals. An experienced fieldworker might identify key places where hedgehogs would go, under a fence, for example, or around a baiting point, increasing the probability of their detection. However, the techniques described above probably offer better prospects of speedy and unambiguous success.

CONCLUSION

Practical experience comparing some of these techniques was reported by Amy Haigh and colleagues (Haigh *et al.*, 2012a). They obtained only a 40 per cent response to a widely publicised questionnaire survey and their footprint tunnels (620 tunnel/nights) mostly detected other species, while traps and thermal imaging detected nothing. Spotlighting proved to be the most fruitful technique (53 hours spread over 23 nights). On average, hedgehogs were detected within 4 nights using this method, whereas it took 48 nights for tracking tunnels to indicate their presence. My own experience and that of my students also indicates that finding hedgehogs is difficult. The best technique we have found so far has been to borrow sexually active male hedgehogs from a care centre and follow them by radio-tracking until they locate the local females, often rather quickly. However, this technique is not always a very practical option.

Marking hedgehogs

Passive implanted transponders ('PIT tags') lodged under the skin are often used to permanently mark pets and laboratory animals. They can be used on hedgehogs too, although they are not cheap and some training or veterinary supervision would be appropriate. PIT tags have the advantage of lasting as long as the animal lives, but there is no external sign of their presence and they can only be read by a special device similar to a barcode reader. Tagged animals can therefore only be recognised by the investigator and no recapture information will be obtained as a result of casual encounters by the public. However, automatic loggers can be set up to record when a tagged hedgehog passes by, through a hole in the fence or at a food bowl, for example. This

FIG 280. If spines are to be marked, using heat-shrink tubing, they should be ones near the head or shoulder where they will be clearly visible if the animal rolls up. A cluster is better than a scattering, as groups are easier to notice in the dark. (Nigel Reeve)

offers the prospect of gathering very useful data on hedgehog numbers and movements once the cost of these detectors comes down sufficiently to allow their widespread deployment.

Sometimes it is desirable to mark hedgehogs so that each can be individually recognised visually (in estimates of population density, for example). It is helpful if the mark can be easily seen in the dark or recognised by members of the public, who can then report the animals they have seen. Externally applied tags that incorporate a telephone number or website address (written or printed on) have proved successful, but they need to be glued to the spines and will fall off after a while. The simplest and cheapest way of giving each hedgehog an individually recognisable mark is to apply a patch of paint to the spines in combinations such as 'left hind quarter + right shoulder' (Morris, 2014). Using water-based emulsion paint is quick, cheap and simple, but the paint wears off after a few weeks (or washes off almost immediately if the hedgehog moves about in wet vegetation before the paint dries). Loss of marks makes identification and population estimates unreliable. More permanent marks using car spray paints usually involve a pungent solvent which may well be distressing for the animal. A neater solution (first used by Andy Wroot) is to use heat-shrink tubing with a number written on it in indelible ink (Fig. 280). A short section of the thin polyolefin plastic tube (1.6 mm internal diameter) can be slid over an individual spine and warmed sufficiently to shrink and remain firmly attached. A tiny drip of superglue inside the tube can be used instead. However, the spine may be shed soon, so several have to be tagged for each animal. Different-coloured plastic tubing can be used to aid speedy identification, although this type of marking is not very conspicuous in the dark. Any form of numbered tag must have the number underlined to ensure it cannot be read upside down, misidentifying the animal. Clipping patches of spines will create a distinctive mark that lasts for many months but is difficult to do because the hedgehog's skin is so mobile that what may be intended as a mark on one shoulder can easily end up appearing as a patch on the back or flank when the hedgehog relaxes its skin muscles. Using anaesthetic to facilitate any of these procedures requires a licence unless undertaken by a vet.

References

Anon (1898). A hedgehog with hairs instead of spines. *Natural Science* 13: 156–157.

Anon (1974). Ministry orders hunt for hedgehog. *Veterinary Record* 95: 6.

Anon (1992). *Prickly Poems*. Hutchinson, London.

Allanson, M. (1934). The reproductive processes of certain mammals, part 7: seasonal variations in the reproductive organs of the male hedgehog. *Philosophical Transactions of the Royal Society B* 223: 277–303.

Allanson, M. & Deanesly, R. (1934). The reaction of anoestrous hedgehogs to experimental conditions. *Proceedings of the Royal Society B* 116: 170–185.

Andrews, P. (1990). *Owls, Caves and Fossils.* Natural History Museum Publications, London.

Arnold, H. (1993). *Atlas of Mammals in Britain.* HMSO, London.

Baaker, S. B., Oretti, T. M., Oesch, R. B., Hazoul, J. G., Brist, M. K. O. & Bontadina, F. B. (2014). Assessing habitat connectivity for ground-dwelling animals in an urban environment. *Ecological Applications* 24: 1583–1595.

Barnes, E. (2017). To what extent are veterinary practices prepared to treat wildlife patients? *The Plymouth Student Scientist* 10: 1–21.

Barnes, E. & Farnworth, M. J. (2017). Perceptions of responsibility and capability for treating wildlife casualties in UK veterinary practices. *Veterinary Record* 180: 197.

Barrett-Hamilton, G. E. H. & Hinton, M. A. C. (1910). *British Mammals.* Gurney & Jackson, London.

Bean, C. (1982). Seeing animals in odd situations. *Countryside Monthly*, August: 397–398.

Becher, S. A. & Griffiths, R. (1998). Genetic differentiation among local populations of the European hedgehog *Erinaceus europaeus* in mosaic habitats. *Molecular Ecology* 7: 1599–1604.

Bell, T. (1874). *A History of British Quadrupeds: including the Cetacea*, Van Voorst, London.

Berry, R.J. (1985). *The Natural History of Orkney.* Collins, London.

Berthoud, G. (1982). *Contribution à la biologie du hérisson (Erinaceus europaeus L.) et applications à sa protection.* PhD Thesis, Faculté des Sciences, Université de Neuchâtel, Yverdon-les-Bains.

Bolfíková B. & Hulva P. (2012). Microevolution of sympatry: landscape genetics of hedgehogs *Erinaceus europaeus* and *E. roumanicus* in Central Europe. *Heredity* 108: 248–255.

Bomford, L. (1979). *Secret Life of the Hedgehog.* Hamlyn, London.

Bourne, V. (2017). *The Living Jigsaw: the secret life in your garden.* Royal Botanic Gardens, Kew.

Boys Smith J. S. (1967). Behaviour of a hedgehog *Erinaceus europaeus. Journal of Zoology*, London 153: 564–566.

Bright, P. W., Balmforth, Z. & MacPherson, J. (2015). The effects of changes in traffic flow on mammal road kill counts. *Applied Ecology and Environmental Research* 13: 171–179.

Bright, P. W. & Hof, A. R. (2016). Quantifying the long-term decline of the West European hedgehog in England by sub sampling citizen-science datasets. *European Journal of Wildlife Research* 62: 407–413.

Brinck, P. & Lofqvist, J. (1973). The hedgehog *Erinaceus europaeus* and its flea *Archaeopsylla erinacei. Zoonoses.* Supplement 1: 97–103.

Brockie, R. E. (1960). Road mortality of the hedgehog *Erinaceus europaeus* L. in New Zealand. *Proceedings of the Zoological Society of London* 134: 505–8.

Brockie, R. E. (1964). Dental abnormalities in European and New Zealand hedgehogs. *Nature* 202: 1355–1356.

Brockie, R. E. (1974a). *Studies on the hedgehog in New Zealand.* PhD Thesis, Victoria University, Wellington.

Brockie, R. E. (1974b). The hedgehog mange mite *Caparinia tripilis* in New Zealand. *New Zealand Veterinary Journal* 22: 243–247.

Brockie, R. E. (1976). Self anointing by wild hedgehogs *Erinaceus europaeus* in New Zealand. *Animal Behaviour* 24: 68–71.

Brockie, R. E., Sadleir, R. M. F. S. & Linklater, W. L. (2009). Long-term wildlife road-kill counts in New Zealand. *New Zealand Journal of Zoology* 36: 123–134.

Brodie, E. D. (1977). Hedgehogs use toad venom in their own defence. *Nature* 268: 627–628.

Buckland, F. (1883). *Curiosities of Natural History*, second series. Richard Bentley & Son, London.

Buckland, S. T., Anderson, D. R., Burnham, K. P. & Laake, J. L. (1993). *Distance Sampling: Estimating Abundance of Biological Populations.* Chapman & Hall, London.

Buckle, A. P. (1975). *Aspects of the relationship between certain epifaunistic insects and their mammalian hosts.* PhD Thesis, University of London.

Bullen, K. (2010). *Hedgehog rehabilitation.* British Hedgehog Preservation Society, Dhustone, Shropshire.

Bunnell, T. (2001). The incidence of disease and injury in displaced wild hedgehogs *Erinaceus europaeus. Lutra* 44: 3–14.

Bunnell, T. (2002). The assessment of British hedgehog (*Erinaceus europaeus*) casualties on arrival and determination of optimum release weights using a new index. *Journal of wildlife Rehabilitation* 25: 11–21.

Burdon, D. & Reeve, N. (1997). *Brachylaemus erinacei*: preliminary data from Jersey and the need for a European recording, monitoring and treatment programme. Second International workshop of the European Hedgehog Research Group, Vienna (not paginated).

Burton, M. (1957). Hedgehog self-anointing. *Proceedings of the Zoological Society of London* 129: 452–453.

Burton, M. (1969). *The Hedgehog.* Andre Deutsch, London.

Cansdale, G. (1970). *Animals of Bible Lands.* Paternoster Press, Exeter.

Cassini, M. H. & Krebs, J. R. (1994). Behavioural responses to food addition by hedgehogs. *Ecography* 17: 289–296.

Christy, M. (1919). The ancient legend as to the hedgehog carrying fruits on its spines. *Manchester Memoirs* 63: 1–14.

Clark, W. E. Le Gros (1932). The brain of the Insectivora. *Proceedings of the Zoological Society of London* 102: 975–1013.

Clausen, G. & Ersland, A. (1968). The respiratory properties of the blood of the hibernating hedgehog *Erinaceus europaeus* L. *Respiration physiology* 5: 2 to 1–233.

Corcoran, C. J. (1967). A case report. *Veterinary Review* 18: 73.

Cott, H. B. (1951). The palatability of the eggs of birds: illustrated by experiments on the food preferences of the hedgehog (*Erinaceus europaeus*). *Proceedings of the Zoological Society of London* 121: 1–41.

Cresswell, P., Harris, S. & Jefferies, D. J. (1990). *The history, distribution, status and habitat requirements of the badger in Britain.* Nature Conservancy Council, Peterborough.

Croft, S., Chauvenet, A.L.M., Smith, G.C. (2017). A systematic approach to estimate the distribution and total abundance of British mammals. *PLoS ONE* 12(6): e0176339. https://doi.org/10.1371/journal.pone.0176339

Davies, J. L. (1957). A hedgehog road mortality index. *Proceedings of the Zoological Society of London* 128: 606–608.

Davies, N. & Griffith, F. L. (1900). *The Mastaba of Ptahhetep and Akhethetep at Saqquareh.* Memoir 8, Archaeological Survey of Egypt, London.

Deanesly, R. (1934). The reproductive processes of certain mammals, Part 6: the reproductive cycle of the female hedgehog. *Philosophical Transactions of the Royal Society B* 223: 239–276.

D'Have, H. Scheirs, J., Verhagen, R. & De Coen, W. (2005). Gender, age and seasonal dependent self-anointing in the European hedgehog *Erinaceus europaeus. Acta Theriologica* 50: 167–173.

Dickman, C. R. (1988). Age related dietary change in the European hedgehog, *Erinaceus europaeus. Journal of Zoology*, London 215: 1–14.

Dillon, P. (1997). *Mammals in Wiltshire.* Wiltshire Archaeological and Natural History Society, Devizes.

Dimelow, E. J. (1963). Observations on the feeding of the hedgehog (*Erinaceus europaeus* L.). *Proceedings of the Zoological Society of London* 141: 291–309.

Dobson, J. (1999). *The Mammals of Essex.* Lopinga Books, Wimbish.

Doncaster, C. P. (1992). Testing the role of intraguild predation in regulating hedgehog populations. *Proceedings of the Royal Society, London B* 249: 113–117.

Doncaster, C. P. (1993). Influence of predation threat on foraging pattern: the hedgehog's gambit. *Revue d'ecologie-terre et vie* 48: 207–213.

Doncaster, C. P. (1994). Factors regulating local variations in abundance: field tests on hedgehogs *Erinaceus europaeus.* *Oikos* 69: 182–192.

Doncaster, C. P., Rondinini, C. & Johnson P. C. D. (2001). Field test for environmental correlates of dispersal in hedgehogs Erinaceus europaeus. *Journal of Animal Ecology* 70: 30–46.

Dowding, C. V., Harris, S., Poulton, S. & Baker, P. J. (2010). Nocturnal ranging behaviour of urban hedgehogs, *Erinaceus europaeus,* in relation to risk and reward. *Animal Behaviour* 80: 13–21.

Dowding, C. V., Shore, R. F., Worgan, A., Baker, P. J. & Harris, S. (2010). Accumulation of anticoagulant rodenticides in a non-target insectivore, the European hedgehog (*Erinaceus europaeus*). *Environmental Pollution* 158: 161–166.

Edwards, J. T. (1957). The Hedgehog. Ch. 7 in *The UFAW Handbook on the Care and Management of Laboratory Animals* (second edition). Tindall Cox, London.

English, M. P. & Morris. P.A. (1969). *Trichophyton mentagrophytes* var *erinacei* in hedgehog nests. *Sabouraudia* 7: 118–121.

Euman, W. (1979). Hedgehogs and cattle grids. *Scottish Naturalist* 15: 21–22.

Evans, E. P. (1987). *The criminal prosecution and capital punishment of animals.* Faber & Faber, London.

Fairley, J. S. (1975). *An Irish Beast Book.* Blackstaff Press, Belfast.

Fairley, J. (2001). *A Basketful of Weasels.* The Author, Belfast.

Fitter, R. S. R. (1949). Checklist of the mammals, reptiles and amphibia of the London Area, 1900–1949. *The London Naturalist* 28: 98–115.

Fowler, P. A. (1988). Seasonal endocrine cycles in the European hedgehog *Erinaceus europaeus.* *Journal of Reproduction and Fertility* 84: 259–272.

Gemmeke, H. (1995). Untersuchungen über die gefahr der sekundärvergiftung bei igeln (*Erinaceus europaeus* L.) durch metaldehyd-vergiftete ackerschnecken. *Nachrichtchtenblatt Deutscher Pflanzenschutzdienst* 47: 237–240.

George, L. MacPherson, J. L., Balmforth, Z. & Bright, P. W. (2011). Using the dead to monitor the living: can roadkill counts detect trends in mammal abundance? *Applied Ecology and Environmental Research* 9: 27–41.

Gransson, G., Karlsson, J. & Lindren, A. (1976). Road mortality of the hedgehog in Sweden. *Fauna och Flora (Stockholm)* 71: 1–6.

Grist, L. (1983). Sleep and dreaming in the three-toed sloth. *New Scientist* 1383 (10 November): 416

Grogan, A. and Kelly, A. (2013). A review of RSPCA research into wildlife rehabilitation. *The Veterinary Record* 172: 211–214. published online doi: 10.1136/vr.101139.

Groves, D. (2013). *The Mammals of Cornwall and the Isles of Scilly.* Environmental Records Centre, Truro.

Haigh, A. (2011). *The ecology of the hedgehog (Erinaceus europaeus) in rural Ireland.* PhD Thesis, University College Cork.

Haigh, A., Butler, F. & O'Riordan, R. (2012a). An investigation into the techniques for detecting hedgehogs in a rural landscape. *Journal of Negative Results: Ecology and Evolutionary Biology* 9: 15–26.

Haigh, A., O'Riordan, R.M., & Butler, F. (2012b). Nesting behaviour and seasonal body mass changes in a rural Irish population of the Western hedgehog (*Erinaceus europaeus*). *Acta Theriologica* 57: 321–331.

Haigh, A., O'Riordan, R. & Butler, F. (2014a). Hedgehog *Erinaceus europaeus* mortality on Irish roads. *Wildlife Biology* 20: 155–160.

Haigh, A., Kelly, M., Butler, F. & O'Riordan, R. M. (2014b). Non-invasive methods of separating hedgehog (*Erinaceus europaeus*) age classes and an investigation into the age structure of road kill. *Acta Theriologica* 59: 165- 171. doi: 10.1007/s13364-013-0142-0.

Harris, S. (1986). *Urban Foxes.* Whittet Books, London.

Harris, S., Morris, P. A., Wray, S. & Yalden, D. W. (1995). *A review of British mammals: population estimates and conservation status of British mammals other than cetaceans.* Joint Nature Conservation Committee, Peterborough.

Harris, S. & Yalden, D. W. (2008). *Mammals of the British Isles: Handbook* (4th edition). The Mammal Society, Southampton.

Herreid ll, C. F. (1964). Bat longevity and metabolic rate. *Experimental Gerontology* 1: 1 –9.

Herter, K. (1938). *Die Biologie der Europäischen Igel. Monographien der Wildsäugetiere* 5: 1–222.

Herter, K. (1965). *Hedgehogs: a comprehensive study*. Phoenix House, London.

Hill, D. & Robertson, P. (1988). *The Pheasant*. BSP Professional Books, Oxford.

Hof, A. R. & Bright, P. (2009). The value of green spaces in built-up areas for western hedgehogs. *Lutra* 52: 69–82.

Hof, A. R. & Bright, P. W. (2010). The value of agri-environment schemes for macro-invertebrate feeders: hedgehogs on arable farms in Britain. *Animal Conservation* 13: 467–473.

Hof, A. R., Snellenberg, J. & Bright, P.W. (2012). Food or fear? Predation risk mediates edge refuging in an insectivorous mammal. *Animal Behaviour* 83: 1099–1106.

Holsbeek, L., Rodts, J. & Muyldermans, S. (1999). Hedgehog and other animal traffic victims in Belgium: results of a countrywide survey. *Lutra* 42: 111–119.

Hoodless, A. & Morris, P.A. (1993). An estimate of population density of the fat dormouse (*Glis glis*). *Journal of Zoology, London* 230: 337–340.

Hubbard, M. J., Baker, A. S. & Cann, K. J. (1998). Distribution of *Borrelia bergdorferi* s.l. spirochaete DNA in British ticks (Argasidae and Ixodidae) since the 19th century, as assessed by PCR. *Medical and Veterinary Entomology* 12: 89–97.

Hubert, P., Julliard, R., Biagianti, S. & Poulle, M. (2011). Ecological factors driving the higher hedgehog *Erinaceus europaeus* density in an urban area compared to the adjacent rural area. *Landscape and Urban Planning* 103: 34–43.

Huijser, M. P. & Bergers, P. J. M. (2000). The effect of roads and traffic on hedgehog (*Erinaceus europaeus*) populations. *Biological Conservation* 95: 111–116.

Huijser, M. P., Mosler-Berger, C., Olson, M. & Strein, M. (2015).. 'Wildlife warning signs and animal detection systems aimed at reducing wildlife-vehicle collisions' (Chapter 24) in *Handbook of Road Ecology* (ed.) R. van der Ree, D. J. Smith & Grilo, C. Wiley-Blackwell, Oxford.

Hyde-Parker, T. (1940). The hedgehog. *The Naturalist* 785: 291–294.

Jackson, D. B. (2006). The breeding biology of introduced hedgehogs (*Erinaceus europaeus*) on a Scottish Island: lessons for population control and bird conservation. *Journal of Zoology, London* 268: 303–314.

Jackson, D. B. (2007). Factors affecting the abundance of introduced hedgehogs (*Erinaceus europaeus*) to the Hebridean island of South Uist in the absence of natural predators and implications for nesting birds. *Journal of Zoology, London* 271: 210–217.

Jackson, D. B. & Green R. E. (2000). The importance of the introduced hedgehog (*Erinaceus europaeus*) as a predator of the eggs of waders (Charadrii) on Machair in south Uist, Scotland. *Biological Conservation* 93: 333–348.

Jackson, D. B., Fuller, R. J. & Campbell, S. T. (2004). Long-term population changes among breeding shorebirds in the Outer Hebrides, Scotland, in relation to introduced hedgehogs (*Erinaceus europaeus*). *Biological Conservation* 117: 151–166.

Jefferies D. J. & Pendlebury J. B. (1968). Population fluctuations of stoats and weasels and hedgehogs in recent years. *Journal of Zoology, London* 156: 513–517.

Jefferies, D. J., Morris, P.A. & Mulleneux, J.E. (1989). An enquiry into the changing status of the Water Vole *Arvicola terrestris* in Britain. *Mammal Review* 19: 111–131.

Jensen, A. B. (2004). Overwintering of European hedgehogs *Erinaceus europaeus* in a Danish rural area. *Acta Theriologica* 49: 145–155.

Johansson, B. W. (1985). Ventricular repolarisation and fibrillation threshold in hibernating species. *European Heart Journal* 6: 53–62.

Jones, C. & Jackson, D. (2009). A first record of latrine use by European hedgehogs *Erinaceus europaeus*. *Mammalia* 73: 145–147.

Judge, J., Wilson, G. J., Macarthur, McDonald, R. & Delahay, R. J. (2017). Abundance of badgers (*Meles meles*) in England and Wales. *Scientific Reports* 7: Article no. 276, published online doi: 10.1038/s41598-017-00378-3.

Kelsey-Wood, D. (1995). *African Pigmy Hedgehogs*. T.F.H. Publications, Neptune City NJ.

King, C. M. ed. (1990). *The Handbook of New Zealand Mammals*. Oxford University Press, Melbourne.

King, C. M. ed. (2005). *The Handbook of New Zealand Mammals*. (Second Edition). Oxford University Press, Melbourne.

Klingmüller, G. & Sobich, E. (1977). Transmission of human leprosy bacteria to hedgehogs. *Die Naturwissenschaften* 64: 645–646.

Knight, M. (1962). *Hedgehogs*. Sunday Times, London.

Kratochvil, J. (1974). Das stachelkleid des ostigels (*Erinaceus concolor roumanicus*). *Acta Scientiarum Natura, Brno* 11: 1–52.

Kratochvil, J. (1975). Zur kenntnis der igel der gattung *Erinaceus europaeus* in der ČSSR (Insectivora, Mamm.) *Zoologické Listy* 24: 297–312.

Kristiansson, H. (1990). Population variables and causes of mortality in a hedgehog (*Erinaceus europaeus*) population in southern Sweden. *Journal of Zoology, London* 220: 391–404.

Kristoffersson, R. (1971). A note on the age distribution of hedgehogs in Finland. *Annales Zoologici Fennici* 8: 554–557.

Kristoffersson, R. & Soivio, A. (1964a). Hibernation in the hedgehog (*Erinaceus europaeus* L.): The periodicity of hibernation of undisturbed animals during the winter in a constant ambient temperature. *Annales Academiae Scientiarum Fennicae*. no.80: 1–22.

Kristofferson, R. & Soivio, A. (1964b). Hibernation in the hedgehog (*Erinaceus europaeus* L.) Changes of respiratory pattern, heart rate and body temperature in response to gradually decreasing or increasing ambient temperature. *Annales Academiae Scientiarum Fennicae* Series A iv. Biologica 82: 1–17.

Kristoffersson, R. & Suomalainen, P. (1964). Studies on the physiology of the hibernating hedgehog. 2. Changes of body weight of hibernating and non-hibernating animals. *Annales Academiae Scientiarum Fennicae*. 79: 1–11.

Król, E. (1985). Reproductive energy budgets of hedgehogs during lactation. *Zeszyty Naukowe* 48: 105–117.

Kruuk, H. (1964). Predators and anti-predator behaviour of the black-headed gull (*Larus ridibundus* L.). *Behaviour Supplement* 11: 1–129.

Kumar, B. & Nijman, V. (2016). Medicinal uses and trade of Madras hedgehogs *Paraechinus nudiventris* in Tamil Nadu, India. *TRAFFIC Bulletin* 28: 7–10.

Le Sueur, F. (1976). *A Natural History of Jersey*. Phillimore, London.

Lever, C. (2009). *The Naturalized Animals of Britain and Ireland*. New Holland Ltd, London.

Lindeman, W. (1951). Zur psychologie des igels. *Zeitschrift für Tierpsychologie* 8: 224–251.

Lovegrove, R. (2007). *Silent Fields: the long decline of a nation's wildlife*. Oxford University Press, Oxford.

Lucas, A. (1997). *Mammals in Carmarthenshire*. The Author, Llandysul, Ceredigion.

Lydekker, R. (1904). Some ancient mammal portraits. *Nature* 70: 207–209.

Macdonald, D. ed. (2001). *The New Encyclopedia of Mammals*. Oxford University Press, Oxford

Macpherson, H. A. (1892). *A Vertebrate Fauna of Lakeland*. David Douglas, Edinburgh.

MacPherson, D., MacPherson, J. L. & Morris, P. (2011). Rural roads as barriers to the movement of small mammals. *Applied Ecology and Environmental Research* 9: 167–180.

Mader, H-J. (1984). Animal habitat isolation by roads and agricultural fields. *Biological Conservation* 29: 81–96.

Mallon, D., Alston, D. & Whiteley, D. (2012). *The Mammals of Derbyshire*. Derbyshire Mammal Group, Chesterfield.

Massey, C. I. (1972). A study of hedgehog road mortality in the Scarborough district, 1966–1971. *Leeds Naturalist* 922: 103–105.

Micol, T., Doncaster, C. P. & MacKinlay, L. A. (1994). Correlates of local variation in the abundance of hedgehogs *Erinaceus europaeus*. *Journal of Animal Ecology* 63: 851–860.

Milsom, W. K., Zimmer, M. B. & Harris, M. B. (1999). Regulation of cardiac rhythm in hibernating mammals. *Comparative biochemistry and physiology A- molecular and integrative physiology* 124: 383–391.

Mitchell-Jones, A. J., Amori, G., Bogdanowicz, W., Kryštufek, B., Reijnders, F., Spitzenberger, M., Stubbe, M., Thisssen, J. B. M., Vohralik, V. & Zima, J. (1999). *The Atlas of European Mammals*. T&D Poyser, London.

Molony, S. E., Dowding, C. V., Baker, P., Cuthill, I. C. & Harris, S. (2006). The effect of translocation and temporary captivity on wildlife rehabilitation success: An experimental study using European hedgehogs (*Erinaceus europaeus*). *Biological Conservation* 130: 530–537.

Moorhouse, T. P., Palmer, C. F., Travis, M. J. & Macdonald, D. W. (2014). Hugging the hedges: might agri-environment manipulations affect landscape permeability for hedgehogs? *Biological Conservation* 176: 109–116.

Moran, S., Turner, P. D. & O'Reilly, C. (2009). Multiple paternity in the European hedgehog. *Journal of Zoology, London* 278: 349–353.

Morris, B. (1961). Some observations on the breeding season of the hedgehog and the rearing and handling of the young. *Proceedings of the Zoological Society of London* 136: 201–206.

Morris, B. & Steel, E. D. (1967). Gastric and duodenal differentiation in *Erinaceus europaeus* and its relationship to antibody absorption. *Journal of Zoology, London* 152: 257–267.

Morris, P. (1966). The Hedgehog in London. *London Naturalist* 45: 43–49.

Morris, P. A. (1969). 'Some aspects of the ecology of the hedgehog (*Erinaceus europaeus*)'. PhD. Thesis, University of London.

Morris, P. A. (1970).. A method for determining absolute age in the hedgehog. *Journal of Zoology, London* 161: 277–281.

Morris, P. A. (1971). Epiphyseal fusion in the forefoot as a means of age determination in the hedgehog (*Erinaceus europaeus*). *Journal of Zoology, London* 164: 254–259.

Morris P. (1972). A review of mammalian age determination methods. *Mammal Review* 2: 69–104.

Morris, P. (1973). Winter nests of the hedgehog (*Erinaceus europaeus* L.) *Oecologia*. 11: 299–313.

Morris, P. (1977). Pre-weaning mortality in the hedgehog (*Erinaceus europaeus*). *Journal of Zoology, London* 182: 162–164.

Morris, P. A. (1979). Rats in the diet of the barn owl (*Tyto alba*). *Journal of Zoology, London* 189: 540–545.

Morris, P. (1983). *Hedgehogs*. Whittet Books, Weybridge.

Morris, P. A. (1984). An estimate of the minimum body weight necessary for hedgehogs (*Erinaceus europaeus*) to survive hibernation. *Journal of Zoology, London* 203: 291–294.

Morris, P. A. (1985). The effects of supplementary feeding on movements of hedgehogs (*Erinaceus europaeus*) *Mammal Review* 15: 23–32.

Morris, P. (1986). Nightly movements of hedgehogs *Erinaceus europaeus* in forest edge habitat. *Mammalia* 50: 395–398.

Morris, P. A. (1988). A study of home range and movements in the hedgehog (*Erinaceus europaeus*) *Journal of Zoology, London* 214: 433–449.

Morris, P. A. (1997). Released, rehabilitated hedgehogs: a follow-up study in Jersey. *Animal Welfare* 6: 317–327.

Morris, P. A. (1998). Hedgehog rehabilitation in perspective. *Veterinary Record* 143: 633–636.

Morris, P. (2014). *Hedgehogs*. Whittet Books, Stansted.

Morris, P.A. & English, M.P. (1969). *Trichophyton mentagrophytes* var *erinacei* in British hedgehogs. *Sabouraudia* 7: 122–127.

Morris, P.A. & English, M.P. (1973). Transmission and course of *Trichophyton erinacei* infections in British hedgehogs. *Sabouraudia* 11: 42–47.

Morris, P. A. & Morris, M. J. (1988). Distribution and abundance of hedgehogs (*Erinaceus europaeus*) on New Zealand roads. *New Zealand Journal of Zoology* 15: 491–498.

Morris, P. A., Bright, P. W. & Woods, D. (1990). Use of nestboxes by the Dormouse (*Muscardinus avellanarius*). *Biological Conservation* 51: 1–13.

Morris, P., Munn, S. & Craig-Wood, S. (1992) The effects of releasing captive hedgehogs *Erinaceus europaeus* into the wild. *Field Studies* 8: 89–99.

Morris, P., Meakin, K. & Sharafi, S. (1993). The behaviour and survival of rehabilitated hedgehogs (*Erinaceus europaeus*) *Animal Welfare* 2: 53–66.

Morris, P. A. & Warwick, H. (1994). A study of rehabilitated hedgehogs after release into the wild. *Animal Welfare* 3: 163–177.

Morris, P. A. & Tutt, A. (1996). Leucistic hedgehogs on the island of Alderney. *Journal of Zoology, London* 239: 387–389.

Morris, P. & Burdon, D. (2008). The hedgehog on Jersey. *Newsletter Société Jersiaise* 49: 8.

Morris, P. A. & Morris, M. J. (2010). A 13-year population study of the edible dormouse *Glis glis* in Britain. *Acta Theriologica* 55: 279–288.

Moss, K. & Sanders, M. (2001). Advances in New Zealand mammalogy 1990–2000: hedgehog. *Journal of the Royal Society of New Zealand* 31: 31–42.

Nelson, S. H., Evans, A. D. & Bradbury, R. B. (2006). The efficacy of an ultrasonic cat deterrent. *Applied Animal Behaviour Science* 96: 83–91.

Neumeier, M. (2016). *Wurfgrössen und Wurfzeiten der Igel in Deutschland.* Pro Igel e.V., Lindau/B.

Omori-Satoh, T. Yamakawa, Y. & Mebs, D. (2016). The antihemorrhagic factor, erinacin, from the European hedgehog (*Erinaceus europaeus*), a metalloprotease inhibitor of large molecular size possessing ficolin/opsonin P35 lectin domains. *Toxicon* 38: 1561–1580.

Orlowski, G. & Nowak, L. (2004). Road mortality of hedgehogs *Erinaceus* spp. in farmland in Lower Silesia (south-western Poland). *Polish Journal of Ecology* 52: 377–382.

Parrott, D., Etherington, T. R. & Dendy, J. (2014). A geographically extensive survey of hedgehogs (*Erinaceus europaeus*) in England. *European Journal of Wildlife Research* 60: 399–403.

Pettett, C. E., Johnson, P.J., Moorhouse, T.P. & Macdonald, D.W. (2017a). National predictors of hedgehog *Erinaceus europaeus* distribution and decline in Britain. *Mammal Review* doi:10.1111/mam.12107.

Pettett, C. E., Moorhouse, T. P., Johnson, P. J. & Macdonald, D. W. (2017b). Factors affecting hedgehog (*Erinaceus europaeus*) attraction to rural villages in arable landscapes. *European Journal of Wildlife Research* 63: 54. doi: 10.1007/s10344-017-1113-6

Plant, C. W. (1979). The status of the hedgehog *Erinaceus europaeus* in the London Boroughs of Barking, Newham, Redbridge and Waltham Forest. *London Naturalist* 58: 27–37.

Poduschka, W. (1977) Das Paarungsvorspiel des Osteuropäischen Igels (*Erinaceus e. roumanicus*) und theoretische Uberlegungen zum Problem männlicher Sexualpheromone. *Zoologische Anzeiger (Jena)* 199: 187–208.

Poduschka, W. & Poduschka, C. (1980). *Geliebtes Stacheltier; verhalten und aufzucht von igeln.* Landbuch-verlag GMBH, Hannover.

Potter, B. (1905). *The Tale of Mrs Tiggy-Winkle.* Frederick Warne, London.

Quilliam, T. A. (1972). Sensory receptors in the oral mucosa of the hedgehog. *Journal of Anatomy* 113: 297–298.

Racey, P. A. (1969). Diagnosis of pregnancy and experimental extension of gestation in the pipistrelle bat (*Pipistrellus pipistrellus*). *Journal of Reproduction and Fertility* 19: 465–474.

Rae, R. G., Robertson, J. F. & Wilson, M. J. (2006). Organic slug control using *Phasmarhabditis hermaphrodita.* *Aspects of Applied Biology* 79: 211–214.

Rautio, A., Valtonen, A., Auttila, M. & Kunnasranta, M. (2013a). The effects of sex and season on home range in European hedgehogs at the northern edge of the species range. *Acta Zoologicae Fennici* 50: 107–123.

Rautio, A., Valtonen, A., Auttila, M. & Kunnasranta, M. (2013b). Nesting patterns of European hedgehogs (*Erinaceus europaeus*) under northern conditions. *Acta Theriologica* 59: 173–181.

Rautio, A., Isomursu, M., Valtonen, A., Hirvelä-Koski & Kunnasranta, M. (2016). Mortality, diseases and diet of European hedgehogs (*Erinaceus europaeus*) in an urban environment in Finland. *Mammal Research* 61: 161–169

Recio, M. R., Matthieu, R., & Seddon, P. J. (2011). Design of a GPS backpack to track European hedgehogs *Erinaceus europaeus.* *European Journal of Wildlife Research* 57: 1175–1178.

Reeve, N.J. (1979). A simple and cheap radio tracking system for use on hedgehogs. In Amlaner, C. J. & Macdonald, D. W. *A Handbook on Biotelemtry and Radio Tracking.* Pergamon Press, Oxford and New York: pp. 169–173

Reeve, N. J. (1981). *A field study of the hedgehog (Erinaceus europaeus) with particular reference to movements and behaviour.* PhD Thesis, University of London.

Reeve, N. J. (1982). The home range of the hedgehog as revealed by a radio tracking study. *Symposium of the Zoological Society of London* 49: 207–230.

Reeve, N. (1994). *Hedgehogs.* T. & D. Poyser, London.

Reeve, N. J. (1998). The survival and welfare of hedgehogs (*Erinaceus europaeus*) after release back into the wild. *Animal Welfare* 7: 189–202.

Reeve, N. J. & Huijser, M. P. (1999). Mortality factors affecting wild hedgehogs: a study of records from wildlife rescue centres. *Lutra* 42: 7–23.

Reeve, N. J. and Morris, P. A. (1985). Construction and use of summer nests by the hedgehog (*Erinaceus europaeus*). *Mammalia* 49: 187–194.

Reeve, N. J. & Morris, P. A. (1986). Mating strategy in the hedgehog (*Erinaceus europaeus*). *Journal of Zoology, London* 210: 613–614.

Reichholf, J. (1983). Nehmen die strassenverkehrsverluste einfluss auf die bestandsentwicklung des igels (*Erinaceus europaeus*). *Spixiana* 6: 87–91.

Robinson, I. & Routh, A. (1999). Veterinary care of the hedgehog. *Practice* 21: 128–137.

Rondinini, C. & Doncaster, C. P. (2002). Roads as barriers to movement for hedgehogs. *Functional Ecology* 16: 504–509.

Roos, S., Johnston, A. & Noble, D. (2012). *UK hedgehog datasets and their potential for long-term monitoring*. BTO research report number 598: 1–63. British Trust for Ornithology, Thetford.

Ruprecht A. (1965). anomalies of the teeth and asymmetry of the skull in *Erinaceus europaeus* Linnaeus, 1758. *Acta theriologica* 10: 234–236.

Saboureau, M. & Dutorné, B. (1981). The reproductive cycle in the male hedgehog (*Erinaceus europaeus* L.): a study of endocrine and exocrine testicular function. *Reproduction, Nutrition, Development* 21: 109–126.

Sainsbury, A. W., Cunningham, A. A., Morris, P. A., Kirkwood, J. K. & Macgregor, S. K. (1996). Health and welfare of rehabilitated juvenile hedgehogs (*Erinaceus europaeus*) before and after release into the wild. *Veterinary Record*, 138: 61–65.

Sanchez-Toscano, F., Caminero, A. A., Machin, C. & Abella, G. (1989). Neuronal plasticity in the hedgehog supraoptic nucleus during hibernation. *Neuroscience* 31: 543–550.

Schäfer, M. W. (1980). Lernleistungen freilebender Braunbrust-Igel (*Erinaceus europaeus* L.): Manipulation, labyrinth, diskrimination. *Zeitschrift für Säugetierkunde* 45: 257–268.

Searle, J. B. & Erskine, I. (1985). Evidence for a widespread karyotypic race of hedgehog (*Erinaceus europaeus*) in Britain. *Journal of Zoology, London*. 206: 276–278.

Shirley, M. D. F. & Lurz, P. W. W. (2010). *Development of a population model for the management of hedgehogs on the Uists and Benbecula*. Scottish Natural Heritage Commissioned Report No.372.

Shore, R. F., Birks, J. D. S. & Freestone, P. (1999). Exposure of non-target vertebrates to second-generation rodenticides in Britain, with particular reference to the polecat *Mustela putorius*. *New Zealand Journal of Ecology* 23: 199–206

Short, M. J. & Reynolds, J. C. (2001). Physical exclusion of non-target species in tunnel-trapping of mammalian pests. *Biological Conservation* 98: 139–147.

Silver, B. (1994). *The Best of Bogor.* 21st Anniversary edition. Silverculture Press, Wellington, New Zealand.

Simpson, A. N. (1912). *British Land Animals and their Habits*. A & C Black, London.

Skoudlin, J. (1981). Age structure of Czechoslovak populations of *Erinaceus europaeus* and *Erinaceus concolor* (Insectivora: Erinaceidae) *Vestnik Ceskoslovenske Spolecnosti Zoologicke* 45: 307–313.

Soulé, M. (1987). *Viable Populations for Conservation*. Cambridge University Press, Cambridge.

Struck, S. (1995). *Ernährung des Igels (Erinaceus europaeus L. 1758)*. Doctoral dissertation, Tierärztiche Hochschule, Hannover.

Sykes, L. & Durrant, J. (1995). *The Natural Hedgehog*. Gaia Books, London.

Tähti, H. & Soivio, A. (1977). Respiratory and circulating differences between induced and spontaneous arousal in hibernating hedgehogs (*Erinaceus europaeus* L.). *Annales Zoologici Fennici* 14: 198–203.

Tapper, S. C. (1992). *Game Heritage*. Game Conservancy, Fordingbridge.

Taylor, J. (2012). *Beatrix Potter's Hedgehogs*. The Beatrix Potter Society, Ambleside.

Taylor, J., Whalley, J. I., Hobbs, A. S. & Battrick, E. M. (1987). *Beatrix Potter 1866–1943: the artist and her world*. Frederick Warne & Co./ The National Trust, London.

Taylor-Page, F. J. (1964). Mammal Report for 1963. *Transactions of the Norfolk and Norwich Naturalists Society* 20: 174–191.

Topsel, E. (1658). *The History of Four-footed Beasts and Serpents*. London.

Trewby, I. D., Young, R., McDonald, R. A., Wilson, G. J., Davison, J. & Walker, N. (2014). Impacts of removing badgers on localised counts of hedgehogs. *PLoS ONE* 9: e95477.doi: 10.1371/journal.pone.0095477.

Tutt, A. (1993). *Alderney's Hedgehogs*. Third Year BSc Dissertation (unpublished).

Uttley, J., Monaghan P. & Blackwood J. (1981). Hedgehog *Erinaceus europaeus* predation of Arctic tern *Sterna paradisaea* eggs: the impact on breeding success. *Seabird* 12: 3–6.

Van de Poel, J. L., Dekker, J. & van Langevelde, F. (2015). Dutch hedgehogs *Erinaceus europaeus* are nowadays mainly found in urban areas, possibly due to the negative effects of badgers *Meles meles*. *Wildlife Biology* 21: 51–55.

Vincent, J. F. V. & Owers, P. (1986). Mechanical design of hedgehog spines and porcupine quills. *Journal of Zoology, London* 210: 55–75.

Visser, M., Rehbein, S. & Wiedmann, C. (2001). Species of flea (Siphonaptera) infesting pets and hedgehogs in Germany. *Zoonoses and Public Health* 48: 197–202.

Walhovd, H. (1975). Winter activity of Danish hedgehogs in 1973/4 with information on the size of animals observed and location of the recordings. *Natura Jutlandica*. 18: 53–61.

Walhovd, H. (1979a). The overwintering pattern of Danish hedgehogs in outdoor confinement, during three successive winters. *Natura Jutlandica* 20: 273–284.

Walhovd, H. (1979b). Partial arousals from hibernation in hedgehogs in outdoor hibernacula. *Oecologia* 40: 141–153.

Wang, Y., Cang, T., Zhao, X., Yu, R., Chen, L., Wu, C. & Wang, Q. (2012). Comparative acute toxicity of twenty-four insecticides to earthworm *Eisenia fetida*. *Ecotoxicology and Environmental Safety*, doi: 10.1016/j.ecoenv.2011.12.016.

Ward, J. F., Macdonald, D. W. & Doncaster, C. P. (1997). Responses of foraging hedgehogs to badger odour. *Animal Behaviour* 53: 709–720.

Warwick, H. (2008). *A Prickly Affair: my life with hedgehogs*. Allen Lane, London.

Warwick, H. (2014). *Hedgehog*. Reaktion Books, London.

Warwick, H. (2016). Britain's hedgehogs: research and the conservation effort in the face of serious decline. *British Wildlife* 28: 78–86.

Warwick, H., Morris, P. & Walker, D. (2006). Survival and weight changes of hedgehogs (*Erinaceus europaeus*) translocated from the Hebrides to mainland Scotland. *Lutra* 49: 89–102.

Watt, J. (1995). *Hedgehogs and ferrets on the South Uist machairs; a pilot study of predation on ground nesting birds*. Unpublished report, Scottish Natural Heritage.

Wembridge, D. E., Newman, M. R., Bright, P. W. & Morris, P. A. (2016). An estimate of the annual number of hedgehog *Erinaceus europaeus* road casualties in Great Britain. *Mammal Communications* 2: 9–12.

White, G. (1883). *The Natural History of Selborne*, with notes by Frank Buckland. Macmillan & Co., London.

White, T. H. (1954). *The Book of Beasts*. Jonathan Cape, London.

Wilson, A., Fenton, B., Malloch, G., Boag, B., Hubbard, S. & Begg, G. (2016). Urbanisation versus agriculture: a comparison of local genetic diversity and gene flow between wood mouse *Apodemus sylvaticus* populations in human-modified landscapes. *Ecography* 39: 87–97.

Wodzicki, K. A. (1950). *Introduced mammals of New Zealand* (DSIR Bulletin No. 98). Department of Scientific and Industrial Research, Wellington.

Wood, J. G. (1876). *Bible Animals*, Longmans Green & Co., London.

Wroot, A. J. (1984). *Feeding ecology of the European hedgehog Erinaceus europeaus L.* PhD Thesis, University of London.

Wroot, A. (1985). A quantitative method for estimating the amount of earthworm (*Lumbricus terrestris*) in animal diets. *Oikos* 44: 239–242.

Yalden, D. W. (1976). The food of the hedgehog in England. *Acta Theriologica* 21: 401–424.

Yalden, D. W. (1980). Notes on the diet of urban Kestrels. *Bird Study* 27: 235–238.

Yalden, D. W. (1999). *The History of British Mammals*. Poyser, London.

Yarnell, R. W., Pacheco, M., Williams, B., Neumann, J. L., Rymer, D. J. & Baker, P. J. (2014). Using occupancy analysis to validate the use of footprint tunnels as a method for monitoring the hedgehog *Erinaceus europaeus*. *Mammal Review* 44: 234–238.

Young, R. P., Davison, J., Trewby, I. D., Wilson, G. J., Delahay, R. J., & Doncaster, C. P. (2006). Abundance of hedgehogs (*Erinaceus europaeus*) in relation to the density and distribution of badgers (*Meles meles*). *Journal of Zoology, London* 269: 349–356.

Index

USEFUL INTERNET RESOURCES

People's Trust for Endangered Species (PTES) – www.ptes.org
British Hedgehog Preservation Society (BHPS) – www.britishhedgehogs.org.uk
Hedgehog Street – www.hedgehogstreet.org
Big Hedgehog Map – www.bighedgehogmap.org

The New Naturalist Library